The Novels of Frances Hodgson Burnett

Frontispiece "She Stepped Into The Gallery Before He Could Protest". The frontispiece is from the first edition of That Lass O'Lowries (Scribner's 1877).

The Novels of Frances Hodgson Burnett

In "the World of Actual Literature"

Thomas Recchio

ANTHEM PRESS

Anthem Press
An imprint of Wimbledon Publishing Company
www.anthempress.com

This edition first published in UK and USA 2022
by ANTHEM PRESS
75–76 Blackfriars Road, London SE1 8HA, UK
or PO Box 9779, London SW19 7ZG, UK
and
244 Madison Ave #116, New York, NY 10016, USA

First published in the UK and USA by Anthem Press in 2020

Copyright © Thomas Recchio 2022

The author asserts the moral right to be identified as the author of this work.

All rights reserved. Without limiting the rights under copyright reserved above,
no part of this publication may be reproduced, stored or introduced into
a retrieval system, or transmitted, in any form or by any means
(electronic, mechanical, photocopying, recording or otherwise),
without the prior written permission of both the copyright
owner and the above publisher of this book.

British Library Cataloguing-in-Publication Data
A catalogue record for this book is available from the British Library.

ISBN-13: 978-1-83998-233-0 (Pbk)
ISBN-10: 1-83998-233-0 (Pbk)

This title is also available as an e-book.

CONTENTS

Acknowledgments		vii
Introduction		1
Chapter One	Learning from Elizabeth Gaskell	23
Chapter Two	Writing as an American: The Portrait of a Washington Lady	53
Chapter Three	Historical Dreamscapes and the Vicissitudes of Class: From *A Lady of Quality* to *The Methods of Lady Walderhurst*	93
Chapter Four	Transatlantic Alliances in *The Shuttle* and *T. Tembarom*	135
Chapter Five	After the Great War: Emerging from the Wasteland in *The Head of the House of Coombe* and *Robin*	171
Bibliography		217
Index		225

ACKNOWLEDGMENTS

The seeds for this book were planted long ago and without my notice. Grace Vasington asked me to supervise her University Scholars thesis on the mythological background of Burnett's *The Secret Garden*. Her research took her to France and the United Kingdom, where she read extensively on the origins and histories of mythological narratives that survive unnoticed as skeletons of story in literary fiction. Her work showed me that Burnett's writing repays thoughtful, close reading. Some years later as I was working on a book of publishing history, my colleague Sarah Winter introduced me to *A Fair Barbarian* in the context of British village fiction along the lines of Elizabeth Gaskell's *Cranford*. A year or two after that, I taught a graduate seminar on Gaskell and Burnett where, with Christina Henderson, Steven Mollmann, Katie Panning, Christiana Salah and Emily Tucker, we read Gaskell's early novels alongside Burnett's. That led to a paper on Gaskell and Burnett at the North American Victorian Studies Association (NAVSA) meeting in Pasadena, California. Later at NAVSA's conference in Banff, Alberta, Sharon Weltman introduced me to Joanna Seaton, who is steeped in Burnett's adult fiction. We discussed the work I had been doing on Burnett and Gaskell, at which point I knew I had to write this book. Over the last two years my colleagues at the University of Connecticut, especially Sarah Winter, Kate Capshaw, Victoria Ford Smith and Margaret Higonnet, supported this work in ways big and small and always important. Genevieve Brassard of the University of Portland offered timely bibliographic advice on women's writing and The Great War. The university's Interlibrary Loan staff has not only helped facilitate the provision of books and articles from other research libraries, they have helped track down periodical sources in some deeply hidden places. The University of Connecticut Scholarship Facilitation Fund has also been generous with financial support. Special thanks to the New York Public Library for access to the Gilder collection. To all I am grateful. But especially to Eleni Coundouriotis, whose intellect, scholarly integrity and moral vision have been a daily inspiration to me for more than two decades, I owe a debt I can never repay. This book is for her and our son, Thomas.

INTRODUCTION

I

Most well known today as the author of the children's classics *The Secret Garden* (1911), *A Little Princess* (1905) and, perhaps still infamously, *Little Lord Fauntleroy* (1886), Francis Hodgson Burnett was for most of her career a serious and ambitious writer of adult fiction. Her first two novels, *That Lass O'Lowries* (1877) and *Haworth's* (1879), garnered strong critical reviews, American periodicals pairing those novels with George Eliot's and Henry James's and announcing in the process the emergence of a significant new voice on the American literary scene. *That Lass O'Lowries* was reviewed with James's *The American* in the *North American Review* in 1877,[1] and the *Southern Review* in its 1879 review of that novel opined that "Mrs. Burnett [...] has come to take the first rank among living American novelists" (n.p.).[2] That same year the *North American Review* paired Eliot's *The Impressions of Theophrastus Such* with Burnett's *Haworth's*; the review states: "When a new writer arrives who is indeed a new voice, and not a confused echo of voices already familiar, the first office of the critic is to ask what results characterize his work and by what methods he achieves his results or makes his impression. Mrs. Burnett [...] has proved herself a distinctly new personality among our novel-writers."[3] Though both reviews seem to concur in their high evaluation of the literary quality of Burnett's early novels, presenting them as vehicles of a distinctive voice that mark Burnett as the preeminent novelist of her time (note the absence of the qualifier "woman" novelist in the first review), there is some suggestive slippage in the language of the second review as Burnett is relocated from the "first rank" of novelists to a "distinctly new personality among novel-writers." First-rate novelist, new writer, distinct personality: taken together, the blurriness of such terms captures the way in which Burnett may be said to have oscillated within the Anglo-American literary field between 1877 and 1924. If one review locates her at the top of the field of literary production, another seems to concur but fudges, shifting terms from novelist to writer and, by implication, from author to personality. The mobility of Burnett's critical location suggests that she was both everywhere and nowhere in the literary field of her time. One way to read her career is as a struggle between her effort to be everywhere in the literary field—as novelist, writer of short fiction, playwright, author of children's books and even as a significant figure in the adaptation of literature to film in the early years of the film industry—and of the self-appointed overseers of literary culture, book reviewers and critics, to define and thus confine her. The dominance of the critics in that struggle can be suggested by an August 20, 1922, *Los Angeles Times* review of Burnett's last novel, *Robin* (1922):

> That Mrs. Burnett handles the situation with consummate art and in so doing tells the most moving story of her career will be the opinion of all lovers of the good, the true and the

> beautiful as expressed in romance, who read this book. Not since Meredith gave free rein to the romantic spirit in the love passages in "The Ordeal of Richard Feverel" has young love been so feelingly and poetically chronicled.[4]

What better way to blunt the literary ambitions and constrain the critical reputation of a woman with the imagination, energy and range to produce high-quality, widely distributed and financially successful literary productions in novel and story for adults and children and in adaptive forms for stage and screen than to praise her "consummate art" to the lovers of Romance.

The tensions just sketched out that are discernible in the language of the critical response to the earliest and the latest novels of Burnett's literary career are an epi-phenomenon of the broad struggles within the Anglo-American literary field at the end of the nineteenth and through the first two decades of the twentieth century. Recent critics of British modernism, literary culture and publishing history have figured those struggles in various though parallel and complementary terms. For example, Peter D. McDonald, drawing on Pierre Bourdieu's distinction between the "'sub-field of restricted production'" and the "'subfield of large-scale production'" (Bourdieu 115–31 cited in McDonald), argues that Bourdieu's distinction captures the "rival extremes, which give the [literary] field its hierarchical structure." Those extremes, McDonald suggests, set "the 'purists' against the 'profiteers'."[5] The "purists" are those who measure literary value in "aesthetic terms; they concern themselves chiefly with the particular demands, traditions, and excellences of their craft; they respect only the opinion of peers or accredited connoisseurs and critics; and they deem legitimate only those rewards, like peer recognition, which affect one's status within the field itself" (13). The "profiteers" in contrast—note the pointedly pejorative quality of the term—rely on "extra-literary principles of legitimacy […] [where] value is measured in strictly economic terms; the agents see their craft […] as a commercial enterprise; the opinion of the greatest number, expressed through sales, is all that counts" (13–14). Of course, such a figuration of struggles within the literary field is an "idealized" binary (14). "Between the two extremes," McDonald notes, "there are a number of positions which combine the two perspectives in various degrees" (14). The implication here is that the opposition between purity and profit has more rhetorical than real value since almost every writer, including such "pure" literary figures as Henry James and Joseph Conrad as McDonald demonstrates, desires a broad readership confirmed and validated by financial success. So when peers and "accredited connoisseurs and critics" rely on that binary to judge the aesthetic originality and power of any particular work and author, consigning works that sell to the merely "popular" and justifying financial failure on the basis of a high cultural aesthetics, it is reasonable to wonder how much praise of aesthetic quality is spiced with more than a dash of financial sour grapes? Answering that question is both helped and complicated when we fold in the matter of gender.

Martin Hipsky suggests two possibilities for women writers of fiction during those years: "By 1880, the year of [George] Eliot's death," he writes,

> evidence suggests that there existed in the world of English letters these two ready-made roles for any would-be fiction writer who happened to be female: on the one hand, there was the

"serious lady novelist," staking her claim to verisimilitude and the complex portrayal of moral problems and psychological truths and thereby taking the mantle of Jane Austen, Charlotte Bronte, Elizabeth Gaskell, and George Eliot; on the other, there were the writers of melodramatic popular novels for the entertainment of the less-educated audience, in a tradition spanning from Ann Radcliff to Mrs. Henry Wood and Mary Elizabeth Braddon. The former category was understood to be a very small club, yet its members were accepted as the peers of the greatest male novelists.[6]

That last sentence helps account for the lack of any gender qualification in the 1879 *Southern Review* assessment of Burnett. Consider these other assessments of Burnett's first novel: the *Atlantic Monthly* (November 1977) compares the novel to those of Charlotte Bronte and Elizabeth Gaskell, claiming "there is not a superfluous sentence in the book";[7] the *Southern Review* (October 1878) calls Burnett "the George Eliot of America" and "the first and best living American novelist"[8] (Eliot too was still alive); three months later that same journal (January 1879) compares her to Dickens in a "kinship of mind and imagination";[9] and in that same month and year the *North American Review* added to the praise, comparing *That Lass O'Lowries* to *Jane Eyre* and *Adam Bede*, announcing the arrival of a new major writer of "original power" and calling the titular character Joan Lowrie "one of the finest feats in modern novel writing."[10] It is clear from those representative reviews that Burnett was welcomed in America as not just a "serious lady novelist" but a novelist of great skill and stature. When we take the *Los Angeles Times* assessment quoted above and the *Chicago Daily Tribune* (1922) review of *Robin*—"It will probably give the tear glands more exercise than anything since 'The Wide, Wide World.' It ought to make Laura Jean Libbey, Bertha M. Clay, Mrs. E. D. E. N. Southworth, and Augusta May Evans shed celestial tears of envy"—[11]together, it is equally clear that at the close of her career she was deemed a "melodramatic" writer of "popular novels for the entertainment of the less-educated audience."

Ann Thwaite in her 1991 biography of Burnett views that change in terms of unrealized potential, stating explicitly that Burnett was a serious author who sold her talent for money. Writing of the transatlantic impact of *Little Lord Fauntleroy*, a book, she notes, that some said "changed relations between America and Britain" for the better (86), Thwaite asserts that *Fauntleroy*'s commercial success "changed her from being a serious writer, striving to master an art, into a craftswoman who had discovered she had the Midas touch." But more than mere touch, making money required work: Burnett as a "pen-driving machine was to become a machine for printing money."[12] While that view certainly can be defended, it is also misleading and unsatisfying for it assumes that Burnett simply rejected her aesthetic ambitions and sensibilities because of a concern for money. It also assumes that since she succeeded in making money she had, by definition, absolutely subordinated her art to that purpose. However, if we place Burnett's work in the context of the changing configuration of the literary field in England and America over the span of her career, we need to acknowledge that the dynamic driving those changes in the assessment of her work was not produced by strictly aesthetic criteria but was generated by developments in an incredibly productive and expansive literary industry. Those developments not only concern distinctions between high and popular culture and the concomitant expansion of the market for popular fiction but also concern, to vary a phrase from Andreas Huyssen, how the idea of popular (or mass) culture was defined as feminine.[13] The literary field, in this formulation, with its distinctions between the high and the low, the aesthetic and the popular, purity and profit, gendered the popular and profitable as feminine as a way to elevate the masculine as aesthetic, the feminine then being (as usual in patriarchy) simultaneously belittled, feared and desired. "Thus," Huyssen writes,

> the nightmare of being devoured by mass culture through co-option, commodification, and the "wrong" kind of success is the constant fear of the modernist artist, who tried to stake out his territory by fortifying the boundaries between genuine art and inauthentic mass culture. Again, the problem is not the desire to differentiate between forms of high art and depraved forms of mass culture and its co-options. The problem is rather the persistent gendering as feminine of that which is devalued. (53)

And, I would add, the devalued is also the desired since what is devalued is, not so paradoxically, money, the marker of value (and the enabler/mediator of material comfort).

The documented material that chronicles Burnett's relationship with Henry James contains small but powerful details that function as symptoms if not comprehensive evidence of the tensions laid out so abstractly above. Burnett and James were well acquainted with each other if not exactly friends. When Burnett's elder son, Lionel, died of tuberculosis at age 16 in 1890 in Paris, James paid a visit of condolence to Burnett in London, an act of "kindness," according to Gretchen Holbrook Gerzina, that Burnett recalled years later with gratitude and fondness.[14] Burnett and James were neighbors in England in the late 1890s, where James was a frequent casual correspondent but an infrequent visitor. Burnett tried to cultivate a friendship, offering, for instance, to support him by attending the debut of his ill-fated play *Guy Domville*, an offer that James fortunately declined, sparing himself the humiliation and Burnett the embarrassment of her witnessing the audience hoot and jeer at the author during the curtain call. Their relationship was restricted to letters in which, according to Gerzina, James was "always the epitome of thoughtfulness." His courtesy on paper, which we will see as unsettlingly overstated at times, and his reticence in person can perhaps be accounted for by the fact that Burnett sold many books and he sold few. "He admitted to his brother [William]," Gerzina notes, of "being somewhat disheartened by the fact that her books sold far more copies than his and, unbeknown to her, had years before written an anonymous and not particularly flattering review of her play *Esmeralda* in the *Pall Mall Gazette*" (208). While it is impossible to know the proportions, it would not stretch the truth to suggest that the aesthetic principles that grounded James's criticism of Burnett's play were leavened by a dose of financial jealousy.

That latter possibility is strengthened when we examine in more detail James's letters to Burnett during the years when they were neighbors in Kent, he at Lamb House in Rye and she at Maytham Hall in Rolvenden. As Ann Thwaite tells it, before leaving London for Maytham, Burnett bought "a set of James' books" and sent them to him "to be autographed." He signed the books and attached the following note when he returned them:

Dear Mrs Burnett

And yet I *lingered*—I never leave your presence and precinct on wings or by leaps—was leaden-footed and most reluctant. And now I'm glad of anything—even anything so dreary as my own books—that may renew our communion.

I am divided between joy at the thought of so many copies sold—my publishers' statement is usually *one* on alternate years—and anguish for your having added that thumping, pecuniary excrescence to the treasure you are lavishing at Maytham.

But I will charge you nothing for the signs-manual. There, don't take them to Maytham (unless you are really otherwise homeless); they will require an extra van. However, if you do, I will speed over and scatter broadcast that I am.

Yours most respectfully,
Henry James (Quoted in Thwaite 184)

While the extravagance of style is certainly very much Henry James, there are three noteworthy things to notice in that note. The self-deprecating reference to the paucity of sales of James's works (one book every other year) is contained within an elaborate allusion to the "treasure" Burnett was "lavishing at Maytham"; the value of James's books marks a damning contrast to Burnett's financial success/excess. The lurking notion here is that his books are expensive and aesthetically demanding, which accounts for their limited sale, but Burnett's wealth, which was based on the sales of her less demanding books, reduces James's books to objects whose value is not aesthetic but monetary, a bit of extra and incidental treasure. The corollary lurking notion here is that for Burnett, that is all his books could possibly be. His compliment masks an insult. And his promise to "speed over" is not kept. As Thwaite puts it, "But when they were both in Kent [...] James did not do much speeding over" (184).

The faintly discernible, simmering resentment in the letter quoted above screams for recognition in an undated letter from that same period. Burnett had sent fruit from her orchard at Maytham to James at Lamb House. Here is the first part of his "Thank You" note:

Noblest of Neighbors and Most Heavenly of Women!—

Your gorgeous, glorious gift shook Lamb House to its foundations an hour or two ago—but that agitated structure, with the light of purpose rapidly kindling in its eye, recuperates even as I write, with a sense of futility, under the circumstances of a mere, economical swoon. We may swoon *again*—it is more than likely (if you *can* swoon from excess of—everything!)—but we avail ourselves of this lucid interval absolutely to *fawn* upon you with the force of our gratitude.

It's too magnificent—we don't deserve the quarter (another peach, please—yet it *is* the 7th—and *one* more fig—it *is* I can't deny it—the 19th!) Well, I envy you the power to make a poor, decent body so happy—and, still more, so proud. The decent body has a pair of *other* decent bodies coming to him for the week's end, from town, and—my eye! *won't* he swagger over his intimate friend, the Princess of Maytham, for whom these trophies and treasures are mere lumps of sugar or grains of salt. (Quoted in Thwaite 184–85)

Such a note, which contains two more paragraphs after the ones quoted, could be written off as hyperbolic humor in a style one might expect from Henry James, but the content is nonetheless odd. After the elaborate cliché of the greeting, James conflates Lamb House with himself, the house recuperating after its swoon "even as I write, with a sense of futility." Is the house's recuperation futile or is the writing futile, James's effort to suggest to Burnett that her gift smacks of economic one-upmanship pointless? As "the light of purpose [rekindles] in its [the house's] eye," one can imagine James's own eyes sharpen with satiric intent, claiming a brief interval of consciousness before being overwhelmed again with some manifestation of excess from Maytham, that is, Burnett. Perhaps if he were to "*fawn*" upon Burnett "with the force of [his] gratitude," the torrent of gifts, which in their excess smack of condescension, would stop. That implication emerges more explicitly in the next paragraph. After the comic images of consumption (7 peaches and 19 figs!), James deftly contrasts his poverty and decency to Burnett's indecent display of wealth, an indecency reinforced by the final comparison between the particularity and quantity of the gifts as they appear in Lamb House and the undifferentiated mass from which they were extracted, the peaches and figs in Lamb House being equivalent to "lumps of sugar or grains of salt" in Maytham. The mask of jest in the note barely conceals an animosity born of pain that energizes the prose. The selective use of italics (in the handwritten letter markers of emphasis rendered as italics in print) emphasizes the general hyperbolic tone more pointedly. As Thwaite mildly observes, "James rather resented a munificence which cast him in the role of comparatively unsuccessful writer" (185).

The undercurrent of palpable pain one can feel in James's note is more visible in a letter he wrote to his brother in 1899 when he was negotiating the purchase of Lamb House.

> My whole being cries out aloud for something that I can call my own—and when I look round me at the splendor of so many of the "literary" fry, my confreres (M. Crawford's, P. Bourget's, Humphrey Ward's, Hodgson Burnett's, W.D. Howellses, etc.) and I feel that I may strike the world as still, at fifty-six with my long labour and my genius, reckless, presumptuous and unwarranted in curling up (for more assured peaceful production) in a poor little $10,000 shelter—once for all and for all time—*then* I do feel the bitterness of humiliation, the iron enters into my soul, and (I blush to confess it,) I weep! But enough, enough, enough! (Quoted in Thwaite 185)

James's anguish about the gap between the "genius" of his aesthetically first-rate literary productions and the second-rate financial return on the material production of those works is a mixture of honest self-assessment and frustration expressed in a way that makes it difficult to discern whether honesty or frustration is the more dominant quality. That instability in tone is also reflected in the contradictory way he represents his fellow novelists—two American men (Crawford and Howells), a popular French poet (Bourget) and two English women (Ward and Burnett)—as both "confreres" (colleagues with a connotation of brotherhood) and "fry," little fish (with James, of course, standing in for the big fish). In James's personal correspondence, then, we can tease out a major fissure in the literary field of his (and Burnett's) time, a fissure that does have an aesthetic dimension to be sure, but one driven more by competition in the literary marketplace than by art as such. As Mary Hammond puts it, "on an ideological level it was sales figures, blatant self-advertisement and financial success which 'feminized' popular literature in the 1880s and 1890s, rather than the formal properties of either realism or romance."[15] Once divergent aesthetic practices (realism variously defined and romance variously practiced) were reinscribed ideologically as high and low, pure and profitable, male and female, the second term in each binary became marginalized, and as feminists critics since Ellen Moers and Elaine Showalter have worked so comprehensively to reveal and to correct, women and the popular were written out of literary history.[16]

Most of the critics I have quoted thus far (among others such as Rita Felski[17]) have worked to reclaim the place of women writers in British literary modernism. But Frances Hodgson Burnett does not appear in any substantial way in any of that work. It is the purpose of this book to include Burnett in the broad reclamation project of popular women novelists as practitioners of forms of popular narrative with similar aspirational drives as those attributed to works of high literary modernism. Hipsky makes a similar point when he writes: "The 'popular sublime,' as embodied in the novels of Marie Corelli and other romancists of the period, strove after a 'transcendence of quotidian reality and the material world' (Felski 120) in a variation of the same mythic and metaphoric quests for transcendence, specific to early twentieth-century forms of social alienation in the metropolitan sphere" (17). I would include Burnett's novels, especially her post-1890s work, in the Marie Corelli "romancist" category. I need, then, to explore why Burnett has not been a subject of such reclamation work in the first place. Then I need to make the case as to why she should be. That will be the burden of the main body of this book, which will comprise a series of contextualized readings of her most ambitious and innovative novels.

II

Burnett's fiction has not been the subject of literary reclamation perhaps because there has been no perceived need to reclaim a writer who seems already to have a clearly defined place in Anglo-American literary history as a writer of literature for children. *The Secret Garden* (1911) has attracted much attention from scholars of children's literature, who have interpreted its mythic, psychological and colonial engagements in addition to its literary sourcing (making connections mostly with the Brontes).[18] There is a hard cover lavishly illustrated Norton Annotated Edition of the novel (2007) edited by Burnett's most recent biographer Gretchen Holbrook Gerzina. *A Little Princess* and *Little Lord Fauntleroy* have also garnered critical attention, the former for thematic reasons related to the colonial context of the story and the latter for historical reasons related to its initial enthusiastic cultural and political acceptance that later transformed into nearly universal condemnation. But the venue that has solidified Burnett's cultural significance as a first-rate children's author has been film and television. What follows is a partial list of English-language productions in reverse order: *The Secret Garden* television productions (2015, forty-two episode series, television movie 1987, seven episode series 1975, eight episode series 1960 and eight episode series 1952); *A Little Princess* television productions (10 episode series 2009, mini-series 1986, six episode series 1973) and under the title *Sara Crewe* (six episode series 1957, six episode series 1951); *Little Lord Fauntleroy* television productions (six episode series 1995, six episode series 1976, three episode series 1966, four episode series 1957); *The Secret Garden* films (1993, 1949 and 1919); *A Little Princess* films (1939 and 1917); and *Little Lord Fauntleroy* films (2003, 1980, 1936, 1926, 1921, 1918 and 1914).[19] Burnett's broader cultural visibility is suggested by two relatively new biographies, one by Ann Thwaite (Godine 1991) and the other by Gretchen Holbrook Gerzina (Rutgers UP 2004), but each ties her fame to her significance as a children's author as evidenced by the full title of each biography: *The Life of Frances Hodgson Burnett author of* The Secret Garden *and* A Little Princess (Thwaite) and *Frances Hodgson Burnett: The Unexpected Life of the Author of* The Secret Garden (Gerzina).

There was a flurry of interest in Burnett's adult novels in the film industry during the last dozen or so years of her life: between 1913 and 1924 there were ten films made of her novels, stories and plays, including adaptations of *That Lass O'Lowries* (1923), *A Fair Barbarian* (1917), *A Lady of Quality* (1913 and 1924) and *The Shuttle* (1918). But as Francis J. Molson put it in a survey of Burnett's publication and critical history, "[V]irtually every standard history of American literature or specialized study of American fiction or drama omits reference to Frances Burnett's writing."[20] That fact remains true today for both histories of American and British literature of the period between 1880 and 1920. The *Columbia History of the American Novel* (1991), for instance, does not mention Burnett anywhere while Philip Waller in his magisterial *Writers, Readers, & Reputations: Literary Life in Britain 1870–1918*[21] alludes to Burnett three times in nearly 1,200 pages of text, each reference drawn from material in Thwaite's biography on such matters as early film adaptations (Waller 10, Thwaite 231–32, 237, and 245–46), public speeches in Burnett's honor (Waller 598–99, Thwaite 164–65 and 170) and celebrity photographs (Waller 354, Thwaite 112 and 214). Alex Zwerdling in *Improvised Europeans: American Literary Expatriates and the Siege of London* devotes two pages to *Little Lord Fauntleroy*.[22] Peter Keating in *The Haunted Study: A Social History of the English Novel 1875–1914* refers to Burnett four times, misrepresenting her when he writes, "Hodgson Burnett lived in Britain for some time and wrote on British themes, but she too was American."[23] (She was born in Manchester, emigrated with her widowed mother and siblings to America at 16, shuttled back and forth between the UK and the United States spending extended periods in both places during all of her writing life, and did not become an American citizen until compelled for financial reasons around 1905, a decision she made "possibly to avoid [her English husband's] claims on her property and income" (Thwaite 216). We might say that she was as American as Henry James was English.) And David Trotter in *The English Novel in History 1895–1920* alludes to Burnett in passing twice.[24] One might think that in the recent reevaluation of the long-standing conviction in literary studies that "realism is inherently superior to romance" (Molson 41), Burnett would have drawn some attention, but in studies as disparate as those by Suzanne Clark (1991),[25] Joseph McAleer (1992),[26] Peter D. McDonald (1997),[27] Nicholas Daly (1999),[28] Mary Hammond (2006)[29] and

Martin Hipsky (2011),[30] Burnett is not mentioned once. Even the one single-volume study of Burnett and her work published in Twayne's English Authors Series (1984) offers this final assessment: "Even the critic trying to resurrect some of Burnett's adult fiction from its near oblivion will probably admit that the survival of *The Secret Garden* as Burnett's masterpiece is just [...]. She deserves a primary place in the annals of children's and popular literature" (Bixler).[31]

III

Excavating Burnett's adult novels from under the layers of neglect and the popular cultural replication and critical praise of her children's stories requires, I think, that we begin by making some distinctions about the range and quality of those novels. A short passage from Thwaite's biography provides a place to begin:

> The *Times Literary Supplement* wrote [in a review of her final novel, *Robin*]: "Lush sentiments flow from her pen with a sweetness that suggests syrup rather than plain ink [...] This is a pity, because once upon a time Mrs Burnett could write differently." She could indeed; if she had died at forty-five, before she had written *Little Lord Fauntleroy*, she might well have had a reputation comparable with Mrs Gaskell's. (240)

To extrapolate from Thwaite's assessment, it is logical to assume that the novels written before 1886 when *Fauntleroy* was published constitute a body of work worthy of the respect afforded Elizabeth Gaskell, who, since the 1960s, has acquired an increasingly important place in studies of the Victorian novel and culture. The question that begs for an answer here is if the pre-1886 work is so good, why neglect it? A corollary that flows from that question is that not all of her novels conform to the same genre, were written in the same style or reveal the same depth of engagement either directly or indirectly with the cultural moment at the time of their composition. Nor do we know, without broad and sensitive re-readings today, how the novels might speak to our current cultural moment. So in much the way she occupied various positions in the literary field during her lifetime, she could be located in various positions in the field of literary and cultural studies in the present. For instance, in the contemporary reassessment of romance written by women in the late nineteenth and early twentieth centuries, the few allusions to Burnett place her squarely in the group of women romance writers. That placement consequently ignores her engagement with mid- and late Victorian realism, and it has not stimulated any reassessment of the depth and complexity of what is considered her romance novels. That is, her novels have been categorized under the broad category of romance; romance itself has been rethought and recalibrated in ways that open up its thematic, ideological, aesthetic richness, but Burnett's "romances" have not been reread. There is a double failure in differentiation here, exemplified oddly in Phylis Bixler's Twayne study, where she organizes Burnett's literary career in the following terms: "From Magazine Fiction to Romance to Realist Novel (1868–84) [...] Popular Romances for Children and Adults (1885–99) [...] Fairy Stories for Children and Adults (1900–1924)" (Table of Contents, n.p.). The pattern of those chapter titles seems circular, from romance to realism, then back to romance with a further move away from realism through fairy stories with the distinction between adult and children's novels being erased. In the end writing for children emerges as the dominant thread that unifies her career, her adult novels subordinated to that purpose.

Based on my reading of Burnett's fiction written for an adult audience, I would classify 14 as full-length novels; there is also a subset of novellas and an extensive bibliography of short stories. While the novellas, such as *A Woman's Will or Miss Defarge* (1888), *The Dawn of a Tomorrow* (1906) and *The White People* (1917), are varied and fascinating in their own right, I will focus on the novels, which appeared in not always chronological clusters at the beginning, middle and end of her writing career. The first cluster, *That Lass O'Lowries* (1877), *Haworth's* (1879) and *A Fair Barbarian* (1881), emerges from the mid-Victorian realist tradition, and they take their inspiration from Burnett's fellow Mancunian, Elizabeth Gaskell. The first two novels, in fact, which are set in Lancashire, England, could be classified as latecomers to the tradition of British industrial fiction of the 1840s while the third novel is squarely aligned with a traditional village fiction inaugurated by Mary Russell Mitford's *Our Village* (1826–32) and confirmed in Elizabeth Gaskell's *Cranford* (1853). The second cluster, *Louisiana* (1880), *Through One Administration* (1883) and *In Connection with the De Willoughby Claim* (1899), is a complex mixture of regional American fiction with, in the case of *Through One Administration* in particular, a heavy investment in what was called the "new fiction" associated with William Dean Howells and Henry James, and in the case of the latter two novels deeply engaged with the social and bureaucratic complexities of political life in Washington, DC. The third cluster, *A Lady of Quality* (1896), *His Grace of Osmond* (1897), *The Making of a Marchioness* (1901) and *The Methods of Lady Walderhurst* (1901), draws on a tradition of historical fiction (the first two titles) and domestic fiction (the third and fourth titles), leavened with more than a touch of sensation in the Wilkie Collins tradition. The fourth cluster, inspired perhaps by a thread of inquiry begun in *Little Lord Fauntleroy*, comprises transatlantic novels: *The Shuttle* (1907) and *T. Tembarom* (1913), which, while ostensibly focused on transatlantic marriages of very different sorts, struggles with contemporary anxieties about familial and national decline in England and American ineptness, through a lack of cultural institutions and practices analogous to European social forms, on the international stage. *The Head of the House of Coombe* (1922) and *Robin* (1922) constitute the fifth cluster. Although those last two titles were written as a single volume, because of their length, at the publisher's insistence they were published as two titles. The first of those novels probes the English experience in the years preceding the Great War, and the second peels back layers of trauma experienced on the home front in London during the war. They are, as I will demonstrate in my last chapter, Burnett's antithetical version of T. S. Eliot's *The Waste Land*.

Within the generic variety of Burnett's novels so briefly sketched above, there are a couple of patterns: first, the novels tend to come in pairs (*A Lady of Quality* and *His Grace of Osmond*; *The Making of a Marchioness* and *The Methods of Lady Walderhurst*; and *The Head of the House of Coombe* and *Robin*), the first pair offering the same narrative first from the point of view of the heroine, Clorinda, and the second from the point of view of her eventual husband, the Duke of Osmond, and the second volume of the other pairs being a continuation of the narrative in the first volume. Second, the plots tend to move in the direction of romance with an emphasis on the moral, spiritual and physical challenges faced by a female protagonist, but rendered in a way that makes the romance marriage plot/consummation merely incidental. Burnett may deploy recognizable romance plot conventions, but she is not interested in those conventions as such. She exploits those conventions in her effort to explore the possibilities of her female protagonists experiencing the world fully through their bodies and reanimating life-denying social conditions through the attunement of their bodies and spirits. In other words, she works to imagine the full being of women in the world.

Given the generic range and imaginative ambition of Burnett's novels, we can push back against Thwaite's suggestion that after the runaway popularity of *Fauntleroy* as a novel, a stage play and a cultural phenomenon (mothers dressing their young sons in velvet coats and frill collars), Burnett was no longer taken seriously by critics, and we can offer some resistance to Molson's assertion that "From 1900 onward, Burnett ceased to have anything significant to say as far as the major journals were concerned" (37). We can begin by looking more closely at what the critics actually had to say about Burnett's novels, pre- and post-*Fauntleroy*, reading with an eye for the details of what the critics specifically notice about the novels and considering to what extent we would evaluate those things the same or differently today. Of *A Lady of Quality*, for instance, Molson observes: "Especially affronted were the many reviewers who [...] were bothered not only by Burnett's romanticism but also by her feminist stance" (36). Molson documents *The Atlantic* reviewer's distress that the heroine of the novel escaped "punishment" for killing the man who stalked her and threatened her life while also noting how the reviewer for the *Critic* found the novel Burnett's best because it "attested to the author's acknowledgement, regardless of cost, that women no longer accept the double standard" (36). I stress those details from Molson's overview of the history or Burnett's novel reviews to suggest that the reviews were more variegated than summary characterizations of trends in the reviews indicate and to highlight that whether writing in mid-Victorian realistic mode or later Victorian and modernist romance mode, Burnett's novels were always engaged with the ideological struggles of their time. And one of those struggles, articulated variously (e.g., the redundant or odd woman, the fallen woman, the new woman and so on) and consistently, concerns the evolving social visibility and broadening range of activity for women. So rather than laying out patterns across the reviews for novels published between 1877 and 1924, which would look in the end like a crazy quilt, a wild mixture of high praise and extreme condemnation with shades or moderation in between, it would be more productive to tease out what Burnett's contemporary critics had to say about her fictional women with an emphasis on Joan Lowrie, Clorinda Wildairs and Emily Fox Seton, the titular heroines of *That Lass O'Lowries*, *A Lady of Quality*, and *The Making of a Marchioness* and *The Methods of Lady Walderhurst*.

One of the earliest reviews of *That Lass O'Lowries* was published in the November 1877 issue of *Atlantic Monthly*. The review opens by observing that the novel's

> essential quality is power. It impresses rather than pleases; it holds rather than entertains; for while it is both entertaining and pleasing in a very marked degree, yet to say that it were

simply that would be to give no hint of its *masculine vigor*, its dramatic intensity, its clear truthfulness to life and the consummate art of its execution. (Italics added, 189)

As an aesthetic judgment, the adjectives "masculine" and "dramatic" refer to the quality of language and narrative focus, but in conjunction with the review's assessment of the novel's protagonist, those adjectives become somewhat agitated: "The prominent character is Joan Lowrie; a sort of queen among her people, self-contained, heroic, masculine in proportions both physically and morally. Few such figures have been seen in fiction" (189). The formulation of a "queen" who is both "physically and morally" masculine may be jarring, but it does gesture toward a degendering of the masculine; that is, if, as the reviewer claims, "[T]he motive of the story is the development of the feminine in Joan" (189), that development builds upon a moral and physical force that is culturally associated with the masculine but may be, in the world of Burnett's novel, the basic ground upon which human beings, men and women, develop in ways peculiar to each individual.

In 1879 in a long review essay in *Southern Review* on a volume of Burnett's short stories and *That Lass O'Lowries*, Mrs. S. Bledsoe Herrick makes a related point:

> Whenever the subject matter of her story has been gathered, however it may be told [...] she reaches down through the external crust of untrained manner, and custom, and speech, and lays hold upon some primal instinct of the race. In fact, the moral beauty and real strength consists in the portrayal of character, whose determining principle is an unswerving loyalty to love or to duty,—sometimes to one, to the exclusion of the other; and sometimes to both—but the key-note to the music of them all is loyalty; and its presence lends all the tenderness and beauty, its lack all the bitterness. (102)

In the abstract, Herrick's assessment seems highly conventional: a woman novelist would perforce conform to the conventions of gender by harnessing her narrative to love or to duty, in either case subordinating herself to the needs of others with loyalty to someone or something outside of herself determining her value. But a counter-reading is possible. By "reach[ing] down through [...] custom" in an effort to make contact with "some primal instinct of the race" (i.e., the human race), Herrick catches a glimpse of Burnett's effort to place socially determined gender constructions of masculinity and femininity in tension with each other, if not to erase the distinction at least to destabilize it and in the process to expand the range of human behavior as that behavior emerges from a ground of physical and by extension moral strength. The idea implicit here is that the more attuned one's body is to the physical realities of being in the world, the moral contours and physical development of the individual life emerge through the interchange between the capacities of the body and the rigors of the material world, a world that includes, of course, other people. So perhaps loyalty of any sort must begin with loyalty to one's self.

That latter point is implicit in the story about the human original upon whom Burnett based the character of Joan. Here in Ann Thwaite's telling, the tale begins with Burnett's observation of a group of factory girls congregated in Islington Square, Manchester:

They were talking loudly, pushing each other, glad to be free. But there was one who was not fooling around. She was knitting a coarse blue worsted stocking. There was something strange and special about her. Frances could not explain it. As she watched, a man came into the Square—a tough-looking man with a moleskin cap pulled over his brow.

"Here's thy feyther!" one of the girls exclaimed. The group stopped laughing and broke up. But the girl knitting went on knitting. When the man swore at her and bullied her and threatened her with his fist, she went on knitting but started to walk slowly out of the square.

"Dom tha brazen impidence!" Frances heard him say. Frances never forget the girl. Fifteen years later, changed into a pit-girl, she was the heroine of Frances' first novel. (15)

The details in that anecdote are striking, the knitting of the stocking, the moleskin cap, the raised fist, the composure of "The Junoesque Factory Girl" (Vivian Burnett, 65). Most powerful, however, is the girl's composure. She responds to her father's threat of violence (a standard image of patriarchal authority) with composure, self-contained and unafraid. The girl is thoroughly embedded in the physical realities of her social and personal circumstance, and awful as they are, she is undaunted, loyal, it is safe to assume, to herself, to the fundamental integrity of the reality of her body/being in the world. In the short autobiography of her childhood, *The One I Knew the Best of All*, which she wrote in the third person, Burnett's reflections on the factory-girl evoke an image of a woman abused, even dismembered, but asserting nonetheless her strength and beauty:

> But she thought of her [the factory-girl] often and pondered her over, and felt her power and mystery. Not until she had given some contemplative thought to various antique marbles, and had wondered 'what was the matter' with the Venus of Milo, did it dawn upon her mind that in this girl in the clogs and the apron she had seen and been overpowered by Beauty such as goddesses were worshipped for, and strength such as should belong to one who ruled.[32]

The vision of the factory-girl and Burnett's comparison of her to a dismembered statue serve as powerful metaphors for Burnett's sense of how the patriarchal society she was born into keeps women constrained through the implicit and explicit imposition of physical force, an idea reinforced by the image of the armless marble statue Venus of Milo, an image of strength and beauty plucked from the ruins of Greek civilization, its disfigurement a symbol of female suffering and dignity.

But the violence figured in that image need not be restricted to physical violence; it can be economic as well. In fact, the roots of the father's violence against his factory-girl daughter most likely had its origins in material deprivation as much as patriarchal authority. As a young girl Burnett's apprehension of that violence was mingled with outrage and a feeling of injustice, emotions that were reinforced in experiences closer to home. She learned first-hand about the economic frailty of women unprotected by a man when, upon the death of her father, her mother took over the family business, which soon thereafter failed. They then were compelled to leave Manchester for the United States, settling near Knoxville, Tennessee, to the place where her father's brother had emigrated some years earlier. There they lived in the post-Civil War years perilously close to poverty until Frances found success selling stories to magazines. Her biographers chronicle those years in detail. My point here is that the line between her perception of her own economic and physical vulnerability and her imaginative engagement with what she sees as the vulnerable position of women more broadly is very thin. Thus, the imaginative investment she makes in the configuration of her heroine's efforts to locate themselves in a position of physical stability and integrity against social structures (and in some cases direct threats of violence from men) that insist on their frailty and dependence is drawn from a deep bank of experience. Her heroines, whether placed in radical or conservative circumstances, find ways to safeguard and develop the potential of their own being in the world.

In a long and miscellaneous piece in the May 1896 issue of the British journal *Pall Mall Magazine*, the novelist and playwright Israel Zangwill offers the most complex and sensitive reading of *A Lady of Quality* of any of the reviews I have seen. Most reviewers responded to the heroine, Clorinda, with either praise or blame, basing their assessments on a standard of conventional morality and psychological plausibility. Zangwill, in contrast, suggests that the novel reveals "the latent Byron in Mrs. Burnett's breast"; he argues that Clorinda embodies a "Nietzsche-like individualism," and in a gesture I find both illuminating and exhilarating, he observes that the story is "a story of 'Tess' triumphant, of the one woman who has conquered Fate."[33] While I object to the metaphor of "Fate" (I would have used the less elegant but more accurate word "patriarchy"), I find Zangwill's defense of the right of Burnett's heroine to defend herself from male violence without having subsequently to pay for that defense in moral condemnation and legal judgment bracing. Reading Clorinda "in the spirit of the Symbolists," Zangwill sees her as a vehicle through which Burnett "says her say on the great problems" (154), but he never says precisely what those "great problems" are. He alludes to the potential influence of the "new woman" novel—"There are [those] who will think the new Mrs. Burnett has caught the infection of the 'new woman,'" he writes—"But this," he observes, "will be unjust. Mrs. Burnett has undergone a slow evolution. They were all Clorindas in embryo—that Lass O'Lowries, Rachel Ffrench, little Sarah Crewe, Bertha Amory, that brilliant Bird of Paradise agonizing in an inward hell" (154). Undefined and rejected as not new, the "great problems" must point toward the long-standing problems for women living in a patriarchal society that subjects them to complex structures of constraint and a moral double standard in behavior and judgment. Clorinda's response to those problems is to redefine herself "as vixen, mistress, and murderess" and wife, "yet remaining withal the matchless Clorinda." So her core integrity, the various placements of her body in the world, where the placements change but her sense of being in her own body remains the same, enables her to find "her soul and her womanhood through all the stress and storm," which, Zangwill observes, "is indeed a bold conception" (154).

Zangwill's praise for the strength of Burnett's "virile, mannish, almost swashbuckling say" through Clorinda on the "great problems" for women is qualified by his perception of an undercurrent of "feminine sentimentality below," which transforms some tragic moments in the novel into "inverted sentimentality [...] something of womanly weakness" (154). What he construes as weakness, however, may be the result of how Burnett redefines strength less as grounded in hardness, gendered as masculine, and more as unfolding expansion of capacity brought out by circumstances; strength is supple, like the power of flowing water, which is an image gendered as feminine. I would then revise Zangwill's closing assessment—"Few lady novelists among her contemporaries have excelled her, either in virility or in femininity, and *A Lady of Quality*, a modern symbolic poem in the guise of an archaic romance, will add a new field to her already ample province" (154–55)—by removing the "or" between virility and femininity and reformulating the expression to "virility in femininity and femininity in virility." What Zangwill's language reflects is a glimmer of understanding of how Burnett's heroines draw on the fullest conception of human capacity, fusing qualities gendered as masculine and feminine in different proportions depending on circumstance, human need and the possibilities of growth.

In contrast to the physical strength of Joan Lowrie and Clorinda Wildairs is the moral strength of Emily Fox-Seton. In the lightly titled "Trips to Book Land" section of the *Los Angeles Times*, Julian Hawthorne reviewed *The Methods of Lady Walderhurst* in a piece called "Frances Hodgson Burnett Creates a New Type in Fiction—and of a Woman, at That." Hawthorne registers a form of strength in that review that seems the antithesis of Joan Lowrie's and Clorinda's virility in femininity, and the way he frames the review seems the antithesis of what became the orthodox critical assessment of Burnett as a writer who sold her genius for money and whose work was unworthy of mention after *Fauntleroy*. With a nod toward *That Lass O'Lowries*, the publication of which "was the beginning of a reputation which has held its own, and has ever and anon increased its stature ever since," Hawthorne offers this assessment of Burnett as an author:

> For although Mrs. Burnett has written a good many books during these thirty years, she has never permitted herself to compromise with her art for the sake of feeding on her popularity [...]. She would want as much as anyone, of course, to make a living: but she could not forecast the flights of her muse or consent to limit them to suit the market. She must write as the god bid her, or not at all. The germ of the idea dawned and gathered force in her mind. *It must be developed according to the laws of its own being.* She would stretch it upon no bed of Procrustes, to be drawn out or curtailed as the exigencies of publication might make expedient. (Italics added, n.p.)

One's first response in reading a passage like the one above may be to think that Hawthorne doth protest too much; why bring up notions like "feeding on her popularity" and limiting ambition "to suit the market" unless those notions were already associated with Burnett. But if we take Hawthorne seriously as a reader of Burnett's fiction (and the fact that he was writing for the *Los Angeles Times* suggests we should), we might find that he helps us to understand what seems to be contradictory impulses in her novels: one will celebrate a woman's defiance to convention, another will insist on passivity and acceptance of the status quo. For readers to take one type as representative over the other type requires that we limit Burnett's choices as a writer according to our own ideological bias. If, for example, I celebrate the audacity of Burnett's conception of Clorinda Wildairs as I do above, I must then be appalled by the characterization of Emily Fox Seton. Here is Hawthorne's description:

> The type to which she [Emily] belongs is new in fiction. She is not brilliant intellectually, not clever, not quick or ready, but in all things she manifests a gentle unworldliness, like that of a good and innocent child, a sweet slowness of mental movement, a naïve and unquestioning faith in things and persons which render her unprepared for evil or hostility. The controlling passion of her tender and pure heart is her worshiping love of her husband. (n.p.)

Such a passage, with its conflation of woman and child and its fissuring of woman and intellect, could be inserted in John Ruskin's "Of Queens' Gardens" (1865) with only minimal editing for grammar. Despite Hawthorne's title, his description reflects the most conventional Victorian female characterization grounded on the ideology of the separate spheres, confirming unambiguously Zangwill's detection of the "sentimentality below" *A Lady of Quality* that takes center stage in *The Methods of Lady Walderhurst*. But if we take seriously the idea that Burnett developed the germ of her narrative conception "according to the laws of its own being," we might ask in the context of her narrative world, how does Emily's character find a path of development that helps her realize her capacities in a way that feels true to her own sense of being, even if that path seems unappealing to us? We might further ask how we might take the depth of Hawthorne's affective response to the novel:

> There are some books which come into one's heart and mind quietly, without knocking at the door, without herald or introduction; there comes with them a sphere of friendliness and sympathy, an assurance of well-doing, a subtle breathing of truth and goodness, which, if there be in us any goodness, truth and human faith and tenderness, draw it forth, and the book thenceforward seems to have become a part of our inner life, a voice out of nature, always speaking to us, but till now never recognized. (n.p.)

Whether we are put off or not by the vocabulary of goodness, well-doing, sympathy, faith and so on in an evaluation of a serious literary work, and whether we are skeptical about Hawthorne's response because it smacks of a socially constructed gender ideology that he is assuming as natural, the idea that reading the novel brought to the surface for Hawthorne an affective dimension of his character that he otherwise would not have recognized speaks to how the heroine takes possession of the reader through the power of narrative.

What I am describing does partake of sentimentality, but it also has a quality of Wordsworth's "unremembered acts of kindness and of love" and is thus something of substance, a kind of strength buried beneath a superficial perception of weakness. So the discourse of reviews that highlight the heroines in Burnett's novels can lead us to think about them less as contradictory and more as protean: strength appears in many guises, even its apparent opposite. Coming to an understanding of the variety and continuity of the heroines that emerged in Burnett's novels—from her youthful insight of the Junoesque pit-girl in Manchester, where she apprehended the possibility that an interanimation of female physical strength and conventional markers of female outer and inner beauty can produce a sense of individual composure defined in the first instance by bodily integrity—provides a through line for my interpretive project in this study.

A selective reading of the reviews of Burnett's novels could be done to arrive at radically different conclusions about the thematic emphases and literary qualities of her work. I could have looked at other reviews and drawn other conclusions about Burnett's novels more broadly but not necessarily about her heroines. They remain in the body of reviews as a whole various and contradictory, similar qualities celebrated or condemned. Joan is strong, Clorinda versatile and physically adept, Emily stoic, long-suffering and immovable. But whether those heroines are read as "reproducing or heroically resisting a univocal dominant ideology" (Felski 142) is not the point. Rather reading Burnett's novels with close attention to her heroines in the context of her originating Victorian context and tracking how that context changes to what recent critics have discussed in terms of popular modernism enables us to recognize in her novels what Rita Felski has claimed for women's popular fiction in the period of high modernism: "popular fiction," she writes, "can more usefully be read as comprising a variety of ideological strands that cohere or contradict each other in diverse ways" (142). The reproduction/resistance dichotomy becomes a way to simplify and, depending on the ideological position of the critic, to praise or blame. In writing about the work of Marie Corelli under the category of "the popular sublime," Felski emphasizes ambiguity, the tension in Corelli's work between "a critical response to irresolvable tensions within the social" and "conservative affirmations of the eternal verities of sexual and racial otherness which are less easily reconciled with any form of resistive impulse" (143). (One's mind might move not unfairly upon reading those quotations to T. S. Eliot, a point I will address at length in the last chapter.) As noted earlier, Burnett's work has not been addressed in the recent reassessments of popular fiction. It should be. For not only do Burnett's novels have the same tensions between resistance and accommodation critics have been exploring in popular modernism, their origins are squarely within the practices of Victorian realism, which Burnett both relies on and reinflects in a way that we might recognize today as Neo-Victorian.

Consider the contrast between Burnett's emphasis on the literal bodily size and strength of Joan Lowrie and Clorinda Wildairs, for instance, and the emphasis in Victorian domestic fiction on the airy, disembodied heroine as angel in the house. Helena Michie addresses that point as follows: "Even though some Victorian works on beauty espouse 'plumpness' in young women, the most positive female characters in nineteenth-century novels are most often frail and weak."[34] She then addresses a gallery of characters from Charlotte Bronte (the contrast between the ethereal Lucy Snow and the voluptuous Ginevra Fanshawe in *Villette*), George Eliot (the plump Hetty Sorrel and the increasingly thin Dinah Morris in *Adam Bede*) and Anthony Trollope (too many characters qualify to list), and draws these conclusions: "bigger, more strikingly beautiful women are somehow suspect" (think of Blanche Ingram in *Jane Eyre*); and "[T]he aesthetic of weakness and hunger only thinly disguises an ideology of male dominance" (22). Thus, male dominance depends on the diminishment of the physical realities of the female body, which must be deprived in one way or another to weaken it, making women fundamentally dependent and subservient. Michie locates resistance to that ideology of male dominance through denying the physical realities of woman's bodies in the poetry of Adrienne Rich in the 1970s. "For Rich," Michie observes, the "abstract" that must be 'broken through' is identified with metaphor and figuration [...]. In "Natural Resources," she insists on literalness [...]. In describing the work of a female miner, she says:

> The miner is no metaphor. She goes
> Into the cage like the rest, is flung
> Downward by gravity like them, must change
> Her body like the rest to fit a crevice.

In resisting metaphor, Rich, along with many other feminists, aligns it with denial of the body. (139)

Rather than a metaphoric "angel," Burnett's first novelistic heroine Joan Lowrie is a miner, who works as hard as any man and has the physical strength beyond the capacities of most of her male peers. There is no way to deny the physical capacity of her body for productive labor. She even has a physical courage beyond the others in the mine, demonstrated by her heroism during a mine accident. And like the pit-girl recollected in Burnett's youth, Joan is under constant physical threat from her brutal father. So even though she is the romantic lead in the narrative, an object of male desire, she too "goes/ into the cage like the rest, is flung/downward by gravity." Burnett, in 1877 not 1977, gives expression to the literality of the female body as a human body, expressive in its capacity for productivity and potential for emotional, imaginative and sexual fulfillment.

IV

In the chapters that follow, I have organized my readings of Burnett's novels based on their generic variety and rough chronology: Victorian domestic realistic novels of the 1870s and early 1880s, American regional fiction in the early to mid-1880s, historical fiction in the 1890s, transatlantic novels in the early twentieth century and post-World War I modernist romance in the early 1920s. There is some overlapping of categories and unevenness in the chronology, which will become apparent in the details of my discussion in each chapter. For the purpose of this introduction, I will lay out the contours of each chapter.

Three of Burnett's first four novels are clearly in the tradition of Victorian domestic realism, a tradition still very much alive in the 1870s. Two are located in industrial settings and the third in an English village. *That Lass O'Lowries* (1877) is an industrial novel, one of a number of subcategories under domestic realism, and is set in a Lancashire mining town. It focuses on the domestic life of Joan Lowrie, who works in the mines, and her drunken brute of a father. Its concerns most broadly are with the plight of the working class. *Haworth's* (1879) is also an industrial novel, but its focus is on the owners of a factory, and the tension between their efforts to develop technology that would displace workers and the workers' resistance to losing their jobs. *A Fair Barbarian* (1881) is an English village idyll, with a difference; it is visited by a brash American girl, whose father had been born in the village before emigrating to the American west as a young man. The girl's arrival threatens the equilibrium of the village. Placing those novels next to the pattern of novels in Elizabeth Gaskell's early career, the parallels are striking. *Mary Barton*, with its focus on working-class suffering; *North and South*, with its focus on the moral tensions among factory owners and between factory owners and workers; and *Cranford*, with its concerns about a traditional English village struggling to maintain its identity in the face of social change arguably provide a pattern of development for an aspiring woman novelist from the very place where Gaskell lived and worked. In this chapter I will explore the relation between Burnett's and Gaskell's early novels in the context of American literary culture at a time when that culture was unsure of its own center of gravity. In order to demonstrate the productive influence Gaskell's work had on Burnett's, I will address the American reliance on British literary precedents in literary culture, notably in *Scribner's Magazine*, which became *The Century Illustrated Monthly Magazine* in 1881; how Burnett deployed those antecedents to establish her literary authority; and then how she may be said to have spoken through those antecedents as she shaped her own identity as an important literary figure even as she created heroines defined more by their vitality than their "wise" passivity.

The fourth of Burnett's novels was published between the industrial and village novels and is a rural American story entitled *Louisiana* (1880), the name of the novel's heroine. That novel has antecedents in Burnett's short fiction, which she had been publishing in popular magazines before achieving success in *Scribner's;* at which point she found support and guidance from the editor, Richard Watson Gilder, considered at the time the arbiter of American literary taste in the genteel tradition. In the second chapter, then, I will address Burnett's American novels, aligning them with American regional fiction and with social realism since that group of novels contains her undervalued political novel *Through One Administration* (1883) and her long delayed multiregional, political and post-Civil War novel *In Connection with the De Willoughby Claim* (1899). Burnett began writing the latter novel before the former; she put it aside and did not complete it until she embarked on writing her historical novels. In *Through One Administration* Burnett probes the desires, doubts, strength and physical beauty of her heroine, Bertha Amory, who builds for herself a depth of integrity in a social milieu that compromises nearly everyone, including Bertha herself. As Henry James had done in *The Portrait of a Lady*, Burnett explores an enigmatic marriage between a strong woman and a deeply manipulative man in a manner that exposes how corruption is masked and normalized. In both novels the blurred boundary between personal ambition for a life of self-fulfillment and a society that turns such ambition into a form of frustrated illusion animates the narratives.

The third chapter will address the historical novels, *A Lady of Quality* (1896) and *His Grace of Osmonde* (1897), with an eye toward how they refract Burnett's contemporary concerns through the prism of historical distance. As Zangwill suggested in his review of *A Lady of Quality*, these novels are best approached as symbols with, I would add, a patina of allegory. Taken together the novels articulate a kind of feminist allegory that challenges gender stereotypes; they introduce the idea of what Angelique Richardson has called "rational reproduction,"[35] a concept Burnett returns to through the remainder of her work, including her two sensation-inflected country house social novels, *The Making of a Marchioness* (1901) and *The Methods of Lady Walderhurst* (1901). Although not historical in setting, those latter novels offer a more contemporary take on re-productive issues by weaving into the narrative elements of personal and social moral degeneration through metaphors of criminality and class conflict. Taken as a group, they extend the feminist concerns of the historical novels to class concerns in the social-sensation novels, in both cases opening social space for individual women, against at times implacable obstacles, to flourish as human beings.

The fourth chapter will address a pair of transatlantic novels, *The* Shuttle (1907) and *T. Tembarom* (1913), which in English country house settings engage Anglo-American kinship and social relations in ways that return to the notion of rational reproduction but sharpen the context through the contemporary fears of degeneration on both sides of the Atlantic. Those novels also deploy elements of sensation fiction, the genre that in the 1860s transformed broad social anxieties into domestic concerns, erasing the boundaries between the public and private, threats to national well-being felt most forcefully as threats to the home. To those themes and generic elements Burnett weaves in an economic thread through the use of American wealth by way of transatlantic marriage to stave off the threat of degeneration through what we might call *ir*rational reproduction: one transatlantic marriage in the novel is irrational, productive of lame offspring; the other transatlantic marriage is rational, regenerating an estate and by extension a nation (Great Britain) through the vitality of a woman.

The fifth chapter will explore another pair of novels, *The Head of the House of Coombe* (1922) and *Robin* (1922), originally written as one, that engage with and refuse the disillusionment of a post-World War I English society defined by fragmentation, social alienation and metaphysical despair. In a generic return to domestic realism, these novels draw on Burnett's career-long experimentation with other generic modes, weaving them together in a story about the growth of two children into adulthood in the years leading up to and then well into the Great War. In the later years of her life, Burnett took a keen interest in psychical research, the occult powers of the mind, an interest shared by figures as diverse as Conan Doyle, William James and Havelock Ellis. Critics have dismissed Burnett's interest, however, suggesting that she was another deluded, grieving mother looking for solace after the death of her favorite child (her son, Lionel, at 16). Based on some of her more incidental texts such as *In a Closed Room* (1905), an illustrated children's book, *The Dawn of a Tomorrow* (1906), a novella turned into a stage play, and *The White People* (1917), another novella about a form of second-sight, Burnett's interest was serious, sustained and in its time a source of productive imaginative response to what felt like in the Great War as the ruin of English speaking culture. (Think of the line from T. S. Eliot's *The Wasteland*, also published in 1922: "These fragments I have shored against my ruins" [l. 430]). In this chapter I will read those novels against Eliot's long poem, arguing for the value of Burnett's turn to physical resilience infused with spirit in the image of heroic maternity against Eliot's synthetic gathering up of pieces that cannot be made whole.

Notes

1 Edward L. Burlingame. "Art. VI.—New American Novels." *North American Review*, vol. 125, no. 258 (September 1877): 309–21.
2 Mrs. S. Bledsoe Herrick. "Frances Hodgson Burnett." *Southern Review*, vol. 25, no. 49 (January 1879): 87–117.

3. Edward Eggleston. "Some Recent Works of Fiction." *North American Review*, vol. 129, no. 276 (November 1879): 510–17 (513).
4. Thomas F. Ford and C. Lillian. "A Chronicle of Young Love." *Los Angeles Times* ("The Literary Page"), August 20, 1922 (Section III), 36, 43.
5. Peter D. McDonald. *British Literary Culture and Publishing Practice 1880–1914*. Cambridge: Cambridge UP, 1997, p. 14.
6. Martin Hipsky. *Modernism and the Women's Popular Romance in Britain, 1885–1925*. Athens: Ohio UP, 2011, p. 21.
7. "Recent Literature." *Atlantic Monthly*, vol. 40 (November 1877): 630–31.
8. "That Lass O'Lowries." *Southern Review*, vol. 24, no. 48 (October 1878): 491–96.
9. Herrick, "Frances Hodgson Burnett," 630–31 and 491–96.
10. Eggleston, "Some Recent Works of Fiction," 510–17.
11. *Chicago Daily Tribune* (July 30, 1922), Section F, 1.
12. Ann Thwaite. *Waiting for the Party: The Life of Frances Hodgson Burnett, Author of* The Secret Garden *and* A Little Princess. Boston: David R. Godine, 1991, p. 86. All subsequent references to Thwaite throughout this book are drawn from this volume.
13. Andreas Huyssen. *After the Great Divide: Modernism, Mass Culture, Postmodernism*. Bloomington: Indiana UP, 1986, p. 48.
14. Gretchen Holbrook Gerzina. *Frances Hodgson Burnett: The Unexpected Life of the Author of* The Secret Garden. New Brunswick: Rutgers UP, 2004, p. 208. All subsequent references to Gerzina throughout this book are drawn from this volume.
15. Mary Hammond. *Reading, Publishing and the Formation of Literary Taste in England, 1880–1914*. Aldershot: Ashgate, 2006, p. 136.
16. Elaine Showalter. *A Literature of Their Own*. Princeton: Princeton UP, 1977 and Ellen Moers. *Literary Women*. New York: Knopf Doubleday, 1976.
17. Rita Felski. *The Gender of Modernity*. Cambridge, MA: Harvard UP, 1995.
18. The most often cited scholar on the Bronte–Burnett connection is U. C. Knoepflmacher. See, for instance, his "Little Girls without Their Curls: Female Aggression in Victorian Children's Literature." *Children's Literature*, vol. 11 (1983): 14–31 and his "Introduction" to the 2003 Penguin edition of *The Little Princess*. For a summary of the scholarship comparing Burnett's *The Secret Garden* to Emily Bronte's *Wuthering Heights*, see the debate in *Connotations* in response to Susan E. James's "*Wuthering Heights* for Children: Frances Hodgson Burnett's *The Secret Garden*," vol. 10, no. 1 (2000): 59–76. The first response by Lisa Tyler is called "Bronte and Burnett: A Response to Susan E. James," vol. 12, no. 1 (2002): 61–66, and the second by Anna Krugovoy Silver is called "*Wuthering Heights* and *The Secret Garden*: A Response to Susan E. James," vol. 12, nos. 1–2 (2003): 194–201.
19. See the Internet Movie Database (IMDb) for more details.
20. Francis Molson. "Frances Hodgson Burnett (1848–1924)." *American Literary Realism, 1870–1910*, vol. 8 (1975): 35–41 (39).
21. Philip Waller. *Writers, Readers, & Reputations: Literary Life in Britain 1870–1918*. Oxford: Oxford UP, 2006.
22. Alex Zwerdling. *Improvised Europeans: American Literary Expatriates and the Siege of London*. New York: Basic Books, 1998, pp. 31–32.
23. Peter Keating. *The Haunted Study: A Social History of the English Novel 1875–1914*. London: Fontana Press, 1991, p. 226.
24. David Trotter. *The English Novel in History 1895–1920*. London: Routledge, 1993.
25. Suzanne Clark. *Sentimental Modernism: Women Writers and the Revolution of the Word*. Bloomington: Indiana UP, 1991.
26. Joseph McAleer. *Popular Reading and Publishing in Britain 1914–1950*. Oxford: Clarendon Press, 1992.
27. McDonald, *British Literary Culture and Publishing Practice*.

28 Nicholas Daly. *Modernism, Romance and the Fin De Siecle: Popular Fiction and British Culture, 1880–1914*. Cambridge: Cambridge UP, 1999.
29 Hammond, *Reading, Publishing and the Formation of Literary Taste in England*.
30 Hipsky, *Modernism and the Women's Popular Romance in Britain*.
31 Phyllis Bixler. *Frances Hodgson Burnett*. Twayne's English Authors Series. Boston: Twayne, 1984, pp. 119 and 128.
32 Frances Hodgson Burnett. *The One I Knew Best of All*. London: Frederick Warne, 1893, p. 75.
33 Israel Zangwill. "Without Prejudice." *The Pall Mall Magazine*, vol. 9, no. 37 (May 1896): 154.
34 Helena Michie. *The Flesh Made Word: Female Figures and Women's Bodies*. New York: Oxford UP, 1987, p. 22.
35 Angelique Richardson. *Love and Eugenics in the Late Nineteenth Century: Rational Reproduction & the New Woman*. Oxford: Oxford UP, 2003.

Chapter One

LEARNING FROM ELIZABETH GASKELL

I

At 18 years old in 1868, Burnett published her first stories in *Godey's Lady's Book*, a popular woman's magazine, and over the next four years "[S]he had stories published […] in every magazine in America, 'except *Harper's, Scribner's* and the *Atlantic*'" (Thwaite 37). She was hesitant to try the latter three magazines because, as she herself put it: "It would have seemed to me a kind of presumption to aspire to entering the actual world of literature" (cited in Thwaite 37). Despite the fact that she stated quite baldly when she sent out her first story to *Ballou's Magazine* that her "object is remuneration," she developed a sense early on that writing strictly for the market was one thing while writing at the behest of her own imaginative impulses and aesthetic vision was another. One question she must have asked herself concerns the principles that might guide her hand were she to write with ambitions of "entering the actual world of literature." We can infer an answer to that question in two ways: by considering the literary field in America in the 1870s and by careful reading of the novels (all first published serially before being published in volume form) she published with Scribner's in the 1870s and early 1880s. One thing we will find is deep points of contact between three of her first four published novels and three of Elizabeth Gaskell's first four published novels. How we might understand that depth of contact depends, in part, on our understanding of Burnett's response to her most immediate literary predecessors and how those predecessors were positioned in the literary field at the time.

Burnett was born in Manchester, England in 1849, the year after Chapman and Hall published Gaskell's first novel, *Mary Barton*, and Burnett lived in Manchester for the next 16 years until 1865, the year of Gaskell's death and the year Burnett emigrated to Tennessee. As her 1893 autobiography of her childhood shows, she read voraciously, everything from the Bible to histories of Greece and Rome to the novels of Sir Walter Scott and Charles Dickens. She read the odd periodical volume as well, even the "*Blackwood*" [sic *Blackwood's Edinburgh Magazine*], "a big book and heavy."[1] Although Burnett's contemporary reviewers detected influences from Dickens, Thackeray, the Brontes and Gaskell on Burnett's early novels, and while Burnett herself alludes to Dickens, Thackeray and their contemporaries in her autobiography, she never mentions or alludes in even the most tangential way to Elizabeth Gaskell, *the* most significant literary figure in Manchester during the years of her formal education in school and her informal education as an insatiable, undisciplined reader. Burnett's ready acknowledgment of the interest and excitement with which she read the great Victorian realists, who were arguably at the height of their powers in the year she was born and through much of her childhood, and her silence about the figure quite literally closest to her own early experiences is surprising, but that silence suggests, I think, how deep Gaskell's influence was, too deep to be named.

During the 1870s, the decade during which Burnett entered "the actual world of literature," the major American literary magazines were reshaping themselves. *Harper's Monthly* had built its reputation (and circulation) by publishing the major Victorian realists in serial before passing the full manuscripts to their book publishing arm for circulation in volume form. In contrast the *Atlantic Monthly* published New Englanders; according to Arthur John some 60 percent of the *Atlantic's* contributors during the 1860s were from New England, notably Emerson, Longfellow and Whittier.[2] That split allegiance in the American literary magazine industry presented a problem for Josiah Holland, the founding editor of *Scribner's Magazine*, who set out to provide a venue to publish American authors in direct competition with *Harper's*, which relied on English authors for much of its content. When Holland found that American writers were hard to find, new writers yet to emerge and established writers loyal to other publishers, he looked abroad. "He personally solicited novels from Charles Kingsley and George Eliot; he authorized the American journalist and diplomat William James Stillman to act as agent for *Scribner's* in England, commissioning him to seek contributions from John Ruskin, Thomas Hughes, William Morris, Algernon Charles Swinburne, and other eminent Victorians" (John 14). The upshot is that American literary taste was continuing to be shaped by the aesthetic practices of English authors even as publishers were searching for ways to foreground the work of American authors, creating a state of literary uncertainty; American literary magazines were venues for a continuing tradition of Anglo-American literature that was being destabilized by unevenly emergent regional American writing. That uncertainty about literary authority contributed to the embrace of Burnett's early English novels: she could be advertised as a new voice in American letters while at the same time writing in an English tradition, her novels set in England, her themes identifiable as part of a familiar genre, her characters' speech regional, English dialect. Consequently reviewers located her work in an Anglo-American tradition, comparing Burnett to Dickens and Eliot, anchoring her among the "eminent Victorians" even as they praised the freshness of her work. That sense of freshness through the familiar, however, captures a tension that can be felt throughout her career while it marks, I suggest, the particular quality of her originality.

If American literary publishing in the 1870s was in a state of uncertainty, characterized by anxiety about the center of literary authority in American letters, the shock in 1880 of George Eliot's death to the Anglo-American literary field exacerbated that anxiety. As Martin Hipsky has pointed out, the literary field in Britain for women became polarized toward the end of the nineteenth century: "Given the lopsided binary 'serious' versus 'frivolous' novel-writing roles, any aspiring young woman writer of the time must have felt powerfully the limited possibilities of the literary field" (28). Because the "serious" side of that binary was identified profoundly with the work of George Eliot, her death stimulated the ambitions of many British women writers. Hipsky puts the point this way:

> [I]n the years following George Eliot's death, the list of those who [tried] to match Eliot's level of achievement is a long one [...]. Patriarchal ideologies notwithstanding, the flourishing

career of such a 'consecrated' and belaurelled predecessor, well within living memory, served as a powerful encouragement to ambitious women romance writers coming of intellectual age in the 1880s and 1890s. (28)

Burnett's place among those so encouraged by Eliot's example and absence is complicated for a couple of reasons. First, her first two novels were published during Eliot's lifetime, one even having been reviewed alongside a work of Eliot's. Any comparisons between her work and Eliot's, then, were living comparisons. Upon Eliot's death, among some reviewers in England and America, Burnett became the figure identified as inheriting Eliot's mantle. Second, the void left by Eliot's death was felt more by Burnett's reviewers than by Burnett herself. Rather than Burnett looking to fill the space in the literary field left vacant by Eliot's death, Burnett's early reviewers placed her there, a lofty eminence from which one could only fall. Burnett's literary career we might say was formed on the bedrock of the Victorian novel before being shaken by uneven and unpredictable forces in the Anglo-American literary field after 1880. Then by the time of the Great War, there was no bedrock of any sort on which to continue to build a literary career, only fragments of stone. With all the flux in the American literary publishing industry accelerated by generational changes at the highest levels of what we might crudely call the literary workforce, and with historical and technological changes in the Anglo-American world that we today associate with high modernism, Burnett's most intimate literary antecedents have fallen by the critical wayside, visible only in side-long glances in the contemporary reviews and later literary scholarship.

Consider in that latter regard how gingerly Ann Thwaite in her 1991 biography addresses the relation between Elizabeth Gaskell's novels and Frances Hodgson Burnett's. The first reference to Gaskell and Burnett occurs when Thwaite notes that on November 24, 1849, the day Francis Hodgson was born, "Not far away, Mrs Gaskell was writing a letter to Charlotte Bronte, congratulating her on *Shirley*. Her own *Mary Barton* had been published the previous year; the Manchester operatives Mrs Gaskell wrote of were the same people who were soon to fascinate the young Frances" (3). That brief passage captures in miniature a typical strategy when Gaskell's and Burnett's names are linked in the scholarship: the happenstance of Manchester residence is raised in order to suggest that they saw similar things, in this case factory operatives. The implication then is that any overlap in literary engagement with working-class life in Manchester at mid-century is a result of place; literary influence is not part of the equation. A more interesting example can be found when Thwaite discusses the death of Burnett's father and the family's financial decline: "Mrs Gaskell's great 'prevailing thought'—'the seeming injustice of the inequalities of fortune'—was already evident to the small Frances" (13). Here Burnett's experience puts her in the place of Gaskell's working-class characters, generating a parallel perception and foreclosing any later literary connection. When Thwaite approaches the possibility that Burnett's literary imagination may have been stimulated by *Mary Barton*, she is careful to overwhelm that possibility by tying Burnett's inspiration for *That Lass O'Lowries* to her memory of the Junoesque factory-girl alluded to earlier, to a series of articles on Lancashire coal mines published in the *Manchester Guardian* during Burnett's visit to Manchester as a young woman, and perhaps to "Kay-Shuttleworth's pamphlet on 'The Moral and Physical Condition of the Working Class Employed in the Cotton Manufacture in Manchester," but, she avers, "[M]ost of the material for *That Lass O'Lowries* undoubtedly came from real life." Burnett, Thwaite notes as an aside, may have been "stimulated by the Reverend William Gaskell's 'Lectures on the Lancashire Dialect' which had been appended to later editions of *Mary Barton*" (46) when she had her working-class characters speak in dialect. That's as close as she comes to suggesting a direct link between the two novels. The material for *That Lass O'Lowries*, it seems, had to come from anywhere but its most obvious source, the Lancashire working-class novel most identified with Manchester, *Mary Barton*. Thwaite, like Burnett, seems hesitant to go there, the influence too deep for delving.

In her 2004 biography of Burnett, Gretchen Holbrook Gerzina explains the relationship between *That Lass O'Lowries* and *Mary Barton* with similar caution:

> Although there is something reminiscent of Elizabeth Gaskell's novel *Mary Barton*, in which a working girl is wooed by the wealthy son of a mine [sic, factory] owner and only finds strength when she works to clear the name of a neighbor accused of the seducer's murder, Frances created in Joan a strong woman immune to traditional seduction and reluctant to marry into a rank above her. (66)

If the imprecise parallel between the heroines of the two novels is the main ground of comparison, then indeed *That Lass* is "something reminiscent" of *Mary Barton*, but the narrative materials in both novels have much more in common than Gerzina acknowledges. Gerzina suggests, however, a deeper connection when she observes that with *That Lass* "reaping strong reviews, and the new book *Haworth's* [also an industrial novel] well under way, Frances was making a strong and viable bid to be considered a writer of industrial novels who followed in the footsteps of those such as Elizabeth Gaskell and Charles Dickens" (70–71). What better way for Burnett to "follow in the footsteps" of Elizabeth Gaskell in particular than to pattern her early novels on the model of Gaskell's, replicating Gaskell's path into the world of "actual literature"? And what better way to make her own name than for Burnett to replicate that pattern with a difference?

There were, of course, other industrial novels set in Lancashire before *Mary Barton*, notably Charlotte Elizabeth Tonna's didactic *Helen Fleetwood* (1840) and Elizabeth Stone's *William Langshawe, the Cotton Lord* (1842), but those novels degenerate into anti-industrial polemic in their exposure of the evils of industrial labor and their defense of middle-class values.[3] Both focalize their explorations of working-class life from the outside in order to document the necessity of social reform. While Gaskell's novel too shows similar documentary and reformist impulses, much of the narrative is focalized from within the working class; readers see through the eyes of working-class characters as they register the physical details of their domestic experience during a time of labor unrest.[4] Characters also speak in Lancashire dialect rather than in the polite tones of the middle class or in ungrammatical syntax meant to suggest working-class speech. Written from the inside as it were, in Gaskell's novel the narrative elements, which are associated with working-class fiction written by mostly middle-class women, are embedded in a texture of language that communicates lived experience. That observation is reflected in the contemporary reviews of *Mary Barton* and in the reviews of *That Lass O'Lowries*.[5]

Within the rich verbal texture of dialect speech that characterizes both novels, there are narrative elements common to both: contrasts between working-class and middle-class life; distinctive personalities among the working class rather than representative types; cross-class romance; ill-fit between a working-class woman and her class position; fallen woman and death of her child and herself; sensational scenes of fire and accidents; the indifference of the industrialist class to worker suffering that changes due to trauma; marriage or its possibility as an amelioration of previous suffering; brutality of working-class men toward working-class women; mixture of sage and comic wisdom among working-class characters; cross-class murder or attempted murder; and the achievement of some degree of cross-class understanding. Many of those elements are shared by industrial novels generally, but all overlap between Gaskell's and Burnett's first novels. But that overlap is of limited importance and even more limited interest for such narrative elements are part of a common mid-nineteenth century narrative stock (what we might think of as a narrative vocabulary) that both Gaskell and Burnett draw on, Gaskell's sources being her predecessors and Burnett's source being Gaskell. What is important concerns what Burnett does differently with those elements, a difference that is a function of context—Gaskell writing in the place she set her novel toward the end of the time in which it is set and Burnett writing in America some 30 years after the time in which the novel is set—and of personal vision and imaginative ambition. Those different places, times and motives constrain and make possible different narrative possibilities. While I will address a number of those possibilities, my focus will be on what Gerzina calls a "new kind of heroine in the industrial novel" (66). That new heroine, Joan Lowrie, is located in the same narrative space as Gaskell's Mary Barton—both for instance are the focal point of a potential cross-class romance and both have close connections to their respective novel's fallen woman—but Joan occupies that space differently. To get at that difference, we must begin with Mary.

The domestic and social space that Mary occupies can be mapped out as follows: domestically she is the only surviving child of John and Mary Barton, who lost a son, Tom, through illness and physical deprivation; the elder Mary dies early in the novel in childbirth; the baby does not survive. As a result, Mary takes a woman's responsibility for her home with her father, becoming the beautiful though young angel in the house and remaining loyal to her father even as he grows bitter through political disappointment, drink and opium. Her father degenerates to the point where he beats Mary, but he quickly repents. Subsequently, having drawn the lot in his trade union's plot for revenge against the factory owners, he murders the mill owner's son, Harry Carson, who had been harassing Mary in his efforts to seduce her while she simply dreams of a better life for her and her father. Mary's social space is limited since John will not allow her to work in a factory, which would, he thinks, make her more independent, so she finds unpaid work as a seamstress. She befriends a neighbor girl and walks the streets between her home and place of employment. Her only exposure to a larger world is when she goes to Liverpool in search of her cousin, who can save her neighbor (and beloved) from a false charge of murder, which her father had committed. Until that point, she leads a passive life, and as can be inferred when we learn that she knows of her father's guilt, her main survival mechanism is silence, a silence reinforced by the injunction of her friend

Margaret Jennings who advices Mary that she "must just wait and be patient" because "being patient is the hardest work we, any of us [women], have to do through life, I take it. Waiting is far more difficult than doing."[6] In her passivity she is quietly protected by her beloved Jem and her fallen Aunt Esther. After Carson's murder, when Mary acts by tracking down her cousin before the trial at which she testifies, she finally collapses, paying for her activity with a serious illness and long-term weakness. The other social space that she could potentially occupy is delineated by her Aunt Esther; beautiful like Mary and beloved by one above her in class, she runs off with her lover, gets pregnant and is subsequently abandoned. She is compelled by circumstances to the streets to provide for her child, who nevertheless dies. This grim litany of domestic depletion, passivity and social threat suggests that Mary's survival is a matter of happenstance. She could have been Esther, and by fleeing to Canada at novel's end, any hope for social change in the industrial setting is muted.

Burnett assembles a similar set of narrative elements—working-class daughter of widowed, drunken and brutal father; cross-class romance; attempted cross-class murder; the fallen woman; a flight from working-class life at novel's end and so on—but builds a very different narrative world. The most significant difference concerns her transforming the passive Mary character into the active, strong, independent character of Joan. That change from passive angel to active woman affects other aspects of Burnett's industrial novel, muting, for instance, the moral framing of the fallen woman narrative and opening up space for working-class and middle-class women to begin to shape their own lives. Burnett builds this changed narrative world through destabilizing the rigid binaries of gender norms for both women and men. She does so not by erasing recognizable socially performed gender roles but by blurring the boundaries between them and showing how socially gendered qualities can be independent of the sexual distinctions of biological bodies.[7]

The opening line of *That Lass O'Lowries* strikes the keynote: "They did not look like women." The "they" are the "'pit-girls,' as they were called; women who wore a dress more than half-masculine [...] some of whom [...] [with] faces as hard and brutal as the hardest of their collier brothers and husbands and sweethearts" (1). Immediately the social construction of gender and the biological division of the sexes are put in tension, the necessities of labor in the mines obliterating "all bloom of womanly modesty and gentleness," signs of one gender convention, and replacing those signs with another, the "unwashed faces" of a "half-savage existence," a masculine gendered image of the male body in a state of nature. This opening move suggests that the masculinizing pressures of industrial labor go against what was understood as the gender norms for women, "modesty and gentleness," and that, Burnett's readers would have assumed, is bad. When Joan Lowrie is introduced in the second paragraph, however, that easy judgment is hard to sustain.

> Most of them [the pit-girls] were young women, though there were a few older ones among them, and the principal figure in the group—the center figure, about whom the rest clustered—was a young woman. But she differed from the rest in two or three respects. The others seemed somewhat stunted in growth; she was tall enough to be imposing. She was as

roughly clad as the poorest of them, but she wore her uncouth garb differently. The man's jacket of fustian, open at the neck, bared a handsome sun browned throat. The man's hat shaded a face with dark eyes that had a sort of animal beauty, and a well-molded chin. It was at this girl that all the rough jokes seemed to be directed. (2)

Like the industrial workers in *Mary Barton*, described as "stunted" (9), the young women look the same, shrunken it seems from the harshness of the work environment; their masculine attire thus is ill-fitting. Not so with Joan. She wears her male jacket and hat as "naturally" as a man, her "sun browned" throat and "animal beauty" evoking a positive rendering of the notion of a "savage existence." In Joan there is little tension between the sex of her body and the gender of her clothing; she seems simply a magnificent human being.

That does not mean that she has been spared the deprivation of her fellow pit-girls. As Paul Grace, the young, effeminate curate, explains to Fergus Derrick, a young engineer from London recently hired at the mine, Joan's mother died "of hard work, privation, and ill treatment," her father when not working in the mine spends his time "drinking, rioting, and fighting," and Joan herself "has borne […] such treatment as would have killed most women. She has been beaten, bruised, felled to the earth by this father of hers, who is said to be a perfect fiend in his cups." What shocks Grace more than those details of Joan's existence is her response to them. "And yet," he explains, "she holds to her place in their wretched hovel, and makes herself a slave to the fellow with a dogged, stubborn determination" (4). Grace's precise choice of words, "dogged, stubborn determination" rather than "dogged, sullen obedience," for example, suggests that Joan holds to her father through choice not necessity. The uprightness, strength, health and beauty of her form are not compromised by her ill-treatment. It is hard to tell whether she is what she is despite her circumstances or because of them. The question of how her strength and beauty could apparently flourish under such conditions seems to be at the front of Derrick's mind as he reflects on what Grace has told him: He "was struck," the narrator observes, "by a painful sense of incongruity" (9).

As readers reflect on that incongruity, we might notice parallel incongruities that reveal something of Joan's metaphoric importance to the novel's engagement with gender. Between the time Grace described Joan's situation and Derrick reflected on it, Grace shares a note he had received from Anice Barholm, the physically delicate and petite daughter of the rector for whom Grace is curate. Grace has fallen in love with Anice, an emotion Derrick perceives when he notices Grace blush as he fetches the note to share. The narrator tells us the note "did not impress him very favorably. A girl not yet twenty years old, who could write such a note as this to a man who loved her, must be rather *too* self-contained and well balanced" (7). Having just registered that assessment, when Derrick thinks of the ill-fit between Joan and her circumstances, the "incongruity" of her life, he wonders aloud, "[I]f she [Joan] had been in this other girl's niche […] if she had lived the life of this Anice—" (9). The "if" is not completed by a then, but one may usefully ask, might Joan also be "*too* self-contained and well balanced"? Might that be central to what perplexes him—that Joan retains her dignity and self-composure under circumstances where a "proper" woman should not, just as Anice maintains her self-confidence and composure in response to being loved when a girl who knew her place would be, at the very least, flustered? In this perceptive and skillful way, Burnett early in the novel suggests that the surface markings of gender may be irrelevant to the depth and strength of character in women; it is the distortions created by social gender distinctions that lead Derrick to the perception of a woman being "*too* self-contained and well balanced," a perception that becomes impossible to maintain for Derrick and for the reader for whom the expression "self-contained and well balanced" woman cannot by the end of the novel contain the adjective *too*.

The tensions between the social conventions of gender and a woman's bodily composure in the world oscillate throughout the novel, conventional notions of gender encouraging sensitive, humane behavior at times and a rejection of those conventions opening space for Joan to be more fully herself. The novel struggles to establish a productive dynamic within what we might call a unified tension between conformity and resistance, both being necessary in varying proportions depending on changing circumstances for women and men to navigate the world with dignity. Conventional gender expectations, for instance, govern Derrick's first personal encounter with Joan. Immediately after Derrick reflected on the possibility of Joan occupying Anice's "niche," he sees a woman sitting at the roadside. As he approaches her, she raises her head, and he sees that "Her face was disfigured by a bruise, and on one temple was a cut from which the blood trickled down her cheek; but the moonlight showed him that it was Joan" (10). He addresses her by name and offers his help, which she resists by wiping the blood away with her own hand and saying, "[I]t'll do well enow as it is" (10). Derrick, ignoring Joan's gesture and words "drew his handkerchief from his pocket, and [...] managed to stanch the bleeding." The narrator describes Joan's reactions: "Perhaps something in his sympathetic silence and the quiet consideration of his manner touched Joan. Her face, upturned almost submissively, for the moment seemed tremulous, and she set her lips together [...]. 'Thank yo',' she said in a suppressed voice, 'I canna say no more'" (11). That exchange is structured by conventional gender expectations, the strong man offering sympathy to the vulnerable woman, whose response hints of submission, all as prelude to the man ultimately mastering the woman. But Joan does not quite play out the role cast for her. She does not submit at that moment, and although she accepts his referral to "Thwaite's wife" (12) for shelter that night, she insists on equalizing the encounter by offering help to him in return: "If yo' ivver need help at th' pit will yo' come to me? [...] 'I've seen th' toime as I could ha' gi'en help to th' Mesters ef I'd had the moind. If yo'll promise *that*—'" (13). He promises. That exchange confirms the narrator's assertion of an equality of strength between Derrick and Joan: "The spirit of determination was as strong in his character as in her own" (11). But despite the symmetry in personal determination, the asymmetries of gender and class suffuse the exchange, and they are simultaneously affirmed and undercut when the narrator closes the chapter with this: "'Good night,' he returned, and uncovering with as grave a courtesy as he might have shown to the finest lady in the land, or to his mother or sister, he stood at the road-side and watched her until she was out of sight" (13). That last sentence registers and destabilizes a range of gender and class relations: between Derrick as upper class and Joan as working class, between upper-class man and upper-class woman, between son and mother, brother and sister. We see in

Derrick's gesture of upper-class courtesy to the working-class Joan the effacement of the borders around each set of gender and class relations, an effacement grounded firmly on the inner strength and bodily symmetry of Derrick and Joan as individuals.

In contrast to *Mary Barton*, where the physical affinity between Mary and her aspiring upper-class lover Harry Carson is shown to be superficial and a moral snare, the physical affinity between Joan and Derrick provides a stable motif throughout *That Lass O'Lowries*, which unties the Gordian knot of the moral dangers of cross-class sexual relations. When Paul Grace is introduced into the narrative, "Derrick strode by his side," the narrator adds, "like a young son of Anak [an Old Testament progenitor of giants]—brains and muscle evenly balanced and finely developed" (4). The authority Derrick carries based on his education and class is affirmed in his physical stature and, as we learn later, his ability to hold his own in a fight. Soon after the encounter between Joan and Derrick discussed above, Derrick shares his thoughts about Joan with Grace: "'Here,' he said, 'is a creature with the majesty of a Juno—though really nothing but a girl in years—who rules a set of savages by the mere power of a superior will and mind, and yet a woman who works at the mouth of a coal-pit,—who cannot write her own name, and who is beaten by her fiend of a father as if she were a dog. Good Heaven! What is she doing here? What does it all mean?'" (15). Derrick's words serve as a corrective to Grace, who when he first commented on Joan at the opening of the novel referred to her as "'[A] fine creature'—and nothing else" (3), all body but no intelligence or character. Derrick sees someone very different, an analog for himself, a mirror of his own physicality and intellect, but in a context that defies the limits of his logic and his imagination. He apprehends the fullness of Joan's capacity as a human being, but her environment, every aspect of her life-world, seems designed to distort her development. Why she isn't stunted like the rest is a mystery.

The novel would seem to set, then, an equivocal situation: on the one hand an attractive, working-class, uneducated "girl" treated "as if she were a dog" by her father clearly needs protection; the conventions of gender and of narrative would predetermine that, but as suggested by the emphasis on the strength of Joan's "will and mind" and on her offer documented above to help Derrick at the mine if ever he needs it, the power relation between the two is less predetermined. As the narrative unfolds, the question of whether Derrick is the protector of Joan or Joan the protector of Derrick is muddled. There are repetitions of the early scene when Derrick binds up Joan's wound and arranges sanctuary for the night, but those scenes are overbalanced by Joan's consistent shadowing of Derrick to ensure that he arrives to his lodging safely each night, putting her body literally between her father, who has vowed to kill Derrick after Derrick defeated him in a fistfight, and Derrick, who has taken his own precautions by carrying a pistol. Here is how he learns of Joan's shadowing:

> But during his lonely walks homeward on these summer nights, Derrick made a curious discovery. On one or two occasions he became conscious that he had a companion who seemed to act as his escort. It was usually upon dark or unpleasant nights that he observed this, and the first time he caught sight of the figure which always walked on the opposite side of the road, either some distance before or behind him, he put his hand to his belt, not perceiving

for some moments that it was not a man but a woman. It *was* a woman's figure, and the knowledge sent blood to his heart with a rush that quickened its beatings. It might have been chance, he argued, that took her home that night at this particular time; but when time after time, the same thing occurred, he saw that his argument had lost its plausibility. It was no accident, there was purpose in it; and though they never spoke to each other or in any manner acknowledged each other's presence, and though often he fancied that she had convinced herself that he was not aware of her motive, he knew that Joan's desire to protect him had brought her there. (93)

The knowledge of Joan placing herself between him and her father may quicken Derrick's heartbeat, marking his hope that her action is for care of him more than a desire to prevent her father from committing a crime that would lead to his own death, but he eventually asks Joan to promise him not to put herself in danger for his sake. "It was that her womanhood,—" the narrator avers, "her hardly used womanhood, of which she herself had thought with such pathetic scorn—was always before him, and was even a stronger power with him than her marvelous beauty" (171). Still constrained by thinking in binary gender categories, projecting an idea of "womanhood" as essential to Joan's identity, Derrick tries to refigure their relation in conventional terms; he cannot understand how it is possible for a woman to interpose her physical strength between two men. Joan rejects his plea, "fur the sake o' [her] own peace" (172). Derrick could not reach the truth behind her refusal, "and would not have reached it if he had talked to her till doomsday." That truth is "that she was right in saying she could not give it up" (172). Here's why: she is unafraid of her father's violence; she knows that there is an unbridgeable social gulf between herself and Derrick; the only thing she had to hang onto is her own endurance, which I would gloss as the strength and integrity of her own body and mental resolve. "There was a gladness" in that endurance, "which she had in nothing else" (173). That gladness, I would argue, is akin to defiance for there is no social script that Joan or Derrick can imagine that would enable them to encounter each other and love each other as equals. So Joan can step out of social scripts, "she could brave darkness and danger [...] she could interpose herself between him and violence," and do those things for the sake of *her* own peace. "But of all this, Fergus Derrick suspected nothing. He only knew that while she had not misinterpreted his appeal, some reason of her own held her firm" (173).

In this existential situation Joan may defy social scripts, but in others she seems to embrace them. The example that challenges my reading the most concerns her conversion from indifference to acceptance of what seems to be conventional Christianity. Unlike in *Mary Barton*, where the discourse of the Bible, as rendered in John Barton's repentance for killing Harry Carson and Mr. Carson's forgiveness of Barton, functions to impose a pattern of meaning for experience after the fact, serving as a way to explain away its pain, Joan's encounter with Christianity begins with a picture first, under which are appended words. Her initial reading is of an image:

Against the end wall was suspended a picture of Christ in the last agony, and beneath it was written, "It is finished." Before it, as Anice opened the door, stood Joan Lowrie, with [the fallen] Liz's sleeping child on her bosom. She had come on the picture suddenly, and it had seized on some deep, reluctant emotion. She had heard some vague history of the Man; but it was different to find herself in the silent room, confronting the upturned face, the crown, the cross, the anguish and the mystery. She turned toward Anice, forgetting all else but emotion. (101)

In the conversation with Anice that follows, Joan accepts a Bible that Anice offers as the only thing that could provide an adequate explanation for what the words "It is finished" mean in the moment pictured. Some days later Joan returns to Anice and says: "'I ha' not getten the words. But I thowt as yo'd loike to know. I believe I' th' Book; I believe I' th' Cross; I believe in Him as deed on it! That's what I coom to say'" (131). In her encounter with the picture and subsequent reflections on "th' Book," for which she has no words, Joan's focus is on the image of suffering, the reality of physical death and the confirmation of the significance of both through the materiality of "th' Book." She is responding, then, not to discourse, not to a narrative of redemption and forgiveness, but to an image of suffering—the "upturned face," the "crown" of thorns—a feeling of "anguish" and then the silence of "mystery." That image seems to confirm the necessity for suffering but the impossibility of attributing any meaning to it. What the image validates is the emotion. Joan may have experienced suffering as her peculiar lot, but the image of the suffering Christ projects that suffering as universal even if its meaning remains opaque.

This nondiscursive reading of Joan's conversion, which the narrator refers to as "Joan's strange confession of faith" in a moment focalized through Anice, is confirmed in the novel by the Reverend Barholm's response to the news of a change in Joan that should for him have confirmed her conversion. Accurately, I think, judging the core of Joan's new faith "emotional," Barholm is

> disinclined to believe in Joan's conversion because his interviews with her proved as unsatisfactory as ever. Her manner had altered; she had toned down somewhat, but she still caused him to feel ill at ease. If she did not defy him any longer or set his teachings at naught, her grave eyes, resting on him silently, had sometimes the effect of making his words fail him. (205)

Barholm's response suggests that Joan's newfound faith involves a rejection of the discourse of Christianity, a resistance to the way Christian discourse has served the interests of the privileged, who understand Christ's suffering as protecting them from having to suffer themselves. Joan's insistence on emotion, on the truth of the body's placement in a world where suffering demands a response, disrupts the formulaic discourse of the rector, "making his words fail him."

Joan's "conversion" highlights one figure in a pattern of change that can be read on the surface as part of her education as a woman who learns to shape her desires in conformity with Victorian middle-class values. She says, for example, in a conversation with the working-class "sage" Sammy Craddock, who accuses her of turning Methodist, that "'it is na Methody so much. Happen I'm turnin' woman, fur I conna abide to see a hurt gi'en to them as has not earned it'" (211). Her definition of "turnin' woman" could just as easily be applied to the notion of becoming a man, who "conna abide to see a hurt gi'en to them as has not earned it." Which is to say that turning a woman in Joan's formulation means becoming a compassionate human being. In that context, then, we can read Joan's "appeal against her own despair" when she says, " 'Is na theer a woman's place fur me I' th' world? Is it allus to be this way wi' me? Con I niver reach no higher, strive as I will, pray as I will,—fur I *have* prayed? Is na theer a woman's place fur me i' th' world?' " (213) as a plea for finding a social space where she can live out her compassion without physical abuse, deprivation and social censure, where her compassion can extend beyond the immediate moments of crisis to help shape a set of social relations where crisis is extraordinary rather than the norm.

An alliance with Fergus Derrick is precisely the circumstance that might enable Joan to find such a space personally through marriage and socially in supporting his efforts to renovate the working environment for all the workers in the mines. Here, for instance, are the plans he presents to the owners of the Riggan collieries: "They were plans for the abolition of old and dangerous arrangements, for the amelioration of the condition of the men who labored at the hourly risk of their lives, and for rendering this labor easier. Especially, there were plans for a newer system of ventilation—proposing the substitution of fans for the long-used furnace" (219). Clearly were those plans put into effect, they would have changed the daily lives of the mining community as a whole, softening the edges of the workers' existence, removing a cause of daily anxiety and even improving worker health, but the owners reject the plans, and Derrick resigns. Before completing his employment, however, there is an explosion in the mine, trapping Derrick and many of the miners deep underground. In a reversal of the gender roles that structured the opening and closing chapters of *Mary Barton*—with Jem Wilson first taking the lead in saving his father and a colleague from a mill fire and then in the end after the trial taking on the care of the delirious Mary—Joan takes on the male role. She leads the rescue team and, followed by Paul Grace, whose hands are described as "feminine" (229) and who "found himself obeying her slightest word or gesture" (231), she finds Derrick, applies first aid in the form of a "brandy flask" (233) and cradles his head in her lap as they are raised to the surface. The frontispiece of the 1877 Scribner first edition pictures Joan holding her "Davy," a miner's lantern, during the rescue in an image that Mark J. Noonan calls "a modern-day Joan of Arc"[8] (see Frontispiece). Derrick is seriously injured, his life in question over many weeks of recovery through which Joan nurses him daily and nightly. Once he recovers, Joan leaves Riggan, feeling herself unfit to be the wife of "a gentlemon" (243). Derrick follows her, confesses his love, to which Joan responds: "I conna turn yo' fro' me," but when he reaches to embrace her in the closing gesture most readers would expect, she stops him, saying, "Not yet […] not yet." "Give me th' time," she pleads, "to make myself worthy" (269).

That plea would seem to negate the finely wrought destabilizing features of a novel that has so powerfully demonstrated the arbitrary and distorting qualities of conventional gender constructions. What happens to that critique when the novel ends in such a conventional way (even if that convention is disrupted by Joan's hesitation)? Jeanette Shumaker argues that the possibility of Joan's union with Derrick is the culmination of her "growth" into a middle-class woman: "Joan's growth," she writes, "despite her background of poverty and abuse, comfortingly suggests that anyone who is motivated to improve can do so—that bourgeois values, behaviors, and consequent economic ease are available to the best members of the lower class."[9] The physically extraordinary Joan, in that formulation, becomes ordinary, a model of middle-class rectitude and decorum. That view of Joan disappears later on in Shumaker's article when she observes that "Joan presents an androgynous contrast to the feminine ideal of the era" (371). Joan is both emblem of and radical contrast to the middle-class model of womanhood. That tension in Shumaker's argument reflects a broad tension in the novel between the evocation of a middle-class feminine ideal that values literacy, sympathy, integrity and community through images of conventional gender stereotypes, as in the figure of Anice, and the extraordinary gender-defiant strength, integrity and beauty of Joan. Perhaps, then, if we read the declaration of love and Joan's plea to work to be worthy of her beloved in the context of what we know about Joan individually, the details of her experiences and the scope of her desires, we can see another dimension to the conventional ending.

What would, we might ask, make Joan unworthy? One answer is her limited acculturation to the social class into which her marriage to Derrick would bring her. Without that acculturation, which need not carry with it a rejection of her social origins, the possibilities for Joan to realize her capacities for personal fulfillment in her marriage relation and for her to finds ways of her own to extend the work of social amelioration for her mining community would be highly constrained. Her hesitation is an argument for education and openness to a broader social experience *for her*. It also suggests a shift from mere endurance to possibility *for her*. Were she to refuse that possibility, she would be closing off analogous possibilities for her mining community. Such possibilities would not mean that she simply becomes an example for other working-class women with the implicit judgment that community structures of working-class life need to be corrected. Whatever the particular shape her life may take as she continues the project of her own development, which she insists on doing on her own, a part from Derrick, her life would grow in relation to her working-class community. In that sense, the conventionality of the narrative closure of *That Lass O'Lowries* feels irrelevant, beside the point, as the convention is woven into the larger tapestry of Joan's life. Joan's individuality carries its own authority.

In Mark J. Noonan's fine study of the *Century Illustrated Monthly Magazine*, he offers this assessment of *That Lass O'Lowries* as a novel of "working-class life":

> Especially when compared to other so-called "realistic" texts depicting working-class life during this period [...], Burnett's work offers a powerful alternative to the competitive worldview seemingly sanctioned by Victorian society. Though Burnett fails to question the socioeconomic system that produces class divisions in the first place, she does eloquently stress the human sensitivity needed to alleviate capitalism's harsh effects. Though perhaps not a fully satisfying solution to a complex situation, her well-wrought vision was deeply humanist and subtly challenged the views of her magazine's exclusively male editorship. (49)

Compare that assessment with Raymond Williams on *Mary Barton* in his *Culture and Society 1780—1950*: "John Barton dies penitent, and the elder Carson repents of his vengeance and turns, as the sympathetic observer wanted the employers to turn, to efforts of improvement and mutual understanding. This was the characteristic humanitarian conclusion, and it must certainly be respected. But it was not enough" (cited in *Mary Barton*).[10] Taken together those comments suggest that Burnett went a long way to replicate Gaskell's social problem novel of 1848 with her own social problem novel of 1877, and that both novels failed to a degree in similar ways. The difference in dates, however, and the difference in place of publication—*Mary Barton* in London and *That Lass O'Lowries* in New York—complicate the parallel. It is well documented that Gaskell's readers were both workers and factory owners in Manchester, and that the labor conditions (wages, strikes, unemployment) were a part of the texture of their everyday lives at the time of publication. There was no parallel situation in the moment of publication for Burnett's novel. The readers of *Scribner's Monthly*, where the novel was originally published serially, were not involved in the mining industry nor were they intimate associates of Burnett at the same time, although some mine owners and mine workers may by chance have read the novel. The relation then between the novels is not between novel and social problem addressed; it is between the earlier and the later novel. Burnett's enterprise was literary practice, not social reform. She did not merely replicate the narrative elements of *Mary Barton* to pursue a similar reformist goal. She seized on those elements, broke them apart, reassembled them and patched in new elements in a way that extended the imaginative possibilities of the form. In Joan Lowrie she fashioned the first in a line of novelistic heroines to come, heroines who challenge gender stereotypes in different ways, from different angles, within different social classes and to different effects. Burnett's next novel, *Haworth's*, which is another industrial novel and like Gaskell's *North and South* focalizes the narrative mainly from the point of view of ownership and management, both redeploys narrative elements from Gaskell's novel and extends her exploration of women who refuse to be fully constrained by the social roles they are asked to play, but *Haworth's* adds a transatlantic element to the narrative and the romance frame resolves nothing.

II

Ann Thwaite's biography of Burnett approaches the relationship between *Haworth's* and Gaskell's *North and South* as obliquely as she had between *That Lass O'Lowries* and *Mary Barton*. As Burnett was writing *Haworth's* Thwaite notes, "she was conscious of looking at the critics over her shoulder this time—just as Mrs Gaskell had been when following *Mary Barton* with *North and South*. 'The difference between this and the *Lass*,' she wrote to [Richard Watson] Gilder, 'is that then I was simply writing a story, and now I am trying to please the critics'" (58). But more than looking over her shoulder at the critics, I would suggest, Burnett was looking pretty squarely at *North and South* itself, drawing on character types, plot elements, dramatic scenes, and social and verbal textures that evoke the world of Gaskell's novel. There is the mill owner who worked himself up from poverty in the figures of Mr. Thornton in *North and South* and James Haworth in *Haworth's*, for instance, each with a supportive and long-suffering mother (the former mother hardedged, the latter gentle and willfully innocent); there is the beautiful upper-class woman who becomes a love interest (Margaret Hale in the former, Rachel Ffrench in the latter novel); and there is a family of working-class characters who become personal interests of the upper-class characters (the Higgins family in the former and the Briarley family in the latter). In both novels the mill owners' businesses fail in part from the effects of a labor strike and in part from investments (in the former a refusal to make a risky investment, in the latter the failure of a series of risky investments), and in both the strike dissipates in a scene where violence is directed at the upper-class woman. And throughout both novels provide details of the texture of working-class homes and the contrasting speech of different class dialects, but both focalize those things through the eyes of the upper-class (or outsider) characters. As she had done in *That Lass*, Burnett deploys those elements from Gaskell's novel, refigures them and adds others to produce a narrative that evokes the social problem novel of mid-century, but refracts the material to produce a text that feels decidedly modern. I would locate that modernity in two features of the novel: the introduction of an American character who brings disruptions to the factory system associated with his scientific/mechanical innovations and his ignorance of the rules of social decorum, and the novel's steady delegitimizing of an assumption of class privilege, which thrives through a double standard of social behavior supported by a moralistic discourse that applies only to the less privileged.

Gaskell's novels, of course, are sensitive to the double standard of moral judgment imposed on the less privileged in their depiction of the fallen woman figure. In *Mary Barton* there is the seduced Aunt Esther, who takes to prostitution to feed her fatherless child, who in turn nonetheless dies, leaving Esther to live out her shortened remaining years judging herself in the strongest, absolute moral terms: "How could she, the abandoned and polluted outcast, ever have dared to hope for a blessing, even on her efforts to do good? The black curse of Heaven rested on all her doings, were they for good or for evil" (206–07). That passage captures the way in which the narrator's language blends with the internal perception of the character, whose thoughts, rendered in indirect discourse ("the black curse of Heaven" is Esther's self-judgment not the narrator's), reveal how deeply she has internalized the moralized social judgment of her suffering. Similarly in Gaskell's *Ruth*, when the fallen titular character thoroughly reforms herself, living what amounts to a saint's life, she dies with a crushing sense of her guilt, which she accepts as her just lot. Her "sin" in being seduced at 16 and parentless must remain within the discourse of absolute judgment even as the novel shows a life that belies that judgment. The fallen Liz in *That Lass* seems immune to any sense of self-judgment. She "falls" twice, first to return to Riggan with her child, and a second time to die, her child having died in the interval. During the time when she and her child were living with Joan, Liz rejects the child, saying with distressing matter-of-factness, "It's nowt but a trouble. I dunnot loike it. I canna. It would be better if it would na live" (67). She feels neither maternal love nor moral revulsion of her behavior and its results. Joan provides most of the basic care for the child, since the child, in Joan's words "seems to worrit her [Liz] to death" (151). In the penultimate chapter when Liz returns, Mrs. Thwaite, who had seen her last, does not quite remember if she asked for her child, but Liz did ask for Joan; "[I]t did na seem to be th' choild she cared about so much as Joan Lowrie" (265). Consequently, when the chapter ends with the image of Liz "with her face downward and with her dead hand against the closed door" of Joan's dwelling (266), we have the iconography of the necessary death of the fallen woman, but its moral, either as a judgment on the woman herself or on the hypocrisy of those who would judge her harshly, is drained away. There is simply the fact of her death. Once the distortions of moral judgment are erased from the narrative, the series of events that lead to Liz's end can be understood for what they are in strictly material, bodily terms.

While there are no Esther or Liz figures in either *North and South* or *Haworth's*, the prospect of a fallen woman hangs over the first novel and the extraordinary, ordinary presence of fallen women and their offspring is visible in the second. Gaskell evokes the shadow of the potential fallen woman in *North and South* through the way she depicts Margaret Hale's hypersensitiveness to any awareness of her maturation as a sexually desirable woman. In her rendering of some events, literal meanings are charged with metaphoric meanings, with the dangers of sexual desire and its potential moral disruptions residing in the metaphors. We can perceive the potential shadow of fallenness in the quality of Margaret's embarrassment after Henry Lennox's surprise proposal of marriage: "Margaret felt guilty and ashamed of having grown so much into a woman as to be thought of in marriage" (27). Rather than being distressed by his presumption, Margaret seems angry at herself, at her body's sexual attractiveness. It is as if the prospect of growing up brings with it sexual danger; to be a woman and to be desired is to be under threat. In her second surprise marriage proposal, this one from Mr. Thornton soon after the near riot during the strike (much more on the significance of that for both novels below), the excess of Margaret's response suggests continued discomfort with her own sexuality. After Thornton declares that he loves her, "as I do not believe man ever loved woman before," Margaret responds, "Your way of speaking shocks me. It is blasphemous" (181). While some of the energy of her response can be attributed to her anger at being misunderstood—their physical proximity during the near riot being misread as a sign of her attraction to him—the excess in its reference to blasphemy equates his desire to possess her as a violation, a desecration of the divine. That reference draws attention away from the carnality that is so central to his proposal, suggesting that the nature of the misunderstanding may be something she fears to confront directly, for were she to do so she would have to work to understand her own sexual desires.

Both proposal scenes are prefaced by moments when Margaret is on public display,[11] the first after modeling the Indian shawls for her Aunt Edith at Harley Street in London and the second after having confronted the strikers openly in the courtyard of Thornton's factory. In both cases the visibility of her body seems to invite both men to try to possess her. The connection between public visibility and the perception of Margaret's body as an object of desire is further reinforced when Thornton sees her with her brother Frederick at the station before Frederick's return to Spain, and Margaret lies about having been there. Thinking that Margaret's brother must be her lover because of the lie, Thornton torments himself: "How could one so pure have stooped from her decorous and noble manner of bearing? [...] And then this falsehood—how terrible must be some dread of shame to be revealed [...] How creeping and deadly that fear which could bow down the truthful Margaret to falsehood!" (259). Thornton's leap from the lie to a language of sexual violation (from "one so pure" to "dread of shame to be revealed") further solidifies the metaphorical link between a woman's public visibility and her sexual vulnerability.

In *Haworth's* Burnett registers the fact that there may be a connection between the people one encounters in the ordinary course of daily life and the roles those people might have in narratives of fallenness. But rather than approaching those connections through the smoky distortions of an increasingly discredited moral discourse around the idea of the fallen woman, Burnett simply notes them. We can see how deftly Burnett discredits the moral judgment of Victorian discourse on the fallen woman in two examples: the introduction of Hilary Murdoch's (the American engineer who works for and befriends Haworth) cousin, a 19-year-old girl of an unwed mother (a cousin of Murdoch's father), and the revelation of the source of funds for the inheritance that Granny Dixon leaves to Mrs. Briarley. In Chapter X Murdoch is summoned to an attic room in Riggan where his father's cousin, Janet Murdoch, lay dying. In the scene that follows, Burnett evokes some standard elements of the fallen woman story: Janet confesses her fallenness by saying, "I am an outcast [...] an outcast!" before describing how her daughter "seemed to fasten her eyes upon me from the hour of her birth, and I have felt them ever since" (63). She is riven with guilt, her daughter a living and perpetual accusation, and she has sent for Murdoch to request that he and his mother take the girl, Christian, in. Without fuss, Murdoch agrees, and Janet says with some surprise: "You are like your father. You make things seem simple. You speak as if you were undertaking nothing." To which he replies: "It is not much to do [...] and we could not do less" (64). Murdoch then fetches his mother, and as they comfort Janet in her dying moments, Janet begs Christian, "Forgive me." "For what?" Christian asks. "But the sentence remained unfinished." Janet is dead, and her daughter looks intently at her while her mother's face became "merely a mask of stone [...] gazing back at her with a fixed stare" (65). So ends the chapter, and in a moment reminiscent of an Emily Dickenson poem, where the hard materiality of the tomb or the buzzing of a fly defies the human effort to project discursive meanings onto death, the tableau of repentance, forgiveness and the assuagement of a necessary guilt splinter against the hard realities of human experience imaged in the "mask of stone."[12] The next chapter begins simply, "They took the girl home with them" (66). In that grimly matter-of-fact way, the residue of Victorian moral sentiment is made irrelevant, evoked only to be corrected.

Such a corrective of sentiment is extended in the Granny Dixon bequest. Just before her death, she reveals to her impoverished, working-class family the source of the wealth that she has been hoarding for more than 60 years: "Does ta want to know where th' money come fro'? Fro' Will Ffrench—fro' *him*. He war one o' th' gentry when aw wur said an' done—an' I wur a han'some lass" (348). The brevity and incisiveness of that revelation is stunning. Will Ffrench is the grandfather of Rachel, the upper-class woman for whom Haworth sacrificed all he had worked for and of whom Granny Dixon says, "she's th' very moral on him" (i.e., her grandfather) (348). Granny parlayed her beauty into financial security, and although it is unclear who Granny Dixon's child or children might be, it is clear that she was by any definition a kept and thus a fallen women. She may not have inspired any affection—she played on her relatives' greed to inherit her money—but she provides a hard-headed reading of what a fallen woman's life might mean were we to abolish moral judgment and sentiment. That life would be as much an open question and just as free from or liable to blame as anyone's. In addition, her equation of her youthful seducer, Will, and his granddaughter Rachel provides a powerful clue to our understanding of the woman who serves as the novel's biggest puzzle: the self-contained Rachel Ffrench.

As was the case in *North and South*, the scene most fraught with the dangers of public exposure is when Rachel Ffrench intervenes between the strikers and the object of their wrath, Hilary Murdoch. Murdoch, the workers believe, has invented a device that will make their labor (and thus their livelihood) obsolete; Haworth circulated that idea in an effort to destroy his romantic rival. As is the case in *North and South*, labor conflict and sexual desire permeate the experiences of key figures in the manufacturing class if not the workers themselves. For Burnett as a writer, that confluence of social and personal tension seems to have focused and energized her narrative. In a letter to Richard Gilder, she described her difficulties in writing the early chapters of *Haworth's* and then identifies the chapter that made everything from that point on smooth sailing:

> After working & going through agonies untold & raving & tearing & hating myself & every word I ever wrote I have suddenly walked out into a cool place & begun to soar & have soared & soared until I don't think I shall return to earth again [...]. The room I have written it [*Haworth's*] in has been a torture chamber & yet at Chapter 27 I am just tearing along & to my utter bewilderment I feel as if I have done something [...] far beyond the *Lass*. (Cited in Gerzina 75)

Chapter 27, oddly enough, is entitled "Beginning," and the extended narrative sequence introduced is of the labor strike and Rachel Ffrench's response to it. It is as if the riot scene in *North and South* inspired what became the imaginative core of *Haworth's*. While Haworth takes active measures to disrupt the strike before it starts, rallying his own men and gauging their loyalties before exploiting the uncertainty of the situation to play a protective role with Rachel, Rachel responds with excitement, relishing, it seems, the opportunity to assert her feminine and class power by an act of public defiance toward both the strikers and toward Haworth himself.

When Haworth rushes into the room to tell Rachel of the strike, he feels as he almost always does in her presence, "unstrung" (184).

> "I've come to tell you not to go out," he said. "There's trouble afoot—in the trade. There's no knowing how it'll turn out. There's a lot of chaps in th' town who are not in th' mood to see aught that'll fret 'em. They're ready for mischief, and have got drink in 'em. Stay you here until we see which way th' thing's going."
>
> "Do you mean," she demanded, "that there are signs of a strike?"
>
> "There's more than signs of it," he answered sullenly. "Before night the whole place will be astir."
>
> [...]
>
> "*Nothing* would keep me at home," she said. "I shall drive through the town and back again. Do you think I will let them fancy that *I* am afraid of them?"
>
> [...]

She left the room, and in less than ten minutes returned. He had never before seen in her the fire he saw then. There was a spark of light in her eyes, a color on her cheek. She had chosen her dress with distinct care for its luxurious richness. His exclamation, as she entered buttoning her long, delicate glove, was a repressed oath. He exulted in her. His fear for her was gone, and only this exultation remained

"You've made up your mind to that?" he said. He wanted to make her say more.

"I am going to see your mother," she answered. "That will take me outside of the town, then I shall drive back again—slowly. They shall understand me at least." (184–85)

Rachel's enigmatic final statement that "they shall understand me at least" raises the question of who else does she want to understand her? How far does the audience for her public display of herself extend? As a representative of her social class (her father has become Haworth's partner in business, an aristocrat dabbling in trade), she relies on the clues of dress, her beauty and the fact that she is publicly known because of her class rank to protect her and to be tools of intimidation; if her social position is unassailable, she is unassailable. But insofar as the former working-class man and current factory owner Haworth assumes any authority over her (her father's economic dependence on Haworth's success reinforces any personal authority Haworth may hope to have over her), there is a gender dimension to her defiance. Her beauty may intimidate but it also attracts, and as a man of working-class origins who is attracted to her and is in fact engaged in an unspoken transaction with her father to buy her (she is the understood price of their partnership), Haworth is the most dangerous of the working men. It is he above all who shall understand her.

Rachel's understanding of Haworth as an extension of the working-class threat to her social position and personal integrity is reinforced by two events: the stone thrown at the near riot and Haworth's physical assault on her body. The near riot begins in a manner reminiscent of the scene quoted above: Rachel dresses for it. After her father and she discuss the fact that their dinner guests would not be coming because of the unrest in the streets, Rachel goes to her room "to prepare for dinner." When she returns, her father is startled by her appearance: "'Why did you dress yourself in that manner?' he exclaimed. 'You said yourself our guests would not come.' 'It occurred to me, she answered, 'that we might have visitors after all'" (232). The visitors, of course, are the strikers, who Mr. Ffrench thinks have come to terrorize him. When it becomes clear that they are after Murdoch, Ffrench's relief is transparent, but he still flinches from any confrontation. Rachel calls out his cowardice. Then she says:

"They shall see *me*. [...] Let us see what they will have to say to *me*."

He would have stopped her, but she did not pay the slightest attention to his exclamation. The window was a French one, opening upon a terrace. She flung it backward, and stepped out and stood before the rioters.

For a second there was not a sound.

They had been expecting to see a man [...] and here was simply a tall young woman in a dazzling dress of some rich white stuff, and with something sparkling upon her hands and arms and in her high-dressed blonde hair.

The rapid shifts in focalization in the quoted passage capture with skill the changing visual emphases from Rachel's self-absorption to her view from inside the French window to the rioters' view from outside it. From there events move quickly: the rioters demand to see Murdoch and his "contrapshun"; Rachel says he has gone "far away," telling "the lie without flinching in the least" (236); and she then offers herself as an object of their violence, saying "If you would like to vent your anger upon a woman, vent it upon *me*. I am not afraid of you. Look at me!" That moment reprises her slow drive through the town during the first stirrings of the strike, and the effect is the same: "The effect of her supreme beauty and the cold defiance which had in it a touch of delicate insolence, was indescribable" (237). The men freeze in their tracks. Then Murdoch arrives, and seeing Rachel's "life [...] was in danger" draws attention to himself, defying the rioters by telling them they are wrong about his invention and that he would in any case never give it up to them. That sets the crowd off. "He saw his mistake in a second. There was a shout and a surging movement of the mob toward him, and Rachel Ffrench, with an indescribable swiftness, had thrown herself before him and was struck by a stone which came whizzing through the air" (239). Murdoch's "sight of the little stream of blood which trickled from her temple turned him sick with rage," and as a similar trickle of blood did with the rioters in *North and South*, it brought them to their senses and they flee. Next, as readers of Gaskell's novel will learn with no surprise: "When they were left alone, Murdoch came and stood near her. He was paler than she, and haggard and worn. Before she knew what he was about to do he fell upon his knees, and covered her hands with kisses," a clear echo of Thornton's surprisingly timed declaration of love to the still unconscious Margaret. Finally, Rachel at first responds with suppressed anger, "then quite suddenly all her resistance ceased and her eyes fixed themselves upon him as if with a kind of dread" (240). The nature of that dread remains undefined, but the threat working-class violence poses to Rachel's social position and the repression of her sexual response to Murdoch both seem at play. As in *North and South* industrial labor, social conflict and sexual desire circle each other in a kind of *carmagnole* as a prelude to the resolution of the tensions among them through the structure of romance—that, I would argue, is what Burnett seems to be setting up, but it would be hard to sustain such a reading by the novel's end.

In *North and South* the industrial and romance plots are resolved in the marriage of Thornton and Margaret, as Margaret throws both her inherited wealth and newly focused social reform activities into Thornton's factory reforms. The competing love interests are more a misperception of Thornton's than real, Margaret's feelings never in doubt to readers; she has no desire for Henry Lennox and the threat of Frederick as a rival is purely a projection of Thornton's jealousy. In *Haworth's*, however, the competing love interests are real and dangerous: out of jealousy Haworth manipulates the workers to take Murdoch's life (a plot that Haworth disrupts in the end), and Rachel toys with Murdoch's affections until she loses interest, at which point her wealthy French lover appears on the scene, their marriage apparently imminent. However, neither that marriage nor any other marriage takes place at the end of the novel; the relationship between Rachel and each love interest is resolved in a different way. In a conversation with her father, Rachel explains why she singled Murdoch out for particular attention: "I must be amused and interested [...] [and] he has managed to interest me [...] [and]

the time has passed more easily [...]. I have gone as far as I choose to go, and it is done from to-night" (271–72). (There are countercurrents in that scene as her father seems to suggest that she cannot simply cast Murdoch off, but when Rachel confronts him with their class difference and asks what he would want her to do, he is silent.) Murdoch takes the rejection badly, and Heathcliff-like, "his face almost wolfish" (309), he haunts the grounds of the Ffrench estate until he purges the pain of his rejection by rededicating himself to the completion of his father's invention. Thwarted love turns out to be the fuel for inventive genius.

Haworth responds to his rejection more directly. He manipulates Rachel into a private meeting where he vents his "rage."

> She saw a look in his eye which caused her to shrink back. But she was too late. He caught her by the arm and dragged her toward him. A second later when he released her, she staggered to one of the rustic seats and sank crouching into it, hiding her face in the folds of her dress. She had not cried out, however, nor uttered a sound, and he had known she would not [...]. "A gentleman wouldn't have done it," he said hoarsely. "I'm not a gentleman." (298)

The precise nature of his violence in the scene is unclear, but its brevity suggests an assault masked as a kiss, the kiss a kind of stone. Thus, Haworth acts out another working-class assault, and when he loses his business in bankruptcy, there is no wealthy woman to save it. Saint Meran, the French love interest, when he learns of Rachel's father's disgrace, goes back to France, leaving Rachel behind, and after his bankruptcy Rachel's father flees Riggan, leaving Rachel alone. The prospect of church bells ringing for any marriage has receded far into the distance.

Among all the narrative elements that *North and South* and *Haworth's* have in common, the resolution of social conflict through the marriage of individuals is clearly not one of them. While we might construct a checklist of cardinal narrative elements (many of which are discussed above) and more incidental narrative elements (such as the visit by the MP from Broxton to honor Haworth's business success at a dinner hosted by Ffrench; the MP declares to Haworth, "I congratulate England upon your determination and indomitable courage, and upon your wonderful success" (340), which echoes a similar dinner marked by similar speeches in *North and South*), the originality of Burnett's novel emerges most forcefully at its close. Murdoch, the American son who completed his English father's invention and thus assured his own personal fortune, is the focus of the ending, not the title character Haworth, who, with his mother's support, has to return to industrial labor to survive. Having emerged from his own dark passages through his efforts to purge the pain of the loss of a love that was never his in the first place—his acceptance of his individual possibilities via the rejection of romance is an apt analog for the novel's rejection of romance—Murdoch embraces his own capacity for labor fueled by imagination, and he sets out to pursue a transatlantic vision of the productive possibilities of labor so defined: "Murdoch had made up his mind as to what his course for the next few years was to be. His future was assured and he might pursue his idlest fancy. But his fancies were not idle. They reached forward to freedom and new labors when the time came. He wanted to be in view, and to fill his life with work" (370). By returning to America, the country where his father had hoped to find the backing to complete and market his invention, Murdoch stitches another thread that links the two countries; America is the place where his fancies for productive labor can take their clearest shape, for there, he believes, his freedom to produce, in a gesture that evokes Thomas Carlyle's gospel of work, can find its requisite scope. He plans, however, to return in a "few years," but to what and for what reason?

Soon after the passage quoted above, and soon after he parts with his cousin Christian with the words, "[T]ry to be happy […] Rachel Ffrench stood before him" (371). The conditions seem set for a reconciliation scene. Rachel is alone, and she regrets her rejection of Murdoch. Her presence takes Murdoch by surprise, but even though Rachel appears to want one, there is no reconciliation. Instead, Rachel names some hard truths that have been felt but not articulated. She admits that she did love him and that she repents her decision to reject him. That admission requires her, though, to violate her dignity: "That it should be I who stooped, and for this—for this! That having battled against my folly for so long, I should have let it drag me to the dust at last" (372). Her consolation, then, is that she was the one who made the choice: "'Is it *my* fault that it is all over?' he demanded. 'Is it?' 'No,' she answered, 'that is my consolation'" (372). As a figure defined throughout the novel by her social class pride, she remains consistent in her acceptance of the consequences of that pride, which is stronger than her romantic desires. In that regard, her closing words are most apt: "'Oh! It was a poor passion, and this is a fitting end to it!'" (373).

Haworth's closes by highlighting two images: a grave and a face. The grave is Murdoch's father's, behind which Murdoch had hidden from the rioters the unfinished invention and upon which he had purged the pain of his thwarted passion by rededicating himself to his father's vision. That vision, once a burden and a specter, becomes his liberation and hope for the future when he makes it his own by completing the invention. The grave whose "silence was like a Presence" (374) links father and son in a story of transatlantic enterprise. But enterprise in and of itself is insufficient. It must be subordinated to a larger vision of social amelioration. And that vision is figured in the image of "a girl in a long cloak of gray almost the color of the mist in which she stood—a slender motionless figure—the dark young face turned seaward" (374). The girl in the cloak is Christian, Murdoch's illegitimate cousin. The chapter wholly devoted to her (Chapter XXXII, "Christian Murdoch") delineates the damaging effects of that illegitimacy to her developing sense of self. She fears the emergence of her own peculiar dark beauty, which she associates with her mother and the unwanted public attentions of men, and when she ventures into the chapel, the "objectionable female figure" of "the 'scarlet woman' […] figured largely and in most unpleasant guise in the discourses of Brother Hixon" (217). She had also crossed paths three or four times as a child with Rachel Ffrench on the continent, encounters both remember well. So while the romance plot of Murdoch and Rachel comes to a "fitting end," it is replaced by the suggestion of another sort of romance. This one involves an Anglo-American man, who is "a gentleman without knowing it" (88) and a young, illegitimate girl, who takes the place of the blonde gentlewoman. The final words of that Anglo-American man in the novel, who imagines the fullness of his personal life to be centered in England as he watches the "dark young" "figure on the shore," are, "'when I return—it will be for you'" (374). In Murdoch's story and his hope for its continuation there are the germs of a broader transatlantic community that Burnett extends in the third of her Gaskell-inspired fictions.

III

If America was in a sense smuggled into the Lancashire industrial environment in *Haworth's*, its symbolic meanings momentary and muted, its broader material connections are implied by the invention the Anglo-American, Murdoch, brought to fruition, which serves as a metaphor for the potential effects of American technological innovation on the English economy. The stakes are public, related to changing conditions of labor and economic interests. In *A Fair Barbarian* America impinges on England in a different form and with a different focus. As Gerzina observes of that novel, it is "about an elegant American who shakes up a small and narrow-minded English village by her refusal to respect their petty and restrictive codes of dress and behavior" (93). That village is called Slowbridge, and it is in the words of a *Harper's* June 1881 review "modeled apparently as much upon Cranford as upon actual places" (861). *Cranford*, as Borislave Knezevic has argued, is part of Gaskell's imaginative effort to present in her novels "fictional mappings of England,"[13] and Slowbridge is presented quite explicitly as "England" in this exchange between Octavia Bassett, the American visitor, and Lucia Gaston, her English counterpart: "'Do you like England?' she [Lucia] asked. 'Is this England?' inquired Octavia" (97). The implied answer to Octavia's rhetorical response to Lucia's simple question is, yes, Slowbridge is, if not England itself, an apt metaphor for a way of life that represents what it means to be English. By establishing Slowbridge as a metaphor for England and presenting Octavia as a representative American, Burnett offers an allegory for a singular Anglo-American character that combines the qualities of stability, decorum, dignity and community associated with the idea of England with an American ideal of energy, innovation, directness and mobility. The fact that the American, Octavia's father, was born in Slowbridge and that her visit (with her father soon to follow) is to her aunt suggests that the allegory of mediation between England and America is a family allegory, a story about the reconstruction of a family that drifted apart. By drawing on the narrative world of *Cranford* in *A Fair Barbarian*, Burnett transforms Cranford's response to the forces of social change embodied in such things as the railroad and the bank failure into an exploration of the forging of a transatlantic identity in response to America's expanding economic importance and visibility in the world. Through the disruptive presence of the beautiful and expensively dressed and bejeweled Octavia, Slowbridge reluctantly but with increasing momentum embraces change in the small, intimate details of daily life, details that in the aggregate suggest a wider horizon of aspiration.

The first sentence of *A Fair Barbarian* reads: "Slowbridge has been shaken to its foundations" (5) by the arrival of Miss Belinda Bassett's (the Miss Matty character) niece from Nevada in "'Meriker'" (8), for in Slowbridge, it seems:

> America was not approved of—in fact, was almost entirely ignored, as a country where, to quote Lady Theobald, "the laws were loose, and the prevailing sentiments revolutionary." It was not considered good taste to know Americans,—which was not unfortunate, as there

were none to know; and Miss Belinda Bassett had always felt a delicacy in mentioning her only brother, who had emigrated to the United States in his youth, having first disgraced himself by the utterance of the blasphemous remark that "he wanted to get to a place where a fellow could stretch himself, and not be bullied by a lot of old tabbies." From the day of his departure, when he had left Miss Belinda bathed in tears of anguish, she had heard nothing from him; and here upon the threshold stood Mary Anne [her servant], with delighted eagerness in her countenance, repeating,—

"Your niece, mum, from 'Meriker!'" (8–9)

Burnett's intimate knowledge of *Cranford* can be felt throughout the passage: the Peter Jenkyns character becomes the brother who left for America, and the allusions to unease associated with the orient and the excesses of the French Revolution from the "panic" chapter become subsumed under America, a country associated here with the violation of all convention. Similarly, the ladies of Cranford's obsession with dress is reflected in Slowbridge with Lady Theobald's (the Miss Deborah character) concern about Octavia's inappropriate dress and with her imposition of a standard of taste that all the other ladies in the town must emulate: "All the ladies of Slowbridge wore caps; and all being plagiarized from Lady Theobald, without any reference to age, size, complexion, or demeanor, the result was sometimes a little trying" (82). Such details permeate the novel; they are woven into the texture of the prose, revealing what a careful reader Burnett was of *Cranford*, and in particular how sensitive she was to the threat to the identity of the Cranford community by the accommodations necessitated by social change.[14]

In *A Fair Barbarian* as in *Cranford* the community's identity is grounded in social custom and anchored by material objects, as evidenced by the centrality of tea parties to community life in both novels, and personal identity seems to be a function of community. Consequently, any change in the community threatens individual identity and any threat to individual identity threatens the community. In *Cranford* one narrative thread depicting a threat to the community is the Signor Brunoni story where the community anxieties associated with his appearance, which is connected to a series of "robberies," dissipate when it is discovered that Brunoni is really a Mr. Brown, an Englishman after all.[15] In *A Fair Barbarian* the threat is from the American girl, who intrudes on the community and threatens its values not only by behaving in ways that do not take those values into account but simply by being open about who she is. When, for example, Octavia announces quite openly that her mother had been a popular actress in San Francisco, who died giving birth at the age of 19, the narrator comments:

The utter calmness, and freedom from embarrassment, with which these announcements were made, almost shook Miss Belinda's faith in her own identity. Strange to say, until this moment she had scarcely given a thought to her brother's wife; and to find herself sitting in her own genteel little parlor, behind her own tea service, and with her hand upon her own teapot, hearing that this wife had been a young person who had been "a great favorite" upon the stage, in a region peopled, as she had been led to suppose, by gold-diggers and escaped convicts, was almost too much for her to support herself under. But she did support herself bravely, when she had time to rally. (21–22)

Miss Belinda's identity is anchored by her domestic, material objects figured in the tea service and teapot, which are, emphatically, "her own" while they are also the objects that facilitate the most ordinary and ritualized community activity, the Slowbridge tea parties. The notion of public display unsettles her fundamentally domestic identity, an identity reinforced by the community activity of taking tea. Her hand, resting on the teapot, enables her to "support herself bravely," the teapot a reassurance of her community values. For Belinda personal identity and community identity are one. Questions of identity, however, concern Octavia as well, and in her relationship with Lady Theobald's granddaughter Lucia, also 19, she strives to find a kind of emotional coherence between her English family connections (and, thus, identity) and her American upbringing and home (and, thus, identity). The riddle Octavia seems set to solve is the possibility of unifying her geographically bifurcated family history and current relations with her personal identity. What community provides the material context and the shared values that can make her identity something more than mere individualism? That community does not yet exist on either side of the Atlantic for Octavia, so she herself becomes the focal point of a transatlantic community in the making, which begins to emerge in a series of personal interactions that reshape Octavia and that transform Slowbridge.

In an effort to manipulate Lucia into marrying a man who, Lady Theobald thinks, would help secure Lucia (and by extension, herself) a fortune, Lady Theobald encourages Lucia to spend time with Octavia after Octavia becomes an object of interest for the, unbeknownst to him, intended. Lucia and Octavia become friends and agree to "help each other" by each telling the other her faults. Lucia says:

> "If you will tell me when I am wrong, I will try to—to have the courage to tell you. That will be good practice for me. What I want most is courage and frankness, and I am sure it will take courage to make up my mind to tell you of your—of your mistakes." Octavia regarded her with mingled admiration and respect. "I think that's a splendid idea," she said. (175)

Unselfconscious courage and frankness are appropriate descriptors of the qualities in Octavia that have so unsettled Slowbridge, in addition to her visually arresting appearance. The first "mistake" Lucia points out to Octavia concerns her hair; the wavy bangs that obscure her forehead, she suggests, make Octavia resemble an actress. Octavia responds by directly cutting off the bangs, an act she instantly regrets, saying that "anyone who was used to seeing [her hair with bangs] [...] would think I looked horrid," to which Lucia replies: "They would think you prettier,—a good deal" (181). Subsequent events confirm Lucia's assessment and Octavia concedes the point, figuratively becoming more herself in adjusting to the expectations of Slowbridge. That physical adjustment extends to Octavia's moral bonding with the town reflected in Reverend Poppleton's assessment of Octavia: "I wish that they [the ladies of Slowbridge] knew her—her generosity and kindness of heart and ready sympathy with misfortune" (193–94), the very qualities the ladies of Slowbridge (and of Cranford) assume among themselves, and that by the end of the novel they recognize in Octavia.

A Fair Barbarian ends with Miss Belinda's brother, Martin Bassett, arriving in Slowbridge with Octavia's fiancé, Jack Belasys, in tow. The wedding takes place is

Slowbridge, affirming the new English grounding of Octavia's American identity and extending that identity to her American husband in a celebration of Anglo-American unity. The Reverend Poppleton officiates, and after the wedding Octavia showers her Slowbridge relatives and friends with gifts, singling out Lucia for special notice with a gift that "dazzled all beholders." The last words of the novel confirm that the wedding represents more than the union of two individuals.

> When she was borne away by the train, with her father and husband, and Miss Belinda, whose bonnet-strings were bedewed with tears, the Rev. Alfred Poppleton was the last man who shook hands with her. He held in his hand a large bouquet, which Octavia herself had given him out of her abundance. "Slowbridge will miss you, Miss—Mrs. Belasys," he faltered. "I—I shall miss you. Perhaps we—may even meet again. I have thought that, perhaps, I should like to go to America."
>
> And, as the train puffed out of the station and disappeared, he stood motionless for several seconds; and a large and brilliant drop of moisture appeared on the calyx of the lily which formed the centre-piece of his bouquet. (258)

The American presence that had so shaken Slowbridge at the novel's opening, in the end, has become, like Octavia, an object of desire; the Reverend Poppleton, representative of the state church, the center of English village life and moral values, is drawn out from the village, yearning for an idea of America embodied by Octavia—youthful, beautiful, wealthy and an agent of social change through the making of a new community where the traditional and the vital interanimate each other. She is also, quite obviously, an object of Poppleton's sexual desire, which becomes sublimated in his wish to go someday to America. Change, thus, does not necessarily mean the uncertainty of an unknown future; it means equally the rediscovery of the past. The tear on the lily, a flower watered with the yearnings of a man representative of the moral core of the nation and suggestive of spring—of Easter renewal—combined with the image of the train, present in embryo an image of the organic growth of an Anglo-American future. The sexual undercurrent of the novel underscores the town's and the nation's need for revitalization.

I am describing here a literary manifestation that anticipates some 20 years in advance what Alex Zwerdling describes as a "displacement of traditional Anglo-American rivalry and mistrust by a new spirit of concord."[16] In Burnett's novel of 1880, deeply responsive to Elizabeth Gaskell's novel of 1853, we see how "traditional mistrust" was woven into the fabric of individual family histories. By presenting an estranged but ultimately reconciled Anglo-American family in the Bassetts, and in basing that family in a village recognizable from its original imaginative manifestation in the 1850s as quintessentially English and fragile, Burnett anticipates a larger cultural project that created conditions within which later political, economic and social accommodations could be articulated. The concessions to their own misjudgment that the ladies of Slowbridge make in their final acceptance of Octavia, despite what they had misperceived as her crass materialism and arrogance, coupled with Octavia's realization that she has much to learn about the importance of community customs and values, anticipate in miniature the concessions, Zwerdling argues, that had to be made between England and America as the center of imperial power shifted from London to Washington after 1898 and the Spanish-American

War. "If Britons and Americans can learn to think of themselves as a single people, fulfilling their joint destiny," he explains, "the unpleasant *fact* of the passage of power from one nation to the other might be ignored. The glorious fate of the 'English-speaking peoples' thus serves as a useful myth to assuage Britain's inevitable resentment" (27).

Burnett's contemporary critics could not have anticipated the thematic resonance of *A Fair Barbarian*, a resonance that became more audible after the turn of the century. Most would have agreed with the reviewer in the April 1881 issue of *The Literary World*, who concluded a review of the novel with these words: "Mrs. Burnett's manner is at her lightest in it, well suited to a sketch designed simply to amuse the reader, with only the faintest shadow of a moral lying within any of its outlines."[17] As I have suggested, however, the comic cultural collisions and reconciliations in *A Fair Barbarian* have a double resonance. The first is literary: that novel and the two industrial novels that preceded it are part of Burnett's effort to establish her literary authority on the model of her most culturally intimate predecessor, Elizabeth Gaskell. In effect, Burnett develops a literary practice in which she deploys recognizable narrative components and refracts her own intentions and writerly voice through those components in order to make them speak differently in a familiar idiom.

In the January 1885 issue of the British periodical *Time* the English socialist, feminist writer Clementina Black (1853–1922) wrote a critical assessment of Burnett's career, "The Novels of Frances Hodgson Burnett," which provides an apt framing of her place in the Anglo-American literary field.[18] The American critical establishment had drawn specific comparisons between Burnett and Dickens and Burnett and Thackeray (see Richard Henry Stoddard's December 17, 1881, piece in *The Critic*, for example)[19] and had placed her among the "seven writers who hold the front rank today in general estimation" (see James Herbert Morse's "The Native Element in American Fiction" in the *Century Illustrated Magazine* in July 1883),[20] but Black's assessment is unusual in the quality of its nuance. Rather than pointing to specific comparisons—such as Stoddard does when he writes, "She impresses me as understanding her suffering and sinning characters as fully as Dickens ever understood his—as having a more genuine affection for them, and as never at any time caricaturing them"—Black identifies a literary strategy that characterizes Burnett's fiction as a whole during the first decade of (and arguably throughout) her career:

> It is not easy to find a final word on Mrs. Burnett's work, or to venture a conjecture as to its further development. It has gone on steadily improving, and its latest level is high. Its weakness, I suspect, lies where much of its charm, and even its strength, lies—in its versatility. Mrs. Burnett reminds us now of one writer, now of another; the likeness is never servile, her work is often equal, sometimes superior to the work resembled, and it has always a distinct flavour of its own, but the flavour is seldom quite so marked as the likeness. As there are people so quick to catch the accent that you may almost guess at their last companion, so you might range Mrs. Burnett's stories each in a different place on your bookshelves, and each beside its literary next-of-kin.

In Black's formulation, the strengths and weaknesses of Burnett's novels are the same; in an argument that smacks of oxymoron, Black asserts that the versatility of the novels is a function of their accentual relations to other novels. Although the accent feels native at first, not long after its origins come to the fore, the voice is not quite native, just as Burnett herself may be said to have been not quite English, not quite American; she writes in one accent and then in the other but in a tenor that is distinctively hers. To locate Burnett's place in the literary field, then, is to locate her in relation to others who preceded her and have stepped aside as it were (as in the death of Dickens in 1870 and George Eliot in 1880), opening a space for her. But she does not fit comfortably into one space; her work, though accented, is her own.

Another way to get at the paradox I have been struggling to pin down is to place Burnett's early novels in the context of the broader publishing practices of the period. In an essay called "Directions and Volume of Our Literary Activities" in the January 1894 issue of *Forum*, Ainsworth R. Spofford, the then Librarian of Congress, wrote the following: "In the field of book literature there appears a marked tendency toward reproduction of standard authors, and this may be hailed as a wholesome symptom both of the public taste and of the judgment of publishers who cater to it. In general terms it may be said that this is an age of compilation rather than creation."[21] The 1880s and 1890s saw an explosion of a series of standard authors produced by publishing giants like Macmillan in England and Harper's in the United States and by a multitude of small publishing houses such as the Dodge Publishing Company in New York and the Henry Altemus Company in Philadelphia. This was also a time when those same publishers printed uniform editions of the work of living authors, marking that work in its material form as the continuation of a tradition. Consequently, when readers took a Scribner edition of a Burnett novel in their hands and noted the embossed cover and the frontispiece and in-text illustrations, the form of the book established a familiarity for readers who would then read the novel in the context of the many novels by other authors that have preceded it. But that familiarity may also have enabled Burnett to inflect her narrative material differently, as suggested by Stoddard's rhapsody over Joan Lowrie:

> She is a glorious creature—elemental, primitive, cast in the mold of the mothers of the [human] race—the daughters of Job, as they live in the vigorous drawings of Blake, or the Daughters of Men, whom the Sons of God saw were fair. She belongs to a sisterhood of heroic heroines whom the novelists of the period are fond of delineating [...] but she overtops them all in massive simplicity and thorough womanhood.

Joan is familiar and unfamiliar, drawn from a complex narrative and visual history but rendered somehow with "massive simplicity," as if the Biblical narrative and romantic illustrations fuse into a figure that is somehow purer, more accessible to Burnett's readers who can feel something of that mythic history in the figure of a working girl.

The second resonance of the cultural collisions and reconciliations in Burnett's early novels is a by-product of the first. That is, in pursuing her literary project throughout her career as a novelist, Burnett provided voice, image and story to emergent political, cultural and literary developments in the relationship between her mother country and her adopted homeland. That is to say, her literary ambitions were enabled and constrained by her particular historical context and her intimate personal history as an Anglo-American woman forging a literary career between 1877 and 1922. Her particular strategy located her in a space on a transatlantic literary field defined by a tension between residual literary values associated with Victorian realism and emergent literary values associated with modernism, a term that points to qualities that also define what Rita Felski calls "the popular sublime." Aspirations toward the sublime in popular forms of narrative, Felski suggests, "seek to familiarize the ungraspable, to materialize the transcendent, thereby setting up a field of tension between the otherworldliness they invoke and its depiction through familiar and established conventions."[22] The difference between that and literary modernism could be articulated by changing the adjectives "familiar" and "established" to "unfamiliar" and "innovative." We might say, then, that Burnett's literary practice was pulled back to the world of Elizabeth Gaskell and forwarded to the world of Henry James then past (or through) James into the world of popular romance, a world that James himself evoked in a high modernist way in, for instance, *The Portrait of a Lady*, his novel that was published serially in the *Atlantic* just prior to the time that Burnett's *Through One Administration* (the central text in my next chapter) was running in *Scribner's*.

Notes

1 *The One I Knew Best of All*. London: Frederick Warne, 1893, p. 110.
2 Arthur John. *The Best Years of the Century: Richard Watson Gilder, Scribner's Monthly, and Scribner's Magazine, 1870–1909*. Urbana: U of Illinois P, 1981, p. 13.
3 See Joseph Kestner's *Protest and Reform* (1985), especially pp. 70–81 and Rosemarie Bodenheimer's *The Politics of Story in Victorian Social Fiction* (1988), especially pp. 69–84 for detailed discussions of Stone's novel.
4 See especially Chapter Six, which contains the well-known description of the typhoid-infected Davenport damp cellar home on Berry Street in Manchester.
5 The deep literary connection between the two novels and Burnett's diversions in her handling of female characterization and the psychology of the fallen women are not, however, registered in the critical history of the Victorian industrial novel. It would be enlightening to place Burnett's two industrial novels in the context of arguments made in, for instance, Raymond Williams's *Culture and Society, 1780–1950* (1958), Louis Cazamian's *The Social Novel in England, 1830–1850: Dickens, Disraeli, Mrs. Gaskell, Kingsley* (1973), John Lucas's *The Literature of Change* (1980), Catherine Gallagher's *The Industrial Reformation of English Fiction, 1832–1867* (1985), Josephine Guy's *The Victorian Social Problem Novel* (1996) and Susan Zlotnick's *Women, Writing, and the Industrial Novel* (1998) among others.
6 For a discussion of the significance of silence in relation to the fallen woman, see Thomas Recchio's "Elizabeth Gaskell as 'A Dramatic Common': Stanley Houghton's Appropriation of *Mary Barton* in *Hindle Wakes*." *The Gaskell Journal*, vol. 26 (2012): 88–102, 127.
7 Gaskell too destabilizes gender norms in *Mary Barton*, but she does so by revealing the nurturing qualities of Jog Legh, who dresses as a woman in his attempt to care for his newly orphaned granddaughter. The cross-dressing Job is also the novel's amateur naturalist.
8 Mark J. Noonan. *Reading the Century Illustrated Monthly Magazine: American Literature and Culture, 1870–1893*. Kent, Ohio: Kent State UP, 2010, p. 49.
9 "A Secret Garden of Repressed Desires: Frances Hodgson Burnett's *That Lass O'Lowries*." *Dickens Studies Annual*, vol. 32 (2002): 363–78 (369).
10 The Norton Critical Edition of *Mary Barton*, edited by Thomas Recchio, 2008, p. 485.
11 For an extended exploration of the significance and dangers for women in the Victorian era to be on public display by venturing into the street unaccompanied or being otherwise visible, see Deborah Epstein Nord's *Walking the Victorian Streets: Women, Representation, and the City*. A willful manipulation and reversal of the dangers of such visibility is enacted by Rachel Ffrench in *Haworth's*.
12 See Emily Dickinson's "I Hear a Fly Buzz" and "I Died for Beauty" for the most apt examples.

13 "An Ethnography of the Provincial: The Social Geography of Gentility in Elizabeth Gaskell's Cranford." *Victorian Studies*, vol. 41 (Spring 1998): 405–26 (405).
14 The Slowbridge of *A Fair Barbarian* might be productively added to the communities discussed in Nina Auerbach's *Communities of Women: An Idea in Fiction* (1978), adding it to the literature of village fiction in England and America in the nineteenth century.
15 For a detailed analysis of that point, see Thomas Recchio's "'Charming and Sane': School Editions of *Cranford* in America, 1905–1914." *Victorian Studies*, vol. 45, no. 4 (Summer 2003): 597–623.
16 Alex Zwerdling. *Improvised Europeans: American Literary Expatriates and the Siege of London*. New York: Basic Books, 1998, p. 22.
17 "Current Fiction." *Literary World*, vol. 12, no. 9 (April 23, 1881): 23, 146.
18 Clementina Black. "The Novels of Frances Hodgson Burnett." *Time*, vol. 12, no. 1 (January 1885): 72–85.
19 R. H. Stoddard. "Frances Hodgson Burnett." *The Critic*, vol. 1, no. 25 (December 17, 1881): 345–47.
20 James H. Morse. "The Native Element in American Fiction." *Century Illustrated Magazine*, vol. XXVI, no. 3 (1883): 362–75.
21 Ainsworth R. Spofford. "Directions and Volume of Our Literary Activities." *Forum* (January 1894): 598–604.
22 Rita Felski. *The Gender of Modernity*. Cambridge, MA: Harvard UP, 1995, p. 120.

Chapter Two

WRITING AS AN AMERICAN: THE PORTRAIT OF A WASHINGTON LADY

I

The three novel sequence established by Gaskell and echoed by Burnett sketched out in the last chapter has an echo in a parallel disruption of that sequence: Gaskell interrupted the serial numbers of *Cranford* in order to write her fallen woman novel *Ruth*, and between *Haworth's* and *A Fair Barbarian* Burnett wrote "*Louisiana*, her first American novel" (Thwaite 65). But unlike the three novel sequence, there is little material connection between *Ruth* and *Louisiana* beyond the happenstance fact that the title of both novels is the name of the main female character and that the concealment of their family names (and thus identities) drives what there is of a plot since in both novels the revelation of the woman's true identity constitutes the crisis. The character Louisiana is, like Ruth, young and naïve, but she, unlike Ruth, is not an orphan, nor is she in her innocence deceived into a fallen state for which she must atone by her own self-sacrificing death. Rather Louisiana, a country girl from the hills of North Carolina, allows herself to be misrepresented by a New York female acquaintance whom she meets at a resort within a couple of hours travel from her home. Struck by the freshness and originality of Louisiana's beauty, the New Yorker, Miss Olivia Ferrol, sets out to enhance Louisiana's appearance by substituting her country dress with a few of Miss Ferrol's own, all high fashion designs from New York. Miss Ferrol's brother Laurence, an aspiring novelist, is soon to follow his sister to the resort. Louisiana agrees to an experiment proposed by Miss Ferrol not to reveal her antecedents to the brother once he arrives, for, as the British periodical *Examiner* (May 22, 1880) put it in its review of the novel, "She [Miss Ferrol] and her brother are both fond of studying 'new types' of humanity" (644). In that way Louisiana becomes an object of analytical interest for the two New Yorkers, a situation with a powerful though implicit harshness.

The following scene captures that harshness.

> One moonlight night, as they [Louisiana, Laurence, and Olivia] sat on an upper gallery, he began to speak of the novelty of the aspect of the country as it presented itself to an outsider who saw it for the first time.
>
> "It is a new life, and a new people," he said. "And, by the way, Olivia, where is the new species of young woman I was to see—the daughter of the people who does not belong to her sphere?"
>
> He turned to Louisiana.
>
> "Have you ever seen her?" he asked. "I must confess to a dubiousness on the subject."

> Before he could add another word Louisiana turned upon him. He could see her face clearly in the moonlight. It was white, and her eyes were dilated and full of fire.
>
> "Why do you speak in that way?" she cried. "As if—as if such people were so far beneath you. What right have you—"
>
> She stopped suddenly. (45–46)

In that early scene the narrative creates the expectation that if Laurence falls in love with Louisiana, the revelation of her identity as one of the putative "new species of young woman" (and of his sister's role in the "trick") will lead to the exposure of the pretense and arrogance of the New York characters. As Ann Thwaite puts it, "The story is far more than a gentle satire on the pretensions of literary New York; it is a passionate defense of the simple, unsophisticated values, of the quiet life Frances had herself known in New Market [Tennessee]" (66). If that were the case, however, the story would have had a far different ending. To paraphrase *The Examiner* review, Louisiana and Laurence do fall in love with each other, "great trouble" does indeed rise between them once her identity is revealed, but the "wounds are ultimately healed" (644) when they marry and settle in New York where, as Burnett explains at the end of the novel, Louisiana's "literary knowledge was something for weak, ordinary mortals to quail before" (162). With that ending it is confirmed that Louisiana does not belong in her original "sphere," for although she, Laurence and their New York friends spend "almost every summer in North Carolina [...] on her native heath," where the narrator notes "numberless new 'types' were discovered" (163), Louisiana is now cast as one of the New Yorkers searching for others who do not "belong to [their] sphere." The world of simple, unsophisticated values that the story defends is relegated to the background of a broader, more engaging world where personal and intellectual growth for women is possible, the life (and culture) of Louisiana's childhood relegated to "a little room, with strange ugly furniture in it" (163), the last remnants of the home she knew as a child.

Slight as the novel seems to be in my summation, more a short story than a novel in conception and execution, the critics received it warmly: one New York critic, for example, called it "a bit of sculpture,"[1] while a Boston critic described the story as "an effective charcoal sketch [...] only the hand of genius could [have drawn]."[2] Clementina Black in her 1885 review writes this:

> To my mind "Louisiana" is the most attractive of Mrs. Burnett's stories. It has not the range and scope of 'Through One Administration,' but it goes to deeper and simpler veins of feeling; its pathos is genuine and irresistible, and it has a certain idyllic perfume which is so rare [...]. "Louisiana" [...] has close affinities to the English school of fiction. It is descended from George Eliot. (81)

Note how even as Burnett shifts her focus from British to American material, aesthetically the British lineage remains central to Black's critical assessment, the thirst for a figure to take the place of George Eliot still apparent. Richard Henry Stoddard, the American poet and critic, in an 1881 essay in *The Critic*, prefaces his assessment of Burnett's heroines by observing that her "pathos [...] is so natural that I am not ashamed of the tears in my eyes; [...] I never question her dominion over me when I am reading her books." Then he draws a contrast between Joan Lowrie (quoted in the previous chapter) and Louisiana, noting how "very different, but very lovely and touching, is that shy, sensitive, rustic little lady, Louisiana Rogers." Both, nonetheless, "represent their sex" even as they "represent [...] the growth and change of [Burnett's] intellect."[3] Stoddard's commentary gestures toward the range of Burnett's conceptualization of the varying strengths of her women characters: from the physical power and individual tenacity of Joan Lowrie, to the self-conscious beauty and enigmatic fearlessness of Rachael Ffrench, to the vitality and social bravery of Octavia Basset, to the quietly intellectual, gentle attractiveness of Louisiana—each quality is depicted in different configurations of bodily attunement to a variety of social worlds. Or as James Herbert Morse in 1883 put it somewhat vaguely but more elegantly: "In the startling smartness of all the women, there was an original way of looking at things."[4] All the *Louisiana* reviews were not uniformly effusive, but as a group they reflect the mixed but generally respectful appreciation and positive aesthetic reception of Burnett's first four novels.

It comes somewhat as a surprise, then, to read the following assessment from the "Literary Gossip" section on "The Recent Work of some American Novelists" in *The Art Interchange*: "'Through One Administration,' the latest work from [Mrs. Francis Hodgson Burnett's] pen, has hardly a redeeming feature. It is unwholesome in tone, sensational, inartistic and intolerably stupid."[5] The shocking harshness of that judgment is mildly echoed in other reviews published during the novel's serial run in the *Century*, which also express a feeling of being let down by Burnett. To quote again from Morse cited above: "Mrs. Burnett [has] sailed into popular favor with the gayest of banners flying. Pathos, humor, sentiment, and all the sympathies came with her first work; sprightliness, dash, vivacity, and all coquetries followed; then the analytic fever set in and left her astray in Washington society, without a guide" (369). Something clearly was changing in the substance and tone of the reviews. Rather than reading that change as reflecting a falling off of Burnett's art, it is more illuminating (and fairer to Burnett) to approach that change in the context of the unstable and changing literary criteria that were emerging in American literary culture in the wake of George Eliot's death and before the split between "purists" and "profiteers" described in my introduction (or in another iteration, between male aesthetic high art and female sensational popular romance) had become clear. Burnett was responding to the emergence of new literary criteria "in the world of actual literature," and she was building on her narrative strengths while attempting something, for her, new. We get a hint of that emergent criteria in Morse's allusion to "analytic fever," a hint more fully developed in this sentence from the *Saturday Review* response to *Through One Administration:* "Mrs. Burnett has apparently made up her mind to show the New World that she can not only write forcible dramatic tales of the familiar European kind, but can rival Mr. Henry James in his happiest mood of ingenious futility.".[6] That straightforward sentence is nonetheless packed with a rich set of associations: the reference to the "New World" captures Burnett's English origins and registers her work as based in a "European" tradition; the locution "forcible dramatic tales" alludes to the quality that critics of her Gaskell-inspired novels almost uniformly noticed—in contrast to depth of character analysis, Burnett revealed qualities of character through action; and the reference to the "ingenious futility" of Henry James registers one consistent critical thread in the literature on James's fiction at the time: the lack of narrative momentum and resistance to closure. Early in Burnett's career, then, her work was in implicit critical contrast to James's, a point illustrated in review essays that addressed their novels in the same critical space.

The sixth article in the *North American Review* (September/October 1877) by Edward Burlingame, entitled "New American Novels,"[7] explored Burnett's first novel, *That Lass O'Lowrie's*, and James's fourth,[8] *The American*. Burnett was fresh on the literary scene, and James had already established a reputation as a critic, essayist and novelist, so it is of little surprise that six pages of the review are devoted to *The American* and two paragraphs to *That Lass*. The final sentence on Burnett's novel captures the measured quality of the review's praise: "It is because it does not 'harry us wi' talk' that Mrs. Burnett's novel is successful above others of its kind" (319). That comment acknowledges the novel's generic pedigree and its emphasis on narrative action while earlier in the review, Burlingame praises Burnett's conception of Joan Lowrie: "Mrs. Burnett's merit lies in this,—that she succeeds in bringing out the whole womanliness of this girl's nature, and in showing her development into an altogether different being, and yet does not call in cant or impossible absurdities to aid her in the task" (319). Taken together the two comments note that Burnett was working within a recognizable tradition and that with her female protagonist, she fulfills a convention of character development without merely following the formulas of the convention. Burlingame's brief critique, then, contains the seeds that produced the broadly enthusiastic assessment of Burnett's early novels. His critique of James in this review, however, helps define the part of the American literary field into which Burnett moved to extend her expressive range as she worked to develop her art as a novelist.

Burlingame opens his review by noting how "exceptional" the reception of *The American* had already been, receiving "more careful and excellent criticism than has fallen to the lot of any other American novel in recent years" (309). James, he asserts, is "a master of the technical portion of his art," but, he goes on to suggest, that begs "the dangerously broad question what a great novel really is." The problem with *The American* (and James's work in general), Burlingame argues, is that the novel appeals "almost entirely—we are tempted to say wholly—to the reader's intellectual side. The enjoyment we derive from it is purely intellectual enjoyment" (310). The problem for Burlingame is not only with James: "It is because Mr. James stands so near the very head of the school in which he has enrolled himself, that what he writes inevitably raises a question as to the limitations of that school," the greatest limitation being that that school allows for "the production of admirable specimens of skillful workmanship instead of real creations" (311). The use of the scientific "specimens" in contrast to the implicit warm blood of a creature animating the word "creations" captures the quality of Burlingame's anxiety about the ascendance of the master's craft. The assumption animating Burlingame's critique is that the intellect may sever art from its connection to felt experience, the affective dimension of human relations. The highest ambitions of realistic fiction—to build the complex relations that bind together social context and the intellectual and emotional development of character, which then provides not just understanding but affective fullness (positive or negative) in a complex life-world for each individual—are closed off by a commitment to method, to mastering a craft. The dichotomy between intellect and creation in Burlingame's review of *The American* is a variation on the pejorative dichotomy between purists, who commit themselves to high art, and profiteers, who write to appeal to a large audience, with this caveat: both purists and profiteers desire readers. So one might inflect that dichotomy as one between a commitment to craft, the shaping power of the mind, and a commitment to affective construction, the shaping of narrative that appeals to feelings, imagination and intellect. The polarized language that characterizes the response to Burnett's *Through One Administration* can be accounted for, then, by the high stakes in the struggle for cultural authority in the "world of actual literature." In that struggle, Burnett's early novels were clearly on the side of Victorian realism, which was beginning to give way to the analytical school associated with James on the one hand and popular romance associated with figures like Mary Elizabeth Braddon, Rhoda Broughton, Maria Corelli, Mona Caird and Sarah Grand on the other.[9] Consequently, a novel that could be read as Jamesian came as a shock to some of Burnett's critics and readers. But the extent to which *Through One Administration* is of the analytical school and the extent to which it has affinities with popular romance is a question that can best be answered through a comparison between it and James's *The Portrait of a Lady*. But because there is such an extensive critical history of readings of James's novel and no sustained critical engagement with Burnett's novel, the comparison proposed needs to be supplemented by a careful, close reading of *Through One Administration* to tease out its particular aesthetic strengths and narrative appeal.

II

The Portrait of a Lady was published in serial parts in *Macmillan's Magazine* in London, beginning in October 1880 and ending in November 1881, and in *The Atlantic Monthly* in New York beginning in November 1880 and ending in December 1881. *Through One Administration* followed in the wake of *The Portrait*, but it was published serially only in the United States, in *The Century Magazine* in New York from November 1881 to April 1883. In that same month and year (April 1883), *The National Review* in the UK published an essay by Arthur Tilley entitled "The New School of Fiction,"[10] which begins by noting that "two of the most successful novels that have been published in this country within the last eighteen months are the work of Americans" (257). One of those novels is *The Portrait of a Lady*, the other William Dean Howell's *A Modern Instance*. Those novels, the essay observes, "bear a strong family resemblance." Part of that resemblance is superficial as "in both there is a charming young woman, who [...] marries a scoundrel; in both there is a silent adorer [...] [and] in both the ultimate fate of the heroine is veiled in enigmatic obscurity." On the surface *Through One Administration* could also claim membership in that family[11] since the resemblances listed map with near precision on features of that novel: a young woman marries a scoundrel, her silent adorer quietly watches over her as protector and her ultimate fate in the end remains an open question. As the fact of such a resemblance among the three novels suggests, the resemblance is too superficial to carry much force. At least between James's and Howells's novels, the resemblance "lies far deeper. It lies in the elaborate analysis of character, in the absence of plot, in the sparing use of incident, in the studied realism, in the conscientious subordination of the artist to his art, in the acute powers of observation, and in the humour" (257), which the essay then suggests is not humor at all because the "writers' gifts" do not "lie specially in that direction." Such qualities, of course, describe "the new school of fiction," which, the critic writes, is "concisely stated" in an article by Howells from the *Century Magazine*. And here is what Howells says about James in that article:

> This school, which is so largely of the future as well as the present, finds its chief exemplar in Mr. James; it is he who is shaping and directing American fiction at least. [Note the hint of ambition to direct British fiction as well in that casual "at least."] It is the ambition of the younger contributors [to American periodicals] to write like him; he has his following more distinctly recognizable than that of any other English-writing novelist [the term "English-writing" rather than American writer confirms the hint buried in the "at least" above]. (258)

So if the qualities of elaborate analysis, lack of plot, submergence of authorial consciousness to the demands of art and so on are the hallmarks of the rapidly solidifying new school of fiction, and if Henry James is the headmaster of that school to which ambitious American authors want admittance, then it makes perfect sense that Burnett, given her ambitions to shape for herself a serious and successful literary career, would explore the extent to which the expressive strategies of the new fiction would serve her narrative ends. She too could write her own portrait of a lady.

As is implied in the negative reviews of *Through One Administration*, the danger for Burnett in launching out in the waters of the new fiction concerns her relationship to her audience. According to Tilley in "The New School of Fiction," the success of *The Portrait of a Lady* "does not imply that [it] enjoy[s] a wide popularity." Quite the contrary, for that novel's success "is confined to a small and select circle of admirers," which includes "the reviewers," who "have been almost unanimous in their praise." Such success may in fact be "the very kind of success which the author most values" (257). Clearly for Burnett, the reviewers were not "almost unanimous in their praise," but based on the fact that throughout her career "she was wildly successful in both America and Britain," that "in the fifty-six years of her professional writing life, no publisher in either America of Britain ever turned down her work" and that she became "the wealthiest woman writer of her time on either side of the Atlantic" (Gerzina xiii), she always enjoyed "a wide popularity." But the contrast between James and Burnett as illustrative of the dichotomy between high art and popular success is simplistic for two reasons: first, James himself very much desired popular success. One of the things that James found heartening about *The Portrait of a Lady*, for example, was that it sold comparatively well. In a letter to Macmillan in London dated December 27, 1881 and written from New York, James expressed contentment, almost happiness with his life in America: "I am struck throughout," he observed,

> with the rapid & general increase of the *agreeable* in American life, & the development of material civilization [...]. Also my book is selling—largely, for one of mine. I hope it is doing something of the kind *chez vous*. I have seen a good many English notices, & appear to myself to have got off on the whole very well. (*The Correspondence of Henry James and the House of Macmillan* 67)

While the "selling" claim is modified by the "one of mine," *The Portrait* was, nonetheless, selling, and that coupled with strong reviews reveals that at least for the moment,

James felt he was achieving that so elusive balance between adherence to the highest demands of art and worldly success.

The challenge in achieving such a balance and the danger of that balance being perceived as necessarily requiring a compromise of one's art to the demands of the world was a recurrent theme in James's work, as Michael Anesko has shown in his study of the economic dimension of James's career. In the chapter called "Accommodating Art and the World" in "*Friction with the Market*," Anesko offers a reading of the end of James's *The Tragic Muse*, where he writes:

> Like the other novels we have examined, *The Tragic Muse* suffers from a problem of completion. Many readers have accepted rather uncritically, however, the simple dichotomy between art and the world that James addressed in his 1908 preface. Seen through that distorting lens, the novel necessarily ends on an unequivocally pessimistic note. The dualistic logic behind such interpretations—that one must choose between art and the world, opt either for artistic integrity or popular success—falsely converts a richly ironic novel into simple melodrama. (138)

In Anesko's formulation, James himself provided the terms by which irony is reduced to melodrama, and those terms are also at play in his discomfort with Burnett's financial success, as we saw in his response recounted in the introduction to her gifts of fruit and his dismissal of her as one of the small fry, falsely converting a "richly ironic" relation to the moral polarities of his personal melodrama.

Second, both James and Burnett had high hopes that their respective novels would represent their highest ambitions, be their best work. As Leon Edel, James's most comprehensive biographer, explains,

> Early in 1880, when T.S. Perry offered to write an article on James's works to date, James told him to wait for the novel he would do that year. "It is from that I myself shall pretend to date—on that I shall take my stand." To Howells he announced that he had found his title—*The Portrait of a Lady*. (252)

Given the fact that he had negotiated "stiff terms for his big novel" (Edel 252) and at the same time projected the book as the one that defined, at least at this point, the quality of his career as an author, the stakes were high. Nonetheless, James was confident, and the reviews for the most part confirmed his confidence. In the *New York Daily Tribune*, Abraham Lincoln's former secretary John Hay characterized the novel thus:

> Of the importance of this volume there can be no question. It will certainly remain one of the notable books of the time. It is properly to be compared, not with the light and ephemeral literature of amusement, but with the gravest and most serious works of imagination which have been devoted to the study of the social conditions of the age and the moral aspects of our civilization.[12]

There are three things of note in that quotation: the reference to "light and ephemeral literature," which are terms that have come to be applied to Burnett's fiction, in contrast to "serious works of the imagination," which are terms that have been applied to James; the broadness of the phrase "social conditions of the age," which begs the questions of whose conditions and where; and "the moral aspects of our civilization," which suggests perhaps the United States since the review was published in New York and the personal pronoun "our" was used, but the lack of specificity (to whom does "our" refer and how broadly does the word civilization extend?) suggests an ethnocentric universalizing of a narrow social group. The implication is that literary value is very much entangled with the views of a privileged social class in Hay's review, and I would argue in the critical assessments of the new fiction more generally.

For a contrasting view of *Through One Administration,* we can turn to Ann Thwaite's biography of Burnett. "*Through One Administration* has been called a political novel," Thwaite writes,

> and indeed it is partly that. Its picture of lobbying, of machinations and intrigues, is vivid and convincing. Frances' portrait of Washington is confirmed by Henry Adams' biographer: "The political tension never relaxed for a moment. A kind of breathlessness was always in the air. Each day during the Washington season some new disclosure, some overwhelming turn, seemed always to lie beyond the corner." Adams reported that Henry James was revolted by the intrigues. Dubious dealings were then, as now, always coming to light. Secretary of State Blaine was reviled as "the continental liar from Maine", when he was found to have been involved in profitable but shady railroad deals. *Through One Administration* examines a "struggling, manoeuvring [sic], over-reaching, ambitious world". (74)

Although Hay's review was contemporary to James's novel and Thwaite's is retrospective, part of a biography written some one hundred years after the novel, the contrast in focus and language is nonetheless instructive. The most obvious contrast between Hay and Thwaite is the specificity of Thwaite's characterization of Burnett's novel. Rather than such terms as "the age" and "civilization," the time and place references are to the "Washington season," and when there are vague allusions to such things as "some new disclosure," the vagueness is clarified by examples, such as "shady railroad deals." For a novelist whose interest in *The Portrait of a Lady* was in part about the effects of a marriage made under false pretenses, the "match maker" as it were being the secret mother of the groom's child, the groom and mother/match maker conspiring to find him a wife with money (the heroine of the novel, Isabel Archer), it comes as a surprise to read Adams's report that James was "revolted" by Washington "intrigues." A comparison of the two novels can help account for that surprise while providing a detailed and textured view of the literariness of Burnett's neglected novel.

The first lines of the portrait of the lady in James's novel (and in Burnett's) are sketched in the first chapter. In *The Portrait* the lady is referred to obliquely while in *Through One Administration,* the lady comes on the scene directly. Men in conversation, however, precede the introduction of the ladies in both novels, their speech set against the backdrop of an imposing English country house in the former novel and in the domestic interior of an affluent scientist's home in the latter. The different settings require different modes of presentation, James evoking a grand historical sweep and Burnett emphasizing the immediate cares of a family at a moment of transition.

Attempting to "sketch" a "peculiarly English picture" at "the hour dedicated to the ceremony of afternoon tea" (17), James writes how

> [T]he house had a name and a history; the old gentleman taking his tea would have been delighted to tell you these things: how it had been built under Edward the Sixth, had offered a night's hospitality to the great Elizabeth (whose august person had extended itself upon a huge, magnificent and terribly angular bed which still formed the principle honour of the sleeping apartments). Had been a deal bruised and defaced in Cromwell's wars, and then under the Restoration, repaired and much enlarged; and how, finally, after having been remodeled and disfigured in the eighteenth century, it had passed into the careful keeping of a shrewd American banker [the old gentleman alluded to above], who had bought it originally because (owing to circumstances too complicated to set forth) it was offered at a great bargain: bought it with much grumbling at its ugliness, its antiquity, its incommodity, and who now, at the end of twenty years, had become conscious of a real aesthetic passion for it, so that he knew all its points and would tell you just where to stand to see them in combination and just the hour when the shadows of its various protuberances—which fell so softly upon the warm, weary brickwork—were of the right measure. (18)

There is not only the micro-history of the American banker, Mr. Touchett, who purchases the English house and grouses at the stupidity of the purchase before learning over 20 years to value its hard-won aesthetic qualities but also the sweep of British macro-history with monarchs, revolution and restoration of which the banker's personal history becomes an extension. That pattern can be read as a personal allegory for James's own ambitions as an American writer who dedicated himself to the daunting task of writing his way into the annals of British literary history, and it is a thematic pattern Burnett would turn to in a series of novels beginning with the children's novel *Little Lord Fauntleroy* in 1886 and more fully realized in *The Shuttle* in 1907.

The Anglophilia in James's description of the house is deepened in the description of the speakers in the chapter. "The old gentleman at the tea-table," James explains, "who had come from America thirty years before, had brought with him, at the top of his baggage, his American physiognomy" (18), while one of the other two speakers, Lord Warburton, "was a remarkably well-made man of five-and-thirty, with a face as English as that of the old gentleman [...] was something else" (19). The only descriptor that follows the reference to American physiognomy is that "he had kept it [his physiognomy] in best order" (18); after the reference to the English face, we learn it was "a noticeably handsome face, fresh-coloured, fair and frank, with firm straight features, a lively grey eye and the rich adornment of a chestnut beard" (19). The third speaker, Ralph Touchett, is the banker's son, an invalid and "an ugly young man" (21).

The conversation among the three is rather strained. "He's a good nurse, Lord Warburton," the father says of his son, to which Warburton replies, "Isn't he a bit clumsy?" "Oh no, he's not clumsy," Mr. Touchett says in defense, "—considering that he's an invalid himself. He's a very good nurse—for a sick nurse. I call him my sick-nurse because he's sick himself" (21). The strain of a bad pun having to be explained characterizes what seems to be light-hearted banter among the three, and from there the conversation gets darker.

> "You young men have too many jokes," the banker says. "When there are no jokes you've nothing left."

> "Fortunately there are always more jokes," the ugly young man remarked.
>
> "I don't believe it—I believe things are getting more serious. You young men will find that out."
>
> "The increasing seriousness of things, then—that's great opportunity of jokes."
>
> "They'll have to be grim jokes," said the old man. "I'm convinced there will be great changes; and not all for the better." (22)

The portentousness of that exchange is not clarified very much by the subsequent reference to the "great changes" alluded to being vaguely "social and political"; the reference hangs there, a reflection of the pessimism of a man toward the end of his life. But the topic quickly shifts from fear of the future to, appropriately, marriage, when Ralph says of Warburton, "He's trying hard to fall in love." To that, the old man replies: "The ladies will save us [...] that is the best of them will—for I make a difference between them. Make up to a good one and marry her, and your life will become much more interesting" (23). Given the fact of the banker's bad marriage, his advice comes across as wishful thinking, especially since we learn that his wife has refused to live permanently with him in his English country house. She is, however, on her way to England with her niece, Isabel Archer, in tow. The chapter ends with this exchange between Warburton and Mr. Touchett:

> "Very likely she's engaged; I've known a good many American girls, and they always were; but I could never see that it made any difference, upon my word! As for my being a good husband," Mr. Touchett's visitor pursued, "I'm not sure of that either. One can but try!"
>
> "Try as much as you please, but don't try on my niece," smiled the old man, whose opposition to the idea was broadly humorous.
>
> "Ah, well," said Lord Warburton with a humour broader still, "perhaps, after all, she's not worth trying on!" (25)

There is non sequitur quality to the dialogue that carries with it a sense of anxiety, despite the "broadly humorous" qualifiers. The announcement of Isabel Archer's impending arrival coming on the heels of the claim that Warburton is "trying hard to fall in love" sets up a narrative expectation that he will fall in love with her, and Mr. Touchett's warning that he "not try on my niece" sets up the requisite obstacle for such a narrative. Colliding with those things is the assertion of hope that a good woman can save a man and Warburton's speculation that Isabel may not be "worth trying on" short-circuits that narrative expectation, the illogic of the dialogue elements suggesting that the obstacle that must be overcome in the love plot is always already impossible to overcome. In addition, the micro-history of the American extending the cultural and aesthetic significance of the historic English country house through the next generation is foreclosed as well since Ralph, the son, is an invalid and unlikely to live long enough to marry and have children. Even though the elements of a love triangle can be discerned, then, they do not take shape. It is as if we know that Isabel, before she is even on the scene, will refuse to step into any narrative that is prefigured for her. That does not mean that elements of such a narrative simply disappear. A potential for the fulfillment of multiple narrative possibilities is evoked then thwarted. That potential and its erasure are plausibly the animating forces that propel the narrative forward. What is implicit in the opening chapter becomes explicit as the novel unfolds.

My reading of the opening chapter of James's *Portrait* mainly unpacks what has been known and accepted for years: the high literary quality of both the conception of the work and its execution, sentence by sentence. The fine balance struck in the chapter is between indicating a thematic core around which the narrative will shape itself and leaving that core implicit enough so that the whole game is not given away. As readers we feel the structure more than see its skeletal form. Set in Washington, DC, *Through One Administration*, as *The Portrait* had done, opens with an expository passage as backdrop to a conversation between men, one a young military officer and the other an older relative, who is both a scientist and professor of entomology.

> Eight years before the Administration rendered important by the series of events and incidents which form the present story, there had come to Washington, on a farewell visit to a distant relative with whom he was rather a favorite, a young officer who was on the point of leaving the civilized world for a far-away Western military station. The name of the young officer was Phillip Tredennis. His relative and entertainer was a certain well-known entomologist, whom it will be safe to call Professor Herrick. At the Smithsonian and in all scientific circles, Professor Herrick's name was a familiar one. He was considered an enviable as well as an able man. He had established himself in Washington because he found men there whose tastes and pursuits were congenial to his own, and because the softness of the climate suited him; he was rich enough to be free from all anxiety and to enjoy the delightful liberty of pursuing his scientific labors because they were a pleasure, and not because he was dependent on their results. He had a quiet and charming home, an excellent matter-of-fact wife, and one daughter, who was being educated in a northern city, and who was said to be as bright and attractive as one could wish a young creature to be. (1)

In contrast to the leisurely opening of *The Portrait*—whose first sentence reads, "Under certain circumstances there are few hours in life more agreeable than the hour dedicated to the ceremony known as afternoon tea" (17)—the paragraph above is dense with information: the opening phrase (even before we get to the main clause) provides both a time reference and an orientation to the narrative as a whole, the "Administration" of a president subordinated to events associated with others; the introduction of the young officer is carried by the main clause. The rest of the paragraph focuses on the professor, whose situation, again in contrast to *The Portrait*, is not embedded in the *long duree* of history but is a product of an inclination to live in the place most congenial to his vocation and his physical comfort. Although Professor Herrick and Mr. Touchett are both wealthy, the professor's wealth is in the service to his scientific interests; it supports a way of seeing that extends to aspects of his personal life as we learn when the narrator describes him in more detail:

> He was a quiet and intensely studious person, taking small interest in the ordinary world and appearing always slightly surprised when his wife spoke to him; still, his manner toward her was as gentle and painstaking as if she had been the rarest possible beetle, and the only one of her species to be found in any known collection, though perhaps the interest she awakened in him was not so great as it might have been under such exceptionally favorable circumstances. (2)

Herrick comes across as an abstracted figure, well-intentioned but whose affect is hesitant, even repressed. What defines him, however, is his power of observation (which he can inflect with feeling, but feeling of manner not of words). Through Herrick, then, the narrator announces seeing—looking, gazing, analyzing, reflecting, examining and other variations—as a thematic concern, a shaping narrative motif. That motif early on in the opening chapter is directed toward Herrick's daughter, Bertha, through an incidental metaphor that could serve as an emblem for Bertha's subsequent experience.

Herrick had not seen his daughter for some years for she had been away at school and just returned after graduation from a college in the northeast. Once at home, she is to "come out" formally, the social occasion that would, by putting her on display (each young woman "coming out" walks on the arm of an escort to the applause of assembled guests), mark her coming of age and thus her availability for marriage. When she returns home, the narrator notes that "to her distant relative [i.e. Tredennis] her arrival was a revelation" as it was also to her father who in response to her coming was "aroused [...] from his entomological reveries" (5). The metaphor emerges in the following dialogue:

> "I do hope you will like me, papa," she said, "when you have classified me."
>
> "Classified you!" said the professor, in some bewilderment.
>
> "Yes," answered Bertha. "You know I always feel as if you might turn me over gently with your finger at any moment, and watch me carefully while I struggled until you knew all about me, and then chloroform me and stick a pin through me with a label on it. I shouldn't like the chloroform and the pin, but I should take an interest in the label. Couldn't I have the label without the pin, papa?"
>
> "I don't know" said the professor, examining her more carefully than ever. "I am afraid not."
>
> After that it became his custom to encourage her to reveal herself in conversation, which it was very easy to do, as she was a recklessly candid young person. (5)

The metaphor, which renders Bertha as insect, is instigated by Bertha's awareness of her father's gaze, a gaze that Burnett has carefully contextualized in relation to the idea of Herrick's daughter reaching sexual maturity. That idea is implicit in a memory the professor recounts almost immediately before the dialogue quoted above. In discussing his daughter with Tredennis, Herrick ruminates:

> "I remember [a girl] I once knew years ago, but that is all. It was when I was a younger man. I think she was a year or two older than Bertha [...]. She used to bewilder me [...] She had gray eyes," he said, in a rather lower voice,—"gray eyes [...]". The professor stood still a moment, regarding the fire abstractly. "*She* had gray eyes," he said again,—"gray eyes!" (4)

The professor's fixation on eyes locates the memory within the motif of sight but with a difference: his memory is from early manhood, a time of his own potential sexual awakening, and the eyes are both what he looks at, and since he sees their color, those eyes were looking at him too in an exchange of gazes. The sexual import in the memory is more felt than stated; Herrick's memory of bewilderment coupled with his disciplined looking at nonhuman objects enacts a pattern of interest and avoidance. That same pattern is embedded in the insect = Bertha analogy buried in the metaphor. Bertha's desire to be gazed upon (and implicitly to return such a gaze) is figured in her "interest in the label": How would she be seen? What language would capture her appearance? And would her appearance represent who she in fact is? The pin suggests a figurative and subtly literal penetrating pain, born, perhaps, of misjudgments and irreversible commitments, and the chloroform implies an effort of forgetfulness, of personal numbing, of entrapment, of hopelessness. No wonder she "wouldn't like the chloroform or the pin." But the metaphor makes it clear there can be no such avoidance.

The pain of not understood and inarticulate frustrated desire that is buried in but also flickering out from the professor's memory of the girl with the "gray eyes" and the metaphorical half-articulated wish to avoid the possibility of a repetition in his daughter's experience strikes the key note for the opening chapter and anchors the emotional repressions that animate much of the narrative. In the conversations between Herrick and Tredennis, between Bertha and her mother, between Tredennis and Bertha, and between Bertha and her father that take up the rest of the opening chapter, we can feel the possibility that desire need not be frustrated. The ingredients for happiness for Bertha and Tredennis are all there, but they are not recognized and remain scattered, uncombined. The professor, we learn, "fell into the habit of talking of the girl [his daughter] to Tredennis" (6). Toward the end of their longest exchange, Herrick animatedly asserts:

> "She might be happy, perhaps—if one thing happened to her [...]. *If* she married a fine fellow, whom she was deeply and passionately in love with."
> "She will be likely to marry the man she loves, sir," he said, in a voice neither clear nor steady.
> "Yes," said the professor; "unless she makes the mistake of marrying the man who loves *her*. She will meet him often enough."

The unsteadiness in Tredennis's voice communicates the yet to be stated (or directly confronted within himself) development of his love for Bertha. But for readers it is clear that one man at the outset who loves Bertha is Tredennis, and the possibility that she also loves him flickers in the dialogue that follows. When he on impulse buys Bertha a bouquet of heliotrope—"'I don't know why, but I thought of you when I saw them' he says to Bertha. 'It's an idea, I suppose'" (11), he hardly communicates passion, but Bertha's response evokes the potential that they both recognize the gesture for what it is, a declaration of love: "'I wish this was my "coming out" night,'" she said. 'I would wear these. You have given me my first bouquet. I am glad of that'" (11). Because it is her first bouquet, however, she has no context for thinking about it; she cannot feel its import in relation to anything else, so she is merely "glad" even as that muted pleasure implies the emergence of her feelings. Tredennis, nonetheless, "felt like a creature slowly awakening to the light of day" (12). His love is figured as light, and when the topic shifts to his departure to the west to take up his army duties, Bertha avers that he "will be a most distinguished person," to which he responds: "I wonder what will have happened to you?" Bertha in her youthful enthusiasm says, "I dare say I should have had a lovely time, and have been very happy." Tredennis "felt himself awakening a little more," so when the conversation turns to the possibility of unhappiness and Bertha responds with a pained expression, Tredennis begins to declare his love: "Don't look like that. It—it hurts me. If any sacrifice of mine—any suffering," but at the moment the professor walks in "and the words were never spoken." A week later Tredennis ships out for the west. As he rode to the station, he "closed his eyes [and] saw […] a bright, pure white figure standing upon the pavement, the night behind it, the great bouquet of white roses in its hand, and the light from the house streaming upon the radiant girl's face" (16). Burnett's deft transformation of Bertha into a "figure," the pronoun she becoming "it," is a brilliant distancing technique. It raises the possibility that the love that Tredennis will feed in his heart over "the eight years that followed" (17)—the first words of Chapter II—will have more than an element of fantasy, the memory of love becoming hard as steel, impossible to dislodge but not of real flesh and blood, a memory not of love but of frustrated desire.

III

My reading of the opening chapters of both *The Portrait of a Lady* and *Through One Administration* does not address the question of literary quality. But literary quality as such does not in itself determine whether a given author or text is a player in the literary field. The fact that both James's and Burnett's novels were reviewed in the same newspapers and periodicals, even at times in the same review, marks their mutual presence in the literary field. I hope thus far to have demonstrated the literariness of both openings via scene setting, dialogue and a configuration of character relationships that implies rather than maps a narrative direction, if not a trajectory of story. Stylistically the novels are very different, however, James's paragraphs dense, his sentences elaborate, his dialogue studied, in contrast to Burnett's more direct and brisker style. Those disparate styles enact different imaginative worlds: *The Portrait*'s Anglo-American world of high culture (spanning the UK, United States and Europe) where his characters possess layered, complex and mostly concealed interiority, and *Through One Administration*'s world of American political culture, intrigue and glimmering surfaces. Readers are left to decide whether the style deployed is appropriate to the world imagined.

The center of the imagined worlds of the novels is the heroine of each, Isabel Archer and Bertha Herrick. In his "Preface" to the New York edition of *The Portrait of a Lady*, James wrote the following about the genesis of that novel.

> Millions of presumptuous girls, intelligent or not intelligent, daily affront their destiny, and what is it open for their destiny to *be*, at the most, that we should make an ado about it? The novel is of its very nature an "ado," an ado about something, and the larger the form it takes the greater of course the ado. Therefore, consciously, that was what one was in for—for positively organizing an ado about Isabel Archer […]. Challenge any such problem with any intelligence, and you immediately see how full it is of substance; the wonder being, all the while, as we look at the world, how absolutely, how inordinately, the Isabel Archers, and even much smaller fry, insist on mattering. (9)

"Insist on mattering" indeed! Let us work backward from the "smaller fry." Recall in the introduction to this book, a letter James wrote to his brother William in which he refers to his fellow authors as " 'literary fry,' my confreres," including on his list Hodgson Burnett. Now make this analogy: James is to Hodgson Burnett as Isabel Archer is to Bertha Herrick, all of whom "insist on mattering." Like Isabel, Bertha "affront[s her] destiny," and like James, Burnett makes an "ado about it." The question seems to be whether the ado is equal to the mattering? The answer to that question in relation to *The Portrait* is an unambiguous yes, given the critical literature that has been written about the book,[13] but given the limited critical literature on Burnett's novel, I will pursue an answer to that question by tracking what seems to be the parallel careers (a euphemism for failed courtships and worse marriages) of Isabel and Bertha. To make that tracking manageable, I will focus on significant scenes that define the courtships, marriages and relationships outside of marriage in each novel. Then I will try to determine to what extent each novel's ending may be read as an "affront" (pun intended) to Isabel's and Bertha's "destiny."

A small moment in Chapter Forty-Seven of *The Portrait* offers an implicit summary of Isabel's history. Henrietta Stackpole, an American reporter and friend, presses Isabel after her marriage to Gilbert Osmond on the fact of her sadness: "She had guessed that Isabel was sad [...] and she had never guessed so happily as that" (a most unhappy use of the word "happily"!). The focalization of that moment shifts from Henrietta to Isabel who half flinches at the fact of being "accused [...] to her face of being wretched. She [Henrietta] was a woman, she was a sister; she was not Ralph, nor Lord Warburton, nor Caspar Goodwood, and Isabel could speak" (399). The men are presented as obstacles to speech, and the absence of her husband from the list suggests he is more than an obstacle; he is an enforcer of silence. Each of the men had proposed marriage to Isabel (Goodwood and Warburton) and/or declared his love (her cousin Ralph), and while they all professed to having her best interests at heart, and while Isabel feels physical desire for Goodwood, principled respect mixed with elements of passion for Warburton and great compassion for Ralph, she will not marry. While her reasons can only be inferred, one possible explanation is that she sees the social role she would have to fulfill in any of those marriages as shaping her life for her in advance, closing off an open exploration and discovery of the world. In other words, she fears the determinations of patriarchal culture. So she marries Osmond, in part, because he seems outside the conventional order, with no social position, no wealth and no ambition other than the aesthetic project of living his own life. Before she can bring herself to say to Henrietta, "No, I don't like him [Osmond]. I can tell you because I am weary of my secret" (400), she has learned that her socially unfettered, unconventional husband whose apparently liberating aesthetic orientation to a world of constraints she finds so attractive has married her for the most conventional of reasons: money. As Osmond says to her in another context, "I'm not conventional: I'm convention itself" (259). She is living, then, the oldest of stories, her life more overdetermined than she could possibly have imagined.

The sequence of her relations with Goodwood, Warburton and Ralph Touchett marks the stages of her progress from ambitious and optimistic girlhood to the horror of her marriage. She had known Goodwood, "a straight young man from Boston" (41) for about a year before her father's death and her aunt's offer to take her to live in Europe. "He was the finest young man she had ever seen, was indeed quite a splendid young man" the narrator notes; "he inspired her with a sentiment of high, of rare respect. She had never felt equally moved by any other person. He was supposed by the world to wish to marry her, but this of course was between themselves" (42). The language in those sentences is poised between the conventions of romance and their simultaneous debunking. Goodwood may have "moved" Isabel more than "any other person," but the word person instead of man qualifies the nature of being so moved. Similarly the idea that the prospect of marriage "of course was between themselves" implies an intimacy that the passively constructed main clause ("He was supposed by the world") freezes in advance. Combine those stylistic features with the fact that "she felt no eagerness to see him" (42) as she anticipated his arrival, and that within "half-an-hour" of his arrival, "Caspar Goodwood [...] took his way back to his lodging with the feeling of a man defeated," romance for Isabel seems impossible. Readers may feel that, but Goodwood "was not, it may be added, a man weakly to accept defeat" (42). When Isabel arrives in England and talks with her cousin Ralph for the first time, he says, "When you do suffer they call you an idiot. The great point's to be as happy as possible," to which Isabel replies: "Well, that's what I came to Europe for, to be as happy as possible" (52). Her prospects for happiness do not include courtship and marriage; as a consequence Goodwood should be out of the picture, but he is "resolute" (42). He travels to see Isabel in Italy and in England at critical moments in the narrative. Each time he renews his suit and is rejected. His final appeal, however, nearly constitutes the last words of the narrative, so clearly the emphasis on Isabel's rejection of a marriage built upon a ground of sexual desire is central to the sense of diminishment and disappointment readers feel at the end of the novel.

A variation on the pattern we saw in Isabel's response to Goodwood's first marriage proposal is repeated in a less straightforward way in the scene of Warburton's first gesture toward a marriage proposal. As we know from the first chapter, Warburton is a guest at Gardencourt, Mr. Touchett's historic country house. On the third day of his visit after Isabel's arrival, Isabel and he are in private conversation. Warburton observes that he doesn't think Isabel's uncle likes him, to which Isabel responds:

> "You're very much mistaken. I've heard him speak very highly of you."
> "I'm glad you have talked about me," said Lord Warburton. "But, I nevertheless don't think he'd like me to keep coming to Gardencourt."
> "I can't answer for my uncle's tastes," the girl rejoined [...]. "But for myself I shall be very glad to see you."
> "Now that's what I like to hear you say. I'm charmed when you say that."
> "You're easily charmed, my lord," said Isabel.
> "No, I'm not easily charmed!" And then he stopped a moment. "But you've charmed me, Miss Archer." (76)

The conversation goes on with more complexity and subtlety over the next two pages, but the undercurrent of flirtation in the above exchange can be felt throughout. Thus, when Isabel reflects on having "heard that the English are a highly eccentric people, and she had even read in some ingenious author that they are at bottom the most romantic of races," she registers a hesitation akin to the one she felt with Goodwood. "Was Lord Warburton suddenly turning romantic," she wonders? "Was he going to make her a scene [...] only the third time they had met?" He does not, being restrained by his "good manners," knowing "he had already touched the furthest limit of good taste in expressing his admiration for a young lady." As they walked back to rejoin the others, Warburton turns to her and says, "I shall come and see you next week." Her inward turmoil and outward response is a mild echo of her refusal of Goodwood's proposal, revealing her awareness that Warburton's returning to see her so soon is a prelude to another:

> She had received an appreciable shock, but as it died away she felt that she couldn't pretend to herself that it was altogether a painful one. Nevertheless she made answer to his declaration, coldly enough, "Just as you please." And her coldness was not the calculation of her effect—a game she played in a much smaller degree that would have seemed probable to many critics. It came with a certain fear. (77)

The fact that the prospect of what is to come produced a mixed emotional response, powerful but not an exclusively painful one, is revealed in the "appreciable shock" that Isabel found not "altogether [...] painful," a complexity of response that she masks in her cool reply: "Just as you please." The question left hanging by the passage is what "fear" her coldness was masking? When Warburton does propose explicitly, the nature of Isabel's fear is clarified.

Warburton's proposal extends over many pages, the following passage being, I think, the definitive one:

> These words were uttered with a breadth of candour that was like the embrace of strong arms—that was like the fragrance straight in her face, and by his clean, breathing lips, of she knew not what strange gardens, what changed airs. She would have given her little finger at the moment to feel strongly and simply the impulse to answer: "Lord Warburton, it's impossible for me to do better in this wonderful world, I think, than commit myself, very gratefully, to your loyalty." But though she was lost in admiration of her opportunity she managed to move back into the deepest shade of it, even as some wild, caught creature in a vast cage. The "splendid security" so offered her was *not* the greatest she could conceive. What she finally bethought herself of saying was something very different—something that deferred the need of really facing her crisis. (99)

For all James's stylistic indirection, the passage communicates sexual desire and Isabel's fear of surrendering to that as a motive for deciding on the terms under which she will live her life. She responds to his words as if they were "strong arms" that become "like the fragrance straight in her face." With the immediate transition from fragrance to "his clean, breathing lips" that evoke "strange gardens" and "changed airs," we have a sequence that communicates seduction and surrender, the arms and lips of the man taking the woman to paradise. Isabel's first impulse is to surrender to the passion of the moment, to "commit" herself to his "loyalty," which the imagery suggests is the loyalty of his body to her body. She quickly, however, perceives a surrender to passion as a trap, "to be caught in a vast cage." Mind intervenes to shock her out of her impulse to listen to her body. She can "conceive" (and the pun between thought and impregnation is not accidental) of something greater, though that something is not named. The strength of the temptation for Isabel is such that she cannot, at that moment, say a definitive no. So she "deferred [...] facing her crisis."

At the end of the chapter, Isabel reflects upon her promise to give Warburton an answer. "She liked him too much to marry him," she thinks, "that was the truth; something assured her there was a fallacy somewhere in the glowing logic of the proposition—as *he* saw it—even though she mightn't put her very finest finger on it." Extending the sexual metaphors from the earlier passage, we can see the "glowing logic" as a figure of desire, Warburton's blood hot, his eyes shining in resistance to hearing Isabel refuse him. He had asked her to marry him, and "[S]he had promised him she would consider his question." But she was not thinking about that. Rather, "she was wondering if she were not a cold, hard, priggish person, and, on her at last getting up and going rather quickly back to the house, felt, as she had said to her friend, really frightened of herself" (101). Fear of herself—a compound of doubt about her judgment and anxiety about her responsiveness to sexual desire—that was the fear her coldness was masking. How was she to do justice to the qualities of her own mind in her quest to experience the world in all its fullness and variety while also growing into full sexual maturity as a woman? It is in that context that we should take the narrator's observation that Isabel, "with all her love of knowledge [...] had a natural shrinking from raising curtains and looking into unlighted corners. The love of knowledge coexisted in her mind with the finest capacity for ignorance" (171).

The repressed sexual energies that are so evident in the prose that animates the narrative engagements with Goodwood's and Warburton's marriage proposals to Isabel are absent in descriptions of her relation to her cousin Ralph, who also loves her, and of her future husband, Gilbert Osmond, who does not. Ralph functions more as Isabel's brother than her lover in the novel; he draws out her affection but not her passion. In the scene when Osmond proposes to Isabel, however, the passion that she had discovered in herself and repressed in fear in response to both Goodwood and Warburton overwhelms her, but it does so in a context where that passion cannot be amplified through the response of another. That is, Osmond is without passion, the painful irony being that that lack of passion weirdly makes it possible for Isabel to feel her own. James prepares Osmond's proposal scene by framing it in reference to the idea that "one ought to make one's life a work of art" (256, Osmond to Isabel). Unqualified, that assertion masquerades as a defensible piece of advice for how to live. Osmond's words, however, come after he and Isabel *jokingly* discuss Warburton:

> "Ah, my English peer left me some time ago." She got up, speaking with intention a little drily.
> Mr. Osmond noted her dryness, which contributed for him to the interest of his question.
> "I'm afraid that what I heard the other evening is true: you're rather cruel to your nobleman."
> [...] "It's not true. I'm scrupulously kind."
> "That's exactly what I mean!" Gilbert Osmond returned, and with such happy hilarity that his joke needs to be explained.

The exchange is more than elliptical, the humor rather strained. The dryness in Isabel's tone and the conflation of cruelty with kindness, while jarring, hardly produce the kind of incongruity associated with humor. The joke is in the tone (hilarity) of Osmond's voice, not in his words. That incongruity is chilling as is the joke's explanation:

> We know that he [Osmond] was fond of originals, of rarities, of the superior and the exquisite; and now that he had seen Lord Warburton, whom he thought a fine example of his race and order, he perceived a new attraction to the idea of taking to himself a young lady who had qualified herself to figure in his collection of choice objects by declining so noble a hand. (253)

The echoes of Robert Browning's "My Last Duchess" make the moment painfully, inhumanly exquisite. Consequently, in the next chapter when Osmond says to Isabel "that I find I'm in love with you," soon thereafter reiterating, "I'm absolutely in love with you," the narrator's comment that "[H]e had repeated the announcement in a tone of almost impersonal discretion" comes as little surprise. As a result, what the narrator then says of Isabel's inner response is a bit of a shock:

> The tears came into her eyes: this time they obeyed the sharpness of the pang that suggested to her somehow the slipping of a fine bolt—backward, forward, she couldn't have said which. The words he had uttered made him, as he stood there, beautiful and generous, invested him with the golden air of early autumn; but, morally speaking, she retreated before them—facing him still—as she had retreated in the other cases before a like encounter. "Oh don't say that, please," she answered with an intensity that expressed the dread of having, in this case too, to choose and decide. What made her dread great was precisely the force which, as it would seem, ought to have banished all dread—the sense of something within herself, deep down, that she supposed to be inspired and trustful passion. It was there like a large sum stored in a bank—which there was a terror in having to begin to spend. If she touched it, it would all come out. (258)

The difference between this proposal scene and the others we have seen is that the language of passion comes from within Isabel, not, as in the other cases, either male figure, Goodwood or Warburton. Osmond's tone is "almost impersonal," his words do not communicate a passion crying out for a passionate response in return. That very coldness may be what causes Isabel to drop her guard to allow the tears that the situation calls for to arise and to feel something inside her—like a bolt moving back and forth. She then projects, from her own inner resources, a golden glow onto Osmond, one we know, given the Browning allusion and the coldness in Osmond's tone, not to be objectively possible. The turn in the passage with the words, "morally speaking," creates a pause, almost like a poetic caesura, before she "retreats" in dread. But unlike the undefined fear alluded to in the earlier proposal scenes, this dread comes from within. She not only dreads the crisis of having to say yes or no (she postpones her answer, and we learn of the engagement indirectly later when she and Ralph discuss it); she dreads that thing that should compel a yes. The passage later, after much qualification, names that thing "passion," which, once allowed to express itself, "would all come out." The chapter ends with Osmond's claim of being "convention itself," signaling, if it were not abundantly clear already, that any pouring forth of Isabel's passion would be like spilling a cup of water in a desert.

The awful enormity of Osmond's cruel manipulation of Isabel has been revealed with narrative relentlessness by the time Caspar Goodwood returns in the final pages of the novel. Goodwood and Isabel meet at Gardencourt, where the novel had opened. She had left Osmond, and all her friends and family understand why she had to leave him, and no one wants her to go back. Goodwood's arrival presents a double temptation: to the author to unite him with Isabel, bringing together the couple whose romance began the novel as it were and whose union after many obstacles would complete a conventional narrative pattern that would surely gratify the novel's readers; the temptation to Isabel is to break the promise she made when she married Osmond and to break the other promise she made to Osmond's daughter that she (Isabel) would return from England. Would Isabel defy narrative convention and return to Osmond, or would she defy social convention (her marriage vows and a personal promise to her stepdaughter) and allow Goodwood to save her from Osmond? The narrative sequence after Goodwood's arrival at Gardencourt extends over many pages, but I will focus on one paragraph that seems to me to capture the essence of the challenge to closure in the novel, and that narrative essence is tied to Isabel's essential character.

The first words Isabel says when she sees Goodwood are "[Y]ou've frightened me" (479). Goodwood asks why she should return to Osmond, why she should "go through that ghastly form" of being a wife in a loveless marriage. Isabel responds, "To get away from *you*!" Then the narrator reveals that with those words Isabel realizes that "she had never been loved before" (480). The choice is stark: return to a loveless marriage in full knowledge that her husband married her for money and that he hates her to boot, or surrender to the arms of the man who has always loved her, with whom she would feel (and, in fact, be) safest and for whom she has felt the deepest physical desire. Goodwood ends his plea to Isabel with: "Were we born to rot in our misery—were we born to be afraid? I never knew *you* afraid! If you'll only trust me, how little you will be disappointed! The world's all before us—and the world's very big." Isabel, as we know, has been afraid throughout the novel, afraid of herself, afraid of her passion, afraid of the physical enticement that Goodwood embodies. A reminder of that fear at this narrative moment undercuts the rhetorical force of the *Paradise Lost* reference to "[T]he world is all before us," a line that comes at the end of that epic poem when Adam and Eve walk out from the Garden of Eden into the beginnings of the vast panorama of human history. Here is the paragraph that follows Goodwood's words:

> Isabel gave a long murmur, like a creature in pain; it was as if he were pressing something that hurt her. "The world's very small," she said at random; she had an immense desire to appear to resist. She said it at random, to hear herself say something; but it was not what she meant. The world, in truth, had never seemed so large; it seemed to open out, all round her, to take the form of a mighty sea, where she floated in fathomless waters. She had wanted help, and here was help; it had come in a rushing torrent. I know not whether she believed everything he said; but she believed just then that to let him take her in his arms would be the next best thing to her dying. This belief, for a moment, was a kind of rapture, in which she felt herself sink and sink. In the movement she seemed to beat with her feet, in order to catch herself, to feel something to rest on. (481)

The language in that passage is consonant with the pattern of language I have tracked across the various proposal scenes, but intensified. Initially language fails Isabel; she can only murmur in response to the verbal pressure from Goodwood that feels like physical pain. When she finds words, those words resist him before her inner perception turns to embrace his assertion that the world is, in fact, big, her inner world especially. Then the language of water—a sea upon which she floats as torrents carry comfort—shifts into the image of Goodwood's arms within which Isabel imagines a figurative death, suggesting a desire for sexual union, a "rapture" rendered as a kind of *liebestod*, a feeling she finds literally destabilizing as she struggles with her feet to find solid ground. That metaphorically establishes the expectation that she will embrace him, find that stability on the ground of his love, leaning on the strength of his body. Instead, the narrator records: "This however, of course, was but a subjective fact, as the metaphysicians say; the confusion, the noise of waters, all the rest of it, were in her own swimming head. In an instant she became aware of this. 'Do me the greatest kindness of all,' she panted. 'I beseech you to go away!'" (481). All of her (or anyone's) inner experience is "a subjective fact," so for her to reject Goodwood because she perceives her experience with him as subjective makes little sense. But if the issue is one of control, of her own need to act under her own volition, her subjectivity not confused with someone else's desire (even if her choice coincides with someone else's desire), then her rejection of Goodwood and her decision to return to Osmond and his daughter Pansy is, painful as that decision may be for Isabel (and for the reader), an assertion of Isabel's freedom to live out the choice she has made. "She had not known where to turn; but she knew now," the narrator observes on the novel's last page. "There was a very straight path" (482). That latter reference evokes a Puritan sensibility associated with the straight and narrow path of John Bunyan's *The Pilgrim's Progress*, but in *The Portrait of a Lady*, there is no spiritually transcendent validation for such a choice, nor are there the consolations of romance. There are the simple facts of Isabel's promise and the strength of her will, morality without metaphysics.

IV

A morality without metaphysics like the one that defines Isabel's choice and that captures the tone at the end of *The Portrait of a Lady* is introduced at the beginning of Chapter II in *Through One Administration* with this revelation about Tredennis's character: "His was a nature to awaken slowly, but to awaken with such strength of feeling and to such power to suffer, at last, as would leave no alternative between happiness and stolidly borne despair" (18). That observation comes at the beginning of Tredennis's eight-year absence from Washington; during that absence while he was serving in the west, he worked to facilitate relations between the American government and the Native American tribal nations. Determined "to achieve practical knowledge [...] with those among the tribes whom it was possible to approach openly he made friends, studying their languages and establishing a reputation among them for honor and good faith" (19). During these years of service, he corresponded with Professor Herrick, who would report on Bertha's doings, her happiness and her character: "I gradually discover her to be full of subtleties," the professor writes in one letter during the fourth year of Tredennis's service in the west, "of which she is entirely unconscious" (20). Tredennis, of course, has been questioning his failure to tell Bertha of his love, rationalizing that the time had not been right, but upon reading the quoted letter, he decides to apply for leave to return to Washington, consoling himself with the thought, "*this* is the time, and it is well I waited" (21). Before he can act, he receives another letter from Herrick with this postscript written on the otherwise blank back page: "Bertha is married" (22). It is four more years before he is called back to serve in Washington, and he arrives days after "the inauguration of a newly elected president." Weary already with the prospect of a loveless life, where his military knowledge will be subordinated to the winds of political expedience and intrigue, Tredennis frames his situation in a way that provides the chronological limits of the novel itself: "'I have come in with the Administration,' he said. 'I wonder if I shall go out with it, and what will have happened in the interval'" (26).

The focus of the interval turns out to be Bertha's life at the center of Washington society, all personal relationships (including her marriage) being inflected by political ambitions—the passage of bills that would benefit certain financial interests, jockeying for government office and so on. The members of society are like elements in an experiment in ethics, with Tredennis as the stabilizer. Burnett sketches her portrait of Bertha as a lady in Washington society by placing her in relation to a series of men: there are three who play primary roles, her husband, Mr. Richard Amory, who Professor Herrick describes as "bright" and "handsome" though "not very robust." He is, nonetheless, "an attractive creature—sensitive, poetic temperament, fanciful" (30), a figure, like James's Mr. Osmond, who lives his life as a kind of aesthetic exercise. There is Bertha's friend, Mr. Lawrence Arbuthnot, whose introduction to the reader is focalized through Tredennis, who "was conscious of feeling secretly repelled by the young man's well-carried, conventional figure and calm, blond countenance,—the figure seemed so correct a copy of scores of others, the blond countenance expressed so little beyond a carefully trained tendency to good manners, entirely unbiased by any human emotion" (41). The third male figure is Tredennis, whom Arbuthnot and Bertha characterize in this exchange: Arbuthnot says that "it shows a great lack of taste in the Indians to have consented to part with him. It appeared to me that he possessed a manner calculated to endear him to aboriginal society beyond measure." Bertha responds: "He is rather rigorous-looking [...] Papa is very fond of him. He turns out to be a persistent, heroic kind of being—with a purpose in life, and the rest of it" (42). That exchange communicates something of the amoral tenor of Washington society (the "and the rest of it" being dismissive of any values not in the service of a peculiar Washington ambition) and the way that moral tenor infects the quality and tone of personal relationships. The exchange also excludes Tredennis from Washington amorality.

An approach to the precise quality of that amorality is provided at the end of Arbuthnot's and Bertha's discussion of Tredennis. Of having just seen Tredennis after his eight-year absence, Bertha comments:

> It certainly was a curious feeling [...]. Everything came to me in a flash. I suppose I am rather a light and frivolous person, not sufficiently given to reflecting on the passage of time, and

suddenly there he stood, and I remembered that eight years had gone by, and that everything had changed. (43)

Bertha goes on to observe that in those eight years "*Everything* has happened to me," to which Arbuthnot pointedly replies, "No—not everything." The insinuation is delicate, easily explained away as vague, but Bertha's rejoinder sharpens the insinuation: "I have grown from a child to a woman [...]. I have married, I have arrived at maternal dignity. I don't see that there is anything else that could happen—at least anything comfortable." Arbuthnot concedes the point, acknowledging in their context the inevitable consequences of infidelity, a point Bertha reinforces when she affirms, "Well, it is very certain I don't want to try anything uncomfortable." She then quotes Montesquieu: "'Happy the people whose annals are tiresome.'" At this point the conversation turns: "I have had," Bertha declares, "no tremendous emotions" (44). Arbuthnot congratulates her on that accomplishment, which produces the following reflections from Bertha:

> "I may not have lived exactly the kind of life I used to think I should live—when I was a school-girl," she went on, smiling; "but who does? —and who would want to when she attained years of discretion? And I may not be exactly the kind of person I—meant to be; but I may congratulate you on that—and Richard. You would never have been the radiant creatures you are if I had ripened to that state of perfection. You could not have borne up under it." (45)

The prose, though not as elliptical as James's, does demand some parsing. The opening sentence establishes an expectation of disappointment to come, Bertha not having lived the life she expected, but rather than disappointment, she suggests that her experience is ordinary; no girl upon reaching maturity would want to hold onto her youthful ambitions and desires. But the ordinariness of her self-interpretation is called into question when she congratulates Arbuthnot and her husband Richard, rather than herself, for her own maturity. Her self-judgment becomes a judgment of the men who, in her turning away from her own striving for "perfection," beam with approval, "radiant creatures" who would have paled in the light of her perfection had she pursued it. One might feel under the banter a note of seriousness, of regret, of self-questioning and of a buried awareness that the standards of social behavior controlled by the male gaze require the obedience, even debasement of women. The end of the conversation communicates something of that: "'No,' she said, 'I am not the person I meant to be, and Colonel Tredennis has reminded me of the fact and elevated my spirits'" (45). The combination of a kind of amoral flippancy and ironic self-judgment with the nearly non sequitur quality of the two halves of the compound sentence (again the tension between disappointment in not being what one meant to be and claiming happiness for that fact) captures the moral and emotional complexity in Bertha's character that the narrative, as in the case of Isabel Archer, will explore.

In both novels the development of and challenges to the integrity of a woman's character, the possibility of a woman genuinely shaping her own life, is explored under the eyes of men, who with a combination of concern, self-interest, genuine affection and incomprehension try to create conditions for the woman to achieve happiness on terms the men think should be her own. That is a reasonable description of the motives that animate Goodwood's and Warburton's marriage proposals, and Ralph Touchett persuading his father to leave seventy-thousand pounds to Isabel is a more disinterested example. As both novels suggest, any effort by a man to enable a woman to be free according to his understanding of what would constitute that freedom merely reinscribes the conditions of patriarchy; the woman's freedom remains dependent on a man's literal or figurative gift. In *Through One Administration* Burnett creates a relentless dramatic situation where the tensions between male ideas of a woman's freedom and the woman's desire to determine for herself what would constitute her freedom play out in variations throughout the novel. In one sense, just as it had done in its serial publication by beginning in the very month when James's was completed, Burnett's novel begins where James's novel ends: with a woman uncertain but determined to figure out how to live in (or through) a loveless marriage. Though Richard Amory is not as overtly malevolent as Gilbert Osmond, he nonetheless subordinates his wife's material and emotional resources for his own egotistical ends. In contrast to Caspar Goodwood, who returns intermittently to try to rescue Isabel from what he sees as her misdirected life, Colonel Tredennis resides near Bertha in Washington and observes her ironic progress as the wife of an aimless but ambitious man in Washington political society. And he does so at the request of Bertha's father.

The narrative momentum of the novel is carried in large part by conversations. Soon after Tredennis's return to Washington, after he had seen Bertha and met her friend Arbuthnot and her husband Amory, and having perceived something undefinable but palpably amiss in his interactions with the three, he visits Professor Herrick and asks whether he thinks Bertha is unhappy. "The professor's reply was simple and direct [...] she has never been happy for an hour since her marriage" (85–86). The professor then explains that Bertha has no illusions about her husband's lack of passion for her; she found out "in two months that he would not have perished if she had discarded him [...]. He did not require her care or sympathy, and [much like Osmond's attitude toward Isabel] the sacrifices she made for him were very simple and natural matters in his eyes" (86). Rather than lamenting her fate or plotting an escape, she accepts the superficial amiability in her daily domestic life and throws herself into her social and maternal duties. "She is too full of spirit to permit herself to be subdued by her disappointment," her father tells Tredennis. "As she cannot retrieve her mistake, she will [like Isabel] make the best of it." The professor then draws this conclusion: "Women are not happy, as a rule [...] they are not happy. I have learned that" (87). That conclusion comes from the professor's trained skills of observation, endorsed, as it were, by the objectivity of his scientific vocation. "I have been studying and classifying all my life," he reminds Tredennis, "and now I sit and look on, and treat human beings as I have treated insects" [but without the chloroform or the pin as Bertha had requested in her youth] (87). What Herrick fears based on his observation is the incredible pain, perforce, Bertha would have to suffer "if her heart were once awakened" (90). He fears, in short, a temptation for adultery, and the man he thinks is on the verge of so tempting her is Arbuthnot. Having revealed to Tredennis that Bertha had regretted not seeing him before her marriage because, she said, Tredennis "was a strong sort of person, and sensible, and—you might rely on his decisions" (85), Professor Herrick makes this request: "I ask you to defend her against this pain [...]. She sees in you the strength she vaguely longed for when she was at the turning-point of her life. Let her feel that it is always near her, and that she may rely upon it now" (90). That request completes the novel's narrative frame. With Bertha as heroine in the center, there are three men vying to be the dominant influence in her life: her husband, who appropriates her money and uses her sexual attractiveness and social instincts to influence politicians who could serve his purposes; Arbuthnot, her potential lover, a man with no resources but looks and charm, who may be angling to exploit Bertha for his own ends; and Philip Tredennis, the physically imposing soldier who loves her but cannot speak of or act on that love based on his own sense of honor and his promise to her father. Those relationships produce throughout the novel unsettling energies that break through the veneer of Washington social vanities. But those vanities have a certain disturbing depth since they can be exploited for hard-edged political purposes concerning land and money and power. Excepting Tredennis, who has his internal struggles, his personal demons to slay, but who remains constant to his promise and true to his values, the basic quality of character for the other two men is tested in the crucible of Washington political society.

Burnett contrasts the collision between unadorned, sincere hard political work and the corrupting frivolities of what she calls the "pretty parlors" (93) of Washington society, and in the process weaves in how misperception, vanity and sexual suggestiveness are products of that collision. Bertha is the medium through which that complex of effects emerges. Tredennis overhears a conversation among Bertha, her husband and Arbuthnot, which begins with Bertha asking this question: "What should I do [...] if I knew nothing of politics?" She then answers her own question.

> There are times when they are my salvation. What should I have done last night with the new member from Arkansas if I had not remembered that he was interested in the passage of the Currency Bill? He is an excellent, solid, sensible creature; we are frivolous, aimless beings compared with him. It is such men as he who do everything worth doing and being done, but he is purely a politician, and he has spent his life in a small provincial town, where he has been a most important person, and he cares as much for the doings of society and discussions of new novels and pictures as I do for the linseed oil market [...]. When I began to ask him modest questions about his bill, his face brightened at once, and he became a self-respecting and well-informed person—at ease with himself and with me [...]. He could not have told whether I was well or ill dressed, but he detected my flimsiness in argument in a moment, and gave me more information in half-an-hour than you scoffers could have given me in a week [...]. he mentioned to Senator Vaughan [...] that I was a most intelligent woman. (93)

On the face of it, the passage points toward a criticism of the social attitudes that would mock a culturally ill-informed, sincere working politician, who is a solid man compared to Bertha's airy socially savvy interlocutors. But their response reverses the direction of the criticism, suggesting that Bertha's sincerity in her description of the member from Arkansas masks her real purpose, to elevate herself as one spoken of among the powerful as "intelligent." "Arbuthnot and Richard burst into the laughter which was always her applause upon such occasions." So her explanation is typical, the narrator's comment suggests; her strategy of seeming to praise a socially inept representative is a dodge to elevate herself. Arbuthnot's comment that follows, however, turns the exchange toward the sexual: "You are Herodias' daughter, dancing for the head of John the Baptist. You are always dancing in a quiet and effective way for somebody's head. Whose would you like next? How does mine strike you?" Those words are both a commentary and a challenge; they suggest that Bertha's exchange with the representative is an instinctive deception that would lead inevitably to his self-destruction. Bertha could not possibly be sincere; her apparent interest is a social trick, a verbal seduction. Arbuthnot's words indicate how fully he understands that. He dares her to seduce him. Bertha's response is ambiguous at best. "'Thank you,' said Bertha. 'Would you really give it to me if I danced for you in my ablest manner; and how do you think it would look on a charger?'" (93). Bertha's choice of the image of a horse focuses the exchange squarely on the body, calling Arbuthnot's metaphorical bluff.

Despite Arbuthnot's and Richard's understanding of the qualities of Bertha's interactions as fundamentally insincere, a form of amusement whose implications they understand and tacitly accept, there is an element of respect in the words she uses to describe the representative from Arkansas. (The representative's response to Bertha suggests he too sees what is genuine in her; he is not a dupe.) Such respect is not only suggested by the directness and specificity of Bertha's terms of praise for him, particularly her reference to his being "at ease with himself"; it is reinforced with great depth and subtlety by Bertha's metaphorical defiance of Arbuthnot when she implies his inability or unwillingness to tie his words to action. The representative has his Currency Bill, something he pursues because he believes it will have a positive effect on the lives of the people he represents, whatever the terms of that bill may be. Arbuthnot has words, which he and Bertha understand as always being just that, words. In addition, the fact that the representative's use of language and his work in the world are mutually reinforcing raises the question of what kind of work could be supported by the way that Bertha, her husband, Arbuthnot et al use language?

The alignment or discontinuity between words and a world of meaningful action has relevance to the two Berthas that Tredennis perceives, the Bertha before and the Bertha after her marriage. The novel evokes those two Berthas in explicit ways and in more indirect ways. The premarried Bertha can be felt in the element of sincerity that survives her superficial, satirical presentation of the representative while the married Bertha can be seen with more force and clarity through the satire that cancels the praise. In so many of the society conversations in which Tredennis takes part, he sees and hears the dynamic described here over and over again, the Bertha he remembers flickering into sight only to fade at the moment of his perception. When Tredennis visits Bertha in the country, where she has taken her children to recover their health outside of the heat of a Washington summer, the contrast between the Bertha he remembers and the married Bertha of Washington society becomes explicit in his consciousness. After he explains to Bertha that he had come in response to her summons instead of her father, who was ill in the city, he pauses to reflect on how he now sees her:

> All the ordinary conventional barriers had fallen away between them [...]. Suddenly he found himself once again side by side with the Bertha he fancied lost forever. All that bewildered

him was gone. The brilliant little figure, with its tinkling ornaments, the unemotional little smile, the light laugh, were only parts of a feverish dream. It was Bertha whose hand rested on his arm—whose fair, young face was pale with watching over her child—whose soft voice was tremulous and tender with innocent, natural tears. (180)

The brittle Bertha of lightly cruel satire recedes in the scene with the distance from the conventionalities of Washington. With the city's affectations suspended in the idyllic background of the country (an old, old literary trope), the emphasis in the passage is on Bertha's naturalness; her physical presence—her hand on his arm, the softness of her voice, the weary paleness of her face—effaces "barriers" between them that the passage names "conventional." How to understand conventional at such a moment poses a problem. The most immediate referent for the word concerns the conventions of Washington society, forms of speech, modes of dress, aspects of decorum and so on. The less immediate but more powerful referent is the convention of marriage, as if the premarried Bertha suddenly has again become real and by implication available. That latter implication of availability, which given the fact of her marriage must mean the possibility of adultery, is something that concerned some American readers during the novel's serial publication.

In a short piece in *The Dial* in October 1882 during the novel's run in the *Century* (formerly *Scribner's*), R. O. Beard includes *Through One Administration* as one of four novels that "trifle with the marriage relation" in an "alarming" way. Beard argues that the plot hinges "upon an attempted disregard of, or a possible escape from, the restraints of marriage."[14] He does not get any more specific than that, but given what we have seen of Arbuthnot and Tredennis in relation to Bertha in this chapter, Arbuthnot could be associated with one who disregards marriage and Tredennis as figuring in its possible escape. Gretchen Holbrook Gerzina documents through Burnett's correspondence how much her own unhappy marriage was on her mind as she wrote *Through One Administration* (Gerzina 100–102). The extent of Burnett's own unhappiness, amounting perhaps to resignation, may have contributed to her closing off any possibility of escape from Bertha's marriage to Richard Amory, even though he at the end of the novel is living ambiguously away from her. So there is no adultery and no divorce; the convention of marriage is unchallenged, and, in fact, as it was in *The Portrait of a Lady*, its force to compel the obedience of women remains as powerful as ever, not despite the exploration in both novels of how marriage can be a form of prolonged agony, but because the novels show that to be the case. Escape for the lady in each novel may be thinkable; it is not doable.

The power of the convention of marriage may be the very thing that enables Bertha and Tredennis to spend days together in the country living a domestic life of profound emotional intimacy and chaste sexual innocence. The following paragraph captures the quality of that domestic interlude:

To find himself sitting at the table alone with Bertha, in her new mood,—Bertha quiet and beautiful,—was a moving experience to him. It was as if they two must have sat there every day for years, and had the prospect of sitting so together indefinitely. It was the very simplicity and naturalness of it which stirred him most. Her old vivid gayety was missing; she did not laugh once, but her smile was very sweet. They talked principally of the children, and of the common things about them; and there was never a word which did not seem a thing to be cherished and remembered [...]. [T]he sun creeping through the vines touched her hair and the child's and made a picture of them. (188)

Rather than a product of Bertha's "new mood," what Tredennis sees is a version of the premarried Bertha of his memory, that memory and present experience fusing in an intensity of happiness. Time seems stopped, their lives centered on "common things around them," household objects, grass, sun, kitchen tables and so on, with no forced emotion, Bertha's smile a natural pulse in contrast to the forced energy of her social gayety. The children vouchsafe the innocence of the domestic space while the sun in the hair of mother and child aestheticizes the scene in an eternal moment. That sense of being out of time reminds readers (and Bertha and Tredennis later on) that the domestic idyll is just that, beautiful but momentary, a reminder of what could have been but is not and cannot be. It is worse than a paradise lost; it is a paradise that never was and the awareness of that fact marks the interlude with a willful blindness.

The brevity, intensity and requirements of will that make the country, domestic idyll possible account for the force of Bertha's reaction once they return to Washington. In their final conversation in the country, just before Arbuthnot arrives to take Bertha back to the city, Bertha tells Tredennis: "All that matters is, that you should know the truth about me,—that I am not to be depended upon, and that, above all, you need not be surprised at any change you see in me [...] when we meet again in Washington." Tredennis then asks, "Are you warning me?" To which Bertha replies, "Yes [...] I am warning you" (218). The nature of the change Bertha projects comes out in a discussion she later has with Arbuthnot about, of all things, a new dress. Calling her new dress "an immense and unqualified success," Arbuthnot then "doubts its power to sustain nature during six or eight hours of a New Year's reception" (236). He then notes, "It is a brilliant thing, and it is not like you in the least." Bertha concurs, calling the dress "a flaring thing" that marks "her new departure" toward becoming "a dazzling and worldly creature" (237). Such a new departure seems hardly new at all, as Arbuthnot observes: "I should scarcely call it a new departure." Externally, the idea of Bertha being "dazzling and worldly" may be an intensification more than a turn to something new, but the something new is an inward departure, an acknowledgment that Bertha, after her idyll with Tredennis, understands fully that her embrace of social power is an inadequate compensation for the deep emptiness of her marriage relation, and that any relationship with Tredennis is impossible. Thus the exercise of social power masks a relational hollowness, becoming an act of despair. "Do you think," she asks Arbuthnot, "if one should do that [be dazzling] *every* day, *every* day, and give one's self *no* rest, that after a while it would *kill* one?" (237). Then she admits, "I don't want to do any of the things I am doing now" (238). Nonetheless she persists, becoming riper for manipulation by her husband as she repudiates that part of herself that she had given expression to in her country interlude.

Burnett creates a richly complicated set of relationships among Bertha and the three men. She is married, has children, but sustains only the most superficial emotional relationship with her husband, a condition he desires and she early on accepted; she has a close relationship with Arbuthnot, developing a language that permits an indirect expression of her deepest feelings and desires, but that remains constrained by the fact of her marriage and the requirements for decorum in the Washington social scene; she realizes the depth of her love for Tredennis but accepts the impossibility of acting on that love, not only repressing but actively distorting her emotion. Those relationships constitute a Gordian knot, and after the idyllic, country interlude, the novel's energy is produced by what we might call the narrative effort to untie the knot. If the knot is made up of the intersection of disparate desires among the three men in relation to Bertha, and if Bertha's character is split between two irreconcilable senses of self, we might be able to configure the knot with Bertha at the center, her husband Amory aligned with Bertha as socialite and potential lobbyist, Tredennis aligned with the presocialite, "natural" Bertha and Arbuthnot aligned with both, his ultimate position within what we might call, to mix metaphors, the moral landscape that Bertha represents an open question. What possible resolution can there be by the novel's end in the metaphoric battle between natural wholeness and cultural corruption, which plays out in Bertha's psyche and in Arbuthnot's ultimate moral choice?

As a representative of cultural corruption, Richard Amory plays a straightforward role. He marries Bertha for her beauty and her wealth; he then uses her wealth (without her knowledge) to invest in land that can become extremely valuable if Congress passes a bill to authorize the building of a railroad line on that land. He then through misrepresentation manipulates Bertha to lobby members of Congress for passage of the bill, a misrepresentation that Bertha more than half understands. In response to his request for her help, she says, "I am not to call it lobbying, am I? What must I call it?" Richard replies: "Don't call it anything." Bertha then pronounces judgment and acquiescence in her response: "What a good way of getting round a difficulty—not to give it a name! It almost obliterates it, doesn't it? It is an actual inspiration. We won't call it anything" (433–34). For the most part her lobbying consists of being a charming hostess at dinner parties and other social gatherings with one unspoken requirement, that she entice the goodwill of the most influential senators through her sexual attractiveness, flirting, like lobbying, without naming the activity. While she is not guilty of the act, she is implicated in the offer of a bribe—she was to offer it to the most powerful (and randy) of the senators at a private dinner, but she did not actually offer the money—and it is through the good offices of Tredennis and of a senator with qualities like the representative from Arkansas she described earlier that her money and reputation are both saved. Amory's guilt cannot be whitewashed, so he flees to Europe.

Arbuthnot, in the meantime, has met and fallen in love with a recently widowed society woman, Mrs. Sylvestre. After various understandings and misunderstandings, Arbuthnot gives over his efforts for political preferment and takes up the serious study of law in Germany. Before he leaves, having given up his courtship because of Sylvestre's wealth and his de facto poverty, Bertha convinces him to see Agnes Sylvestre one more time. "Don't be too proud, Larry;" she says, "don't reason too much. If people are true to each other, and content, what does the rest matter? I want to know that someone is happy like that. I wish it might be you" (546). And he does, in fact, become "happy like that," happy in his productive work and happier in his relationship with his wife. With the figure of Richard pulling Bertha deeper into artifice and dishonesty on the one hand and with

Arbuthnot finding happiness in work and in a truth-based, loving marriage in response to Bertha's guidance, Bertha's two selves are externalized, objectified by the narrative. That would seem to set up a resolution that brings Bertha and Tredennis together, but Tredennis, with the advent of a new administration, had been assigned to active duty in the west where he is killed in battle saving a child during an attack on a settlement. Bertha hears the news at a social gathering, the words mixing with the strains of a waltz as she rushes "through the whirling crowd of dancers" (562) on her way home. With Amory in Europe, she is alone with her father, and she says to him before closing herself off in her children's room as the novel ends: "I have suffered […]. I have been broken; I have been crushed. I knew that I should never see him again, but he was alive. Do you think that I shall someday be punished enough?" (563).

The novel's last view of Amory provides one possible, unsettling answer to that last question. After his studies in Germany, where he was for six months while Agnes remained in Washington, Arbuthnot travels to Paris to attend a series of lectures. Agnes joins him there.

> It was when they were in Paris that they had the pleasure of meeting Mr. Richard Amory, who was very well known and exceedingly popular in the American colony. He was in the most delightful, buoyant spirits; he had been very fortunate; a certain investment of his had turned out very well, and brought him large returns. He was quite willing to talk about it and himself, and was enraptured at seeing his friends […]. He seemed, however, to have only pleasantly vague views on the subject of the time of his probable return to America.
>
> "There is no actual necessity for it," he said, "and I find the life here delightful. Bertha and the children will probably join me in the spring, and we may ramble about for a year or so." And he evidently felt he had no reason to doubt the truth of this latter statement. (553)

That Bertha would not return to Amory as the father of her children is rendered as a possibility in the last sentence above, but there is little else in the novel to support the idea that she would deny her children a father or refuse a reunion. However, the contrast between the inner life of Amory (such as it is) and of Bertha could not be more jarring; without a hint of legal recourse, or any intention on her part to change her situation, Bertha had decided, it seems, like Isabel Archer, to suffer.

V

After *Through One Administration* was published as a single volume in the United States and in three volumes in the UK,[15] the reviewers began to respond more favorably to it. *The Nation* (United States), which had been dismissive of Burnett's first three novels, noting, for instance, that *Haworth's* "does not amount to much,"[16] says this in its review of *Through One Administration*:

> The book is well worth reading, as all of Mrs. Burnett's are […]. As a social study it presents many curious features, and perhaps the only reason why it is not already attracting more attention as a fresh specimen of the American novel, is that we have not yet got the news of the way it is looked at in England.[17]

The reviewer seems to have reassessed the quality of Burnett's earlier novels based on his positive response to this one even as he hedges, waiting for the reviews from England. But the *Nation* review was printed at the end of June, and a month earlier, on May 12, one of the most authoritative journals in England, *The Athenaeum*, reviewed the novel in terms that link it to Burnett's earlier industrial novels while emphasizing its affinities to the new fiction of Henry James.

> "Through One Administration" [...] is, in the main, a novel of character. The book is comparable with Mr. Henry James's "Portrait of a Lady" [...]. The method of analysis, the attention to details, and the brilliancy and cleverness displayed in the conversations, constantly recall Mr. James's well-known manner, and his characters have perhaps suggested something to Mrs. Burnett. Her characters, like his, surprise the reader by their extraordinary quickness in guessing half-hidden meanings, and have another point of resemblance in their tendency to an excessive refinement of sensitiveness. The pathetic power which Mrs. Burnett showed so fully in "That Lass O'Lowries" is exhibited in many a touching scene in her new story, which is only to be found fault with because it is too touching. The strain is continuously severe, and even the sad end comes as a sort of relief. But, in spite of all this, the book is one of great interest and striking ability.[18]

The emphasis on dialogue, character and feeling is reminiscent of the reviews of Burnett's two Lancashire novels, a connection made explicit in the allusion to her first, *That Lass O'Lowries*, and the emphasis on analysis, wit and subtlety points to her effort to work in new novelistic modalities in the wake of and in competition with Henry James. Her first five novels straddle what we might call the melodramatic realism of the industrial novels of Elizabeth Gaskell and the hyper-interiority of the new fiction, also a mode of realism,[19] paradoxically already "well-known" through Howells and James. She was successfully building a literary career that, in the words of Arthur Hobson Quinn in 1936, gave her "a right to claim a place with the most logical of realists" (490), locating her in the vicinity within the literary field that had been occupied by George Eliot (who had died three years before the volume publication of *Through One Administration*) and that Henry James was striving to inhabit. The English and American reception of the volume publication must have come as a gratifying surprise to Burnett, who found committing to a schedule of serial publication before having completed the book and having to respond to her editor's intervention put a severe strain on the novel's imaginative integrity: in a letter to a friend she described the serialized novel as "a broken backed, ineffectual, incomplete, aimless travesty of what would have been the best thing I ever did—if my friends of the *Century* had let me alone" (cited in Gerzina 101). While her ambition remained to do "the best thing," and her accomplishment in *Through One Administration* absolutely belies her self-judgment, she was clearly frustrated with the terms of play within the literary field, terms dictated in large part by her relationship with the man who had welcomed her into the "world of actual literature," the editor of *Scribner's* (later *The Century*) Richard Watson Gilder.

Burnett's first submission to *Scribner's* was rejected because of its length. Gilder closed the rejection letter with this: "Who are you? You write with a practiced hand and we shall always be glad to hear from you. Stories should not be more than eight or ten pages in length" (cited in Thwaite 40). Described by Gerzina as her "break through story' (47), Burnett's "Surly Tim's Troubles" was accepted in a letter dated February 23, 1872, in which Gilder emphasized how the folks at *Scribner's* had "all wept sore over 'Surly Tim'. Hope to weep again over MSS from you" (cited in Thwaite 40). From that point on, Gilder took it upon himself to guide Burnett into the literary field. He began by inviting her to New York, he later accepted a revised version of the story originally rejected and he "gave her a list of books she should read" (Thwaite 42). As she submitted more work for publication, their working relationship became more intimate. In a letter dated October 23, 1877 that intimacy is hard to miss.

> I wrote a scene [in "Haworth's] this morning which I believe will make you quiver. And the sole object of my literary existence is to make R.W. G. quiver. I am not afraid of you now as I was in the first chapters which I wrote and rewrote five times [...] but I like to try things on you [...] I write something and then gloat over it. "Possible effect upon R.W.G.?" I say "He will quiver."[20]

Such intimacy does little to mask the power dynamic that fuels it; the physical impact of Burnett's writing on Gilder serves as an objective correlative of her effort to attain some power in her relationship with him through her own verbal–physical appeal. So while Burnett may have claimed that her literary apprenticeship "came to a close after the publication of the little sorrowful Lancashire story" (cited in Gerzina 47), that apprenticeship was only beginning as she and Gilder worked closely together until the publication of *Through One Administration* when, she might more justifiably have said, her apprenticeship was over.

What had changed? One answer to that question is given in Thwaite's biography, where she argues that Burnett, in essence, subordinated her literary talent for money, becoming merely a craftsman with words, a writing machine. (See my discussion of that in the "Introduction.") It is the case that the apparently straight line of development that one can trace from *That Lass O'Lowries* to *Through One administration* is clearly disrupted after the publication of the latter novel; it is less obvious that that disruption is caused by Burnett's chasing after wealth. She did become wealthy to be sure, but that in itself bears no relation, as I argued earlier, to the imaginative ambition of her work and the quality of her writing. Insofar as her first five novels displayed variations on the real strengths of her woman protagonists—the physical and moral strength of Joan Lowrie, the physical bravery of Rachael Ffrench, the forthrightness and affective wisdom of Octavia Basset, the intellectual power of Louisiana and the social power of Bertha Amory—we might look to the areas where Burnett began to exercise her own particular strengths for her own ends within the literary field. Once she was firmly oriented in that field, she no longer had to struggle to be taken seriously as a literary figure. She no longer needed Gilder's guidance; she wanted, as her letter quoted above indicates, for her "friends of the *Century* to leave [her] alone." Most simply she wanted full control of her own work.

That desire gains more force when we consider how the strain in her relationship to Gilder as editor had become a part of public discourse. In "Our New York Letter" published in *The Literary World* on January 23, 1886, the following paragraph appeared:

> Mrs. Frances Hodgson Burnett, who formerly wrote regularly for the *Century*, story after story following each other in rapid succession, has not written anything for that magazine for nearly

four years. I happen to know the cause of this: When Mrs. Burnett sent the last chapters of *Through One Administration* to the *Century*, the editorial censor of that magazine [Gilder], fearing to shock some of his squeamish readers [...] took the liberty of making important changes in the denouement of the story without consulting the author. Mrs. Burnett was highly offended [...] [and] must indeed have keenly felt the unwarranted liberty taken with her story, for she has deliberately sacrificed a very handsome income which she made from her contributions to the *Century*. In the mean time she is obliged to seek other less prominent and less profitable market for her literary productions.[21]

Elements of that paragraph can be read affirmatively, for instance the implication that she is surrendering income for pride of literary ownership; and elements of the paragraph can only have stung, for instance the jab at the speed of her contributions, the assumption of knowledge of her feelings and the claim of diminished quality in the non-*Century* venues of publication. Burnett responded on February 19, 1886 in a letter published in *The Literary World* on March 6 of that year: "I have been much annoyed by the constant repetition of the story of a quarrel between myself and the editor of the *Century* [...]. But it finally tires me to see for the thousandth time a story which is really without any foundation whatsoever." She then points out that her relations with the *Century* staff, especially with "Mr. Gilder," have always been "friendly and agreeable." Then she points out that the story is the opposite of the truth before then correcting it at some length:

For some time before writing "Through One Administration" I had been very much exhausted by over-work. While writing it I was rapidly breaking down. When I finished it I was too tired to have any interest in it left. I wrote two endings, however, merely because having written the one finally published I was haunted by another, in which Bertha Amory died and Tredennis lived—and the only way to rid myself of it seemed to be to write it down. A few days later I went to New York and saw Mr. Gilder, giving him the two terminations.

"There can be no greater proof of my complete exhaustion," I said, "than that I have actually not an atom of proper artistic feeling about this. If I were in a normal condition, *one* of these terminations would be inevitable and as immovable as Fate, and no other one would be possible; but here are the two and I am so worn out and indifferent that I will leave you to choose between them."

"But," said the gentleman who had been represented as engaging in mortal combat with me, and arranging my story according to his own views, "that is out of the question. Nothing would induce me to assume such a responsibility. The public is waiting to hear what *you* have to say, not what I have to say. I will tell you what I will do; I will have them both put into proof and when you read them in print you may have a choice."

So the proofs were sent to me, and after reading both I said: "The one in which Tredennis dies is more tragic and unbearable, and so is more likely to be true. You shall take that." And he took it, while I retained the other one, which I keep in Washington and read sometimes to intimate friends.[22]

Burnett's story sounds too good to be true, but I suspect it is, but only in part. Her deep weariness from overwork is well documented by her biographers, but as we saw above in her desire to be left alone by her *Century* "friends," she did feel interfered with in ways that were damaging to her own sense of the "truthfulness" and aesthetic power of her novel. Her retaining both endings, reserving one to read to her "intimate friends," reveals a desire to retain control of versions of the story outside the fact of publication. As if in a figurative circular dance that draws eyes to the center from every direction, the vacillation between letting Gilder choose, then acquiescing and choosing herself, and then, in a sense, not choosing at all by retaining the rejected conclusion provides some access to the intensity of Burnett's desire to assert her artistic prerogatives, revealing the conflicting external pressures she had to reconcile within herself. At the heart of this struggle for artistic control is the fact of gender difference, specifically male editors mediating female expression in conditions where sexual desire, whether acted on or not, is at play.

In the "Prologue" to her biography of Burnett, after noting that Burnett's son, Vivian, wrote a biography of his mother in order to "circumvent the gossipmongers" and that her daughter-in-law Constance wrote another one for "young adults," Gretchen Holbrook Gerzina writes this tantalizing sentence: "Even so their children, Frances's beloved granddaughters, grew up to be women who never spoke of 'that woman,' even though their financial security resulted from her hard work and her literary and dramatic successes" (xii). Such, what is the right word—caution?—suggests that there were details of Burnett's sexual experience, beyond the facts of her divorce and distasteful remarriage, "the biggest mistake of her life" as Gerzina puts it (214), that would not bear careful scrutiny. Neither biography provides much insight into the precise details that account for Burnett's granddaughters' hesitation to acknowledge her, but based on some correspondence that both biographers cite, it is possible to infer Burnett's posthumous reputation within her family had something to do with the frankness and honesty of her expressions of the sexual aspects of female experience. A hint of the quality of that frankness can be discerned in the letter that claims the power to make Gilder "quiver" quoted above, the woman figuratively seducing the man through her writing.

In the summer of 1881 while Burnett was writing *Through One Administration*, she was also working on a play, *Esmeralda*, with a coauthor, William Gillette, the actor who created the famous image of Sherlock Holmes with the pipe and deerstalker hat on stage. Gilder had arranged accommodation for her at a hotel in Long Beach on Long Island, which was close enough to Manhattan for Gillette to join her to work on the play. In a letter to Julia Schayer, Burnett recounted one of Gillette's visits:

> Mr Gillette comes out to me and we are convinced that we are working on the play—only the sea and the sand and the sky and things, don't you know? This morning we simply played with sand and he said it rested him to look at my tennis suit, which he is amiable enough to think one of the prettiest things he ever saw. Yes, dearest, I know what you are saying in your little mind, but when I tell you in confidence that he is engaged to be married and things, and is supposed to be densely in love, you will know he is quite safe and accusations are quite needless. (Cited in Thwaite 76)

The vagueness of a series of references in the letter gives the game away: "and things," "don't you know," "your little mind," "supposed to be densely in love" and so on all dance around the facts of a flirtation grounded on a mutual acknowledgment of sensual pleasure, a reciprocal awareness of each other's bodies. The claim to being "quite safe" because of his proximity to marriage without mentioning the fact of her own marriage provides license for a pleasant defiance of decorum. In another letter to the same correspondent, Burnett explains that Gilder's wife Helena approved his proposal to take Burnett (who Gilder referred to as "this girl") to Long Beach "and keep her all night?" Helena thinks the plan fine saying, "You couldn't do it if she was not married, but under the circumstances it is perfectly proper" (cited in Thwaite 77). Marriage, it seems, is an instant inoculation against sexual desire! The letter goes on to describe how Gilder and Burnett spent the time together:

> We rambled about on the beach and grubbed in the sand and then went back to the hotel [...] and dined on the immense piazza, and then went back to the beach and sat in the sand again and bayed at the moon and talked and talked and talked, and I sang little songs, and things loomed up generally as they haven't in a long time, and we sat there until midnight and then went and had lemonade on the porch, and he said he was afraid to leave me for fear I would say something interesting after he was gone and finally we retired, and as all our baggage consisted of one small pocket-comb, we had to perform our toilets with it by turns—he throwing it over my transom, and I returning it under his door. (Cited in Thwaite 77–78)

As in the Gillette letter, the vagueness of the noun "things" carries as many meanings as a reader might want to attach to it. The emphasis on talk, the reluctance to part, the singing, the returns to the beach, the obvious not wanting the night to end present a picture of young love with all its enthusiasms and celebrations of small pleasures. The details, were they in reference to a younger couple rather than two figures already married to others, would come across as boding well for the future of the relationship because of the sheer joy expressed in each other's company, but the details do not play that way as a prelude to adultery. The tension between the tone of the letter and the situation of those described in it may account for Thwaite's one sentence comment on it: "It is perhaps significant that this episode seems to mark the end of the close relationship between Gilder and Frances" (78). When we place the Gillette and Gilder Long Beach episodes next to another letter from that same time, we get a sense of the nature of the danger they both may have felt in their experience of mutual pleasure with Burnett. The letter describes a swimming instructor, whom Burnett calls "A Greek God in bronze":

> He is the most wonderful creature. His physique is perfection, simple and pure. I never noticed a man's body before. I was always so actively employed searching for their brains—but his—Mon Dieu! Gott im Himmel! Santa Maria—and things! He wears a dark-blue woven, tight-fitting garment, reaching to the knee and leaving his superb arms and divine antique legs bare [...]. And that is not the worst of it, either. The color of him, Julia, the color of him! He is sun-burned all over—the most exquisite pure bronze! I grow wild and will have to erase!—and far be it from me to presume to ask him how much it is a lesson. (Cited in Thwaite 77)

The letter recounts the discovery of the sensual beauty of a man's body for Burnett, again the vagueness of the reference to "and things" being pregnant with implications. The language in the letter evokes a vocabulary that has traditionally been used to capture the male gaze of a young woman as a "simple and pure" creature whose dress and bodily form are anatomized by the eyes of the man. Here that power is reversed, the woman's gaze the objectifying agent, the man's brains dismissed as irrelevant, the man simultaneously reduced to and celebrated as a body. There is even a comically reverent echo in the evocation of Gott in Himmel to the idea of the beautiful woman being akin to deity, the male body stimulating cries of divinity in German, French and with an extra twist of irony, Mary the mother of God in Spanish. For all the excess, the humor, the exaggeration, the letters taken as a group communicate a developing sense in Burnett of the possibility of achieving gender equality by deploying the matter-of-course prerogatives of male expressions of sensual pleasure through the eyes and words of a woman. She is not playing with the trope of a woman using her powers of seduction to control a man, nor is she implying anything immoral in a woman's self-awareness as a sexual being. She is simply enacting the right of a woman to be human.

Something of the fine balance I am trying to suggest here, between unsanctioned desire and a natural, sensitive responsiveness to the realities of the body, can be found in an undated, rather cryptic letter in the Gilder Collection. From Burnett to Gilder, the letter refers to "those Long Beach people," so it might have been written around the same time as the others quoted above. In it Burnett asks Gilder to "let me know when you are coming" before ending with this: "I must confess to being impatient to try to see if the harp is your Stringed instrument, with a view to seeing if you vibrate and if [illegible] & to what extent."[23] Here the woman's gaze is both sensual and experimental, erotic and scientific, the style on the page as much in control as the writer desires to be in the world. That tension between deeply personal attractions and the requirements of the imagination for an ambitious writer in a changing literary field marks a stage in Burnett's transition from apprentice, dependent on the approval of the man who invited her into the world of actual literature, to autonomous author, ready to build on what she learned during her apprenticeship while responding in her own way to the range of possible forms of expression available to her. Surely one of the things she learned in the years 1877–83 when she published the five novels discussed so far is how particular literary genres can both constrain and enable the realization of a literary idea. Her apprenticeship was served, we might say, among literary purists, James being one of her "confreres," working through past forms in order to forge something new. But because she did not develop her work along the lines of the new fiction, with its hyper-refinement of high style, does not automatically align her with literary profiteers, with their putative subordination of allegiance to a literary ideal in order to fatten their purses. In fact, after *Through One Administration* Burnett did not publish another novel for 13 years. According to Thwaite, she "was unable to write—and so she was ill. Or she was ill and so she was unable to write. They [sic] called it a 'nervous prostration'" (88). Gerzina put it more directly: "But it is probably just as true to say that she was, quite simply, worn out" (102).

The depth of her fatigue is a reflection of the depth of her commitment to succeed as an author of novels, not just a writer of stories. She expended all of herself in her work, and in the years that followed when no physical cause could be isolated for the extent and length of her suffering, she turned to metaphysics, or "mind-healing," for a cure, exploring but never committing to Christian Science, Hinduism and theosophy among others (see Thwaite 88 ff. and Gerzina 103 ff.). When she could not marshal the energy to begin another novel—she had started *In Connection with the De Willoughby Claim* before writing *Through One Administration* but put it aside and did not publish it in volume form until 1899—she managed to write the one story that made her fortune, cemented her fame and did the most long-term damage to her literary reputation: *Little Lord Fauntleroy*. Today that story is known more by misrepresentation than by actual reading, and, despite the fact that the story ran serially in the children's magazine *St. Nicholas* beginning November 1885, it is not absolutely clear whether Burnett wrote the book for a child or adult readership.[24]

Any ambiguity in that regard is apt for *Fauntleroy* sits at the intersection of the three paths that Burnett trod in her career; in addition to being a novelist and a children's author, she was also a playwright of both adaptations from her own books and of original plays, some coauthored. She had been involved with the theatre by necessity with the publication of her first novel and the nearly immediate unauthorized dramatic adaptations that followed, most notably the one by Charles Reade. With the publication of *Fauntleroy*, however, and another unauthorized dramatization, Burnett took the matter of a novelist's right to hold copyright over stage adaptations to court. She won and wrote her own highly successful adaptation.[25] Such comprehensive literary activity is more akin to Charles Dickens, who wrote *A Child's History of England* serialized in *Household Words*, later published in three volumes, and who was involved extensively in amateur theatricals in addition to his dramatic public readings, than it is Elizabeth Gaskell. Particularly with the success in theatre, it is a level of activity that James also aspired to, primarily because the theatre was more profitable than publishing, but failed to achieve. The stage success of *Fauntleroy* added to the novel's sales of multiple editions accelerated Burnett's financial independence.

The 13 years between novels were highly productive in terms of Burnett's broadening literary and cultural significance, the personal freedom enabled by financial success and the increasing understanding of the mind–body connection she achieved through her search in her illness for peace and physical wholeness. We can detect in the productivity of those 13 years the image of a woman working to realize as comprehensively as she could her full creative, social and personal powers, unconstrained by the complex of dependencies that enmeshed most other women at the time. In the eight novels that followed *Through One Administration*, Burnett performs a series of thought experiments where she imagines, at different times and in different places, the possibilities for individual women to grow into and then live out their full potential in the unity of mind and body. In her early novels, her women embody potential more than realization: *That Lass O'Lowries* ends with Joan in a liminal space; *Haworth's* celebrates Rachael French's physical courage but condemns her moral softness; Octavia in *A Fair Barbarian* stimulates change but does not stay to nurture it; the titular character in *Louisiana* ends up more shaped by her new environment in New York than a shaping influence either there or in North Carolina; and Bertha in *Through One Administration* lives a life of misjudgment and frustrated desire despite her capacity for a far fuller and more productive life. In each case the women are placed in relatively contemporary social environments rendered in a realistic mode, their lives constrained by the social forces Burnett could see at work in her own social world. When Burnett turned again to the novel in 1896, she wrote a historical novel set in England in the early eighteenth century during the reign of Queen

Anne. That novel, *A Lady of Quality*, and its heroine Clorinda Wildairs will anchor the next chapter.

Notes

1. "Recent Literature." *The Manhattan* (1883–1884), vol. 2, no. 1, 7 (1883): 88.
2. "Current Fiction." *The Literary World; a Monthly Review of Current Literature* (1870–1904), vol. 11, no. 10 (May 8, 1880): 153.
3. R. H. Stoddard. "Frances Hodgson Burnett." *The Critic* (1881–1883), vol. 1, no. 25 (December 17, 1881): 345–47.
4. James H. Morse. "The Native Element in American Fiction." *Century Illustrated Magazine* (1881–1906), vol. XXVI, no. 3, 7 (1883): 369.
5. "Literary Gossip." *The Art Interchange: A Household Journal* (1883–1904), vol. 10, no. 6 (March 15, 1883): 67. I should note that this review was written in response to the serialization of the novel. The reviews after it was published as a single volume were generally more positive.
6. "Through One Administration." *Saturday Review of Politics, Literature, Science and Art*, vol. 55, no. 1444 (1883): 383, 837–38.
7. Edward L. Burlingame. "Art. VI.—New American Novels." *The North American Review* (1821–1940), vol. 125, no. 258 (September 1877): 309–22. Burlingame was an editor at Scribner's, Burnett's New York publisher. See Thwaite, p. 73.
8. *Watch and Ward* (1871), *Eugene Pickering* (1874), *Roderick Hudson* (1876, in the critical literature generally regarded as his first novel) and *The American* (1877).
9. Braddon is best known for her sensational novel of 1860, *Lady Audley's Secret*. Reprints of Broughton's *Not Wisely, but Too Well* (Victorian Secrets, 2013) and *Belinda* (Virago, 1984), of Caird's *The Daughters of Danaus* (Feminist Press, 1989) and of Sarah Grand's *The Beth Book* (The Dial Press, 1980) and *The Heavenly Twins* (The Echo Library, 2007) mark a consistent contemporary interest in the new woman novel, which is reinforced by an increase in critical interest. See, for example, Lloyd Fernando's *"New Woman" in the Late Victorian Novel* (Pennsylvania State UP, 1977), Gail Cunningham's *The New Woman and the Victorian Novel* (Macmillan, 1978), Ann L. Ardis's *New Woman, New Novels: Feminism and Early Modernism* (Rutgers UP, 1990), Lyn Pykett's *The "Improper" Feminine: The Women's Sensation Novel and the New Woman Writing* (Routledge, 1992) and Teresa Mangum's *Married, Middlebrow, and Militant: Sarah Grand and the New Woman Novel* (U of Michigan P, 1999).
10. Arthur Tilley. "The New School of Fiction." *The National Review*, vol. 1, no. 2 (April 1883): 257–68.
11. "The Modern School of Fiction" (October 29, 1882). *Chicago Daily Tribune* (1872–1922) reviews the three novels together, noting "There are no full-blooded men and women, but plenty of mannikins."
12. John Hay. *New York Daily Tribune* (December 25, 1881): 8.
13. A quick search of the Modern Language Association International Bibliography database produces 406 entries, including books, articles, book chapters and doctoral dissertations. And that only scratches the surface of critical productivity on James and his signature novel.
14. R. O. Beard. "A Certain Dangerous Tendency in Novels." *The Dial*, vol. II, no. 30 (October 1882): 110–12 (110).
15. In the May 12, 1883 number of *The Athenaeum* the novel is advertised as follows: "At all the libraries, in three volumes, *Through One Administration* by the author of 'A Fair Barbarian,' 'That Lass O'Lowries,' 'Haworth's,' 'Louisiana,' & c." "Frederick Warne & Co. Bedford Street, Strand" was the publisher.
16. *The Nation* (October 23, 1879): 278.
17. "Recent Novels." *The Nation* (June 28, 1883): 552–54 (553).
18. "Novels of the Week." *The Athenaeum* (May 12, 1883): 600–601 (600).

19 Arthur Hobson Quinn. *American Fiction: An Historical and Critical Survey.* New York: D. Appleton-Century, 1936.
20 From the Gilder Collection in the New York Public Library. Used by permission.
21 "Our New York Letter." *The Literary World: A Monthly Review of Current Literature* (January 23, 1886): 28.
22 "Correspondence. Mrs. Burnett and the Century." *The Literary World* (March 6, 1886): 82.
23 I transcribed the letter written in Burnett's rather florid, difficult to decipher hand. From the Gilder Collection, New York Public Library. Used by permission.
24 See Thwaite, where she raises the question, "Was [*Fauntleroy*] really a children's book?" (93 ff.).
25 For details of the issues involved in that copyright case, see Gerzina 120–21. The "Copyright—Dramatization of Novel—Injunction" was published in *The Albany Law Journal: A Weekly Record of the Law and Lawyers* vol. 38, no. 13 (September 29, 1888): 256–58.

Chapter Three

HISTORICAL DREAMSCAPES AND THE VICISSITUDES OF CLASS: FROM *A LADY OF QUALITY* TO *THE METHODS OF LADY WALDERHURST*

I

Burnett's silence as a novelist lasted 13 years, a period she spoke about in an interview with Marie A. Belloc published in *The Idler* (UK 1896). Asked about the fact that during those years she had been "writing about, and chiefly for children," Burnett responded:

> Yes, but that has been the result of circumstances. Since my great bereavement of five years ago [the death of her eldest son, Lionel, in Paris at the age of 16], I have not had the courage to look upon life with sufficient interest to build comedies and tragedies upon it. Children I could write about, because they do not seem quite to belong to the world. During the last year I have been physically and mentally stronger, and have written my first novel since *Through One Administration*.[1]

Critics read that novel, *A Lady of Quality*, refracted through Burnett's previous work, but unlike the response to *Through One Administration*, which was read in relation to Burnett's Lancashire novels, *A Lady of Quality* was evaluated in relation to her previous novels and to her more recent, and widely acclaimed children's books, including *Editha's Burglar* (1886), *Little Lord Fauntleroy* (1886) and *Sara Crewe* (1888). In contrast to *Fauntleroy* in particular, with its emphasis on moral rectitude and social decorum, the libertine world of the late seventeenth and early eighteenth centuries of *A Lady of Quality* came as a shock to some critics, and even today readers can be made uneasy reading it. Anne Thwaite, for instance, in the "Foreword and Acknowledgements" section of her sympathetic biography of Burnett, writes that "*The* [sic] *Lady of Quality* [...] has no permanent value. I would not recommend it to anyone" (xi), and when I taught the novel in a graduate seminar on Gaskell and Burnett in the second decade of the twenty-first century, a number of my students were taken aback by the rendering of Clorinda, seemingly unable to process the moral challenge she presented to them. Those small details coupled with the inclusion of the novel on a banned books list sponsored by the Evanston, Illinois Public Library in 1902, a list that included Thomas Hardy's *Jude the Obscure* (listed just below *A Lady of Quality*), Boccaccio's *Decameron*, Kate Chopin's *The Awakening* and Frank Norris's *McTeague* among others, are symptoms of the novel's power and seriousness of purpose.[2] "It was as if," as Thwaite writes elsewhere in her biography, Burnett "had been deliberately setting out to refute Henry James' charge that most of the stuff that was reaching him from America seemed to have been written 'by eunuchs and sempstresses'" (153), a jab that could have landed on the author of *Fauntleroy* but would have been countered by the "Nietzsche-like individualism" (Zangwill 154) of Clorinda in *A Lady of Quality*.

Zangwill's linking of Clorinda and Nietzsche captures incisively how unsettling Burnett's contemporary readers found the novel and something of the novel's continuing capacity to challenge readers today. Nietzsche, of course, is the philosopher whose concept of the *Übermensch* (literally "overman," more commonly referred to as "superman") is associated with the desire to realize the full capacity of an individual's humanity in the world (rather than in an afterlife) by overcoming all social and moral strictures that would constrain one's scope of action. He introduces the word in the "Prologue" to his poetically aphoristic volume called *Thus Spoke Zarathustra*:

> Once the soul looked contemptuously on the body, and then
> that contempt was the supreme thing: the soul wished the
> body meagre, ghastly, and famished. Thus it thought to escape
> from the body and the earth [...].
> But my happiness should justify existence itself! [...]
> I want to teach men the sense of their existence, which is the
> Superman, the lightning out of the dark cloud man.[3]

Note in those lines the celebration of the human body, which, in defiance of concepts of the soul, refuses to be "meagre, ghastly, and famished"; contempt of the body is replaced with an embrace of physical wholeness, the raison d'être of existence being the happiness experienced through the body. Lightning, then, is not an infusion of energy from outside the body; it is the imaging forth of the spark of life that is "the Superman" (*Übermensch*) itself. Buried in the concept of the *Übermensch* is the idea of radical wholeness, where the duality of body and spirit, intellect and affect is shown to be life-negating. The relevance of Nietzsche to Burnett is not a poetic projection coming from her critic and friend Israel Zangwill; it can be shown through an exploration of Burnett's emphasis on bodily power—the capacity for literal physical force emanating from the unity of body and mind in women and men—in how a healthy body is so central to the experience of happiness, and in the necessity to ground morality on a basic of respect for the physical well-being and autonomy of every individual, but especially of women.

This brief Zangwill-inspired excursion connecting Burnett and Nietzsche suggests that *A Lady of Quality* can be read as a thought experiment, not a philosophical novel as such but a historical novel distanced enough in time to allow for socially sensitive material to be handled without reserve. The connection between the historical novel as a genre and social concerns of the time of writing is made indirectly in the Belloc interview with Burnett quoted above. After Burnett points out that her new novel "is laid in the reign of Queen Anne," Belloc says, "I need hardly ask you, Mrs. Burnett, if your latest work is a problem novel?" (648). Prefacing a question by stating it need not be asked makes the question rhetorical, a statement that Burnett half-rejects and half-concedes. First, the rejection: "Heaven forfend," Burnett declares, "that my poor *Lady of Quality* should be called a problem novel!" Next, the concession: "The heroines of such books beat their breasts, and tear their hair, and call themselves sentimental, bad names to the emotional delight and hysteric admiration of all beholders. My heroine does not. Perhaps that is the problem." Earlier in her response Burnett suggests that authors write "problem" novels "as if in default of having anything real to write about, one trumped up a popular question." Burnett's ambition, then, for *A Lady of Quality* is to write an historical novel that engages a problem of substance, nothing "trumped up" for the moment but something that is actual in the moment but has also been historically a real problem rather than an ephemeral one. Burnett's further elucidation in her response reveals that she knows the problem that Belloc was alluding to, the woman question, which she redefines as follows: "The man and woman question has no interest for me." Making the case that issues related to women's equality in marriage, politics, the professions and so on cannot be addressed apart from the role of men in those areas, bringing both female and male roles into question, Burnett argues that "[W]e are not to be divided into mere men and women; we are human beings who are part of each other. Each part should be as noble as the other, and the one who is stronger should teach the other strength." The thought experiment Burnett's words imply is to imagine the possibility of a woman being fully human in a world that in its social configuration and daily cultural practices relegates women to a position dependent on the authority of men (i.e., patriarchy). To imagine that is to project an ideal that would challenge both the social realities in the historical past of the novel and of the contemporary present of the reader. Burnett concludes her Belloc interview by articulating in general terms such an ideal. "The ideal woman," she explains,

> must be a strong creature, self-controlled and tender. She must have no small, illogical tempers or petty jealousies or shifty little cowardly tricks. She must have the reason and sense of honour and justice which one expects from the ideal man. It is my opinion, in fact, that the ideal woman, among quite a number of other things, should be "a perfect gentleman." (648)

Rejecting misogynist clichés, Burnett's ideal emphasizes the positive virtues of strength, composure, tenderness, reason, honor and justice. Those ideals may be associated with men, but traditionally men have been held up as the normatively human with women defined as lesser. Consequently, Burnett inflects those positive qualities as human qualities, the ideal woman becoming the ideal human.[4] The majority of reviewers of *A Lady of Quality* did not perceive that ideal in the figure of Clorinda; they tended to judge her humanity as unfeminine and immoral. A minority of reviewers took a more nuanced view.

The keynote for the skeptical reviews was struck in *The Interior* (United States) where the reviewer states: "Certainly it is, from the standpoint of the Young Person, the most flagrantly impossible book offered to decent readers in many a day. 'Jude the Obscure' was loathsome and terrible, but 'A Lady of Quality,' is subtly pernicious, and to a more dangerous degree."[5] The capitalized reference to the "Young Person" reveals how the memory of *Fauntleroy* lingered with the reviewer, but the comparison with Hardy's *Jude* captures the reviewer's recognition of the adult, literary ambitions of the book. Such a bifurcated response accounts for the sentence that follows the one quoted: "The story

[…] is of intense interest notwithstanding its faults." The point the reviewer makes is that the skillful writing masks the morally questionable content of the novel, hence its subtle perniciousness that goes beyond the presentation of a multiple murder then suicide committed by a child "because we are too menny" that occurs in *Jude*. George Preston, the reviewer for *The Bookman*, develops the *Jude* comparison further. Calling *A Lady of Quality* "the most startling literary event of the month […] right in the midst of the alarm raised by *Jude the Obscure* sounding a tocsin at the least sign of immorality in fiction," Preston goes on to contrast Clorinda with Arabella from *Jude* (the titular hero's first wife). He points out that Arabella was guilty of breaking only one of the Ten Commandments while Clorinda broke nearly all of them: "There may be an exception," he writes, "but scarcely more than one or two." He then offers this daunting (but highly questionable) catalog:

> She remembers the Sabbath Day only to further worldly schemes; she honours not her father, nor her sisters, nor any living creature; she swears unceasingly until she learns that profanity is not the vogue; she lies, not economically, like Arabella, but prodigally to both friend and foe; she covets wealth and rank, and wins them by deceit crueler than Arabella's deception of Jude; she rids herself of an old lover when wanting a new one, not by brutal candour, as Arabella dismisses Jude, but by murdering him and concealing the crime.[6]

The critic's moral outrage builds through four columns of print, his sentences seasoned with claims such as, despite the work maintaining "an artistic semblance of reality," it is nonetheless (or all the more) "insane and pernicious" (157).

Such reviews from the secular press make the review in *The Catholic World* appear measured and judicious, which, despite its conclusion that "The Lady of Quality is hardly lady or woman, but a monstrous literary *lusus naturae*," it arguably is.[7] Sensing, perhaps, some of the thinking Burnett shared with Belloc on her views of the ideal woman being a gentleman, that is, being human, the review rejects that possibility in its axiomatic assumption that if a woman does not conform to the gender stereotypes of a lady, she is either base or unnatural. The crux can be found in the review's second paragraph:

> The great aim of many authors now is to present woman in new lights. The more startling and unreal, the better the effect, so it is thought. The Lady of Quality is certainly a startling creature. The idea seems to have been suggested by a statue of the Sphinx or similar chimera—one half the creature beast, the other part woman. (271)

Here the unity of a woman's physical body (as opposed to an etherealized disembodiment of the "moral" woman) and the soul/intellect that animates that body is fractured, the woman's bodily strength turned bestial, the prospect of her being fully human rendered as a monstrous impossibility. That point is reinforced later in the review when the writer observes: "There are far too many flashes of glowing animalism in the descriptive parts of the story, suggesting a want of sympathy with the spiritual side of womanhood," but the writer backs off the severity of that observation by adding, "which may be unjust to the author" (272). That relative clause with its conditional "may" certainly expresses doubt about being unjust to Burnett while also opening up the possibility that the review is, in fact, misrepresenting the novel. Calling this review measured and judicious, then, may be justified in comparison to the aggressively negative reviews, but such a judgment is questionable in relation to the more engaged positive reviews.

Jeanette L. Gilder begins her review in the *Chicago Daily Tribune* by comparing *A Lady of Quality* to *That Lass O'Lowries*:

> In this, her new novel [...] Mrs. Burnett has returned to her older and better manner. Here we find the author of "That Lass O'Lowries," and I for one in reading it am glad to forget the author of that popular but very sentimental story "Little Lord Fauntleroy." I will not go so far as to say that "A Lady of Quality" is better than "That Lass O'Lowries," but I will say that it is as good, and that is high praise indeed.[8]

Gilder reads *A Lady* clearly in reaction to *Fauntleroy*, closing her review with gratitude that Burnett's latest novel is able "to take the taste of the mawkish Fauntleroy out of our mouths," and the aspect of the novel that accounts for its ability to do that is its "virility," the same virility "that made [*That Lass O'Lowries*] a literary sensation of the better sort." Even after *Fauntleroy, Editha's Burglar* and *Sara Crewe* the critic sees Burnett coming back to her true vocation as a novelist in the tradition of Victorian realism. Given the fact that Thackeray (*Henry Esmond*), Gaskell (*Sylvia's Lovers*) and George Eliot (*Romola*) all wrote at least one historical novel—we can add Burnett's immediate contemporary Charles Reade, who wrote an unauthorized dramatic adaptation of *That Lass* to the list—seeing Burnett's move to a new genre as a kind of return makes good sense. But it is also a departure in terms both of genre and of theme: "The scene is laid in England and the action takes place at the end of the seventeenth century, but the newest of 'new women' might envy the independence of Clorinda Wildairs." In that sentence Gilder registers the thematic freedom Burnett's turn to the past enables her, and, in the process, suggests a way of reading the novel that culminates in Zangwill's celebration of its "Nietzsche-like individualism."

The *New York Times* review, published a week after Gilder's, can serve as a bridge to Zangwill's more radical reading. Entitled "A Tale of Queen Anne's Reign," the review calls *A Lady of Quality* "an excellent specimen of the modern novel," that, like *Jude the Obscure*, "will be attacked with vehemence [...] [and] praised intolerably" as it is "read by everybody who reads fiction of the higher class and probably by many others."[9] The review then focuses exclusively on Clorinda, whom the reviewer calls "one of the most piquant, irresistible, and audacious character studies in modern fiction [...]. Neither Hardy nor Meredith has imagined a more remarkable woman." After summarizing Clorinda's career and commenting on its significance in relation to heredity, environment, religion and so on, the penultimate paragraph of the review emphasizes a quality that fits comfortably under the label Nietzschean:

> But the most striking quality of Clorinda is her superb selfishness, which is not presented as a vice, and which is her dominating trait from first to last. It governs her every action, the few evil, the many beneficent. Her noble charities, in her later years, are all due to it—to her belief in herself, her self-love, her exaltation of herself over others. In other words, Clorinda,

though never a pagan, is never a typical Christian. What is esteemed the very essence of Christianity she disregards all together. (31)

"Superb selfishness" that extends beyond good and evil as it accounts equally well for both categories of action captures the spirit of the *Übermensch* quite succinctly, and it is that spirit that animates Zangwill's fusion of Clorinda with the heroine from a Hardy novel not called *Jude the Obscure*.

Soon after his reference to the "Nietzsche-line individualism of *The Lady of Quality*," Zangwill corrects the reviewers who had condemned Clorinda on the basis of her lack of plausible psychology. He writes: "to approach the character Clorinda on the side of psychology were ungrateful to a story conceived rather in the spirit of the Symbolists."[10] Working from a conception of art that emphasizes the intuitive, the a-logical (as opposed to the illogical) and the expansive, Burnett creates "a story of 'Tess' triumphant, of the one woman who conquered fate." The reference to Tess triumphant conjures an image of Tess walking away after her stabbing of Alex,—her rapist, stalker and oppressor—liberated and not subject to self or external judgments of guilt that feel so contrary to the emotions conjured when Tess finally asserts her responsibility to herself. In that reading, Tess does not enact revenge; she simply claims her right to be. The reference to Tess also recalls the subtitle to the novel, "A Pure Woman." "Clorinda as vixen, mistress, and murderess," Zangwill asserts, "suggests the latent Lord Byron in Mrs. Burnett's breast." That shift in gender, from the pure Tess to the libertine Byron, resonates with Burnett's gender disregarding ideal woman, and it argues for a way of reading Clorinda that oscillates between human qualities associated with gender in order to blur the distinction. With gender distinctions unstable for readers of *A Lady of Quality*, it becomes possible to think critically about how the very same actions taken by a woman or a man mean different things when they are, in fact, substantially equivalent.

This interpretive reading of Zangwill's review is consonant with Burnett's explicit ideas about gender, which she articulated in a speech at a dinner held in her honor by the London Authors' Club in the spring of 1896 soon after the publication of *A Lady of Quality*. Gerzina provides an account of the event:

> Dressed in masses of fluffy chiffon, and with a tall osprey rising from her fair hair, she delivered a talk about being a pioneer in a new country. "In the course of what occasionally appears to be a somewhat protracted existence, I have never yet discovered a good quality—or a bad one—which seemed to have a gender," she told the audience of men and women. "As to one's success in the work one does, surely that is not a question of gender either. The big world settles that." (185)

She then points out that Burnett talked next about Clorinda, before offering the following evolutionary vision of the future:

> I think it probable that—say a hundred years from now—a woman may stand as I do, in some place such as this, the guest of men who have done the work all the world has known and honored, and she will be the outcome of all the best and most logical thinking, of all the most reasonable and clear-brained men and women—women and men—of these seething years.

She will have learned all the things I have not learned, and she will be a woman so much wiser and more stately of mind than I could ever hope to be—she will have so much more brain, so much more fine and clear a reason, that if we were compared we should scarcely seem to be creatures of the same race. And of this woman I say, "Good luck to her, great happiness, fair fortunes, and all the fullest joyousness of living; all kind fates attend her, all good things to her—and to the men who will be her friends."[11]

That such a vision of the future grew out of an exploration of the past communicates something about the constraints Burnett feels for women in the present and her desire, like George Eliot's, for her work to be judged as work, not as woman's work. As Gerzina observes in her commentary on Burnett's speech, Burnett was looking "ahead to the Virginia Woolfs of the world, unborn or in their infancy, and both envied and saluted them" (186). One might speculate that in her heart, Burnett also wanted already to be them, but since that cannot be the case under the social conditions that prevailed at the time, Clorinda could be a version of the woman to come. The past, in Burnett's historical fiction, becomes a way to imagine the future.

II

The intersection between gender and history permeates *A Lady of Quality*, whose historical distance and generic affiliation are announced in its full title: *A Lady of Quality. Being a Most Curious, Hitherto Unknown History, as Related by Mr. Isaac Bickerstaff but Not Presented to the World of Fashion Through the Pages of the Tatler, and Now for the First Time Written Down.* That title echoes an eighteenth-century practice by naming the fictional narrator and the periodical through which the story could have been but was not presented. When Burnett's reviewers addressed history in the novel, they emphasized the relation between the novel's language and the period that language was supposed to reflect. The last sentence of the *New York Times* review is representative: "The phraseology often seems affected, and the author is always thinking more of the traits and moods of her heroine than of the fashions and manners of the time in which she lived." The emphasis is on verisimilitude, whether the language in the novel accurately presents the physical details of the time announced in the title; history, for the reviewer, becomes a picture frozen in the past with no relation to the present. The focus on the heroine "over the fashions and manners of the time" removes the heroine from history even as history is dissevered from the movement of time. Contrary to the *Times* reviewer's assumptions, in his classic study of the historical novel, Avrom Fleishman has pointed out that "[A] reliving of past experience," in the historical novel, "invariably evokes life in the present, for historical life is understood only in its connection to present life." In doing so, however, "[A] work of historical art generates an esthetic distance from the present as well as from the past; it allows us to see not only others but ourselves in history."[12] The creation of that double distance enables one to think historically, which, as Christina Crosby puts it, "is to comprehend, after the fact, the significance of the fact, to reconstruct, as best one can, the historical event, to grasp how it emerged from the past and how it carries within it the germ of the future."[13] If some historical fiction, however, does not set out to recreate historical events as such but to conjure the distance of the past in the service of fictional character and story, we can think of character itself, in this case Clorinda, as an event. Even though *A Lady of Quality*, as fiction, is not itself reconstructing a historical event after the fact, it is injecting into the affective history of the reader a new subjectivity that emerges from the evoked past to bring forward in the present "the germ of the future." So at the moment of reading, readers experience the subjectivity called Clorinda as she emerges from the past into the present experience of the narrative; Clorinda's subsequent afterlife then in its impact on the subjectivity of readers extends into the future in ways that can neither be calculated nor fully known.

The analogy I have just drawn between how to think about historical event and fictional character is not absolutely dependent on any given novel being defined generically as historical, for character always precedes readers who experience the narrative in present time. In that way to think historically is like reading, where the interplay between past and present cannot be consummated in a future totality because the future is, to paraphrase Mikhail Bakhtin, always an open question, unfinished. Thinkers may theorize history based on teleological models or, as Crosby puts it, in "profoundly theological ways" (144), as if history has a goal whose contours can be perceived as providing the shape of history as a totality, but those models remain abstractions in relation to human experience in the midst of an unfolding history. One way to read Burnett's investment in gender through her creation of Clorinda, then, is as an effort to explore how a subjectivity gendered female may emerge from the past, and through her unpredictable, particular experience struggle to shape her own history both within and in opposition to teleological models. In *A Lady of Quality* that struggle is against the social and historical determinations associated with patriarchy.

The novel opens in extremis with Sir Jeoffry Wildairs of Wildairs Hall, a "place [that] was like pandemonium,"[14] riding out to hunt with his hung-over, half-nauseous, ill humored, coarse, scandalous companions while his wife had just an hour earlier delivered her ninth child. All the children were girls, and only two others were still living. Just as Sir Jeoffry is set to leave the hall, his wife's servant rushes to him to request he attend to his wife, who wanted him to know "that she felt strangely" (5). Because none of his children had been sons, "he considered each of his offspring an ill turn done him," he responds, "[T]ell her I had gone hunting and you were too late"; he then rides off, his "fellow-roysterers [...] who had caught at the reason of his wrath, grinning as they rode" (5). The scene shifts from the grotesque Sir Jeoffry to his wife Daphne, who was 15 when they married and called by her friends "Titania for her fairy slightness and delicate beauty" (6). We learn that Sir Jeoffry courted her vigorously, her head was turned and she married him thinking she was "the luckiest young lady in the world." With the physical toll of each birth and Sir Jeoffry's increasing anger as each is a girl, Daphne's beauty fades quickly, and as the novel opens, "[S]he is alone, and she knew the time had come for her death" (7). These early pages, with their emphasis on the physically powerful and demanding man taking a wife for reasons of lust and patrimony only to be disappointed and subsequently rejecting both wife and children, set up an allegory of patriarchy. In that allegory, the woman is reduced to her body for its beauty and capacity to bear male children; when that body fails to deliver boys and its beauty fades, her value becomes less than nothing. In the physical contrast between the robust man and physically drained woman, the moral effect is equivalent to torture and murder, the natural functions of the woman's body denatured, the man a rapist and killer.

Daphne's dying reflections go some way to confirm the harsh outlines of this allegory:

> "Nine times like this," she panted faintly, "and 'tis for naught but oaths and hard words that blame me. When 'twas 'My Daphne,' and 'My beauteous little Daphne,' he loved me in his own man's way. But now—" She faintly rolled her head from side to side. "Women are poor things," a chill salt tear sliding past her lips so that she tasted its bitterness, "only to be kissed for an hour—and then like this—only for this and nothing else. I would that this one [her newborn] had been dead." (9)

Nine pregnancies after being "loved in a man's way" lead unremittingly over time to the life being drained from her body, her beauty fading as her life fades, the only acquisition from her marriage being pain. In that context her contemplation of infanticide is the next logical step in the life-denying sequence. But as she "lay staring at her child and gasping, her thin chest rising and falling convulsively," and though "the glaze of death [was] stealing slowly over her wide-opened eyes," she sees the child's strange but natural beauty. Whispering to herself, she says, "[S]he—she will be like—Jeoffry—and like *me*." The narrator registers the pronoun *me* as having "a shuddering sound." Fearful then of the consequences of her child's female beauty in the hands of "her father and no mother" (and perhaps later in the hands of a husband or lover), she concludes that "only evil can come to her." The best thing to do under such circumstances as she whispers to her daughter is to "stop thy breathing […] 'twould be fairer" than to let her live a woman's life under a brutal man supported by a patriarchal system.

> She gathered up all her dying will and brought her hand up to the infant's mouth. A wild look was on her poor small face, she panted and fell forward on its breast, the rattle in her throat growing louder. The child awakened, opening great black eyes, and with her dying weakness its new-born life struggled. Her cold hand lay upon its mouth and her head upon its body, for she was too far gone to move if she had willed to do so—but the tiny creature's strength was marvelous. It gasped, it fought, its little limbs struggled beneath her, it writhed until the cold hand fell away, and then its baby mouth set free, it fell a shrieking […] fierce and shrill […]. 'Twas not a thing to let its life go easily, 'twas of those born to do battle. (10–11)

By the end of the chapter, the contours of the allegorical tale begin to emerge. The child, in defiance of the logic of a woman's life under patriarchy as experienced by her mother, refuses to avoid confronting that life by resisting her mother's efforts to save her from the battle. She is determined by nature to fight against male oppression, to change its determinations for herself as a way to break the totalizing force of patriarchal control. That allegorical frame, however, is troubled by a pointed natural detail: "She will be like Jeoffry and me." Her natural strength, then, her fierce resistance is associated with the masculine energies and brutalities of her father. Thus, if she is "born to do battle," that battle must, perforce, take place against a world dominated by men with the weapons deployed by men. As a first step, she will have to do battle within herself. Because the power of patriarchy is shown to be grounded on physical strength, and physical strength is the keynote struck in the hours after her birth, the child must learn to use her physical strength—as opposed to her ethereal beauty expressive of spiritual purity, which becomes a vehicle of redemption for men—as her most basic weapon to carve out a life for herself on her own terms. Such a battle cannot be won in an absolute sense; gains can be partial, uneven and cumulative over time. Or there may be no gains at all. The final image of the opening chapter captures those conflicting possibilities. When the nurse reenters the room after Daphne's death, she finds her "lying stone-dead, her poor head resting on her offspring's feet and her open glazed eyes seemed to stare at it as if in asking Fate some awful question" (11). After figuratively (and probably at times literally) being trampled under the feet of her husband or kneeling before him, her head resting on the ground as she pleads for respect and succor, Daphne's head rests on the feet of her hours-old girl child, whose visage is the last thing reflected in her eyes. The substitution of the image of the infant girl for the image of the brutal father ending on the note of "some awful question" leaves open whether the meaning of the awful question becomes clear in the girl's awe-inspiring growth into wholeness or the horrifying repetition of the assertion of the power of a patriarch? The setting of the novel in an historical past creates enough distance from the moment of writing to bring out the allegory in bold relief, while the convergence of Clorinda's life story with the 1890s transatlantic debate about the emergence of the new woman provides an immediate and changing context for Burnett's readers to transform the allegory into the symbolic, to read it, perhaps, as Zangwill did.

III

After her mother's death, Clorinda is raised by servants, her father refusing to have anything to do with her. Nonetheless, as she grows she resembles her father. The butler puts it this way: "[S]he is as like Sir Jeoffry in her temper as one pea is like another." The housemaid amplifies that assertion by adding, "[A]nd she will be of his build, too [...]. What mishap changed her to a maid instead of a boy, I know not. She would have made a strapping heir." She has "the thigh and shoulders of a handsome man-child," the housemaid concludes. Clorinda's nursemaid counters that "She will be a handsome woman, though large in build it may be" (17). Those gossipy observations capture in miniature the way the language used to define Clorinda throughout the narrative oscillates between genders, at one moment praising her masculine strength and another her feminine perceptions. "She has her father's long limbs and fine shoulders," her nursemaid continues, "and the will to make every man look her way" (18). Whether the allusions are masculine or feminine, however, the emphasis is almost always on her physical power and strength of will, but in her early years masculine allusions tend to dominate. Consider the words she exchanges with her father when she chances to meet him for the first time when she is 6 years old. Having wandered into her father's wing of the house, she finds his powder horn; she seizes it and spills the powder on the floor as she plays. Her father sees her and shouts: "Blood and damnation on thee, thou impudent little baggage [...]. I'll break thy neck for thee, little scurvy beast" (24). Her response does him one better: "'Damn *thee*! Damn *thee*!' she roared and screamed, flogging him [with her riding whip]. 'I'll cut thy liver from thee! Damn thy soul to h—l'" (24–25). As a pair they sound like Heathcliff and the young Hareton in Emily Bronte's *Wuthering Heights* as they bond through the medium of curses. More pointed, perhaps, is the description of her beating her father with a whip, an image that emphasizes the strength of her arm and her readiness to strike. The encounter with her father captures in miniature the general condition of her childhood. The narrator summarizes that condition thus: "Uncivilized and almost savage as her girlish life was, and unregulated by any outward training as was her mind, there were none who came in contact with her who could be blind to a certain strong, clean wit and unconquerableness of purpose for which she was remarkable" (40). She is both girlish and savage with an unfolding relentlessness of purpose.

As Clorinda grows the masculine and feminine allusions blend in a paradoxical erotic androgyny. "She spent her days," the narrator explains, "with her father and his dissolute friends, treated half like a boy, half like a fantastical queen until she was fourteen" (41). Just before her 15th birthday the local chaplain, who was dispatched by a local neighbor to remonstrate with Jeoffry Wildairs for bringing up his daughter as a boy (the locals are fixated on the girl wearing breeches), he finds "a beautiful youth" and is taken aback when the servant addresses that youth as "mistress." "And this was she," he thought, "this fine young creature who was tall and grandly enough built and knit to seem a radiant being even when clad in masculine attire!" (42). Note how the masculine qualities of height and physical amplitude are presented as the vehicle through which Clorinda's feminine "radiant being" is visible. Once he registers Clorinda as female, when she escorts him to see her father, the chaplain struggles not to look at her the way he feels irresistibly drawn to do. "She led the way, holding her head jauntily and high, while he cast down his eyes lest his gaze should be led to wander in a way unseemly in one of his cloth. Such a foot, and such—!" (43). The female body that radiates through male signifiers becomes, for the chaplain, unspeakable, even as he cannot help being drawn to look against his better judgment. This scene confirms her nursemaid's observation when Clorinda was three about her "will to make every man look her way." It also registers how she can transform her precocious physical and mental force into a heightened version of traditional feminine beauty, turning that beauty into a weapon.

At the end of the chaplain's visit, Clorinda agrees not to wear breeches when she hunts. She does so not in acquiescence to his request but through her own judgment about how best to make her way in the world as she grows out of her "boyish maiden charm," recognizing that in her social world "her market must be made" (47). Her father had squandered the family fortune, she had to marry well, so she works to transfigure herself into something more than a mere beauty. At the stroke of midnight of her 15th birthday, she appears before her father and his carousing guests in opulent formal dress, "which showed off her grandeur [...] [her] mien so dazzling that every man sprang to his feet beholding her." She regards the guests, all men, with "her lips curving in the triumphant mocking smile of a great beauty looking upon them as vassals." Before anyone can speak, she cries, "Down upon your knees [...] and drink to me kneeling. From this night all men must bend so—all men whom I deign to cast my eyes on" (56). With that grand declaration Clorinda announces her intention to deploy her personal force through the conventions of gender. She reverses her self-presentation from her feminine radiance emerging through, even being enhanced by her masculine dress, as we saw in the chaplain's perception of her, to a representation of female beauty that is animated by the vitality of her exuberant physical strength. That strength is confirmed over and over again by her prowess as a rider, who can break any horse to her will, but that strength is at the service of her desire to shape and control her own experience as a woman, an experience that is constrained, perforce, by the social conventions of her time. The narrator makes the point as follows:

> The high courage and undaunted will which had been the engines she had used to gain her will from her infant years, aided her […] to carry out what her keen mind and woman's wit had designed, which was to take the county by storm with her beauty, and reign toast and enslaver until such time as she won her prize of a husband of rich estates and notable rank. (58)

Her design may be the most conventional of all for a woman of her class and circumstances, but for her that convention is the medium through which she can continue to assert mastery over her environment.

The novel's emergent allegorical shape can be described as a fracturing of the androgynous unity of Clorinda's infancy into a dominant feminine identity whose masculine qualities remain in her physical strength and her bodily attunement with her environment. Then, once Clorinda gives herself fully to her feminine identity, her life is defined by her search for a masculine counterpart. Much like the poet in Percy Shelley's narrative poem "Alastor," who dreams of his female counterpart and spends the rest of his short life in pursuit of what is little more than a vision, Clorinda's conventional path is not motivated only by wealth and social position. She is looking, as Alastor had done, for a "mate," a word that in the context of the novel has both biological and spiritual resonance, the body being the physical manifestation of the soul. Of the three men who form in different ways a relationship with Clorinda, only one represents the mutuality of body and soul that resonates with Clorinda's apprehension of her best self. The first relationship is defined exclusively in terms of the body, the second in terms of the soul; in each case they appeal only to a part of Clorinda's full humanness. The third, however, completes her in being her mate, which in the terms established by the novel itself means a return to the wholeness of her androgynous childhood through the necessary, adult other, the female and male reconstituting the androgynous whole.

Clorinda's first relationship is with John Oxon, whom she meets as a guest of her father's.

> He was […] twenty-four years of age, and a man, while she was fifteen and a woman, but being so tall and built with such unusual vigor of symmetry, she was a beauteous match for him, and both being attired in fashionable masculine habit, these two pretty young fellows standing smiling saucily at each other were a charming, though singular spectacle. (50)

Focalized through the other guests, that description is consonant with the chaplain's first impression of Clorinda, the mutual saucy smiles adding a more explicit erotic component. Oxon vows to seduce her, and his friends mock that vow as a pretense. To prove his success, he bets that he will return from a tryst with a lock of Clorinda's hair as evidence that he has possessed her. He succeeds, then rejects her as he pursues a wealthier bride, fully expecting that henceforth Clorinda will be cowed in his presence, ashamed and fearful. When his pursuit of the other woman fails, he requests to see Clorinda at the site of their earlier tryst. She speaks:

> "You thought to see a woman crushed and weeping, her beauty bent before you, her locks disheveled, her streaming eyes lifted to Heaven—and you—with prayers, swearing that not Heaven could help her so much as your deigning magnanimity. You have seen women do this before, you would have seen *me* do it—at your feet—crying out that I was lost—lost forever. *That* you expected! 'Tis not here."
>
> Debauched as his youth was, and free from all touch of heart or conscience—for from his earliest boyhood he had been the pupil of rakes and fashionable villains—well as he thought he knew all women and their ways, betraying or betrayed, this creature taught him a new thing—a new mood in woman—a new power which came upon him like a thunderbolt.
>
> "Gods!" he exclaimed, catching his breath and even falling back a pace. "Damnation! You are *not* a woman!" (119)

Here Burnett is playing with the convention of the fallen woman whose virginity, once lost, makes her anathema as the bride of an honorable man. The seducer then can rescue her, only subsequently to shame her again when the prospect of a wealthy bride appears. Clorinda refuses to surrender to the power of that convention. The tryst for her is more an error in judgment than it is a mark of sin. She has lost nothing of value but rather strengthened her will. No one can make her fall if she does not choose to fall herself. If a man can "sin" without loss of dignity, so can a woman. "I am a woman," she cries, "who would show other women how to bear themselves in hours like these" (119). She ends the meeting with this: "Then [...] *go!*—back to your kennel!" (121). It seems a decisive victory made possible by Clorinda's fundamental lack of physical fear, for without fear Oxon cannot intimidate her. The physical mirroring described in their first meeting is more than surface appearance; she is a physical match for him in bodily strength. That symmetry becomes important later in the narrative when Oxon stalks her in his effort to prevent her from marrying her "mate." But in the meantime, she achieves her ambition for wealth and social position when she marries the kind, grateful and elderly Lord of Dunstanwolde.

While it is an exaggeration to argue that Dunstanwolde represents a response to Clorinda's hunger of soul, he does appeal to the noncorporeal aspect of her being. Through him she learns that male–female relationships can be built on trust and that sustaining that trust can test and strengthen her will. Here is how she explains it to her sister, Anne: "I love my Lord of Dunstanwolde as well as any other man, and better than some, for I do not hate him. He has a fine estate and is a gentleman [...] [he] gives me wealth and rank and life at Court. I give to him the thing he craves with all his soul—myself. It is an honest bargain, and I shall bear my part of it with honesty" (133). Given the social world depicted in the novel, her declaration of simple honesty is more attractive than it is emotionally cold. She shows she understands her husband's desire, and while she does not "crave" him as he does her, she is determined to be a good wife. "I have no women's virtues," she explains to her sister, "but I have one that is sometimes—not always—a man's. 'Tis that I am not a coward and a trickster, and keep my word when 'tis given" (133–34). The net effect is that she learns to respect her husband and herself as his wife (135). The marriage is short-lived, Dunstanwolde dying of heart failure after less than two years. Clorinda's capacity for faithfulness was well tried over that time, however, for between the time when she promised herself to Dunstanwolde and they actually married, he introduces her to the man who is her absolute counterpart in both body and soul, the man who under other circumstances would have been mate. That man is Dunstanwolde's kinsman, the Duke of Osmonde.

One evening Dunstanwolde observes how strange it is that "being past his callow youthful days," Osmonde has yet to marry. Clorinda disagrees, saying, "There is no strangeness in it." In the exchange that follows she makes a distinction between simple marriage and the idea of mating, the latter being an ideal that structures the second half of the novel; it is also a concept Burnett will return to throughout the second half of her life as a novelist. Here is how Clorinda introduces it:

> "A man like him must mate as well as marry, or he will break his heart with silent raging at the weakness of the thing he is tied to. He is too strong and splendid for a common woman. If he married one, 'twould be as if a lion had taken to his care a jackel or a sheep. Ah!"—with a long drawn breath—"he would go mad—mad with misery." (139)

Her words create the image of a man superior, if not a Nietzschean superman, then one whose capacities require far more than a world of conventions could satisfy. They also imply a view of marriage as containing a biological imperative to choose a spouse whose physical attributes mirror the best in the other as well as creating the greatest possibility to produce biologically and mentally strong offspring. Such a view of marriage as a form of mating is associated, as Angelique Richardson has shown, with the idea of rational reproduction central to the discourse surrounding the new woman.[15] Dunstanwolde's response suggests the aptness, given the terms of this novel, of Clorinda being Osmonde's mate, and his precise phraseology reveals that at heart he himself understands that. "He [Osmonde] should have a goddess," Clorinda's husband says. "He should hold a bitter grudge against me, that I, his unworthy kinsman, have been given the only one" (139). When we begin with Clorinda's matter-of-fact acceptance of her asymmetrical marriage, then fold in Dunstanwolde's deep gratitude and contentment with what he experiences as the gift of his marriage and then add the realization that Clorinda and Osmonde are a truer match, each with the same physical and mental superiority to ordinary folk, we can see how Burnett sets up another narrative convention involving infidelity rather than fallenness. But in contrast to Clorinda's defiance of Oxon in which she breaks the latter narrative convention, her absolute self-control (and Osmonde's) in deference to the legal bond of marriage quietly obliterates the former convention. There is no fall; there is no infidelity. There is only human will and human experience where, in the end, the weaker give way to the stronger.

When Dunstanwolde dies, as in his age and physical frailty he must, Clorinda goes into mourning for 18 months, after which, as a rich and still quite young widow, she returns to society where inevitably she and Osmonde find each other. Of Clorinda the narrator explains:

> There were, in [her] strange nature, depths so awful and profound that it was not to be sounded or to be judged as others were. But one thing could have melted or caused the unconquerable spirit to bend, and this was the overwhelming passion of love—not a slight, tender feeling, but a great and powerful one, such as could be awakened but by a being of as strong and deep a nature as itself—one who was in all things her peer. (198)

Such a love is not romantic, a soft and tender passion; it is a responsiveness of Clorinda's total being to her "peer in all things," a physical and mental match in equal measure clear-eyed and strong of will. In her widowhood as her mind turns to Osmonde, she inwardly acknowledges his power to compel her response. "She did not think this as a romantic girl would have thought it; it was revealed to her [...] by a shock like terror. Here was a man who was of her own build, whose thews and sinews of mind and body were as powerful as her own" (200). The grammatical passive construction of "it was revealed" conveys the force by which Clorinda's recognition of Osmonde as her mirroring other moves her to see him as the only thing that can complete her sense of self and confirm her purpose for being in the world. He, like she, has "thews and sinews" that knit together body and mind into a powerful whole, their individual strengths enhanced in the unity of their relation. It is as if they are the couple Tennyson prophesied at the end of *In Memoriam*, "a closer link/ Betwixt us and the crowning race" ("Epilogue," ll. 127–28), the final stage up on the evolutionary scale. But Oxon, thwarted in his own marriage ambitions, renews his pursuit of Clorinda, who is no longer poor and even more beautiful than ever. He wants to complete a romance narrative that Clorinda wants no part of, and in his insistence, he becomes part of a larger narrative of justice.

Oxon's frame of mind is captured in the following passage:

> There had been a time when without this woman's beauty he might have lived—indeed he had left it of his own free, vicious will; but in these days when his fortunes had changed and she represented all that he stood in most desperate need of, her beauty drove him mad. In his haunting of her, as he followed her from place to place, his passion grew day by day, and all the more gained strength and fierceness because it was so mixed with hate. (208)

Today we would call Oxon a classic stalker, obsessed, driven by hate that he deludes himself into thinking is love. Obsessed with their youthful tryst, at which time Clorinda had foolishly pledged her love for him, Oxon is frustrated by having lost the lock of hair he had cut from her, without her knowledge, as proof of her promise. Not being able directly to confront her, he pursues her, appears at odd and sundry times and places around her while she fluctuates between ignoring and defying him. Burnett figures their tension through Clorinda's breaking of a horse named Devil. "The great brute who dashed and plunged and pranced beneath her seemed to have sworn to conquer her as he [Oxon] had sworn himself." Oxon taunts her, saying, "You will not conquer him," to which Clorinda replies, "I will unless he kills me." Oxon then wishes that he himself could be the one to do that: "He will kill you," he says to her, before expressing this threatening wish, "I would were I in his shoes" (209). Clorinda, of course, "with the air of a great rough man" (211), tames the horse, bystanders crying in their excitement, "the beast gives way! [...] She has him!" Oxon is watching too, and when he sees Clorinda's success, he "turned pale as death" (210). Metaphorically, then, their struggle ends with Clorinda ascendant and Oxon in fear. Doubly galling to Oxon is the appearance of Osmonde, who when he is together with Clorinda the onlookers perceive that "their love shone like the light of day itself through poor conventions" (215). In the background, then, of the extended conflict between Oxon and Clorinda, with Oxon playing the villain in a narrative of lust and revenge, is the shimmering fact of the love of the soon to be mated couple to whom Oxon's "romance" "counted for naught" (215).

Just as the battle between Clorinda and the horse Devil is resolved in her triumph, so her conflict with Oxon, who does find the missing lock of hair, ends with absolute certainty. Following her more persistently and pressing her harder, Oxon succeeds in convincing Clorinda to let him escort her home to "speak to [her] in private" (233). There Oxon reminds her of her girlhood promise as he dangles the lock of hair before her. He threatens to tell all to Osmonde, and as he recounts the tale he adds his own inflection to it, making it the old story of sexual intrigue and betrayal:

> I will tell him all the story of the rose garden and the sundial, and the beauty who had wit enough to scorn a man in public that she might more safely hold tryst with him alone. She had great wit and cunning for a beauty of sixteen. 'Twould be well for her lord to have keen eyes when she is twenty. (240)

Unlike what he had done earlier, when he assumed that Clorinda would react to seeing him again with shame, he interprets Clorinda's experience for her overtly as shameful, drawing an analogy between his mind and hers in an effort to reduce her to his level of baseness. But as Clorinda had done earlier, she refuses to play her part. Rather than defiance, however, she tells him a truth that he does not fully understand: "'All that you can say I know,' she said; 'all that you can say. And I love him. There is no other man on earth. Were he a beggar I would tramp the high road by his side and go hungered with him. He is my lord and I his mate—his mate!'" (240). That which Oxon hears is a declaration of love for the other man; what Clorinda means is a declaration of her most profound attachment to the other as her mate, the one with whom she best realizes the fullness of her own being, as he does with her, in a relationship that defies convention. As destined mates they need no external confirmation. Their story cannot be plugged into any other narrative. While she understands fully the drift of Oxon's tale, for her it defies sense. Oxon cannot see all that, but he does understand her claim of equality between herself and Osmonde. So he extends his fallen woman story: "'He is a high and noble gentleman, and wants no man's cast-off plaything for his wife" (240). Clorinda, then, the narrator observes, "breathed" rather than spoke these words in response: "'And once [...]—and once—I loved thee—cur!'" (241). Oxon's reaction draws the tale he is telling to its most tawdry conclusion: "'Loved me!' he said. 'Thou! As thou lovest me—and as thou lovest him—so will Moll Easy love any man—for a crown!'" (241). What an elegant way to say, "you whore!"

Throughout the narrative Burnett has emphasized the integrity of Clorinda's body, so the mere fact that she had a single sexual experience in her youth does not change what her body can do and what it means for her. That coupled with Osmonde's knowledge of the fact of her first marriage and widowhood, with the sexual knowledge that entails, suggests that for him Clorinda's value is not tied to an idea of female purity, which ultimately serves the power of patriarchy. Oxon then is exploiting the social conventions of the marriage market and the moral conventions that enable male control of female bodies to disrupt a development toward human freedom and integrity, both things that Clorinda and Osmonde by their very nature resist. Feeling Oxon's insult and threats (recall his wish to kill her) in her body, a feeling that had been built up over weeks, months, even years as Oxon dogged Clorinda's steps, she responds to his words with action: "Her whip lay upon the table, she caught and whirled it in the air. She was blind with the surging of her blood and saw not how she caught or held it, or what she did—only that she struck!" (241). At that moment, Clorinda asserts ultimate mastery over him as Oxon lies dead at her feet. Her blood cooling, Clorinda, with "the look of a creature who, being tortured, the worst at last being reached, begins to smile at fate" (244). That observation is far more complex than it first appears, for the worst being reached for a torture victim would be that victim's death. But here the worst is the death of the perpetrator. Were his death known, he would go from perpetrator to victim; Clorinda, the stalked, threatened and cornered woman would be judged as guilty.[16] The obvious question that situation raises is what to call Clorinda's action: self-defense, murder, accident, chance, justice? The remainder of the novel struggles with that question, suggesting an answer we might say is all of the above—except murder.

The general narrative strategy after the novel recounts Oxon's death is to contrast what the rest of his life might look like in its relations to other people's lives (particularly young women's) and the life Clorinda subsequently leads. The contrast is made most clearly in Clorinda's efforts to restore the many young girls (mainly from country villages) who were ruined by Oxon. Her life of good deeds, centered on redressing his sins, functions as a way to make the case that the practical result of active goodness in the world overrides an act of killing in self-defense, or even one that is anything less than unambiguous, premeditated murder. There remains, however, something intractable about the killing that neither Clorinda's redemptive actions nor her heroic maternity (she bears six strapping children worthy of the virtues of her husband) can quite remove. We see that most clearly in the last conversation between Clorinda and her sister Anne toward the end of the novel. Anne, it seems, has for years assumed that Clorinda had murdered Oxon; she knew, for instance, where the body was hidden. "It has done me to death, this knowledge," Anne says, "and before I die I pray you tell me" (353). Clorinda seems taken aback by the idea that Anne thought that she (Clorinda) had murdered Oxon, so she explains:

> "I think 'twas God himself who did it," she said, "though 'twas I who struck the blow. He drove me mad and blind, he tortured me and thrust to my heart's core. He taunted me with that vile thing nature will not let women bear, and did it in my Gerald's name, calling on him. And then I struck with my whip, knowing nothing, not seeing, only striking like a goaded, dying thing. He fell—he fell and lay there—and all was done." (354–55)

While everything she says squares with the novel's presentation of the history leading up to the event, the grating element in her explanation is its beginning, "I think 'twas God himself who did it." That assertion sounds less like explanation or even justification than it does blame, as if Clorinda and Oxon were puppets and God the puppet master, a kind of reinstatement of the justification for patriarchy. But it is also possible that the concept of God stands in for the concept of justice.

Clorinda's explanation also puts pressure on the logic of the imperatives of the freedom of her own being and her right not to be oppressed by the man, Oxon, whose behavior maps most closely on her father's (who himself had hoped for Oxon's success). Within the symbolic logic of the novel (what I have called its allegory), Oxon and Clorinda's father represent the worst aspects of a patriarchy that defines itself through its social structures that enforce and its narrative conventions that naturalize women's subordination. Osmonde exists outside of that version of patriarchy since his full humanness is judged as complete only in relation to his union with Clorinda, his mate. So while the reference to a God who did it would nullify Zangwill's reading of Clorinda as "Tess triumphant," the last words of the novel reinstate that reading with Clorinda and her mate Gerald rendered as evolutionary harbingers of a future freedom from the oppressions of patriarchy, whose rationale depends upon social structures animated by ego, physical force and the lust for power. "'Here sleeps by her husband the purest and noblest lady God e'er loved, yet the high and gentle deeds of her chaste, sweet life sleep not, but live and grow, and so will do so long as earth is earth" (363). As Tess had done in Hardy's great novel, Clorinda lived and died a pure woman, a "chaste" life not being dependent on her body being throughout life untouched. But unlike Tess, who could not escape the patriarchal imperative that the woman must pay, Clorinda lives out her life as part of the evolutionary development that depends on the attunement of human being and the natural world. In her epitaph, God and evolution are not in tension; evolution is the means by which Clorinda, Osmonde and their children live out God's blessing. For Burnett, in contrast to Tennyson's searing question in *In Memoriam*—"Are God and Nature then at strife?" (55, l. 5)—God provides the energy that animates the human body and all that grows on the earth. Morality is the natural result of the body's and mind's attunement to those energies, which by their very nature foster health and growth. In that way she effaces the notion of God as father, and thus as authorizer of patriarchy, and through her novel she presents a narrative of the natural justice of human equality with women and men living out the same moral imperatives for human health, growth and fulfillment through reciprocity.

IV

His Grace of Osmonde (1897) serves as an experiment in point of view, the incidents in that novel being identical to those in *A Lady of Quality* but rendered throughout from the perspective of Osmonde. Although some reviewers found such a retelling original, it is not unprecedented; the repetition of the same story from multiple characters in Robert Browning's *The Ring and the Book* (1868–69), the piecing together of a single narrative from multiple sources in Wilkie Collins's *The Woman in White* (1859) and the competing points of view in Charles Dickens's *Bleak House* (1853), for instance, suggest such experimentation was widespread in the nineteenth century. Nonetheless George Preston in *The Bookman* begins his review of the novel by proclaiming that "In giving a second version of this amazing tale [*A Lady of Quality*], Mrs. Burnett has done a daring thing," before he concludes that "after all, nothing vital seems to have come from this hearing of the man's side of the story of which the woman's side has already been told."[17] Most other reviews reflect a similar disappointment, one noting rather concisely that Burnett "has forgotten the existence of Realism."[18] Realism, however, as my reading of *A Lady of Quality* amply demonstrates, is not the mode Burnett was working in despite her emphasis on the historical in both novels. Burnett evokes an England in the late seventeenth and early eighteenth centuries through forms of language and details of reference to dress, attitudes and customs, in order to create a space distanced from her present historical moment, where she can experiment with thinking differently about gender relationships under a patriarchal social system. That difference concerns conceptualizing a woman as physically strong and adept at activities gendered masculine (such as hunting, cursing, drinking, fighting and general assertions of will) as even the most masculine of men, and it means conceptualizing a man who embodies masculine qualities of physical strength and self-control in addition to qualities of deference, sensitivity and self-denial for the sake of others, qualities associated with that figure gendered most feminine, the angel in the house. The point of such a thought experiment seems to me to create a collision between the social, moral and legal conventions of a patriarchal culture and a morality of individual growth. That growth is tied to the idea of a healthy, strong body as a vehicle for the expression of a higher morality, whose roots and fundamental energies are enmeshed in the natural world. History, in Burnett's two historical novels, becomes a kind of dreamscape, opening a space to project desire as myth.

His Grace of Osmonde replicates and expands Burnett's thought experiment, linking her myth of equality between female and male bodies to contemporary concerns about social degeneration and the responsibility of women to redress that concern. That linkage helps account for her emphasis on mating as opposed to mere marriage, and on the role Clorinda and Osmonde play in rejuvenating local lands and defending the nation abroad. In the midst of nearly universal negative reviews of *His Grace*, something of what I am pointing to here emerges into visibility. The reviewer for *The Academy Fiction Supplement*, who complained about her forgetfulness of realism, praises the beauty of her conception of Osmonde:

> [T]he unaided workings of enthusiasm have produced in his Grace of Osmonde a figure of undeniable beauty. We have so much conscious art now-a-days, so much realistic prying and anatomizing, that the sight of something purely ideal and warm from the heart is moving and delightful. All Mrs. Burnett's literary sins may be all but forgiven, for the really fine conception which accompanies them. And yet the pity of it that her ideal man and woman are not more lifelike! His Grace [...] is so pleasing a figure that it is a shame to find fault. His picture should certainly be acquired by readers, to be placed side by side with that of his wife, a lady of quality. (123)

The rejection of "conscious art" gestures toward the mythic feel of Burnett's conception of the human body, a notion akin to William Blake's celebration of "the human form divine" in his poem "The Divine Image." The suggestion that Osmonde's portrait should be placed side by side with Clorinda's renders their physical form aesthetic images that might echo the shimmering, energetic bodies in Blake's illuminated poems. Taken together the conceptual and the physical image become one, the body representing a change of consciousness.

Such a change, at least for Osmonde, is presented as possible in an otherwise damning review of the novel in *The Chap Book*. Condemning the character Osmonde as an adult "prig" on the model of Fauntleroy, the reviewer speculates about what Burnett could have done in the novel.

> If Mrs. Burnett had cared to attempt it, there is indeed a really interesting story to be written about a certain type of modern man who has arisen alongside of the modernest [sic] woman. The man has more than old-time chivalrous devotion to woman, is violently respectful of her, and hopes to keep himself more or less pure for her sake. The love of such a man for a woman who lets herself go, who takes to herself all the privileges and all the cheapnesses [sic] of modernity, and who in many ways seems endeavoring to arrive at the point from which the modern man departed, is an admirably humorous and novel theme. The meeting of Lord Fauntleroy, no longer little, and Beth perhaps, fresh from her Book, is what Mrs. Burnett could have done, and what she has failed to do.[19]

Surely the reviewer must have recognized elements of what Burnett did, in fact, do in *His Grace of Osmonde* in order to come up with his explanation of what he claims she failed to do. For instance, Osmonde does "keep himself more or less pure" for Clorinda's sake while Clorinda in her youthful masculine exuberance seems to aspire for what Osmonde transcends. But the review assumes an attitude of realism while at the same time essentializing women, who, the review suggests, in claiming privilege to occupy space in the socially constructed male sphere must "let herself go," be cheapened by modern life and therefore must be in need of being put back into her place (the woman's sphere) by the masterful man. Unable to imagine the artificiality of the gendered separate spheres, the review manages nonetheless to capture a small part of Burnett's effort to efface those spheres, and by linking Burnett's novel to Sarah Grand's *The Beth Book*, he inadvertently captures Burnett's engagement with issues central to the new woman novelists.

Toward the end of *The Beth Book*, as Beth reflects on her life in London, the narrator alludes to an experience similar to John Oxon's stalking of Clorinda and draws a broad conclusion from the fact that there is redress for the woman:

> She occasionally experienced the sickening sensation of being followed about by one of those specimens of mankind so significantly called "sly dogs" by their fellow-men. They made themselves particularly objectionable in Kensington Gardens and Hyde Park; but she found that an appeal to a policeman or a Park-keeper, or to any decent workman, was enough to stop the nuisance. Genuine respect for women, which is an antidote to the moral rottenness that promotes the decay of nations, and portends the indefinite prolongation of the life of the race, is of slow growth, but it is steadily increasing among the English-speaking peoples. (494)

Like the last paragraph of *A Lady of Quality*, this passage from *The Beth Book* presents an evolutionary hope, but instead of the mythic resonance of Burnett's novel, Grand emphasizes small, practical steps that combine social organization (police and park-keepers) and individual rectitude (decent workmen). Instead of a gradual emergence of higher human beings where biological sex determines nothing in advance, Grand imagines slow changes in social arrangements where "genuine respect for women" becomes not only the moral ground upon which society rebuilds itself but also the antidote to moral and physical degeneration of "the race," that is, humankind. Burnett's vision is not bureaucratic and more comprehensive. She is less interested in thinking about respect for women as a purely practical matter and more interested in reimagining male and female relationships as human rather than gendered, and she founds her hope for the future "of the race" in how appropriate mating functions as a vehicle through which nature improves the human lot. She celebrates, then, both biological sex and the cultivation of the land, healthy versions of both being essential for the well-being of individuals and of the nation. That is the animating vision in her transatlantic novels, but its contours are visible in *His Grace of Osmonde*.

Osmonde's thinking about the relations between the sexes is stimulated when he learns about the lot of Clorinda's mother. He wonders why it is "that women who had not the happy fortune of his mother seemed at so cruel a disadvantage—that men who were big and handsome having won them, grew tired of them and cast them aside, with no care for their loneliness or pain?" That thought registers two things: the role of sheer chance in a woman's lot and the centrality violence (or its potential) based on brute, masculine physical strength has as an instrument of chance. His next thought confronts the contradiction between notions of supernatural agency and individual responsibility. "Why had God so made them that they seemed helpless as poor driven sheep? 'Twas not fair it should be so—he could not feel it honest, though he was beset by grave fears at his own contumacy since he had been taught that God ordained all things." Osmonde admits much in that thought: he questions God's fairness and honesty on the one hand before tacitly acknowledging his own culpability in perpetrating a divine justification for what is nothing less than the abuse of women. But he hedges a bit, claiming that he "had been taught" those things, so he need not believe them. In that context, his next question becomes more rhetorical than real: "Had he [God, note the lower case of the pronoun] ordained this, that men should be tyrants, and base, and cruel, and that women should be feeble victims who had but the power to moan and die and be forgotten?" (41). Buried in that question is the statement that nothing has of necessity predetermined male tyranny or female victimhood. As human actions sustained by a patriarchal social order, they can be changed by redefining sexual relations on a biological model tied to an evolutionary view of nature. For Osmonde such a change begins with himself.

Once he has formed a nonoppressive ideal in his mind about the relations between the sexes, Osmonde determines that the way the male self is gendered in his culture needs to be overcome, for that self is built from ego and a will to power, particularly power over women. He thus sets himself "to be stronger than [his] very self, so that naught can betray me—no passion I am tormented by, no anger I would conceal, no lure I would resist. 'Tis a man's self who oftenest entraps him. The traitor once subdued, life lies at one's feet" (70). To be stronger than himself is to be stronger than the cultural definition of the masculine self, which, when it acts out of unreciprocated passion, or anger, or relentlessly pursues a base end, is admired for showing strength and ambition. His effort, then, is to imagine a self, free from social determinations. By extension, for that self to find a mate, there too social determinations must not be in play. Consequently, Osmonde reflects, "'Tis sure nature makes one man for one woman, one woman for one man—as it was in the garden when our first parents loved" (72). The Garden of Eden trope may be overused, but in this case it is framed within a discourse of nature, and it functions to mark a presocial space, outside of the history of patriarchal culture. Because the garden image comes from the *Bible* there is more than a little irony that Burnett uses it in that way; however, that use is consonant with her effort to replace an asymmetrical view of sexual relations to one of reciprocity (which should not be confused with the hierarchical notion of complementarity). She may not be able to change a patriarchal vocabulary, but she can inflect the words differently.

She can also inflect gender markers differently, as she did in *A Lady of Quality* when she rendered the erotic energies generated by Clorinda in male garb standing next to Oxon just before her birthday transfiguration. In this latter novel Burnett evokes similar energies. As Osmonde listens to his uncle, Lord Dunstanwolde, tell the story of Clorinda's childhood, Dunstanwolde says that "The blood of the fierce devils who were chiefs of her house centuries ago woke in her veins at her birth. 'Tis strange indeed, Gerald, how such things break forth—or slumber—in a race" (88). Dunstanwolde then waxes eloquent about how "splendid" were Clorinda's ancestral devils, who could laugh at death and "endure in silence horrors almost supernatural" (89). Osmonde's inward response to the story is to think that "[A] girl child of twelve rollicking in boy's clothes was not a pleasing picture [...] and certainly not such as should set a man's heart beating and his cheek to flame when he heard stories of her fantastic life and character." That thought registers, as if he were a reader of an erotic tale, his bodily response to the idea of such a human being, his racing heart, his flushed face. He perplexes himself in the moment; he "frankly felt himself restless and ill at ease" (89). To ameliorate his perplexity, his mind turns to the most conventional of patriarchal thoughts: "'Twould have been safer for her to have died beneath her dead mother's body," Osmonde comments to Dunstable, "almost fiercely." "Yes, safer," Dunstanwolde replies, "Yet what a woman!—What a woman!" With those words, the novel notes, "he broke off speech" (91). That collision, between conventional language of gender and the defiant physical fact of Clorinda's being, neutralizes the power of language. A human figure that embodies a deep history of family endurance, who is a woman in male attire superior in male attributes to the bawdy coterie of men that surround her and who also decenters the moral certainties and unsettles the erotic energies of a young man in line to be the patriarch of his family and a representative of his nation, is not better off dead. In the end, her life gives meaning and takes meaning through her reciprocal bond with that young man who moves from wishing she had died to declaring, "A barbaric fantasy that a woman needs a master. She who is strong enough is her own conqueror—as a man should be master of himself" (164–65). In that formulation there can be no mastery of the other; the only true mastery is of the self, which in terms of this novel is by definition false, for that self is a social fabrication.

Burnett's conceptual ambitions in her second historical novel *His Grace of Osmonde* are often in excess to what her prose can carry out. That excess can be felt most forcefully in her effort to refigure the moral discourse around Clorinda's killing of John Oxon.

In the description of the killing in *A Lady of Quality* it is clear, as we have seen, that Clorinda strikes after intense provocation and, arguably, actuated by simple self-defense. Were Osmonde, for instance, to have walked in during the confrontation, intervened and struck Oxon, killing him, a strong case could be made that he did so to protect Clorinda. There would be neither legal nor moral jeopardy. When a woman defends herself, the moral calculus is different. Within the symbolic logic of both novels, however, Oxon is aligned with the forces of degeneracy and corruption while Clorinda is aligned with the forces of life. Oxon is by any measure an abuser of women. He impregnated many, one of whom kills her child at birth and is later hanged for infanticide and another of whom dies in childbirth along with her stillborn child. Clorinda makes it her task to find as many of his victims as she can in order to stabilize their lives and give them a future. So strictly in terms of the most clear-eyed moral calculus, condemning Clorinda for killing Oxon is unjust. The novel's language makes it emotionally difficult to accept that conclusion, though, and the question that raises is whether the difficulty is a failure of art or a marker of how conventional moral discourse that tends to function in absolute terms—something is either right or wrong—retains its power over readers. It is a bit of both. Consider this explanation for the killing given in the last pages of *His Grace*:

> One frantic, unthinking blow struck in terror and madness had ended him and all his evil doing, but left her standing frenzied at the awfulness of the thing which had fallen upon her soul in her first hour of Heaven. And all her being had risen in revolt at this most monstrous woe of chance, and in her torture she cried out that in that hour she would not be struck down. (462–63)

Acting out of "terror and madness" she strikes down an evil man, an awful act that taints her anticipation of happiness in her upcoming marriage to Osmonde, her "first hour of Heaven." The killing in the next sentence becomes a function of "chance," and her first response to that notion is that she would not allow chance to do the same to her. The "awfulness," then, that readers may attribute to the act of killing itself, does not necessarily refer to that but to the prospect of the killing impinging on her happiness. That tension is enhanced by the conflation of Christian discourse in the reference to "Heaven" and the agency of chance. What produces the discomfort may be the simple fact that the killing is not acknowledged for what it is, a killing performed by one human being on another either under the canopy (or figurative eyes) of heaven or through the agency of chance. The result, in terms of the discourse, is to produce moral confusion. Clorinda's own explanation does little to mitigate that confusion: "Of ending his base life I had never a thought," Clorinda cries in her explanation to Osmonde, "though I had thought to end my own. But when Fate struck the blow for me, I swore the carrion should not taint my whole life through" (463). There is a similar tension in her words: Oxon's baseness created the conditions for the act; her impulse to kill herself captures her recognition that despite the provocation, she had, herself, struck the blow; the rationalization sets in with "Fate struck the blow for me." After one more moral jab at Oxon, "the carrion," Clorinda ends with the defensible notion that under the circumstances his death was just. Her thinking when all the facts of the case are considered seems right, but as we read, it feels wrong. That tension captures the duality that Clorinda felt within herself, a discomfort that actuated her acts of redress toward Oxon's victims. In that light, justice is not an absolute resolution that emerges in a moment of clarity; it is an imperative that stimulates moral action. Justice itself may be said then to recede, as each moral action begets another. Justice functions as an actuating principle rather than a condition of judgment.

When Osmonde learns the truth about Oxon's death, "he could look upon it with just, unflinching eyes" because he knows "'tis in *myself* to have struck the blow [...] [and] to have hid [the body] as she has done; for naught would have torn her from me!" (464). His words echo Clorinda's at the time of the killing. What compels both is their relationship and how that relationship can be the lifeblood for a rejuvenated community. Zangwill's judgment of the "Nietzsche-like individuality" of Clorinda needs some modification, for she does not, like Nietzsche's superman, rise above human morality in her drive to realize the fullness of her strength; she realizes her strength through another in a relation of reciprocity, which functions as a bonding energy for the five villages that compose Osmonde's estate and for "the miserable, long-neglected village of Wildairs." That village is described as follows:

> Falling walls, rotting thatches, dirt and wretchedness were to be seen on all sides; cottages were broken-paned and noisome, men and women who should have been hale were drawn with rheumatism from mouldering dampness, or sodden with drink and idleness; children who should have been rosy and clean and studying their horn books, at the dame school, were little, dirty, evil, brutal things. (328)

Although the novel does not go on to detail how the cottages were repaired, the villagers finding employment (presumably by participating in the repairs), the school reformed, and the men, women and children returned to health, it does emphasize that the changes depend upon Clorinda engaging with the villagers "as if they were human beings like herself" (329). The implication is that in her treating the villagers like human beings, they become human beings; the project of revitalization thus becomes a community project. Such projects are central in Burnett's subsequent novels as she details how the economic, architectural, agricultural and interpersonal aspects of community renewal can be fueled by the love between two individuals. The general narrative pattern where romance is defined in terms of physical mutuality and psychic attunement as the anchoring point around which communities are revitalized, and where a human future is fed by cycles of reciprocity, comes into visibility in Burnett's historical novels. In her country house and transatlantic novels that pattern becomes more pronounced, the romance subordinated to the work of rebuilding community in the face of violence and abuse. Although the word was not in popular use at the time, we can say that Burnett's interests become more ecological in the last third of her career. That certainly is the case in her most well-known and widely respected children's novel *The Secret Garden*, the seeds of which were planted in her strange and anomalous novel *In Connection with the De Willoughby Claim*.

V

Burnett began writing *In Connection to the De Willoughby Claim* in 1880, the same year she published *Louisiana* and two years before *Through One Administration*, but it was not finished until 1899. The vicissitudes of the manuscript, which Gerzina characterizes as having "been limping along for some twenty years" (212) and that Thwaite quotes Burnett herself as calling "the fiend" (74), are documented in their respective biographies. Given the uneven history of its composition, it should not be surprising that the novel in the end seems a pastiche of past work and an anticipation of future work. The reviewer for *The Hartford Courant* has this to say about the novel's setting: "The scene of the story is partly in the South, partly in New England, and partly in Washington; the scheme lends itself to a variety of description that is attractive, though there is no question that the pictures of Southern life are the best."[20] That description captures the transitional quality of the work, its southern material looking back to *Louisiana*, its Washington material anticipating *Through One Administration*, and its New England material turning out to be, for her future work, a dead end. The *Chicago Daily Tribune* reviewer captures the pieced-together-feel of the novel deftly: "If Frances Hodgson Burnett had been able to maintain the delightful success of the first eleven chapters of her new novel, the story would have been a masterpiece. Unhappily, there is a distinct break at this point, and what follows in apparently written in another mood."[21] It is fair to say that the moods clash as the novel shifts from setting to setting, but in the quality of the relationship between Tom De Willoughby and his informally adopted illegitimate daughter Sheba, there is an integrity of conception that softens the novel's architectural flaws.

Tom De Willoughby is six feet five inches tall and fat. The son of a judge in eastern Tennessee, De Willoughby fails to complete his training to be a doctor and is rejected by the woman who subsequently marries his handsome and more accomplished brother. He flees to western Carolina where he opens a general store and runs the post office in an isolated, mountain town. No one there knows his antecedents. When a man and a pregnant woman from the outside take refuge in an abandoned house outside the town, De Willoughby helps deliver the child; the woman dies and the man runs off, leaving the baby behind. Once Burnett establishes that situation, she captures with fine precision the emotional quality of Tom's determination to take the child in care. A local woman, whom he had asked to help him get the things required to care for a newborn, gives him a book entitled *Advice to Young Mothers*. He records having received the book in his "memorandum-book." Here is Burnett's rendering of the scene:

> Then he made as he stood up before the looking-glass and in the flickering light of the candle, an entry which was as follows: "Advice to Young Mothers, Brough and Bros." He made it with a grave countenance and a business-like manner, and somehow, owing it may be to the small size of the room, its low ceilings and many shadows, or the flickering of the candle, his colossal height and breadth of body and tremendous look of strength had never seemed so marked nor appeared so to overpower the objects surrounding him. (85)

One way to read that paragraph is to emphasize the contrast between the title of the book and the description of the massive male figure who is preparing to read it, with an emphasis on the humor generated by the incongruity. Another is to note his "grave" and "business-like" determination to take the book seriously, his masculine strength preparing to serve the requirements of being a "young mother." Burnett encourages the latter reading, having De Willoughby remark: "If a man ain't a young mother […] I guess he can get the good of it, if he gives himself time. And what she [the child] wants [...] is to get as good a start as if she had a young mother." We can see in this sequence Burnett's critique of gender that began with the physical strength of Joan in *That Lass O'Lowries* and extended to the powerful physical versatility of Clorinda. Here gender is bent the other way, the powerful male having to subdue his body and teach it tenderness, making tenderness rather than force his second nature: "And he sat down and pulled off his right boot in so absorbed a frame of mind, that he aroused presently with a start to find that he was holding it as if it had been made of much less tough material and required handling tenderly" (85). Rather than the woman figuratively becoming the man, the man figuratively can become the woman, and both can become the mother.

Reading that moment as an element in Burnett's unsettling of conventional gender constructions emphasizes De Willoughby's individuality. If we read the moment ecologically, however, we can begin to track how Burnett works to embed human relationships as a part of the complex, organic and dynamic web of nature. That is, to provide a fuller human meaning to Tom's life, the novel not only traces his individual growth through his relationship with Sheba, it places that relationship within a narrative framed by intergenerational relationships. Those relationships are not only essential for the happiness of individuals, the novel shows, they provide the means by which human energies converge with the juices of renewal that animate nature because reciprocal, human relations are part of an ecological whole. This point is implied, of course, by Tom's and Sheba's relation, which is itself intergenerational. Nonetheless, their relationship is oddly cut off; it is not connected to the larger ecology that provides order, joy and growth. Consider in that regard how Tom is cut off from his family, living in exile as it were, and how Sheba is also in exile, her mother dead and her father having refused to acknowledge her. Through the following three passages, we can trace how the novel ends their exile, embedding them within the ecological web from which Tom acknowledges he had been excluded.

> "There must be happiness on earth somewhere," [Tom] would say. "Somewhere there ought to have been a woman I belonged to, and who belonged to me. It ought all to have been as much nature as the rain falling and the corn ripening in the sun. If we had met when we were young things—on the very brink of it all—and smiled into each other's eyes and taken each other's hands, and kissed each other's lips, we might have ripened together like corn. "What is it that's gone wrong?" All the warm normal affections of manhood, which might have remained undeveloped and been cast away, had been lavished on the child Sheba. (257)

Tom figures his happiness not just in terms of finding his female counterpart, what we can think of as an analogous though less superlative mating as that between Clorinda and Osmonde, he figures his desire for such happiness as a part of the elements that animate the earth, the vivifying moisture of rain and the slow processes of the growth of grain; the latter of which he equates with reciprocated bodily contact in the repetition of the words "each other's" tied to eyes, hands and lips. Without such reciprocity, he cannot develop as a human being, and even though the child Sheba provides what the narrator calls "his domestic circle," it is impossible for her to compensate fully for what has "gone wrong." While there is an element of humor and charm when Tom tells Sheba that she is "a pretty numerous young person," because she stands in for "a man's wife and family, and mother and sisters, and at least half a dozen boys and girls" (257–58), that humor masks a burden impossible for any child to bear. Consequently, the novel shows how Sheba has to begin to form her own patterns of reciprocity, first with the earth represented metaphorically as a garden, then with her male counterpart and finally with her biological mother.

> It was a heavenly, warm spring morning, and Sheba [...] wandered into the garden to wait [for Tom] among the flowers. The rapturous first scents of the year were there, drawn by the sun and blown by vagrant puffs of wind from hyacinths and jonquils, white narcissus and blue violets. Sheba walked among the beds, every few minutes kneeling down upon the grass to bury her face in pink and yellow and white clusters, inhaling the breath of flowers and the pungent freshness of the sweet brown earth at the same time. She had lived among leaves and growing things until she felt herself in some unexplainable way a part of the world they belonged to [...]. The birds were singing and nest-building this morning, and, as she hung over a bed of purple and white hyacinths, kneeling on the grass and getting as close to them as she could, their perfume mounted to her brain and she began to kiss them. (247)

I have quoted that passage at some length to capture how the lushness of Burnett's language performs Sheba's immersion in the elements and energies of the garden, the reciprocity contained in the phrase "inhaling the breath of flowers," which attributes the flowers' ability to exhale the breath that Sheba inhales, capturing the essence of the moment. It is a scene of quasi-sexual congress without a hint of cupidity, filled with rapture, perfumes, touching and kisses that provide Sheba with an inchoate sense of her place within an ecological system, but to complete her sense of ecological wholeness, of deep and resonant attunement with her natural, human environment, she needs her own mate to appear, who does in the figure of the young Rupert De Willoughby, Tom's orphaned nephew.

Rupert, orphaned by events related to the Civil War, enters the narrative in search of his uncle. On the night he arrives at De Willoughby's house, he first sees Sheba, narcissus in her hair, standing on a small balcony outside her window. She sees him too. "They stood and looked at each other quite simply, as if they did not know they were strangers. A young dryad and faun meeting on a hilltop or in a forest's depths by moonlight might have looked at each other with just such clear, unstartled eyes, and with just such pleasure in each other's beauty" (253). Clearly each has found the one and only mate, a fact the narrator signals but that they at the moment do not quite recognize. As it happens Rupert is there to enlist his uncle's help to make a claim in Washington for his family's lands, which had been confiscated by the government during the war. Tom agrees to help, and the narrative recounts their efforts to procure a hearing for their claim. Hardship ensues, Sheba is alienated from the garden that had provided such deeply felt though inarticulate meaning as she grew to maturity and Rupert has to learn something of the ecological wisdom Sheba had experienced before the narrative reaches its end.

After the resolution of their claim in Washington, Tom, Sheba and Rupert return to North Carolina, having while in Washington discovered the truth of the circumstances of Sheba's birth and the identity of her mother. That night Tom sits on his front porch and reflects on his past: "There had been nights like this in the days when he had been a big, clumsy young fellow, wild with hopeless love for Delia Vanuxem" (443), the woman who had rejected him and married his brother. He glances toward the garden and sees Sheba and Rupert, now newly married. "They're pretty safe" (444), Tom says, before the narrator captures the scene.

> Rupert and Sheba walked slowly side by side. They saw and felt everything. If a bird stirred with a sleepy sound, they stopped to listen and smiled tremulously at each other. More than once Sheba knelt down and hid her face among the flowers, kissing them. Her arms were full of white blossoms. She and Rupert had made white garlands for her hair and waist, such as she had worn the night he had first seen her standing on her little balcony. When Rupert held her to his side, the scent from their crushed petals filled the air they breathed. The early night was at its stillest and fairest, and the moonlight seemed to flood all the world. (444)

Sheba is no longer waiting for Tom as she had in the earlier garden scene; she is with her mate, who seems to complete the ecological system, adding that element of human reciprocity to the inter-animation between the garden and Sheba in a dream of prelapsarian wholeness, the scent of the flowers and the breath of the woman and man mingling in the still, night air. The flowers are no longer named, their distinctness absorbed within the symbolism of a marriage that marks the unity of human being and nature. In this idyllic picture, there is one piece missing: the human link to past generations, which will metaphorically transform the ecological system as closed, functioning only for exceptional souls in fleeting moments of harmony to an open system that can be disrupted and destabilized before being reset and renewed.

"They had planned weeks ago," the narrator explains, "the things they were going to do. They were going to say good-night to the small mound at Blair's Hollow" (444). The small mound is Sheba's mother's grave, the woman who had died in despair, cut off from family, alienated from social connections and out of tune with nature, her most natural function of giving birth having been judged as unnatural, a sin, a symbol of disharmony and defective morals. She thus had to be cut off from the cycle of generations, if not perpetually despised then at least forgotten. In gentle defiance of all that, and to redress her mother's suffering by reconnecting her to family, nature and the movement of generations on the earth, Sheba "knelt down beside [her mother's grave] and began to lay her bridal blossoms on the grass-covered earth. Rupert stood and watched her. His heart beat with reverent, rapturous tremor. She looked like a young angel" (444). More forest nymph than Christian spirit, Sheba's action brings her mother into the moment of Sheba's full maturity, marked by the fusion of her sexual, moral and aesthetic energies; her body and Rupert's seem to tremor in tune as Sheba makes her final gesture to draw her mother back onto the earth and into the garden from which she was forced, enacting a pattern of life her mother had been denied. "She bent down and laid her cheek upon the grass; her arm was thrown out as if she clasped something to her girl's breast" (444–45). That something, figuratively, is her mother, upon whose breast she lays her head and whose form she encircles in her arm. With that gesture she, Rupert and her mother are all healed by being drawn back into harmony within themselves and within the world that made them. With Sheba's final words—the last words of the novel—"I am happy. Oh, do you hear [mother]? Do you hear?" (445), the ecosystem is complete.

VI

After the 20-year ordeal of *In Connection with the De Willoughby Claim*, Burnett completed her next novel somewhat faster. Written at the urging of Gilder for *The Century Magazine* and published simultaneously in *The Cornhill Magazine*, *The Making of a Marchioness* (1901) took "only ten days" to write (Gerzina 225). It appeared in three installments in June, July and August of 1901 before being published as a single volume by F. A. Stokes in New York and Smith, Elder in London (the publisher of *The Cornhill*). Soon thereafter she published a sequel called *The Methods of Lady Walderhurst* (1901) followed by both novels in a single volume called *Emily Fox-Seton* (Stokes, 1909) with illustrations by C. D. Williams. The venues of publication confirm Burnett's continued presence as a literary novelist, *The Cornhill* in particular linking her to Thackeray (the magazine's first editor), Gaskell, Anthony Trollope, Wilkie Collins, Thomas Hardy and Henry James, all of whom were published serially in that periodical. That connection is especially apt given the policy of Reginald John Smith, the editor of *The Cornhill* from 1898 to 1916, who, as Barbara Quinn Schmidt observed, produced a "safe reliable magazine" by looking back to the editorial practices of his father-in-law, George Smith, who founded the magazine in 1859.[22] But when one thinks about a sensation novelist such as Collins or a novelist of tragic modernism such as Hardy, for example, it is hard not to wonder what "safe and reliable" might mean. The mere fact of working within established genres does not in itself suggest caution, nor does an editorial policy that models itself on the magazine's early successes. As Burnett had done when she drew on Elizabeth Gaskell as a model to establish her career, she worked within established genres but varied details of characterization and narrative tropes (such as the fallen women) in order to make those genres speak differently. So while the Emily Fox-Seton novels may glance back to older forms— *The Making of a Marchioness* seems a character sketch similar to Burnett's own *Louisiana* and *The Methods of Lady Walderhurst* is clearly a sensation novel with similarities to both Mary Elizabeth Braddon and Wilkie Collins[23]—the question is to what use she puts those forms, to what extent do they open up new ways of thinking about established narrative tropes or in what ways might such narrative tropes be made to speak with freshness and originality? A starting point for answers to those questions is contained in the subtitle to Julian Hawthorne's *Los Angeles Times* review of *The Methods of Lady Walderhurst*, from which I quoted in the introduction to this volume: "Frances Hodgson Burnett Creates a New Type in Fiction—and of a Woman, at That."[24] As I suggested earlier, that "new type" can be read as an old type, the woman as angel in the house; we can thus take Emily as the antithesis of Clorinda. To do so, however, would be to ignore what Burnett presents as Emily's essential strength, a strength defined by her positive lack of self-consciousness.

That lack of self-consciousness accounts, I believe, for the essential quality that leads the narrator to assert that Emily "was rather early Victorian" (98). Probably the most articulate (though overwrought) spokesman for what it means to be early Victorian is Thomas Carlyle, whose two essays "Signs of the Times" (1829) and "Characteristics"

(1831) are the lead entries in George Levine's anthology called *The Emergence of Victorian Consciousness* (1967).[25] Carlyle opens "Characteristics" with reference to the "Physician's Aphorism" that "the healthy know not of their health," which, he writes, "holds no less in moral, intellectual, political, poetical, than in merely corporeal therapeutics" (39). Later in the essay he addresses what he calls the moral power of conduct:

> The good man is he who works continually in well-doing; to whom well-doing is as his natural existence, awakening no astonishment, requiring no commentary; but there, like a thing of course, and as if it could not but be so. Self-contemplation, on the other hand, is infallibly the symptom of disease, be it or be it not the sign of cure: an unhealthy Virtue is one that consumes itself into leanness in repenting and anxiety; or, still worse, that inflates itself into dropsical boastfulness and vain glory; either way, it is a self-seeking; an unprofitable looking behind us to measure the way we have made: whereas the sole concern is to walk continually forward, and make more way. If in any sphere of Man's Life, then in the moral sphere, as the inmost and most vital of all, it is good that there be wholeness; that there be unconsciousness, which is the evidence of this. (44)

In Carlyle's formulation the good man or woman is revealed through moral conduct that by definition is not self-seeking since such conduct must perforce be unselfconscious. For any life to be whole, it must be moral, morality being for Carlyle equated with vitality, those energies that are most conducive to engendering life. I will return to this quotation at the end of my discussion of Emily Fox-Seton, but for now the passage serves to frame most accurately Burnett's central conception of Emily's character. Reinforcing Hawthorne's reading of Emily, the *New York Times* reviewer writes this: "Emily goes on being dearer, more unselfish, more tenderly considerate of everybody else to the end of the chapter; one of those rare beings dowered with unconsciousness of self […]. Her creator has nowhere shown higher art than in limning this portrait."[26] So even though the British reviews of the novels were less sympathetic, one reviewer for instance describing Emily as both "charmingly tactful" and "marvelously stupid,"[27] the American reviewers recognized the characterization of Emily as exemplary of Carlyle's healthy, whole man, whom Burnett presents as a belated though vital early Victorian woman during the last years of Queen Victoria's reign.

In order to explore the potential power of Carlyle's radical unconsciousness of self to be effective in the world, Burnett combines the trope of the odd, or redundant, woman with the genre of sensation, *The Making of a Marchioness* squarely informed by the former and *The Methods of Lady Walderhurst* decidedly energized by the latter.[28] The first novel of the pair focuses, as *Louisiana* had done, on the events that led up to the marriage of the heroine, but unlike Louisiana, who is an attractive only child on the brink of maturity, Emily Fox-Seton is in her thirties with a kind of beauty not immediately apparent on superficial observation. As the narrator explains:

> She was thirty-four and a well-set-up creature, with fine square shoulders and a long small waist and good hips. She was a big woman, but carried herself well […] her big eyes [had] a fresh look which made her seem rather like a nice overgrown girl than a mature woman whose life was a continuous struggle with the narrowest of mean fortunes. (14)

Although she began life in comfortable circumstances, her mother's annuity ended at her death, compelling Emily to hold a litany of "respectable" jobs; at 18 she worked as "an assistant teacher" before taking a job as a "nursery governess" and then as a "reading-companion to an unpleasant old woman in Northumberland" (16). That old woman left Emily a small sum in her will and the advice that she should make herself "useful to a lot of helpless creatures who will pay [her] a trifle for looking after them and the affairs they are too lazy or too foolish to manage for themselves" (17). With no father, no brother, no husband and no profession, Emily has no clear social place of her own, hence her redundancy. She is, to borrow the title of George Gissing's 1893 novel, one of *The Odd Women* or, as we might put it today, a member of the precariat, a kind of social nonentity in danger each day of falling into abject poverty. Burnett captures how Emily's social precariousness renders her empty in the eyes of others when she describes the moment of her departure from London to the village of Mallowe. On the platform "a tall man with a square face" looked "admiringly" at a fashionably dressed young girl as she entered a first-class carriage, but "[A]s he passed close to Emily, he stared through her head as if she had been transparent or invisible" (48). As it turns out both the girl and Emily are on their way to Mallowe Court, one of the Walderhurst estates, but when the footman sent to drive them to the estate pilots the girl to the carriage, he "merely touch[ed] his hat quickly to Emily, being fully aware that she could take care of herself," knowledge he gleaned, apparently, just by glancing at her (50).

The combination of invisibility, precariousness and an assumption of self-sufficiency clings to Emily's character throughout the narrative, as closely as her bodice does to her torso. Most of the novel is set in Mallowe Court, where Lady Maria, Lord Walderhurst's aunt and one of the women who employs Emily to do the things she is too lazy to do, has invited three women for an extended stay knowing that each hopes to win Walderhurst's hand. He, in his early fifties, is widowed and childless, in possession of magnificent family diamonds and "not only has three superb places, but has money enough to keep them up" (67). In contrast to the three women suitors, one a clever and well-read young widow, another a wealthy athletic American and the third a beautiful, ethereal English woman just of age and in love with someone else, Emily has no designs or stratagems. She is simply "a perfectly healthy woman, with a palate as unspoiled as that of a six-year-old child in the nursery. Her enjoyment of all things was so normal as to be in her day and time an absolute abnormality" (74). So as the novel unfolds, Emily remains in the background, always friendly and supportive of the three women, solicitous of their well-being without thinking about her own. Lady Maria describes Emily's behavior as pandering: "There is such comfort in being pandered to by a person who is not even aware that she is pandering. She doesn't suspect that she is entitled to thanks for it" (80). That observation, representative of others like it in the novel, captures something in the way Emily's actions are perceived by others rather than what her actions may actually mean. That is, if Emily does not perceive herself as pandering, which involves indulging questionable desires in others, to perceive her actions as such reveals more about Lady Maria than it does about Emily. The larger point that emerges from that distinction is that Emily's actions defy the social terms that others use to define them. It is as if her responses to others and her actions in the world are outside of social determinations; she acts always as one human being responding to another, her consciousness centered on the other person, never on herself, until, that is, she is forced to confront her own precarity.

Despite the material abundance and social rank of Emily's informal employers and acquaintances, Emily's resources are minimal, her home a bedsit in a working-class house in Mortimer Street, London, held by a Mrs. Cupp and her daughter Jane. The Cupps admire Emily for the class markers of her speech, education and manner, but in terms of material realities, Emily is dependent on them. When during her visit to Mallowe Court Emily receives a letter from Mrs. Cupp informing her that they are selling the house and relocating to Chichester to live with her widowed brother, Emily is compelled to consider herself:

> The friendliness of the two faithful Cupps and the humble Turkey-red comforts of the bed-sitting room had meant home to Emily Fox-Seton. When she had turned her face and tired feet away from discouraging errands and small humiliations and discomforts, she had turned them toward the bed-sitting room, the hot little fire, the small, fat black kettle singing on the hob, and the two-and-eleven-penny tea set. Not being given to crossing bridges before she reached them, she had never contemplated the dreary possibility that her refuge might be taken away from her. She had not dwelt on the fact that she had no other real refuge on earth. (157–58)

With the minimal domestic security that she had suddenly stripped away, she has to think about her situation "with a suddenly realizing sense" (158) that reduces her to tears. She had read the letter while walking out on an errand, and she says, "I *am* tired. But I must get on, really" even as "the mist in her eyes prevented her seeing the path before her" (158). Walderhurst, who had ridden out in search of Emily, finds her in tears. When he asks the cause of her tears, she tells him her story, to which he responds: "I came here, in fact, to ask you if you will come and live with me?" (177). Emily fears the meaning of the question, recalling "stories of transgressions, of follies, of cruelties" and thinking of the fact that as in her own case, "[T]he lives of well-born struggling women were so hard" (177–78). All she can muster as a response is a woeful "Oh!" (178), the narrator noting that "she was so without help or stay" (179). She has no defense from being a kept woman until Walderhurst clarifies his meaning "even with some irritation": "I am asking you to be my wife" (180). Walderhurst's irritation is born less of impatience than it is of surprise by Emily's not taking his meaning as directly and simply as he meant it, for he could not enact the social script required of a man of means in need of a wife. Here is how the narrator retrospectively presents the moment, half focalized through Walderhurst's eyes and half interpreted by the narrator:

> Walderhurst has never told her that the most beautiful moment of her life was undoubtedly that in which she stood upon the heather, tall and straight and simple, her hands hanging by her sides, her large, tear filled hazel eyes gazing straight into his. In the femininity of her frank defenselessness there was an appeal to nature's self in man which was not quite of earth. And for several seconds they stood so and gazed into each other's souls—the usually unilluminated nobleman and the prosaic young woman who lodged on a third floor back in Mortimer Street. (179)

Here Walderhurst sees her fully, openly, her hands by her sides, her body framed by a backdrop of heather, her gaze direct, her eyes glittering with tears. She is defenseless against any masculine misrepresentation (i.e., attack on her integrity), and in her innocent openness he sees nothing to attack and everything to embrace. Nature in the scene is transfigured (nature being in the sentence "not quite of earth"), and as her body and his stand face to face, they are more than mere bodies; the unilluminated and prosaic become incarnate souls. The burden of that passage is to render what Walderhurst sees and what his seeing means, but that meaning is something he could never tell. Like Emily's "Oh!," his perception defies words, the collision between the illuminated, unconventional couple and the most conventional of social forms (a marriage proposal) dislocating the couple from the convention, thereby revitalizing the social form as emergent from a genuine feeling between two individuals rather than the convention itself defining in advance the roles to be fulfilled.

That sense of genuine feeling uncompromised by the demands of social roles and status is recapitulated early in *The Methods of Lady Walderhurst* when Lady Maria reflects, "I believe she's in love with him, as if she was a nurse-maid and he was a butcher's boy" (4). Although Emily's feelings may be uncompromised by social roles—the narrator posits that Emily "represented something [...] primitively of the emotions" (20)—her social precarity is very much a part of those feelings, the prospect of an impoverished old age having fed a daily anxiety that she strove to repress. "[I]t was not only the living from day to day that made one anxious," she tells Lady Maria, "it was the Future! [...] I have been so frightened sometimes in the middle of the night, when I awakened and thought about living to be sixty-five, that I have lain shaken all over [...]. I had nobody—nobody" (4–5). Her love for Walderhurst is mixed with intense gratitude, a condition that must perforce sustain a sense of inequality in the marriage, for the fact that Walderhurst has raised Emily out of poverty seems to permeate her thinking at every level, "her care of herself" becoming an effort to "render [herself] worthy of his qualities and tastes" (16). His qualities and tastes, however, "were of no exalted importance in themselves" (16). Because his life had been "entirely self-absorbed" (14) and "that it required an effort to reconcile [himself] to the fact of a woman's being continually about" (15), the qualities that Emily perceives him to have are such that "no other human being would have assented to. She felt that he had condescended to her with a generosity which justified worship. This was not true, but it was true for her" (16). The brief moment of mutual illumination prior to his proposal of marriage at the end of *The Making of a Marchioness* is dimmed by the economic realities that determine social class along with the gender politics that would reinforce the assumed necessity of a woman's dependence on a man. The challenge for Burnett seems to be credibly to show how, through the transformations opened up by the power of narrative, it may be possible for the inequalities of class and gender to be subordinated to the mutual desires of equal hearts. She approached that task by removing Emily from the muted narrative world of unsentimental romance, where the seeds of genuine feeling are planted in a soil defined by practicalities, and placing her in the frenetic narrative world of the sensation novel.

The reviewer for the British journal *Academy* judged that generic turn as a "descent to melodrama,"[29] while the reviewer for the *New York Times* argues that "[I]n less gifted hands the story would have fallen over the precipice of the kindly sensational, but in spite of a sort of Wilkie Collins conspiracy, the tale is firmly held back from so much as the border of melodrama."[30] The oxymoron, "kindly sensational," suggests something of the reviewer's feel for what Burnett does differently with the sensational in her novel; she sets a sensational plot in motion in order to subordinate it to the stirring of deep and genuine affection between the two characters who spend most of the novel apart, Emily and Lord Walderhurst. In so doing Burnett introduces character types and narrative situations drawn from sensation fiction, but she subdues one of the dominant features of the sensational, that is, exaggeration. In her groundbreaking study, *The Maniac in the Cellar*, Winifred Hughes emphasizes the links among exaggeration, melodrama and the sensation novel. She identifies exaggeration as the "instinctive realm of melodrama" and argues that "everything in a sensation novel is larger than life; intensified, distorted, prodigious; invested with the quality of nightmare. Humanity is seen *in extremis*, perpetually at the point of crisis."[31] In assembling the elements that would constitute a perpetual crisis, Burnett generates narrative energies of sensation on the one hand and attenuates those energies on the other. Those countervailing forces do not emerge through the structure of the novel but are generated moment by moment as the story unfolds. We see an early example of that when Walderhurst's distant relative and potential heir to his estates, Alec Osborn and Osborn's wife, are introduced.

Emily has learned about Captain Osborn in conversation with Lady Maria. Readers learn more as the conversation recedes and the narrator's omniscience takes over. Although he is not a "near relation" to Walderhurst, he is "the next of kin" (26), who, the narrator observes, when he heard about Walderhurst's marriage while in India, "shut himself up in his quarters and blasphemed until his face was purple and big drops of sweat ran down it" (27). He then decides to return to England "for a long leave" (26). His wife, Hester, is "an Anglo-Indian girl," "interesting and clever" with "a good deal of odd un-English beauty [...] so sinuous of lithe, slim body, that among native beauties she seemed not to be sufficiently separated by marks of race" (29).[32] Early in their marriage when Osborn told her of his prospect to inherit the Walderhurst estates, the vision of being taken home "to a life of English luxury [...] haunted her in her sleep"; in her anguish she suggests to her husband that "there were occult things to be done" to ensure his inheritance (30). Osborn believes that Hester "knew such curious, intimate things" that "in England she might be a sort of sensation" (34). In that way Burnett nods to the sensation genre by introducing two character types familiar to readers of Wilkie Collins, the drunken impoverished near heir to an estate who will do anything to obtain it (think Sir Percival Glyde from *The Woman in White*) and the oriental other bent on using occult arts and even violence to procure a treasure (think the Indian jugglers intent on returning the gem to India in *The Moonstone*). In addition, Emily herself evokes a sensation novel type: the younger, poor and attractive woman bent on exploiting the wealth and position of a lonely, older, titled man (think Lucy in M. E. Braddon's *Lady Audley's Secret*). Emily does not, however, play true to type.

In his paraphrase of one definition of the sensation novel articulated in Canon Schmitt's *Alien Nation: Nineteenth-Century Gothic Fictions and English Nationality*, Andrew Radford writes:

> Schmitt construes the genre as not simply embracing, but advertising with an impish zeal its mixture of a plethora of conflicting ideological and literary elements within the bounds of

a single opus. Indissolubly intermingled in the narrative fabric are elements from the seedy underworld and the rarefied domestic refuge, the lunatic asylum and drawing room, showing the "overlap" of patrician and criminal trespasser. These effects, according to Schmitt, "depend upon figurative miscegenation" at all levels.[33]

While "impish zeal" would be an exaggeration to describe Burnett's deployment of the sensational, she does evoke the seedy and the rarefied, the criminal and the domestic, the lunatic and the ordinary with a sly humor and steady moral compass. And she makes miscegenation literal in the figure of Hester. The sequence that describes Walderhurst's explanation to Emily about the Osborns' impending visit and Emily's subsequent first impressions illustrates how Burnett weaves those elements into "the narrative fabric." Walderhurst opens the conversation by observing that he knows Lady Maria had already told Emily who the Osborns are and why they would visit their kinsman. He then says:

> She has been definite enough to explain that I consider Osborn altogether undesirable. Under the veneer of his knowledge of decent customs he is a cad. I am obliged to behave civilly to the man, but I dislike him. If he had been born in a low class of life, he would have been a criminal [...]. Any number of people would be criminals if circumstances did not interfere. It depends a good deal on the shape of the skull [...]. Osborn's skull is quite the wrong shape. (36–37)

Shielded by his putative good birth, Osborn is, nonetheless, a criminal by nature, his moral character visible to anyone who knows how to look, according to Walderhurst. Emily, however, sees things differently. "She had accepted," the narrator writes, "everything she had ever heard said in a pulpit" and thus "she believed that people who were bad were bad from preference" (36–37), so she would judge Osborn herself once she met him. Then, when "Captain Osborn brought the skull in question into the room, covered in the usual manner with neatly brushed, close-cropped hair, Emily thought it a very nice shape indeed." Seeing nothing unsettling in Osborn's appearance, Emily is further reassured when she compares the "nice shape" of Osborn's head to her own knowledge of phrenology: She "found [his skull] a trifle hard and round-looking and low of forehead, but not shelving or bulging as the heads of murderers in illustrated papers generally did. She owned to herself that she did not see what Lord Walderhurst evidently saw" (37).

Her attention next shifts to Mrs. Osborn, whom she finds to be "beautiful in an odd way. Every movement of her exceeding slimness was curiously graceful [...]. undulating" (38). The hypnotic serpentine suggestiveness of "undulating" coupled with Emily's perception of Mrs. Osborn's "long, drooping, and dense black eyes" extends the orientalist references from the narrator's earlier description, but Emily's sense that she (Mrs. Osborn) "had such a lovely, slow, shy way of lifting [her eyes] to look at people" softens those references, suggesting that Mrs. Osborn is simply a reticent, even demure young woman who defers to others, someone, as Emily further perceives, who "seemed like a schoolgirl" (38). Such mixing of the oriental and the ordinary, the criminal and blandly handsome compromises the simple ideological binary of the degenerate aristocrat and devilish oriental against the morally superior and innocent legitimate landed proprietor and his chosen bride. Burnett develops that figurative moral ambiguation when she takes account of Emily's reflections on the Osborns as claimants to the property that she has married into.

> Emily was the kind of mistaken creature whose conscience, awakening to unnecessary remorses [sic], causes its owner at once to assume all the burdens which Fate had laid upon the shoulders of others. She began to feel like a criminal herself, irrespective of the shape of her skull. Her own inordinate happiness and fortune had robbed this unoffending young couple. She wished that it had not been so, and vaguely reproached herself without reasoning the matter out to a conclusion. At all events, she was remorsefully sympathetic in her mental attitude towards Mrs. Osborn. (38–39)

Although the narrator judges Emily as fundamentally mistaken, her sense of her own criminality does reflect her narrative role as a kind of Lady Audley claiming property that by moral if not strictly legal right should pass on to others. Her guilt, then, is situational rather than moral, circumstances, to reverse Walderhurst's earlier claim, interfering to transform the feel of her luck from something wonderful to something criminal, "irrespective of the shape of her skull." The relative truth of the narrative situation in all its moral ambiguity is summed up in a conversation between Emily and Lady Maria that follows the Osborns' first appearance. Emily expresses her pity for them while Lady Maria cautions her from showing "them all sorts of indiscreet kindnesses." Lady Maria charges Osborn with being "odious, and the girl," she says, "looks like a native beauty. She rather frightens me." Emily dismisses the "odious" charge and counters the "native" claim with the assertion that Mrs. Osborn "*is* pretty." Lady Maria's fear is rather misplaced, she suggests, since Mrs. Osborn "is frightened of us, really" (40). The ambiguation of the evil–good moral binary produced by the destabilization of the ideological figuration of sensation narrative character types will, as the narrative unfolds, be disambiguated. How to do so is the challenge to Burnett's art.

Burnett meets that challenge by showing that character types are produced by the projections of others; then by defining character by actions and the degree to which those actions are motivated by a relationship rather than purely self-interest, she reveals the complex of human motive that is lost when character is judged by type. The clearest instance of Burnett's strategy is Mrs. Osborn's ayah, an Indian servant Ameerah. Mrs. Cupp, who has joined her daughter Jane at Mallowe Court to serve Emily Walderhurst, views Ameerah in the most stereotypical racial and cultural terms. "She knows her betters when she sees them," Mrs. Cupp remarks, "and has pretty enough manners for a black [...]. I wonder if she's ever heard of her Maker, and if a little brown Testament with good print wouldn't be a good thing to give her?" Mrs. Cupp later presents Ameerah with the Testament, who receives the gift as follows:

> Ameerah, in whose dusky being was incorporated the occult faith of lost centuries, and whose gods had been gods through mystic ages, received the fat, little brown book with down-dropped lids and grateful obeisance. These were her words to her mistress: "The fat old woman with protruding eyes bestowed it upon me. She says it is the book of her god. She has but one. She wishes me to worship him. Am I a babe to worship such a god as would please her. She is old, and has lost her mind." (154–55)

The passage is focalized through Ameerah, the racially tinged gaze of Mrs. Cupp reversed as Ameerah defines the giver of the Testament in terms of her physical features, her obesity and "protruding eyes." Ameerah's perception of the materiality of the Testament itself diminishes its authority, the word of God, for Mrs. Cupp, reduced to a "fat, little brown book" that resembles the "fat old woman" who gave it. The narrator's view takes Ameerah's side, comparing the deep antiquity of Ameerah's gods to Mrs. Cupp's singular god in a stroke of common-sense logic that on its own terms is hard to refute. The benevolent Christian Mrs. Cupp is rendered a mad old woman in her inability to make any effort to perceive Ameerah's full humanity and the specificity of her cultural difference. In that context, Ameerah's gestures of deference, her "down-dropped" eyes and "grateful obeisance," reveal her understanding of the limitations of Mrs. Cupp rather than being marks of deceptive servility. In the passage the meaning of the racially tinged language is reversed, character revealed as individual rather than type.

The pattern where character type is made ambiguous in the way the narrative uses language to mediate character relationships is replicated on the level of action in the plot. At first glance, the plot seems unambiguous: Osborn feels cheated of his rightful inheritance and will stop at nothing to gain it; his wife shares his interests while also desiring English luxuries for herself as a response to her mixed-race experiences in the Anglo-Indian community in India; Ameerah, Mrs. Osborn's ayah, is connected to the idea of the occult, ancient powers of the mysterious East, who will stop at nothing to serve Mrs. Osborn's interests. On one side, then, the male figure has two women supporting his efforts to secure an inheritance. On the other side there is the absent male figure serving England's colonial interests in India, whose pregnant wife is left alone to protect her husband's interests by defending herself and her unborn child from Osborn's attempts to kill her. The plot unfolds slowly with Emily never quite fully certain that the attempts on her life are real or accidental. "They may be as innocent as I am," she thinks. "And they may be murderers in their hearts. I can prove nothing, I can prevent nothing" (194). She also believes that she can say nothing: "[W]hat would she appear to her husband, to Lady Maria, to anyone in the decorous world, if she told them that she believed that in a dignified household, an English gentleman, even a deposed presumptive heir, was working out a subtle plot against her such as might adorn a melodrama?" (192). Consequently, it appears she can play the role only of the passive victim, hoping that her husband will return in time to save her.

The simple lines of conflict laid out in that plot summary are complicated, however, as the women begin to form unspoken lines of sympathy with each other. The most powerful bond forms between the two pregnant women, Mrs. Osborn and Emily Walderhurst. Once she realizes that her husband is serious in his desire to kill Emily, Mrs. Osborn's mind turns to a memory of Emily bringing gifts for her unborn child, and she "heard again [...] the nice, prosaic emotion of her voice as she said: '*Don't* thank me—don't. Just let us *enjoy* ourselves.'" That memory juxtaposed against her increasing knowledge of her husband's capacity for murder brings Mrs. Osborn up short: "She was not strong enough," the narrator explains, "to stand the realization that she had become part of a web into which she had not meant to be knitted" (200). She determines that "there was a thing that must not be, and she herself must come between" (201). Then when Osborn manages to poison Emily's drink, Mrs. Osborn dashes the drink from her hand before informing Emily of the reality of the plot against her. "You represent the thing," Mrs. Osborn tells her, "that we have the right to *hate* most on earth." To which Emily asks: "Do *you* hate me?" Mrs. Osborn explains that, yes, sometimes she does, but "[W]hen I do *not*, I actually believe it is because we are both—women together" (208). The expression "women together" gestures toward their shared pregnancies, which as a reality shared only by women carries more value than the potential for either child to inherit an estate. At that moment the two women are in solidarity with each other, not in the service of their respective men.

Ameerah too shares in the symbolic logic of the solidarity between the two pregnant women against Captain Osborn, for her relationship with Hester Osborn began when Hester was a child; as her ayah, she cared for her as a kind of surrogate mother. After Hester's confession to Emily, Ameerah recognizes the break Mrs. Osborn has made with her husband's project, and she turns against him too. The significance of that turn is emphasized in the novel's last page, which reports on Captain Osborn's death. After his failed effort to dispose of Emily, Osborn returns to India with his wife and Ameerah. His drinking intensifies, and he progresses from verbal to physical abuse of Hester. Ameerah loads a gun that Osborn thinks unloaded, and in his carelessness, he kills himself, his plot to cause Emily's "accidental" death rebounding on him. His manner of death also demystifies Ameerah's putative occult powers, for she is merely a careful observer of human behavior; she put the means of his death in his own hands and he simply acted in character. After Osborn's death, Emily invites Hester, her child and Ameerah to return to England. The novel ends four years later with Hester's explanation of the manner of Osborn's death. After detailing her beatings, Osborn's increasing degeneration and Ameerah's actions, Hester muses: "Before I married Alec, I did not understand how one human being could kill another. He taught me to understand, quite. But I had not the courage to do it myself. Ameerah had." The flat, matter-of-fact quality of that explanation, coupled with the fact that there is no possibility that Ameerah would be charged with any crime, conveys a sense of the ordinary; as John Oxon's was, Alec Osborn's death is simple justice.

Like Clorinda, the women in *The Methods of Lady Walderhurst* are also, quietly, Tess triumphant, the unsettling realities of the man's death and the actions that led to it absorbed within a pattern of domestic life built on human relationships actuated by care. But there is a cost; suffering leaves its marks. Because the plot moves from clear lines of conflict to ambiguous allegiances to relationships finally being disambiguated, the last sentence of the novel cannot suggest a return to clarity. "And while Lady Walderhurst sat gazing at her [Hester] with a paling face, she began quietly to eat the little buttered scone" (304). In the "paling" of her face, Emily's suffering is reactivated as she learns of Hester's suffering. It is also enhanced by the knowledge that Osborn's death was no accident, Ameerah having arranged it in defense of Hester. His "accidental" death, however, can also be seen as the final act in Osborn's plot to kill Emily herself. As she had done in *A Lady of Quality*, Burnett does not inject an element of guilt in the killing, which is the end point of a sequence of events Osborn himself set in motion. Emily's body may register the weight of events, but her mind turns to the continuation of her domestic life in the consumption of "the little buttered scone." In that small act, she offers comfort to Hester as she tells a tale that had been weighing on her for years. And in offering that comfort, Emily signals her persistent orientation to work, as Carlyle put it, "continually in well-doing," which is as "natural [as her] existence," which should awaken "no astonishment" and which requires "no commentary [...] as if it could not but be so."

In the five years from 1896 to 1901 Burnett continued to experiment with new ways to conceptualize her heroines. While the uneven development of Joan Lowrie, Rachel Ffrench, Christian Murdoch, Octavia Bassett and Bertha Amory may, as Israel Zangwill argued, have been consummated in the symbolic meanings of Clorinda's career, Clorinda also marks a departure. In the earlier novels Burnett had emphasized the individual development of her women protagonists; in each case (except for Octavia Basset) the novels end with the women fronting the future alone, Joan insisting that she be educated before she will consent to Derrick's proposal, Rachel rejected by her French lover and spurned by Murdoch, Christian left behind as Murdoch leaves for America and Bertha trapped in a marriage with a man who betrayed her. The women retain their integrity (except for Rachel Ffrench to some degree) by having the strength to carry on in the world despite the quality of their relationships with others. Each woman must find a way to make a life for herself. Clorinda would seem to be a culmination of Burnett's effort to imagine the possibility for a woman to shape her own life and achieve happiness on her own terms by both resisting and exploiting the social structures that would subordinate her to men. And that is true up to a point. The difference between Clorinda and the women protagonists who precede her is the emphasis on her finding a specific mate, something more than Burnett suggests in the relationships depicted in her earlier novels. Joan Lowrie and Derrick may be in love and Bertha Amory and Tredennis may be too, but there is little sense of the absolute necessity of their being together for each woman to realize her full humanness. Burnett shifts from focusing on the woman's individual growth as the central element in her self-definition to exploring how the fullest expression of one's humanness can occur only in a certain kind of relationship.

In *A Lady of Quality* that relationship is defined in heightened terms, the emphasis on exceptional physical strength and beauty as the foundation for an instinctual morality. Added to that is a bio-mystical element, the physical attraction triggering a sense of a common spirit, even a singular soul. The distancing of the historical narrative, which enables an allegorical reading of character with the action of the plot producing a kind of dreamscape, provides an aesthetic logic to such a conception of character. In contrast, *The Methods of Lady Walderhurst* offers a muted relationship; Emily, though a woman of some stature, is self-effacing while Walderhurst is phlegmatic, self-absorbed and emotionally distant. On the one hand, Emily idolizes Walderhurst, blinding her to his actual physical and emotional qualities, and on the other Walderhurst takes Emily for granted, assuming she will simply cater to him, make his life more comfortable. The contrast between the two novels is from the extraordinary to the exceedingly ordinary. As, what we might call, the narrative disposal of the aggressive male figure in each novel suggests, however, the novels do intersect, with Emily and Clorinda sharing a similar freedom from conventional social expectations. In addition, while the sexual energy so evident in the relation between Clorinda and Osmonde is missing between Emily and Walderhurst, the novel demonstrates a similar bio-mystical bond between them.

Burnett renders the physical basis of the bond Walderhurst increasingly feels with Emily while he is in India in this simple, declarative sentence: "He wanted to see his wife" (274). His mind then immediately turns to picturing her eyes and the blood rushing to her face as he recalls how "impressive" her physical presence is. He feels most forcefully that "his affection for her had warmed" (275). When he arrives at their London house, he finds Emily near death after she had given birth to their son. As he listens to an account of the birth, Walderhurst bursts out with "I would have strangled the boy with my own hands rather than lose her" (284), in that moment recasting his marriage from a social form to produce an heir to a means by which he and the woman whose body and spirit enliven him can be physically and legally one. "In this manner, it seemed, did a rigid, self-encased, and conventional elderly nobleman reach emotion. He looked uncanny" (282). The clear implication is that Walderhurst becomes authentically human when he gives himself to another in a relationship that obliterates self-conscious as the other takes precedence over self. The test of the reality and power of such a relationship comes as Walderhurst struggles to save Emily's life by willing her back to consciousness, not through consciousness of herself but of him:

> What he hoped or intended to do he did not explain to himself. He was of the order of man who coldly waves aside all wanderings on the subjects of occult claims. He believed in proven facts, in professional aid, in the abolition of absurdities. But his whole narrow being concentrated itself on one thing,—he wanted his woman back. He wanted to speak to her. (290)

So he does; he speaks to her, softly whispering her name in her ear, hour after hour until she opens her eyes and says, "It—was—you!" (298). He, giving himself fully to her, and she, hearing only his voice, find life in each other. Youth, physical force and external beauty, though nice, are not required for the experience of a total human attunement that transfigures even the most ordinary of lives.

The next two phases in Burnett's career as a novelist are animated by qualities that surface in the five novels discussed in this chapter but become central in the novels that follow. The paragraph in *A Lady of Quality* that gives an overview with few details of Clorinda refurbishing Wildairs Hall and the adjacent village is a harbinger of the long-term rebuilding project central to Burnett's most important transatlantic novel, *The Shuttle*. Fused with that rebuilding, even, we might say, a prerequisite for it, is stimulation of the bio-mystical energies at play in Burnett's historical and country house novels. The general pattern I am gesturing toward here is visible if undeveloped in an exchange between Dr. Warren and his wife in *The Methods of Lady Walderhurst*. Before they get to know Emily well, they speculate about her origins and what for them is her confounding behavior. Once they take on her full care together, after learning she is Lady Walderhurst, Mrs. Warren talks with Emily at length. Emily, the narrator writes, "learned to reveal herself in simple talk with Mrs. Warren." In conversation with her husband, Mrs. Warren observes

"[T]hat an adoration such as hers could exist in the nineteenth century is—," before her husband, laughing, interrupts her with these words: "Almost degenerate" (264). The term degenerate plays, of course, on the reputation of the sensation novel, but it also names a cultural anxiety that seized the imaginations of ordinary Britons in 1895 with the publication in English of Max Nordau's *Degeneration*, which was cited in the press as evidence of the roots of degeneracy in the trial of Oscar Wilde. Superficially the word indicates a deterioration of the tacit values that help structure social behavior and maintain social stability, and the joke here is that it is being applied to a woman whose behavior models the most stable of social values. After his laugh, Dr. Warren reflects and changes his term: "Perhaps it is regenerate" (265). The question concealed in the joke concerns not so much the evidence for social degeneration but the possibility of transforming those negative energies in the service of regeneration. In Burnett's novels of 1895–1901 the possibilities of individual regeneration through bio-mystical attunement carries most of the burden of the narratives. In her transatlantic novels the inter-animation between personal and social regeneration takes on a heavier thematic burden.

Notes

1. Marie A. Belloc. "Mrs. Hodgson Burnett: A Famous Authoress at Home." *The Idler*, vol. 9 (1896): 645–48 (648).
2. "Western Town has Literary Censors." *New York Times* (July 6, 1902): 9.
3. Friedrich Nietzsche. "Prologue." *Thus Spoke Zarathustra*. Thomas Common (trans.). New York: Modern Library, 1917, pp. 25–26.
4. Nancy Armstrong has famously argued in her *Desire and Domestic Fiction* (Oxford, 1987) that the "modern individual is first and foremost a woman" (6), and that became the case, in part, through the narrative transformations of the novel.
5. "New Books: A Little Fiction." *The Interior* (April 9, 1896): 473.
6. George Preston. "Mrs. Burnett's New Book." *The Bookman* (April 1896): 156.
7. "Talk about New Books." *The Catholic World* (May 1896): 271.
8. Jeanette L. Gilder. "'A Lady of Quality' by Frances Hodgson Burnett." *Chicago Daily Tribune* (March 1, 1896): 40.
9. "A Tale of Queen Anne's Reign." *New York Times* (March 8, 1896): 31.
10. Israel Zangwill. "Without Prejudice." *The Pall Mall Magazine*, vol. 9, no. 37 (May 1896): 153–57 (154).
11. "A Speech by Mrs. Burnett." *New York Times* (August 16, 1896): 23, 187. Cited in Gerzina.
12. Avrom Fleishman. *The English Historical Novel: Walter Scott to Virginia Woolf*. Baltimore: Johns Hopkins Press, 1971, p. xii.
13. Christina Crosby. *The Ends of History: Victorians and "the Woman Question."* New York: Routledge, 1991, p. 144.
14. *A Lady of Quality, Illustrated with Scenes from the Photoplay*. New York: Grosset & Dunlap (n.d., c. 1925), 1896, p. 2.
15. Angelique Richardson. *Love and Eugenics in the Late Nineteenth Century: Rational Reproduction & the New Woman*. Oxford: Oxford UP, 2003.
16. Had Osmonde done the killing after discovering Oxon in Clorinda's rooms threatening her, Osmonde would have been guiltless, his act judged as protecting the integrity of his intended wife. The logic is if a man kills in defense of a woman, he is merely protecting his own; if a woman kills in defense of herself, she is liable for murder because she does not own herself.
17. George Preston. "His Grace of Osmonde." *The Bookman* (December 1897): 355–56.

18 *The Academy Fiction Supplement* (December 11, 1897): 122–23 (122).
19 "Reviews": "Fauntleroy in Later Life." *The Chap Book* (February 1, 1898): 251.
20 "The New Publications." "Strong Work in Mrs. Burnett's Latest Novel." *The Hartford Courant* (December 16, 1899): 17.
21 "Books of the Week." "Mrs. Burnett's New Novel." *Chicago Daily Tribune* (December 9, 1899): 10.
22 Barbara Quinn Schmidt. "Introduction, *The Cornhill Magazine*: Celebrating Success." *Victorian Periodicals Review*, Special Issue, *The Cornhill Magazine* (Fall 1999): 202–8.
23 In addition to the volumes on sensation fiction by Winifred Hughes and Andrew Radford cited below, see also Thomas Boyle's *Black Swine in the Sewers of Hampstead: Beneath the Surface of Victorian Sensationalism* (Viking, 1989), Nicholas Rance's *Wilkie Collins and Other Sensation Novelists* (Fairleigh Dickinson UP, 1991) and Ann Cvetkovish's *Mixed Feelings: Feminism, Mass Culture, and Victorian Sensationalism* (Rutgers UP, 1992).
24 Julian Hawthorne. "Trips to Bookland: Frances Hodgson Burnett Creates a New Type in Fiction—and of a Woman, at That." *Los Angeles Times* (March 16, 1902): C6.
25 George Levine (ed.). *The Emergence of Victorian Consciousness: The Spirit of the Age*. New York: Free Press, 1967.
26 "Mrs. Burnett's New Story." *New York Times* (March 1, 1902): BR 2.
27 "Novels." *The Saturday Review* (January 25, 1902): 115.
28 In 2012 ITV in the UK broadcast a one-hour thirty-five-minute television film adaptation of *The Making of a Marchioness* and *The Methods of Lady Walderhurst* under the title *The Making of a Lady* and directed by Richard Curson Smith. The screenwriter, Kate Brooke, disposed of the first volume in minutes, focusing the bulk of the film on the sensational aspects of the second volume. Hester was played by a mixed-race actress.
29 "Fiction." *The Academy* (December 14, 1901): 592.
30 "Mrs. Burnett's New Story." *New York Times* (March 1, 1902): BR 2.
31 Winifred Hughes. *The Maniac in the Cellar: Sensation Novels of the 1860s*. Princeton: Princeton UP, 1980, p. 22.
32 Since Anglo-Indian generally refers to one born of English parents in India, that term may be misleading as it applies to Hester. Her exact parentage is vague, and her description produces a mixed-race image; she is then most likely a child of miscegenation, making her a racial other in both India and England.
33 Andrew Radford. *Victorian Sensation Fiction: A Reader's Guide to Essential Criticism*. Basingstoke: Palgrave/Macmillan, 2009, p. 75.

Chapter Four

TRANSATLANTIC ALLIANCES IN *THE SHUTTLE* AND *T. TEMBAROM*

I

Burnett's transatlantic literary interests have been visible in her work as early as *Haworth's* (1879), and, as documented in Chapter I of this volume, in *A Fair Barbarian* that interest was central to the plot of the American girl's rejuvenating disruption of an English village. With the publication of *Little Lord Fauntleroy* (1886), however, which came out during Burnett's silence as a novelist between *Through One Administration* (1883) and *A Lady of Quality* (1896), Burnett's transatlantic engagement took on heightened importance for herself as a writer and for her readers on both sides of the Atlantic.

Although the contemporary reviews were enthusiastic, *Little Lord Fauntleroy* as a novel for children and as a character did not age well. The American reviewer for *The Eclectic Magazine of Foreign Literature* in November of 1886 begins by claiming that Burnett's "juvenile story adds another laurel to a lady who as worthily won high honors in more serious and pretentious fiction." In addressing the aesthetic merit of the tale, the reviewer notes that "[T]he story is charmingly told, and none but a practiced literary artist, whose sympathies, too, were deeply in her work, could have used her material with such simple, yet telling, effect."[1] Such commentary captures both Burnett's status as a novelist while gently suggesting a shift in her cultural visibility toward children's literature. *Fauntleroy*, the reviewer concludes,

> is worth a cartload of the rubbish which often goes under the name of juvenile literature [...]. It can hardly fail to make the name of Mrs. Burnett a delight among a great throng of readers whose plaudits should be little less pleasant to her than the approval of those who judge her by her novels written for a mature public. (715)

To capture the quality of that "delight" we can turn to the review written by Louisa May Alcott, which closes with this eulogy to the power of Burnett's tale and those written by other women who possess "the tender wisdom of motherly hearts": "Let us hope that these delightful stories may be multiplied rapidly, for they do the old as much good as the young, and refresh tired eyes and anxious minds like spring air and a glimpse of green grass and daisies after city streets and the dull rooms where daily work goes on."[2]

The cloying language of Alcott's review hints at a feeling of revulsion that developed as a reaction to the overwhelming popularity of the book. The combined forces of praise and revulsion blended over time in a way that catapulted the titular character to a level of fame that enhanced and overshadowed the status of his creator. As a writer for the

New York Times observed in a short essay on the change in child heroes from "the child as the antechamber to heaven to the child as pure animal" written in the aftermath of Burnett's death in 1924, "Frances Hodgson Burnett secured the strongest lien on fame that any writer of fiction can aspire to—the creation of a character rather than a book. Fauntleroy has an assured place in the gallery of immortal children,"[3] a place so assured that the headline of Burnett's obituary in the *Chicago Daily Tribune* proclaims, "Mrs. Burnett, 'Fauntleroy' Author, Dies."[4] To tease out the tension between Fauntleroy's fame and his infamy, we can turn to two retrospective essays, Arthur Maurice's "Best Sellers of Yesterday" and John Beffel's "The Fauntleroy Plague," published in *The Bookman* in 1911 and 1927, respectively.[5] In the course of re-presenting the plot, characters and dialogue of the novel through copious quotations from the text, Maurice manages to convey a laudatory image of Burnett's place in literary culture more broadly. He begins by quoting Richard Henry Stoddard's favorable comparison of Burnett to Dickens where Stoddard writes: "She impresses me as understanding her suffering and sinning characters as fully as Dickens ever understood his" (35). He reproduces the citation from British authors given to Burnett for securing dramatic copyright against "the English play pirates" (37) who made a practice of stealing novelists' work for stage productions. He adds two pictures of Burnett's son Vivian, who was the well-documented model for Fauntleroy as a character. One of the pictures shows Vivian in what came to be embraced (or eschewed) as Fauntleroy dress, lace collar and all. He offers two images of "The Secret Garden" with Burnett herself in one, along with a photograph of the entrance hall to Burnett's Washington residence where she wrote the story. The last image in the piece is of Reginald Birch, the well-respected illustrator for the first and a number of subsequent editions, a gesture that nods toward the aesthetic investment Burnett's publishers made in her work. The implication is that on a basic level, *Little Lord Fauntleroy's* qualities as a story and its history of composition, publication and visual adaptation can encapsulate the high quality and importance of Burnett's literary career writ large. But, Maurice concludes, *Little Lord Fauntleroy* "meant more than" those things. "It meant the writing of one of those rare books that the hypercritical may condemn as melodramatic and over sentimental, but that somehow seem never to lose their youth or their power to touch the hearts of all but the dullest and most unimpressionable of readers" (45). Sixteen years later, John Beffel would beg to differ.

For Beffel, the power of *Little Lord Fauntleroy* did more than touch hearts, it lacerated them, or to use Beffel's own words in reference to what he calls the Fauntleroy plague, "[I]nevitably the soul of many a boy in the nineties was seared by this weird pestilence" (136). After the publication of the book and then its adaptation on stage, the plague took root with the help of "designers of juvenile wear," who fed the vogue among mothers to dress their sons with

> long curls, velvet jacket and pants, lace collar and cuffs, and velvet tam-o'-shanter [...]. Other manufacturers climbed on the band wagon. One turned out decks of miniature playing cards bearing pictures of the characters in the play. Perfumes were named for Little Lord Fauntleroy; a song was written about him; statuettes in his likeness came onto the scene, in metal, plaster and chocolate; and toys bore his name, first expensive and then cheap ones.

Such madness, according to Beffel, the contagion "heightened by maternal pride [...] continued for ten years," but the vague memory of the Fauntleroy plague continues to exist as a shadow in popular memory through the pejorative use of the name Fauntleroy in colloquial speech even today. The quality of the anecdotes that permeate Beffel's essay conveys the narrative energy that accounts for Fauntleroy's pejorative persistence. "In Davenport, Iowa, in the year of the Burnett play's opening, an eight-year-old burned down his father's barn because he was compelled to dress up in Fauntleroy fashion," writes Beffel. He continues:

> In Madison, Wisconsin, a kid with brick colored curls battled in vain to be severed from them. After he had been inserted forcibly into velvet jacket and pants, he walked up to a policeman in front of the principal hotel there and deliberately kicked the bluecoat in the shins to call attention to his plight. In Worcester, Massachusetts, another victim of the plague traded off an expensive Fauntleroy suit to passing gypsies for some old clothes bearing patches which the local sufferer considered admirable. And in Lexington, North Carolina, Roswell Robbins, son of a prominent lawyer there, snipped off his golden curls with a pair of scissors and cut away a large patch on his head in emulation of his father's bald spot. (135)

Beffel, of course, is engaging with the epi-phenomenon of the book rather than the book itself, and his painfully comic anecdotes of the way the pestilence affected its young male sufferers beg a number of questions, the most obvious being a simple, Why? Why would American mothers in large enough numbers embrace Fauntleroy's image with such enthusiasm and tenacity? This second question contains within it an answer to the first: What is the nature of the anxiety, bordering perhaps on fear, which would fuel such a maternal rush to impose an identity on American boys from the late 1880s through the turn of the century? So one answer to the "why" is anxiety, but anxiety over what?

To address that question, I will draw on Alex Zwerdling's *Improvised Europeans: American Literary Expatriates and the Siege of London* (1998), a book that Ruth Bernard Yeazell has called "A shrewd and convincing history of the making of Anglo-American modernism."[6] In his discussion of the many versions of the "story of an American heir to a British estate" (30), Zwerdling singles out *Little Lord Fauntleroy* as an "experiment in the genre." "Burnett's story," he writes, "of how the impoverished American-reared child of a British aristocrat and an American girl unexpectedly becomes the heir to an earldom 'caused a public delirium of joy.'" Such joy was not only felt by general readers, it was shared by those in positions of political power. Prime Minister Gladstone, for instance, was an "enthusiast," who reassured Burnett personally that "'the book would have a great effect in bringing about added good feeling between the two nations and making them understand each other'" (cited in Zwerdling, 31). Zwerdling speculates:

> Precocious Little Lord Fauntleroy [himself] has a clear sense of his political mission. He tells an American friend before reluctantly setting out for the old country, "If I have to be an earl, there's one thing I can do: I can try to be a good one. I'm not going to be a tyrant. And if there is ever another war with America, I shall try to stop it." That such monosyllabic wisdom out of the mouths of seven-year-olds should have been taken seriously by prominent grown-ups in England and America suggests the powerful hunger for familial and national reconciliation it was intended to feed. (31)

Zwerdling argues that *Fauntleroy* "is an unalloyed romantic fantasy" that "concedes nothing to reality" (31). The reality he refers to is the decline of Britain and the ascendance of the United States as a world power. That reality transformed the "reverent picture of the mother country" among the American political elite into an "image of Britain as a baffled, geriatric old man or shrunken old woman," with "the British Isles reduced to the fringes of an American archipelago spanning the Atlantic" (32). Under such circumstances, the historical tensions between the two countries needed to be soothed by what Zwerdling calls "the reconciliation fantasy." That fantasy was built on a "compensatory myth" of racial unity between Britain and the United States. The English journalist William Stead in 1902 wrote of his own nation: "If we are afflicted with national vanity we can console ourselves by reflecting that the Americans are only giving to others what they inherited from ourselves. Whatever they do, all goes to the credit of the family. It is an unnatural parent who does not exult in the achievements of his son."[7] In Stead's formulation, since America is the offspring of Britain, what he calls the Americanization of the world should be considered more accurately as the world "Anglicized" (1). In the context of *Little Lord Fauntleroy*, it would seem that the first step in the American task to "Anglicize" the world is to re-Anglicize Britain itself. As Christopher Hitchens observed in 1990, the "special," familial relationship between Britain and the United States "is really at bottom a transmission belt by which British conservative ideas have infected America, the better to be retransmitted to England."[8] That, it would seem, is Fauntleroy's real political mission.

In Britain, then, *Little Lord Fauntleroy* assuaged anxieties about national decline as the young Anglo-American boy reestablishes the ideal of the gentleman within one aristocratic family, the boy himself by virtue of his youth being uncorrupted with moral energies powerful in their purity. Because his resemblance to his father is so emphasized in the story, his arrival at Dorincourt Castle is more a return; when he stands next to his grandfather at the end of the tale, his inheritance of the estate no longer in question, his American associations are absorbed by the imperatives of British family history, his natural relation to his grandfather presenting the idea of family as more determinative than national differences or geopolitical competition. Fauntleroy embodies physical and moral health against the symptoms of degeneration exhibited by his grandfather, and by his youth ensuring a longer future for the stability of the estate, he also embodies a symbolic response to fears of national decline. Britain has such an appeal that at the end of the story, Fauntleroy's American friend, the grocer Mr. Hobbs, repudiates his earlier denigration of all things British and aristocratic as he embraces the importance of ancestors (what he calls "auntsister") and the social value of earls. He acknowledges the appeal of the United States "for them that's young and stirrin'" (290), but he chooses to sell his "corner store in New York, and settle in the English village of Erlesboro" (289). As a group, Fauntleroy, the Earl of Dorincourt and Mr. Hobbs represent a simultaneously comic, naïve and sincere version of the idea of the Anglo-Saxon alliance under which all would be well.[9]

British mothers, however, did not dress their boys in Fauntleroy garb. American mothers did.[10] That suggests that the anxieties *Fauntleroy* enabled Americans to process were more personal, closer to ordinary homes and not easy to ameliorate through narrative idealism. If as Britain's geopolitical power declined as America's strengthened, there is no need for anxiety if Stead's view is right; it is a matter of family, the son building on the inheritance from his parents. As long as the notion of a single, Anglo-Saxon race destined to "Anglicize" the world could be believed, there would be little to fear for Anglo-Americans. But Anglo-Americans were afraid in the midst of their emergence on the global stage, and what they feared was what was called at the time, "race suicide."[11] We can turn again to Zwerdling for context. Broadly speaking, until the early 1880s, European immigrants were welcomed in the United States "because their arrival in great numbers was treated as an international vote of confidence in the democratic experiment." By the mid-1880s, however, faith in "America's ability to absorb and assimilate vast numbers of strangers [...] seemed suddenly to evaporate."

> What had changed was the immigrant pool. In 1882, for instance, over three-quarters of arriving immigrants had come from "Nordic" countries like Britain, Germany, and Scandinavia, while those from southern and eastern Europe accounted for only an eighth of the total. By 1905, the proportions were nearly reversed, with over three-quarters emigrating from countries like Italy, Austria-Hungary, and Russia and less than a quarter from northern and western Europe. In the year 1907 [the publication date for *The Shuttle*] nearly a million of these "new" southern and eastern European immigrants poured into the country. Clearly if this trend continued [...] America would no longer be able to call herself an Anglo-Saxon nation. (44)

Race was at the heart of what was perceived as a problem. With the development of new racial taxonomies in books such as William Ripley's *The Races of Europe* (1899), which divided Europeans into different racial groups, the northern Teutons, central Alpines and southern Mediterraneans in addition to the Slavs, who populated both Europe and Asia, the new immigrants were said to have distinctive "cranial shapes and characteristic strengths and weaknesses," which were over time "interpreted hierarchically" with Teutons (aka Aryans) at the top and Mediterraneans (southern Italians and Greeks) at the bottom. By 1911 such a racialized approach to immigration was codified in a US congressional report of forty-two volumes initiated by a Senator Dillingham. Volume Five was called a *Dictionary of Races of People*. In that volume Italians are divided into two races, the northern associated with the Alpine and the southern associated with, to use the dictionary's term, the "negritic" peoples of North Africa. Volume Thirty-Eight is called *Changes in Bodily Form of Descendants of Immigrants*, and it contains the commissioned anthropometric studies of the physiognomy of immigrants carried out by Franz Boas.[12] Clearly the physical appearance of the new immigrants unsettled many Americans who saw themselves in the image of those from the mother country. Because physical appearance was thought at the time to be a mark of character, the darker races being morally inferior to the lighter ones, the imperative of assimilation carried with it more than the new immigrants adapting American cultural practices; it required a change in their appearance, hence the optimism of Volume Thirty-Eight where Boas claimed that within one generation under the shaping influence of environment, medicine, hygiene and culture, the new immigrants' bodies began to conform to an Anglo-Saxon ideal. From our perspective today, what I am describing sounds crazy, but between 1886 when the Haymarket Riot in Chicago took place (and also the publication date of *Little Lord Fauntleroy*) and 1924 when the US Congress passed the most restrictive immigration bill to date, there was a modulating and persistent expression in the press, in academic research and in popular literature of race panic.[13] Such race panic surely felt like a threat not just to the hegemony of the American governing classes but also to the integrity of the American middle-class home. Anna Wilson has argued that Fauntleroy "represents a boy functioning as a female substitute" (235, see note 10). If we take that insight and link it with the threat of the new immigration to the middle-class American home, American mothers' embrace of Fauntleroy's image projected literally onto their sons can be read as a form of symbolic self-defense. If the home is under threat, and the home is the fundamental building block of the nation, it may have felt like a national duty.

What the sources of the British and American enthusiasm over *Little Lord Fauntleroy* have in common, despite the obvious differences, is anxiety about the degeneration of the human body, which perforce serves as a harbinger for the degeneration of the nation. As Stephen Arata has shown, "[I]n the last years of the nineteenth century English writing […] [a]cross disciplines and genres [articulates] the same anxieties concerning the collapse of culture, the weakening of national might, the possible fatal decay—physical, moral, spiritual, creative—of the Anglo-Saxon 'race' as a whole."[14] In order to tease out one strand of this multidisciplinary discourse of decline, Arata focuses on what he calls "the pseudo-science of degeneration theory," which, he suggests, is the counterpart to the "better-documented" Victorian belief in progress. Beginning with the work of Benedict-Augustin Morel in the 1850s, "the study of degeneration was at once a branch of biology and a form of cultural criticism" (2). Arata explains how Morel approached degeneration through his specialization in cretinism, always within the context of the relationship between the individual and the nation: "Degeneracy afflicted the individual, but its supposed causes (poverty, malnutrition, prostitution, crime, alcoholism, pollution) and effects (sterility, madness, imbecility, suicide, revolution) reached deep into the collective life of the people" (3). In the work of Max Nordau entitled *Degeneration* (1895), a text that journalists drew on to explain what was at stake in the trial of Oscar Wilde,[15] the concept is not confined to the urban masses but extends to the upper classes. "Nordau," Arata explains, "took pains to insist that the degenerate population 'consists chiefly of rich educated people' who, with too much time and means at their disposal, succumb to decadence and depravity" (35). Degeneration, it seems, was a concept that in the minds of the middle class applied to the decay of the aristocratic and working (or simply impoverished) classes, and as a form of middle-class "popular wisdom […] [it] received its most compelling articulations in the highly commonsensical modes of popular fiction" (4). The themes Arata evokes in his rendering of the late nineteenth century notion of degeneration—a debauched aristocracy, a debased working class (both urban and rural), the linkage of degeneracy and drunkenness and violence, and so on—are clearly central to Burnett's novels in the wake of *Through One Administration*. The drunken, carousing Sir Jeoffry Wildairs and the sexually promiscuous, stalking villain John Oxon in *A Lady of Quality* and *His Grace of Osmonde* and the violent, wife beating, murderous Alec Osborn in *The Methods of Lady Walderhurst* are the obvious examples in novels that one might place in the literary field on the border between "actual literature" and popular fiction.

In those cases, however, decay seems more a result of individual behavior with little to suggest a broader application to society writ large. In *Little Lord Fauntleroy* the Earl of Dorincourt seems to anticipate character as representative of a social pattern of degeneration, his elder sons having modeled his self-indulgent behavior and his youngest dying early, but in the end he is retrievable, his apparent degeneration a function of his selfishness rather than a result of family decay. *Little Lord Fauntleroy* is then, as Zwerdling has argued, a reconciliation fantasy, a passing on of wealth, power and responsibility from Britain to America and then back to Britain via an American return. In *The Shuttle*, however, Burnett is far more interested in the idea of degeneration in the context of her lived experience in the United States in the years of race panic spurred by the "new immigration" and in relation to her lived experience in England, where she rented Maytham Hall in Rolvenden, refurbished its gardens and lived the life of "Lady of the Manor."[16] Burnett worked to assuage anxieties related to fears of degeneration on both sides of the Atlantic; she did so by exploring two transatlantic marriages contracted in the context of the necessity to save the decaying English estates.

II

The Shuttle obsesses over the problem of degeneration. After Bettina Vanderpoel, the heroine of the novel, is given an unplanned, impromptu tour by Lord Mount Dunstan of his ancient, neglected and still majestic country estate, during which he tells her his family's story of decline, she reflects on what she had seen and heard as follows:

> To be able to look back through centuries and know of one's blood that sometimes it had been shed in the doing of great deeds, must be a thing to remember. To realize that the courage and honour had been lost in ignoble modern vices, which no sense of dignity and reverence for race and name had restrained—must be bitter—bitter! [...] The worst of it for him was that he was not of that strain of his race who had been the "bad lot." The "bad lot" had been the weak lot, the vicious, the self-degrading. Scandals which had shut men out from their class and kind were usually of an ugly type. This man had a strong jaw, a powerful, healthy body, and clean, though perhaps hard, eyes. (147)

Mount Dunstan's story of decline is a familiar one: a noble, aristocratic family that has played a part in the development of national and local identity, traditions and prosperity is debased by the self-indulgence of its heirs, who within two generations drain all wealth and vitality from the family and the land. Note how in Bettina's thoughts the family debasement can be seen in the body by contrast: because Lord Mount Dunstan is not of the "bad lot" of his race (i.e., his ancestry), he is healthy, powerful and clean, the opposite of debased. In terms of contemporary theories of degeneration, Mount Dunstan is a positive manifestation of the negative atavism of Mr. Hyde;[17] instead of atavistic strength being figured as unrestrained, animalistic violence as with Hyde, for Mount Dunstan strength is a resurgence of the primal, creative energies of his ancient ancestors. Bettina registers that idea in her subsequent reflection on Mount Dunstan as "The First Man of them, who hewed his way to the front, who stood fierce in the face of things, who won the first lands and laid the first stones, might have been like him in build and look" (147).

The locution, "The First Man," evokes not only the first of Mount Dunstan's ancestors, it suggests the biblical first man, Adam, who by virtue of being first is genetically pure, untainted by social vices.

With the concept of the first man, Bettina's thoughts take another turn: "'It's a disgusting thing,' she said to herself, 'to think of the corrupt weaklings the strong ones dwindled down to. I hate them. So does he'" (147). By attributing such a thought to Bettina, Burnett indirectly introduces the idea of a woman's responsibility to do something to correct the continued production of "corrupt weaklings," to act, in short, on her hatred of them, that hatred being a function of her devotion to her race. The next turn in her thoughts indicates one direction for such action:

> There had been many such [corrupt weaklings] of late years, she knew. She had seen them in Paris, in Rome, even in New York. Things with thin or over-thick bodies and receding chins and foreheads; things haunting places of amusement and finding inordinate entertainment in strange jokes and horseplay. She herself had hot blood and fierce strength of rebellion, and she was wondering how, if the father and elder brother [of Mount Dunstan] had been the "bad lot," he had managed to stand still, looking on, and keeping his hands off them. (147)

Her disgust leads to violent thoughts, but clearly such thoughts are untenable; exerting physical force against those with "receding chins and foreheads" can be only an empty gesture. A better response is to do something productive, or to put it more precisely, something reproductive. It is on this point *The Shuttle* can be aligned with the "New Woman" novel and the idea of "rational reproduction."

In my discussion of *A Lady of Quality* I evoked Angelique Richardson's connection between the new woman and rational reproduction in the context of the idea of Clorinda and the Duke of Osmonde being physical equivalents of each other, ideally suited to produce strong, healthy children through mating, marriage as such being incidental to that imperative. In Richardson's chapter, "Women and Nature," she discusses Frances Swiney's *The Awakening of Women; or, Women's Part in Evolution* (1899) in terms of a theory of degeneration. "As she [Swiney] saw it," Richardson writes,

> "from the time that woman lost her power of selection, and man exercised upon her the abuse of sexual excesses, the race began to degenerate". She urged women to choose life partners "as to character rather than talent, to healthiness and purity of body and mind, rather than to affluence of position and station." (50)

The inability of women to choose and the possibility of restoring that ability, the association of aristocratic men with sexual excess (and drunkenness and venereal diseases) and the possibility of restoring moral and physical health to such men: those things are at stake in a woman's choice of a man with whom to mate. As part of its fascination with and revulsion against degeneration, *The Shuttle* teases out the implications of each choice. One marriage in the novel plays out the consequences for a woman who has been deprived of choice by a degenerate man while the events that lead to the prospect of a contrasting marriage depict how a woman's choice of a mate is ultimately subordinated to the natural energies that resist degeneration and work perpetually to renew the vitality of the race. In that latter formulation race refers to a familial line of descent and to the concept of a people, such as the Anglo-Saxon/Anglo-American race, as a whole.

The Shuttle is structured on the contrast between two American sisters and heiresses, Rosalie and Bettina Vanderpoel, who are each connected to the last surviving male inheritors of rundown, impoverished country estates, Sir Nigel Anstruthers of Stornham Court and James Hubert John Fergus Saltyre, fifteenth Earl of Mount Dunstan. Rosalie, the elder and weaker sister, is duped into marrying Sir Nigel, who needs her wealth to both restore his estate and to enable him to live in a manner he deemed appropriate to his rank and adequate for his appetites; Bettina, the younger and stronger sister, becomes entangled with Lord Mount Dunstan, who also needs money to restore his estate, but who finds the idea of marriage to an American to attain that money impossible to entertain. It would, he thinks, be an affront to the pride he feels for his ancestral line of descent. We can place those pairs of relationships in the context of Frances Swiney's theory of degeneration, with Rosalie and Sir Nigel representing the loss of a woman's choice in the face of male sexual excess, and with Bettina and Lord Mount Dunstan representing a woman's rational choice being in tune with a man's in the service of the imperative of the health of the race, in defiance of any consideration of wealth and status. In tracing how the novel renders the history of those relationships, it is possible to discern the contours of a grand transatlantic alliance, the precise terms of which come as a surprise.

Burnett introduces Rosalie Vanderpoel in the context of the metaphor she chose for the title of her book: the image of the shuttle equates the instrument that moves the thread back and forth in weaving to the image of ships carrying people back and forth across the Atlantic.

> It was in comparatively early days that the first thread we follow was woven into the web. Many such have been woven since and have added greater strength than any others, twining the cord of sex and home-building and race founding. But this was a slight and weak one, being only the life of one of Reuben Vanderpoel's daughters—the pretty little simple one whose name was Rosalie. (2–3)

Rosalie is drawn into the transatlantic weave after being selected by Sir Nigel to be his wife. Sir Nigel, though a baronet and possessor of Stornham Court, is, in his own words, "much worse than a beggar" (7). America, having been "discovered" by the English aristocracy "as a place where [...] one might marry one's sons profitably" (7) was where Sir Nigel's mother dispatched him to find an American bride with money. Although marred by "a heaviness of feature the result of objectionable living," Sir Nigel "was a man of good figure and a good voice," who exploited the social effects in New York of his "'English accent'" (5–6). Rosalie is pretty and petite, "with a childlike simpleness of mind." As the narrator notes, "she was exactly the girl to find Sir Nigel's domineering temperament at once imposing and attractive, so long as it was cloaked by ceremonies of external good breeding" (9). Sir Nigel exploits the myth of English cultural and social superiority, seducing Rosalie with the prospect of living the elegant life of the wife of a landed English lord. His apparent charm, however, masks his calculation for he "was cold-blooded enough to see that her gentle weakness was of value because it could be bullied, her money was to be counted on because it could be spent on himself and his degenerate vices and on his racked and ruined name and estate" (11). For him the stakes are high, but all he needs to secure his prey are his voice and his manners as Rosalie chooses social position over "purity of body and mind." Although Sir Nigel's sexual excesses and capacity for violence are not openly revealed until later in the novel, by the end of the first chapter the contours of Swiney's theory of degeneration can already be discerned. Rosalie's sister, at the time only 9 years old, is sharp enough to see it. '"He'll do something awful to you,'" Bettina says to Rosalie. '"He'll nearly kill you. I know he will'" (12).

Before he nearly kills her, however, he diminishes her through a combination of bullying and condescension, so that relatively soon after Rosalie settles in at Stornham Court "Sir Nigel had managed to convey to her that in England a woman who was married could do nothing to defend herself against her husband, and that to endeavor to do anything was the last impossible touch of vulgar ignominy" (28). The fact that Rosalie should feel the need to defend herself in the early days of her marriage is chilling in itself, but Sir Nigel's success in convincing her that she is to blame through behavior that would be judged as vulgar reveals how easy it is for him to exploit Rosalie's (and Americans' more generally) sense of social inferiority. Sir Nigel's mother aids him in that latter task. "Since Nigel has married you," she says to Rosalie, "he has, of course, a right to expect that you will at least make an effort to learn something of what is required of women in your position" (37), the primary requirement being to surrender all her financial resources to her husband, something that "[T]he law used to settle [...] definitely" (26). The appeal to what the law used to require is a cynical gesture to past traditions, suggesting that since Rosalie is inhabiting a titled country estate, she must conform to all traditions, even those not legally sanctioned.

Such pressures on Rosalie, combined with the long-standing tensions between Sir Nigel and his mother, disorient her. She cannot comprehend the emotional tone of her new home. The narrator provides painful insight into the quality of that tone when she addresses Nigel's relationship with his mother: "They were both bullies and each made occasional efforts at bullying the other without any particular result. But each could at least bully the other into intensified unpleasantness" (37). That intensified unpleasantness culminates in a scene that occurs after Rosalie discovers that Sir Nigel had prevented her family from making a visit and that he is determined to continue to do so. When Rosalie protests, he and his mother berate her with assertions such as: "If she had been an Englishwoman, well born, and of decent breeding, all her fortune would have been properly transferred to her husband," but because she has not done that, she is held in contempt by "all people who had been properly brought up and knew what was in good taste and of good morality" (50). The baseness and hypocrisy of such claims are clear to Rosalie, who defends herself by mocking her own belief in the value of their being "aristocratic" and by judging Nigel for pressing her so harshly for money "that I daren't offer to a decent American who could work for himself" (50). Those words, which link Sir Nigel to the idleness of the basest of the nonworking poor, fusing a view of degeneration from the top and from the bottom as described by Arata, enrage Nigel, who strikes her. Before she falls, Rosalie reveals that she "might have a son." Then "[S]he fell in a shuddering heap" striking her head against "an oak chest and lay upon the floor, her arms flung out and limp, as if she were a dead thing" (50). But Nigel only "nearly killed her," as Bettina had predicted. Rosalie recovers to deliver a humpbacked son, the implication being Nigel's attack on her is the cause of the boy's deformity. In the context of the theory of degeneration at play in the novel, that deformity marks the next stage of decay as the corrupt moral weakling in a declining family fathers an ill-formed son.

The decay of the Anstruthers' baronetcy, in terms of both land and people, need not be absolute. As a counterforce to the theory of degeneration that dominates the international marriage narrative of Rosalie and Sir Nigel is an exhilaratingly positive form of gender-based social Darwinism as figured in the relationship between Rosalie's younger sister, Bettina, and Bettina's father. That counterforce is enacted in such plot details as Bettina's arrival as an adult at Stornham during a time when Sir Nigel is traveling on the continent with his Spanish paramour. Her response to the parallel condition of Rosalie and the estate is to dedicate herself to the restoration of both through care of Rosalie's physical and mental health and through the refurbishment of the house, stables and gardens of Stornham Court. A conversation between Bettina and Lord Mount Dunstan helps contextualize Bettina's actions as more than the whim of a rich woman with the means to redress the wrongs committed against her sister; the details suggest that her actions are part of the long-term natural and social development of women. The conversation is rich and allusive, so it will take a bit of unpacking to reveal its layers.

It begins when Bettina takes Mount Dunstan into the gardens she is restoring at Stornham. As she explains how she had been so ignorant of the varied patterns and processes by which flowers can be brought to bloom at different times of the year, she describes her feelings as she observed "a bed of transplanted things that seemed to droop too long." She tells how "they slowly lift their heads [...] as if to listen to a Voice calling." Focusing then on a single rose, she renders her experience of its revival: "Once I sat for quite a long time before a rose, watching it. When I saw it *begin* to listen, I felt a little trembling pass over my body [...]. It was Life [...] coming back in answer to what we cannot hear" (276). This vision of and feeling for a rose being reanimated by the nutrients from the earth is for Bettina an image of life itself; she later says that in the garden she felt as if she were "standing close to the Secret of the World," a secret, I would argue, that becomes accessible as one's body achieves attunement to the energies of growth, decay and renewal in nature. Such an attunement to the animating currents in nature stimulates in Bettina an understanding that those currents can also animate the growth and renewal of ties between human families and the land they occupy and, ideally, care for. That shift in perception marks a transition from feeling to thought, from emotion to intellect. Mount Dunstan recognizes something of that as he ponders how unusual it is for a woman to come from outside England to manage a restoration project at Stornham. But this woman, he recognizes, "illuminated" her efforts by "an intelligence at once brilliant and fine" (278). Finding her sister in such distress upon her arrival, and with the husband gone (his mother had died some years earlier), there was no obstacle to her simply taking Rosalie back to New York. Bettina, however, decides to restore the estate because of the child. He may be deformed, but he is the heir to the estate, and the estate is entailed; it must go to him. To break the entail would be to disrupt the multigenerational link between a family and the land, severing in the process the secret of life that binds people to the earth; the obligations of care such a link requires are human relationships that sustain families and renew communities over generations.

That such a vision could be discerned as animating the intellect of a woman perplexes Mount Dunstan. "He wondered at first […] how a girl had learned certain things she had an obviously clear knowledge of." But "as they conversed he learned" that Bettina "had acquired […] almost unconsciously a remarkable education" (278). The narrative renders that education as her genetic inheritance from the "strong and fine intelligence" of her father. As she grew up, her father took her traveling with him, shared with her his business plans, operations and successes; he talked with her frankly and fully. Bettina explains: "He trusted me. He told me of great things even before he talked of them to men." In other words, he treated her as a fully capable human being, unhampered by the assumed limitations of her gender. "He once said," Bettina explains to Mount Dunstan, "that it was a part of the evolution of race that men had begun to expect of women what in past ages they really only expected of each other." Mount Dunstan's response is hesitant; he seems unable to think beyond gender binaries. He says, "You mean—absolute faith—apart from affection" (279)? Faith in a woman because of affection for her he understands; faith in a woman as faith in another human being poses a problem for him. In order to be aligned with the "evolution of race," to avoid being trapped by a sense of the past that he fears closes off his future, he has to get past that problem; he has to learn to see Bettina fully as a human being. That does not require a rejection of sex, quite the contrary. It does require that sex not be tied to the social constructs of gender. The complex challenge, then, that Burnett poses to herself in *The Shuttle* is to reconcile her drive to show how her main protagonists, Bettina and Mount Dunstan, can bring out the full humanity of each other in a way that eliminates the distortions of national difference, gender pressure, economic inequality and personal pride while at the same time aligning them with deep family and national histories. Her primary strategy seems to be to look back to the beginning of particular family histories, leap over the traditions that accumulate over time and reassert the positive atavistic power of those family stories as formative and restorative for the nation.

As I noted above, Burnett opens the novel by introducing the metaphor of the shuttle, which, she writes, "was guided by the great hand of Fate" to weave a web linking Britain and the United States in order for those nations to take their "place in the making of world history." Although she does not use this explicit vocabulary, her readers at the time would recognize that opening as a gesture toward the dream of an Anglo-Saxon alliance that would form, in the words of Sir Charles Wentworth Dilke, a "Greater Britain."[18] Here is how he presents that idea in the "Preface" to his book of that name published in 1869: "In 1866 and 1867, I followed England round the world: everywhere I was in English-speaking, or in English-governed lands. If I remarked that climate, soil, manners of life, that mixture with other peoples had modified the blood, I saw, too, that in essentials the race was always one" (vii). Actuated by a vision "of the grandeur of the race, already girdling the earth, which it is destined, perhaps, eventually to overspread," Dilke places America at the center of that vision:

> In America, the peoples of the world are being fused together, but they are run into an English mould: Alfred's laws and Chaucer's tongue are theirs whether they would or no.

There are men who say that Britain in her age will claim the glory of having planted greater Englands across the seas. They fail to perceive that she has done more than found plantations of her own—that she has imposed her institutions upon the offshoots of Germany, of Ireland, of Scandinavia, and of Spain. Through America, England is speaking to the world.[19]

The "offshoots" Dilke alludes to are all from Western Europe, representatives of the old immigration to America; he also assumes an organic unity of growth between England and America, ignoring efforts in the United States to build something new. That something new is explicit in Ralph Waldo Emerson's essay "Nature," in which he asks, "Why should we not also enjoy an original relation to the universe? Why should not we have a poetry and philosophy of insight and not of tradition, and a religion by a revelation to us, and not the history of theirs?"[20] But in the years after Emerson in 1836, Dilke in 1869 and Burnett in 1907, the tension between the idea of America forging its own future in opposition to the English traditions of its cultural inheritance and Dilke's assertion that English laws and language are in America's blood "whether they will or no" disappeared in the face of the new immigration, Dilke's view taking on a new importance on both sides of the Atlantic. The weaving that Burnett evokes in her opening, then, functions as an instinctive response to fears of degeneration and the decline of empire in Britain and fears of race suicide by degeneration in the United States. "Men thought but little," she writes "of either web or weaving [...] for the time unconscious of the strength of the thread thrown across thousands of miles of leaping, heaving, grey or blue ocean" (1). In that formulation the shuttle is weaving together the frayed threads of organic Anglo-American/Anglo-Saxon unity, but unlike Dilke's vision of world dominance, Burnett's vision turns inward. She is not concerned with matters of empire, nor does she engage directly with questions of immigration. Her interest is on the intersection of the personal, the local and the national.

Burnett's introduction in the first chapter of the Vanderpoel family history establishes that pattern of interest. The Vanderpoels, Burnett explains, "were [...] of the Americans whose fortunes were a portion of the history of their country. The building of these fortunes had been a part of it, or had created epochs and crises" (3). Burnett presents history as it is built upon the accumulated acts of individuals; consequently, she chronicles the development of the Vanderpoel family over four generations, with Bettina Vanderpoel being the representative par excellence of the fifth. "The first Reuben Vanderpoel [...] was the lauded hero of stories of thrift and enterprise." He may have been "practical, sordid, [and] uneducated," but he had "genius [for] commerce"; he was also wise enough to marry "a trader's daughter," who shared "his passion for gain." Together they founded the family fortune, which their son, the second Reuben Vanderpoel, built upon to create "a fortune as much larger than the first as the rapid growth and increasing capabilities of the country gave him enlarging opportunities to acquire." The quality that made the family unique "was not so much that they wished to be rich as that Nature itself impelled them to collect wealth as the load-stone draws towards it iron" (4). The growth of the family wealth mirrors the expansion of the country, both actuated by the vital energies of the place and the historical moment. The family and the nation grew together, mutually transforming each other. "After the second generation the meagre and mercantile physical type of the Vanderpoels improved upon itself," Burnett writes with a kind of evolutionary flourish, and the focus of the evolutionary gesture is the woman. "Feminine good looks appeared and were made the most of," the innuendo referencing sexual selection providing the next stage in the family's climbing upward on the evolutionary scale, a point reinforced by the fourth Rueben Vanderpoel's comment to his daughter about her part in the "evolution of race." By the fourth generation, the "brown-stone mansion" the family built had become a symbol of American affluence; it was thought of through popular press accounts as the "personal possession" of townsfolk from New England to the Rocky Mountains (5). Burnett thus presents the Vanderpoel family history as the representative, even archetypal, American social narrative where human enterprise and the productivity of the land interanimate each other in a dance of parallel development.

The degenerative counterforces at play in the figure of Sir Nigel Anstruthers exert pressure on such an archetypal, evolutionary narrative; his visit to America to barter for a wife as described above serves as a parody of the story of the first Reuben Vanderpoel. Though not a "genius of commerce," Sir Nigel comes to New York with a kind of mercantile interest, and he uses all the personal attributes he can muster, and his rank, to achieve his end. The crucial difference between the two, however, is that Sir Nigel is out of tune with the productive potential of the time and place. Unlike the first Reuben who was "compelled by nature," paradoxically forgetful of self in his pursuit of wealth, Sir Nigel's motive is self-indulgence; he takes pleasure in inflicting pain, on asserting his power over others. In that light, one of the central tensions in the novel is between Bettina's evolutionary narrative and Sir Nigel's trajectory of degeneration. The novel does not simply place those narratives in opposition with the obvious conclusion being that evolution must prevail. Rather the novel struggles to reconcile the two narratives, to fuse them together in order to transform the degenerative within the generative. That requires that the evolutionary narrative not be linear, moving on a steadily upward path, but that it turn back and recoup some of its original energies. The novel achieves that through the story of Lord Mount Dunstan, whose own visit to America functions as a parody of Sir Nigel's parody.

III

As the first Reuben Vanderpoel had done, and as Sir Nigel's New York journey echoed as parody, Mount Dunstan traveled to America to make his fortune, but unlike Vanderpoel and Sir Nigel, he failed. Using the little bit of money he could squeeze out of his decaying estate, Mount Dunstan, under the name of Jem Salter, travels to the American West to establish a sheep farm. In a scene parallel to the one described above, when Bettina walked Mount Dunstan through the gardens of Stornham Court, Mount Dunstan walks Bettina through the grounds of his estate. Because they had met earlier on the crossing from New York to Liverpool, she knew he had been to the United States without knowing his identity or purpose. When she finds out who he is, she asks: "Did you like America?" to which he responds: "Hated it. I went there lured by a belief that a man like myself, with muscle and will, even without experience, could make a fortune out of small capital on a sheep ranch. Wind and weather and disease played the devil with me. I lost the little I had and came back to begin over again—on nothing—here!" (144). Bettina asks what he means to begin again? He replies: "To begin to build up again, in one man's life, what has taken centuries to grow—and fall into this" (144). His response to the situation he shares with Anstruthers is to act differently; rather than looking for a wife he looks to work, which Bettina observes, is "a splendid thing to do" (144) because she too, she admits, is "a sort of commercial working person [...] [who] resent[s] seeing things lose their value" (145). Anstruthers's reaction to his family's degeneration is to exploit the qualities of debauchery and immorality to manipulate others and to accelerate his own degradation, a point confirmed by the deterioration of his body as the novel develops. Mount Dunstan's reaction is to resist, to begin again, to become, as his founding ancestor Red Godwyn had been as well as the first Reuben Vanderpoel, like "The First Man," if not an originator, then a rejuvenator. Bettina suggests that he might begin the restoration "at the fences," her own starting point for the restoration of Stornham Court.

In the pattern I have teased out here, Bettina is a gender-inflected evolutionary advance from the first Reuben Vanderpoel, a woman of intelligence, practicality and fearlessness, qualities shared with her idea of the first man. (Recall on this point Burnett's assertion that for her the perfect woman would be a perfect gentleman.) Sir Nigel is the inverse, a degenerate, immoral, self-absorbed, bullying and fearful. Mount Dunstan is associated more with a theory of degeneration than he is with evolution. He has more in common with Anstruthers than he does with Bettina. By the time he was born, his older brother, Lord Tenham, "had reached a premature and degenerate maturity"; he was also a close associate of Sir Nigel's. The two of them, we learn later, were involved in a "shameful scandal" compounded of sexual excess and physical abuse, which Mount Dunstan compares to the early history of his ancestors: "Savagery in savage days had its excuse," he thinks. But his brother's and Sir Nigel's brutality "is the beast sunk into the gibbering, degenerate ape" (185). When that scandal happened Mount Dunstan was still a child; his brother fled and, "after descending into all the hells of degenerate debauch," died, followed soon thereafter by his father, who had lived "long enough to make himself something horribly near an imbecile" (180–81). In the tradition of the Victorian sensation novel, debased bloodlines end in insanity, the only thing Mount Dunstan stands to inherit. But in his youth, Mount Dunstan had resisted the influence of father and brother; he lived in reclusive humiliation, inwardly rebelling against them as he spent hours in the family library, reading histories of "his own people." The local vicar, Mr. Penzance, befriends him and acquires an understanding of Mount Dunstan's humiliation; Penzance also sees that Dunstan's native pride could not develop into healthy self-confidence as long as he was tarred with the same brush as his father and brother. Nonetheless, Penzance perceives a core of strength: "It sometimes thrilled him to see in the big frame and powerful muscles, in the strong nature and unconquerable spirit, a revival of what had burned and stirred through lives lived in a dim, almost mythical past." Penzance's insight reverses the parallel between Anstruthers and Mount Dunstan, for Mount Dunstan does not embody the next stage of family degeneration; he is a revival. "Students of heredity knew that there were curious instances of revival of type," Penzance muses, and he wonders "[W]hy might not one fancy [...] this strong thing reborn, even as the offspring of a poorer effete type" (183). Why might Mount Dunstan not be a reversion to Red Godwyn, the first man of his family's history? If he is, the savagery he would have been capable of in savage times can become moral strength and physical persistence, the power to work "in well doing," Penzance as vicar might have hoped. As the theory of degeneration plays out in the stories of Anstruthers and Mount Dunstan, the latter's reversion to an earlier type turns out to be an advance. He reembodies what Penzance later thinks of as "Primeval Force" (185).

In the turn to the primeval, Burnett redirects the tension between theories of evolution and degeneration to an evocation of the divinity of human labor, which converts brute force into productive work. If degeneration is evidenced by atavistic brutality, and if evolution moves to ameliorate gender binaries in a unified vision of human integrity and strength, a rekindling of primeval energies aligns human change with the eternal powers of renewal that animate nature. Here is how Mr. Penzance puts the idea as he contemplates Mount Dunstan's "big back and body": "Primeval Force—the thin-faced, narrow-chested, slightly bald clergyman of the Church of England was thinking—never loses its way, or fails to sweep a path before it. The sun rises and sets, the seasons come and go, Primeval Force is of them, and as unchangeable" (185). Note how the religious elements in those sentences—the speaker of the Church of England deploying a conventional Christian language of an unchangeable God who never fails to guide the believer aright—are subordinated to natural processes, the power of the deity ascribed to "Force." Brief as the passage is, it nonetheless depends on a fusion of the concepts of God, natural force and human work articulated by Thomas Carlyle in his *Sartor Resartus* (1836).

> Well sang the Hebrew Psalmist: "If I take the wings of the morning and dwell in the uttermost parts of the universe, God is there." Thou thyself, O cultivated reader, who too probably art no Psalmist, but a Prosaist, knowing God only by tradition, knowest thou any corner of the world where at least Force is not? [...] Thinkest thou there is aught motionless; without Force, and utterly dead?[21]

In that brief passage, Carlyle redefines God from the animating power in the universe to "Force," which, like God and like the seasons, is "unchangeable." The passage suggests not that force is one of God's instruments but God itself; God becomes a tradition, force the reality. Once Carlyle decenters the concept of God and replaces it with force, he subordinates force to the imperative of human labor. In a reflection on the fire viewed from a distance at the center of a blacksmith's forge, Carlyle addresses his reader as follows:

> Thou fool, that smithy-fire was (primarily) kindled at the Sun; is fed by air that circulates before Noah's Deluge, from beyond the Dog-star; therein, with Iron Force, and Coal Force, and the far stronger Force of Man, are cunning affinities and battles and victories of Force brought about; it is a little ganglion, or nervous centre, in the great vital system of Immensity. Call it [...] an unconscious Altar [...] whose dingy Priest, not by word, yet by brain and sinew, preaches forth (exoterically enough) one little textlet from the Gospel of Freedom, the Gospel of Man's Force, commanding, and one day to be all-commanding. (54)

From the biblically poetic "wings of the morning" that lead one to God, to God being redefined as force, to force being the one constant through all of time (i.e., from at least the time of Noah's flood) and throughout all space (i.e., the Dog-star, Sirius, the brightest star visible from earth), to force being under the hammer of the strong arm of man whose very being is defined by the imperative to work, Carlyle articulates a vision of the perpetual renovating power of human labor. For Carlyle, work is the essential moral imperative that gives meaning to individual lives and the communities that comprise those lives, and work is the keynote that rings throughout *The Shuttle*.

IV

The pattern sketched above of evolutionary forward momentum pressing against the retrograde forces of degeneration which are reconciled through the productive imperatives of work is reinforced by the novel's presentation of the relation of the United States to England. The retrograde forces are stimulated by books, "cheap, pirated editions of English works [...] [that] brought before American eyes soft, home-like pictures of places which were [...] the birthplaces of fathers or grandfathers." Such images of "home" through the "power of nature caused a stirring in the blood [...] and awakened something akin to homesickness, though no man called the feeling by its name" (51). The evolutionary forces are rendered in the American project itself, to build a new country, inhabit new spaces and experience new things: "In the United States of America, which had not yet acquired the serene sense of conservative self-satisfaction and repose which centuries of age may bestow, the spirit of life itself is the aspiration for change." The contrast between "aspiration for change" standing in for "the spirit of life" in the United States and the "self-satisfaction and repose" that characterizes England in that sentence carries with it an implicit moral judgment; self-satisfaction connotes complacency, even smugness while repose evokes the supine, both resistant to change and thus, by the logic of the sentence, life-denying in that there is no project, nothing to work toward. For the United States:

> Ambition itself only means the insistence on change. Each day is to be better than yesterday, fuller of plans, of briskness, of initiative. Each today demands of tomorrow new men, new minds, new work. A today which has not launched new ships, explored new countries, constructed new buildings, added stories to old ones, may consider itself a failure, unworthy even of being consigned to the limbo of respectable yesterdays. Such a country lives by leaps and bounds. (52)

Nostalgia and such ambition must be hard to reconcile, as if an immovable object (nostalgia) blocks the passage of an irresistible force (ambition). Perhaps reconciliation is not what is needed, however. What happens when nostalgia is disrupted? To begin to answer that question, consider what Bettina tells her father: "It is England we love, we Americans [...]. What could be more natural? [...] It is only an English cottage and an English lane, whether white with hawthorn blossoms or bare with winter that wakes in us that little yearning, groveling tenderness that is so sweet. It is only nature calling us home" (95). It would be hard to find a better evocation of the quality of feeling, a "groveling tenderness," that an aesthetic production of nostalgia creates in an American who feels bereft of culture. As Bettina's train carries her from London through the Kent countryside to

Stornham Court, she thinks she sees "the England of Constable [...] and Miss Austen" and then comments to herself: "That is so American [...] the habit of comparing every stick and stone and breathing thing to some literary parallel" (101). The imagined fathers and grandfathers putatively born in English villages are as real as the literary sources that produce the images of their habitation. When Bettina arrives in Stornham village, however, present reality impinges on the workings of nostalgia; the England of Constable and Austen clashes with the actual village she enters. Her reaction is not a shocked repudiation of the invented memory of her literary-fed imaginative nostalgia; rather, she responds to the collision between nostalgia and the present with an impulse to work.

This is what she sees in Stornham village: "Her pulse beat a little more hurriedly as the brougham entered Stornham village. It was picturesque, but struck her as looking neglected. Many of the cottages had an air of dilapidation. There were many broken windows and unmended garden palings. A suggested lack of whitewash in several cases was not cheerful." Anticipating an image out of a Jane Austen novel, her heart rate increases as she perceives an overall aesthetic impression; then the details impinge, replacing the picturesque with the dilapidated. "I know nothing of the duties of English landlords," she says softly to herself, "but I should do it myself" (103), the "it" being to fix the windows, mend the garden palings and whitewash the walls of the cottages. She is in for further surprises as she sees the park gateway is "out of order," and the diamond-shaped windowpanes in the nearby lodge are damaged. Those preliminary shocks are merely preparatory for what she experiences when she sees what has become of her delicate, fetching sister: "Twelve years should not have changed a pretty blond thing of nineteen to a worn, unintelligent-looking dowdy of the order of dowdiness which seems to have lived beyond age and sex. She looked even stupid, or at least stupefied" (105). Rosalie presents a different order of problem than the village and estate. "Her spirit and her health are broken," Bettina observes. "Her prettiness has faded to a rag. She is as nervous as an ill-treated child. I do not know where to begin with her" (113), but begin she must. It is her nature, for "[H]er pulses beat too strongly, her blood ran too fast to allow of inaction of mind or body [...]. Disorder filled her with a sort of impatience which was akin to physical distress" (112). Bettina may have been born to wealth; she was also born to work.

Here is how the narrator explains Bettina's essential nature:

> If she had been born a poor woman she would have worked hard for her living, and found an interest, almost an exhilaration, in her labour. Such gifts as she had would have been applied to the tasks she undertook [...]. Imagination and initiative could make any service absorbing [...]. [I]f she had been a nursemaid, the children under her care would never have been sufficiently bored to become tiresome or intractable [...]. She would not have left them alone so to speak. In obeying the mere laws of her being, she would have stimulated them. (112)

Bettina's genius for living, one might say, is her ability to exert the full force of her human potential into productive labor, forgetful of herself. Those qualities—unselfconsciousness and a will to work—are qualities associated with Carlyle's "dingy Priest" alluded to in the quotation above, that priest being representative of the shaping force of man. Bettina's father indirectly acknowledges that view when he tells her that she "ought to have been a man" (112). To that, Bettina says, no. "[O]ne is either born like that, or one is not," Bettina argues. "Sometimes I think that the people who must *act* are a distinct race. A kind of vigorous restlessness drives them [...]. [T]here has always been as much for women to do as for men" (113). The point for Bettina is not one of gender; it is of being a certain kind of human being. From her perspective her nature cannot be measured in terms of its compatibility with social constructions of masculinity with the mark of her development being its similarity to a man's. Rather she is of a race, a human grouping of men and women who share qualities that do not fit already established patterns. In terms of the evolutionary trajectory of the narrative, she represents a new stage.

Something to that effect comes out in a conversation between the vicar Penzance and Mount Dunstan. Penzance introduces the topic of Bettina when he tells Mount Dunstan of Bettina's surprising arrival at Stornham village. Alluding to the isolated, even distressing, circumstances of Rosalie, noting how "unexplainable" it is "that none of her family ever appeared," Penzance exclaims with some surprise: "Now—apparently without having been expected—the sister appears" (188). Not only is her arrival surprising, so is her person: "I heard today that she seems an unusual young woman, and has beauty," says Penzance, to which Mount Dunstan replies: "Her eyes and lashes are remarkable. She is tall. The Americans are setting up a new type." Two men discussing a woman as a new type based on her beauty and stature is ordinary enough; they could simply be alluding to changes in fashion, tall women becoming more the thing than the "slender, fragile little women" that used to come from America. More than beauty and stature are at play, though. Penzance explains:

> "She has made a curious impression. She has begun to do things. Stornham village has lost its breath." He laughed a little. "She has been going over the place and discussing repairs." [...]
> "That is practical," [Mount Dunstan] commented.
> "It is really interesting. Why should a young woman turn her attention to repairs? If it had been her father—the omnipotent Mr. Vanderpoel—who had appeared, one would not have wondered at such practical activity. But a young lady—with remarkable eyelashes!"

The humor in the exchange results from the men's fixation on Bettina's beauty via the synecdoche of her eyelashes and the contrast between that and Bettina's "practical activity." That activity calls for a different kind of response than they seem able to muster until Penzance says this: "It allures me. Unknown quantities in character always allure me. I should like to know her. A community like this is made up of the absolutely known quantity—of types repeating themselves through centuries. A new one is always a startling thing" (189). The shift in pronouns from "she" to "it" marks how Penzance thinks about Bettina's presence. His focus shifts from surface to depth, from appearance to character, so when he says he would like to know "her," his desire is to plumb her character, assess her humanity. The emergence of a new type draws him more than the length of Bettina's eyelashes even though the eyelashes (and the eyes that they frame) cannot be ignored.

The productive tension between Bettina's practical energy and her personal beauty can be discerned throughout her work with the local artisans as she plans and they execute the restoration work for both the village and the estate. After Bettina's initial conversations with the carpenter, the saddler and the blacksmith, the men gather at "The Clock" to discuss "the new young lady from the court [who] had been to see them." Fox, the saddler, is the first to talk.

> "This is what she said," Fox's story ran, "and she said it so straightforward and business-like that the conceitedest man that lived couldn't be upset by it. 'I want to see what you can do,' she says. 'I am new to the place and I must find out what everyone can do, then I shall know what to do myself.' The way she sets them eyes on a man is a sight. It's the sense in them and the human nature that takes you in." (207)

As in the conversation between Penzance and Mount Dunstan, Bettina's eyes are emphasized but not for their feminine appeal. Her eyes support the honesty and directness of the interaction between two human beings, the difference in sex lightly registered ("the way she sets them eyes on a man is a sight") but subordinated to her clarity of mind and "human nature." Because of Bettina's wealth she certainly would have the authority that would be granted to a man under similar circumstances; her exercise of that authority is cooperative, however. She does not issue commands; she inquires and tests before she can configure her own role in the grand project. Tread, the blacksmith, recognizes that, for in response to Fox's story, he says: "Yes, it's sense […] her looking at you as if she expected you to have sense yourself, and understand that she's doing fair business. It's clear-headed like" (207). When we consider the inverse power dynamics of class (where Bettina is dominant) and gender (where the men have priority) in the interaction Tread is reacting to, we can detect that for Tread those asymmetries disappear in a "clear-headed" balance of mutual good sense and equity; Bettina assumes a common humanity, orients herself toward Tread (and the other craftsmen) on that assumption and Tread responds in kind.

The craftsmen end their conversation with a discussion of this question: "Where's the money coming from?" Tread offers the obvious answer, "It'll come from America," and he then provides this explanation:

> "She [Rosalie] came here with plenty [of money], but Sir Nigel got a hold of it for his games, and they're the games that cost money. Her ladyship wasn't born with a backbone, poor thing, but this new one [Bettina] was, and her ladyship's father is her father, and you mark my words, there's money coming into Stornham, though it's not going to be played the fool with. Lord, yes! this new one has a backbone and good strong wrists and a good strong head, though I must say"—with a little masculine chuckle of admission—"it's a bit unnatural with them eyelashes and them eyes looking at you between 'em. Like blue water between rushes in the marsh." (207)

Even though Bettina's beauty, with strong overtones of sexual allure—Tread offers a sensual simile that equates her eyes to rushing water—emerges in the last words of the conversation, the recognition of her sexual appeal does not dominate; it seems more afterthought than the central element that commands the goodwill of the men. The most direct appeal is to the strength of Bettina's body and mind, a strength that functions as an extension of the power of her father while at the same time being clearly Bettina's own.

Her qualities are her qualities. Her physical beauty still has the potential to compromise any recognition of her capacity to do practical work in the world, but in the series of examples explored in this section, her beauty comes in the wake of her practical energy and receptive intelligence.

Burnett's presentation of Bettina as a new type, a woman who possesses qualities of character traditionally associated with an idealized definition of man while retaining physical qualities traditionally associated with an idealized sexual attractiveness of a woman, serves as a narrative vehicle to transform the tension between the evolutionary force of development and the degenerative forces of retrogression, where retrogression becomes a version of development by way of restoration. Development becomes a kind of return. As a capstone to that point, we can look at two passages, one that captures the reflections of Lord Dunholm, holder of the one estate in the novel that had prospered rather than fallen into decay, and the other where Bettina recounts her motives for wanting to restore Stornham Court and village. On a visit to Stornham Court performed after the restoration was well in hand, Lord Dunholm reflects on the woman responsible for the changes so visible in the estate. "The change," he thinks, "suggested magic" performed by a woman who represents something new:

> She was not of the curious, exotic little creatures, whose thin, though sometimes rather sweet, and always gay, high-pitched young voices Lord Dunholm had been so especially struck by in the early days of the American invasion. Her voice had a tone one would likely remember with pleasure. How well she moved—how well her black head was set on her neck! Yes, she was a new type—the later generation. These amazing oddly practical people had evolved it—planned it, perhaps bought—figuratively speaking—the architects and material to design and build it—bought them in whatever country they found them, England, France, Italy, Germany—pocketing them coolly and carrying them back home to develop, complete, and send forth into the world when their invention was a perfected thing. (256)[22]

Although Lord Denholm dismisses his thoughts as merely the "humour of his fancy," they clearly capture the novel's evolutionary discourse associated with Bettina, linking her development to a national project rather than the fluke of a singular family. Based on the logic of Dunholm's thinking, America is personified as a social engineer involved in a eugenics experiment; Bettina is the result of combining the best physical, intellectual and moral qualities from throughout Western Europe. To borrow Dunholm's words, "figuratively speaking" Bettina serves as an American eugenics export, bringing the best combination of European genetic material back to England where she can reverse the processes of moral and material decay by restoring England to its original state. In the novel that original state is associated with a revival of patriarchal medievalism, where a vision of organic community subsumes the subordination of social classes within a model of mutual responsibility, the prosperity of each social class depending on the prosperity of the others.[23] Here is how Bettina explained it in a letter to her father:

> When I walk down the village streets, faces appear at windows, and figures, stolidly, at doors. What I see is that, vaguely and remotely, American though I am, the fact that I am of "her ladyship's blood," and that her ladyship—American though she is—has the claim on them

of being the mother of the son of the owner of the land—stirs in them a feeling that I have a shadowy sort of relationship in the whole thing, and with regard to their bad roofs and bad chimneys, to their broken palings, and damp floors, to their comforts and discomforts, a sort of responsibility. That is the whole thing, and you—just you, father—will understand me when I say I actually like it […]. There is something patriarchal in it which moves me. (221)

That passage renders a shadowy set of associations and relationships that take on substance as Bettina acts on what she calls "a sort of responsibility." She first registers a recognition that the villagers assume that the possessors of Stornham Court have a claim on them, an expectation of commitment to serve the interests of the estate. That claim is mediated by the idea that such a claim depends on the fact of a relationship; thus the villagers and the estate are answerable to each other, and with Bettina being the most resourced figure in the estate, she must accept a particular responsibility. The reference to patriarchy, then, is framed by Bettina's recognition of the intimate codependence of village and estate; given her placement in that community, she functions as the patriarch, whose role she defines as follows:

To feel that every man on the land, every woman, every child knew one, counted on one's honour and friendship, turned to one believing in times of stress, to know that one could help and be a finely faithful thing, the very knowledge of it would give one vigour and warm blood in the veins. I wish I had been born to it, I wish the first sounds falling on my newborn ears had been the clanging peal from the old Norman church tower […]. Still, though the first sounds that greeted me were probably the rattling of a Fifth Avenue stage, I have brought them *something*, and who knows whether I could have brought it from without the range of that prosaic, but cheerful, rattle. (222)

The source of the patriarch's power is not defined by authority in the abstract; power is a function of intimate, interpersonal knowledge. The patriarch in Bettina's formulation here builds trust through offering friendship, acting honorably, providing help at need and remaining faithful to those who have come to rely on those qualities. The effect is not only on the well-being of the villagers; their trust warms the blood of the patriarch and stimulates bodily vigor. At Stornham Court, the Anstruthers' men had through generations abandoned any patriarchal responsibility for the health of the community. For them class hierarchy means obedience of the lower to the higher, the only responsibility of the higher being to themselves in pursuit of their own pleasures. Once the social bond is broken, the lifeblood of the community bleeds away; the decay of the cottages and estate buildings is a symptom of the decay of the social body. So much blood, figuratively speaking, had been lost that renewal could not begin to emerge from within the remnants of the community. *Something* needed to come from the outside, but that something had to be capable of being absorbed into the lifeblood of the community. More than Bettina's money is needed for her to accomplish her goal to revitalize the village and estate, although that money figured in the "rattle" of the "Fifth Avenue stage" is essential as well. A new human type needs to become part of the community, infusing new blood, new energy, new life into it. The only way that Bettina can fulfill her vision of the responsibility of the patriarch, or, in her father's words, to realize the "idea of the lord of the land" (223), that "lord," of course, being a woman, is to become a permanent part of the community, to play the part of the First Woman to Mount Dunstan's First Man.[24]

That is where the novel ends, with the evolved woman of the new type poised to marry a "curious revival of type" (183), Mount Dunstan, in a closing chapter titled "The Primeval Thing." In that chapter Reuben Vanderpoel finally arrives at Stornham where he meets Mount Dunstan and engages in long conversations with him that were "of absorbing interest to both. Each presented to the other a new world, and a type of which his previous knowledge had been but incomplete" (510). In that latter sentence divisions between the old and the new, the past and the present are fused under broad notion of a "new world" referring to both the past associated with Mount Dunstan and the present with Mr. Vanderpoel. As the two men's interests become absorbed into each other's, so their worlds fuse. Vanderpoel comes to think of himself as "a romantic New York man of business" while Mount Dunstan's pride in family history and of place dissipates into the present that left little "space or thought for poor things" (511). The novel's final vision blends the deep past ("the primeval thing") and a future-oriented present on the verge of making history. As he muses in conversation with the vicar, Penzance, Mr. Vanderpoel sees Bettina and Mount Dunstan as fully and mutually human, their social circumstances irrelevant to the power of their being:

> "There is a great primeval thing which sometimes [...] occurs to two people" he [said]. "When it leaps into being, it is well if it is not thwarted, or done to death. It has happened to my girl and Mount Dunstan. If they had been two tinkers by the roadside, they would have come together, and defied their beggary. As it is, I recognize, as I sit here, that the outcome of what is to be may reach far, and open up broad new ways."
>
> "Yes," said the vicar. "She will live here and fill a strong man's life with wonderful human happiness—her splendid children will be born here, and among them will be those who lead the van and make history." (511)

Vanderpoel's reference to hypothetical beggary is a way to suggest that social constraints, be they of class or nation, disappear in the face of the evolution of the "race" spurred by the physical vitality and unique reciprocity between that rare primeval man and woman, the revival of the primeval type being the catalyst for future change. Bettina may seem reduced in the end to a woman bearing children to carry on her husband's name and legacy, but she does so, compelled by forces that make a negative social judgment of that fact irrelevant. Whatever future children she may have and however they may "lead the van," they are an extension of the restoration of life in the community. Burnett turns her contemporaries' fantasies of Anglo-Saxon union as a way to sustain world dominance for the English-speaking race into a domestic Anglo-American union where the power that has real, lasting value is the power of relationship, the power of community, the power of a paradoxical female-centric patriarchy that is always life affirming even as, in the novel's last words, "the Shuttle in the hand of Fate [...] weaves [...] its yet vague and uncompleted design" (512).

The domestic emphasis in *The Shuttle* of an Anglo-American alliance centered on the rehabilitation of a decaying England has its origins in Burnett's biography. As my reading of that novel suggests, Burnett's sympathies rest with England and America; she sees each nation as incomplete without the other in such a way as to blur any distinction in identity. In an interview she gave to *Harper's Bazaar*, she discussed her own identity as both: "'But I am English. I am both English and American. I am more of one until the other of me is denied, and then I'm that; and taken altogether, if I were not English, I should not be American; if not American, not English. In fine, I must be both or not at all" (cited in Gerzina).[25] As the *Harper's Bazaar* interviewer implies when she writes, "she was born in Manchester, England, not coming to this country till she was entering upon young lady-hood, and following which she has lived always half of the time in England," her sense of the Anglo-American alliance is grounded in her own bodily experience. Even though *The Shuttle* in its broad outlines is clearly a romance, or as the *Chicago Daily Tribune* reviewer put it, "'The Shuttle' is no more and no less than [...] a fairy story although it incorporates a great many ideas which will fool the incautious adult into thinking it something less inherently fascinating,"[26] the narrative materials emerge from Burnett's knowledge of the world as it is. Consider in that regard Burnett's probing of Sir Nigel's obsession with Bettina. After the narrator reports a conversation Sir Nigel had with an erstwhile Spanish lover, Teresita, who tells him that something is "eating him up," someone you love but "who will not look at you," the narrator probes the extent of Nigel's self-knowledge:

> He [...] cursed himself because he could not keep cool. It was part of his horrors that he knew his internal furies were worse than folly, and yet he could not restrain them. The creeping suspicion that this was only the result of the simple fact that he had never tried to restrain any tendency of his own was maddening. His nervous system was a wreck. He drank a great deal of whisky to keep himself "straight" during the day, and he rose many times during his black waking hours in the night to drink more because he obstinately refused to give up the hope that, if he drank enough, it would make him sleep [...]. His secret ravings would not have been good to hear. His passion was more than half hatred, and a desire for vengeance, for the chance to reassert his own power, to prove himself master, to get the better in one way or another of this arrogant young outsider and her high-handed pride. The condition of his mind was so far from normal that he failed to see that the things he said to himself, the plans he laid, were grotesque in their folly. The old cruel dominance of the man over woman thing, which had seemed the mere natural working of the law among men of his race in centuries past, was awake in him, amid the limitations of modern days. (434–35)

That passage unpacks the workings of an alcoholic mind that filters and remixes feelings, desires, frustrations and plans through the haze of constant, partial drunkenness. His awareness of the stupidity of his own behavior and his inability to restrain himself are recognizable attributes of alcohol addiction. His rationalization to drink more to overcome the effects of excess drink is a classic alcoholic move. When his alcohol addled mind reaches to conceptualize the cruelty of his desires as the workings of the natural order and refuses to acknowledge "the limitations of modern days" (something Bettina earlier in the novel alludes to as simply laws that protect women from abuse), his personal torment and the historical moment coalesce in the clarity of Burnett's understanding.

The Sir Nigel that emerges in that passage, and in any number of other passages that render his stalking of Bettina within the walls of Stornham Court and out on the estate grounds, is described by the *New York Times* reviewer as "a Jack-in-the-box goggling on a coil wire."[27] If he is right, then Burnett lived during her years at Maytham Hall with such a "Jack-in-the-box." In Gretchen Holbrook Gerzina's telling, Stephen Townsend, whom Burnett married in 1900 after divorcing her husband Swan Burnett a year earlier,[28] "had bouts of jealous anger in which he berated and threatened her, followed by periods of calm. Now [once they were married] he began to act out in front of friends and servants, accusing her of the most egregious improprieties, screaming at her, and making threats. He had bullied and blackmailed her into marriage, and she feared he was mad" (217). In a letter to Katherine Thomas dated May 24, 1900, Burnett wrote: "It is even worse than I thought it would be. I am certain it is not sanity I have to deal with in this violent madly jealous and strangely spiteful & malignant nature. I never saw or heard of anything like it. It *could* not be a sane thing" (cited in Gerzina, 217). It is in the context of the parallels between Burnett's second husband, who was English, and Sir Nigel in the novel that Gerzina discusses the center of gravity in the book. Burnett "used the book," Gerzina writes, "to praise all that was good about America and Americans: energy; a knack for commerce, whether in millionaires or in newsboys [...] a belief that one could rise through the caste system over the generations by working hard; a sense of being responsible for one's own living" (246). Based on such praise for Americans in *The Shuttle* and based on letters Burnett wrote to Richard Watson Gilder, her first editor, that emphasized her balanced perspective on things English and American ("balancing the scales of justice" is the phrase Burnett uses in the letter), and based on the fact that Burnett became a naturalized American citizen some time at the end of 1905 or soon thereafter, Gerzina concludes that Burnett "finally had resolved the issue of her nationality and come down on the side of America" (247). It is more likely, however, that Bettina, whom Burnett calls in another letter to Gilder, "the New American Woman" who has "taken possession of both" England and America, represents the unified English-American, American-English identity Burnett described to the *Harper's Bazaar* interviewer five years earlier. Given how Burnett emphasizes that it is Bettina's control of money augmented by her strength of character that enables her to defend herself from male oppression, it is likely that Burnett's becoming a naturalized citizen may have been a way to protect her American sourced wealth from Townsend (see Thwaite, for example).[29] In either case, the intersection between Burnett's life and the structures of romance in the service of shaping a myth of Anglo-American unity points to Burnett's effort in her next published story to create a myth less dependent on transatlantic relations and national boundaries.

It took Burnett over six years to write *The Shuttle*, a length of time that suggests, as was the case with *In Connection with the De Willoughby Claim*, that there was a thread of central interest that was struggling to emerge. That thread appears with great clarity in *The Secret Garden* (1909), her most fondly remembered children's story that appeared between *The Shuttle* (1907) and *T. Tembarom* (1913). The thread I am alluding to, of course, is of the garden as a metaphor for the human body. In *The Shuttle*, for example, restoring the gardens at Stornham Court is the centerpiece to the restoration of the estate and the village, and at the end of the novel the prospect of restoring the gardens at Mount Dunstan anchors the vision of the future. But the garden is more than a metaphor of the health of the estate, the village and by extension (and tradition) with England as a nation; it is tied specifically to Bettina, who more than finances the garden's restoration. The garden becomes an extension of herself even as she draws vital energies from it. The point emerges with some clarity in a conversation Bettina has with Kedgers, the head gardener at the court. Toward the end of a cholera epidemic, which hit the hop pickers on Mount Dunstan's estate particularly hard, word is that Mount Dunstan himself has contracted the disease. Waiting to hear the tolling of the church bell that would confirm his death, Bettina goes to Kedgers as he was "clearing flower beds and preparing them for their winter rest" (464).

> It was good, normal, healthy work to do. The scent of the rich, damp, upturned mould was a good thing to inhale. They walked from one end to another, stood before clumps of shrubs, and studied bits of wall. Here a mass of blue might grow, here low things of white and pale yellow. A quickly-climbing rose would hang sheets of bloom over this dead tree. This sheltered wall would hold warmth for a Marechal Niel [a type of yellow rose].
> "You must take care of it all—even if I am not here next year," Miss Vanderpoel said.
> Kedgers' absorbed face changed.
> "Not here, miss," he exclaimed. "You not here! Things wouldn't grow miss." (465)

In the midst of uncertainty, the garden remains, stark and elemental. It calls for labor and enlivens the breath as it warms the body; it also teases the eyes with the prospect of future blossoms of various color. Kedgers perceives Bettina's distress as she listens for the death knell even as the quality of her distress is softened by the image of the "quickly-climbing rose," which would absorb the "dead tree" within its "sheets of bloom," the image of a shroud becoming a living thing. The prospect of being separated from the garden intensifies Bettina's distress; Kedgers notices that "she did not look quite like herself […] [perhaps] she had a headache, or was low in her mind" (465). A moment like this suggests that the garden represents something deeper than a metaphor for abstractions like estates, villages and nations. As a symbol the garden at such moments eschews more obvious external determinations, as Burnett feels her way to redefine the garden not as metaphor or even as myth but as a real, material place that calls on human beings to recognize they are part of an ecological system. In this formulation the symbolic enables contact with the real; the garden may represent a demi-earth while also being earth itself. We saw Burnett's earlier effort to form such a conception of the garden in scenes with Sheba and Tom and then later Sheba and Rupert in *In Connection with the De Willoughby Claim*. In the context of the novel as a whole, though, those scenes are incidental, a part from the larger social tapestry; they seem a little unreal. In *The Shuttle* the restoration of gardens is a significant part of the larger social tapestry while also being thematically central to the novel's imaginative integrity. But in *The Secret Garden* Burnett's ecological conception of the garden finds its purest and fullest expression.

V

The gentle implication in *The Shuttle* that one's bodily health is in a reciprocal relation to the health of a garden (or of the local ecology more generally) becomes the governing concept of *The Secret Garden*.[30] The emphasis emerges most starkly with the depiction of the sickly, young Colin, who lives as an invalid convinced he is going to die (after he first becomes a hunchback) but who is brought into bodily health by the secret garden. Before revealing the garden to him, Mary wonders whether she can trust him to keep it a secret, and she decides he could, for "[T]he grand doctor had said he must have fresh air and Colin had said that he would not mind fresh air in a secret garden. Perhaps if he had a great deal of fresh air and knew Dickon and the robin and saw things growing he might not think so much about dying" (132). In those two simple sentences, Mary projects something of her own experience of attuning her body to the natural world onto Colin. The emphasis on air, rather than being a trope for imaginative inspiration, is constrained materially to bodily respiration, the energized body itself becoming transfigured. As Martha observes to Mary: "Th' air from th' moor has done thee good already [...] Tha'rt not nigh so yeller and tha'rt not nigh so scrawny. Even tha' hair doesn't slamp down on tha' head so flat. It's got some life in it so it sticks out a bit" (132). Here the synecdoche of the enlivened hair represents the more diffuse energies from the air that permeate Mary's body, energies that draw her out of herself into relation with the moor-side landscape and the half-cultivated, half-wild garden. She thus thinks of herself as a "creature" (132), and one of the earliest signs of Colin's turn toward life is his observation a page later that "I am a boy animal" (133). Such small moments typify the novel's overall design, which within a domestic ecology redresses physical alienation with bodily wholeness and interpersonal reconciliation.

The agency through which that design is made manifest is what the children in the garden, Mary, Dickon and Colin, call "magic." In a conversation between Dickon and Colin immediately after Colin has gotten out of his wheelchair and stood on his own for the first time, Dickon notes that Colin was able to do that because he stopped being afraid. Colin agrees before he asks: "Are you making magic?" Dickon responds with: "'Tha's doin' Magic thysel' [...]. It's same Magic as made these 'ere work out of the earth,' and he touched with his thick boot a clump of crocuses in the grass." Glancing down at the crocuses, Colin says, "aye [...] there couldna' be bigger Magic than that there—there couldna' be" (196). Magic is identified with the vital energies in nature that link the earth, sun and all living things into a life-renewing and life-sustaining system. Consequently, when Colin makes magic, he simply gives himself to those vital energies, which earlier in the tale Dickon described as "watchin' an' listenin' an' sniffin' up th' air an' [getting] soaked through wi' sunshine" (162) in order for Colin to heal. For his illness was neither in his body nor exclusively in his mind; it was a function of a failed relation to the world, a lack of attunement with nature and with his fellow human creatures, including his father.

Through such a concept of magic, Burnett is refracting another concept articulated by Thomas Carlyle, "Natural Supernaturalism," which the critic M. H. Abrams has defined as "the general tendency [...] in diverse degrees and ways, to naturalize the supernatural and to humanize the divine" (68). For Abrams, Carlyle's term looks back to the first generation of romantic poets, William Wordsworth in particular, who wrote in his long autobiographical poem *The Prelude* how men "as natural beings in the strength of nature," live in "the world / Of all of us, the place in which, in the end, / We find our happiness or not at all" (cited in Abrams).[31] For a poet like Wordsworth, to see the supernatural in the natural requires the special mode of vision vouchsafed to those of superior perception, such as a poet like himself.[32] For Burnett, the experience of magic in the very substance of nature is available to everyone, even necessary for everyone. We can take Wordsworth's "Lines Written a Few Miles above Tintern Abbey, On Revisiting the Banks of the Wye during a Tour, July 13, 1789" as an example to pin down the difference.

Wordsworth's poem, as its title indicates, chronicles a return to a natural landscape the speaker had left five years earlier. After a verse paragraph that surveys the scene, the beginning of the second verse paragraph presents what might be called a physiology of the memory of homely, natural scenes:

> Though absent long,
> These forms of beauty have not been to me,
> As is a landscape to a blind man's eye:
> But oft, in lonely rooms, and mid the din
> Of towns and cities, I have owed to them,
> In hours of weariness, sensations sweet,
> Felt in the blood, and felt along the heart,
> And passing even into my purer mind
> With tranquil restoration: (ll. 24–32)[33]

While in *The Secret Garden* and in "Tintern Abbey" there is an interchange between the body and nature, in the poem that interchange is mediated by the mind; it is as much a function of memory as it is experience; memory produces "sensations" that then course through the blood and heart on their way to a "purer mind," the body being a vehicle that then is transcended. To be in nature, then, requires an act of mind; for Burnett to be in nature is an experience of the body. Whereas for Wordsworth the feelings produced by the memory of the beauteous forms of nature may be the source of "that best portion of a good man's life" (l. 34), the interchange of the mind and nature resulting in a kind of instinctive moral goodness, for Burnett a bodily attunement with the natural world includes by definition attunement with one's fellow beings, morality a function of relationship, the ecology of the garden being a moral ecology.

That the magic in nature provides the energies that link material ecology to moral ecology is established by the layers of association that adhere to the garden. We learn, for instance, that the old gardener, Ben Weatherstaff, has kept his job after Colin's mother's death and the closure of the garden "because she liked" him and was so "fond" of the garden. When Colin learns that, he says: "It is my garden now. I am fond of it" (198). With those words, he accepts an inheritance from his mother, taking the first step to restore his family (his father, himself and his cousin Mary) in relationship with each other and with the wider community in the figures of Mrs. Sowerby and her son Dickon. Such a restoration, in fact, is the unspoken object of what Colin calls his "scientific experiment," which he bases on his belief that "there is Magic in everything, only we have not sense enough to get hold of it and make it do things for us—like electricity and horses, and steam" (207). The first purpose of Colin's experiment is to bring himself into health, but that becomes secondary to a larger goal: to bring him into a familial relationship with his father. At the end of the chapter called "Magic," Colin expresses that goal after he has learned to walk and can feel his body gaining strength day by day as he spends more time with Mary and Dickon in the garden:

> No one is to know anything about it until I have grown so strong that I can walk and run like any other boy. I shall come here every day in my chair and I shall be taken back in it. I won't have people whispering and asking questions and I won't let my father hear about it until the scientific experiment has quite succeeded. Then sometime when he comes back to Misselthwaite I shall just walk into his study and say "Here I am; I am like any other boy. I am quite well and I shall live to be a man. It has been done by a scientific experiment." (214)

Colin's determination to first accept his unspoken inheritance of the garden from his mother and second to absorb the magic of that place to fulfill his new desire to live wholly extends the power of the magic to reach his father on the continent. As Mrs. Sowerby exclaims to Colin: "Eh! Dear lad! [...] Thy own mother's in this 'ere very garden, I do believe. She couldna' keep out of it. They father mun come back to thee—he mun!" (243). Much as the dead branches become the boughs upon which drapes of new roses are hung, so Colin's dead mother functions to draw her still living connections back into relation through the ecological system of the garden.

As Colin increases in health and strength, his father, while "wandering in the Norwegian fjords and the valleys and mountains of Switzerland" (245) begins to feel, "for no reason that he knew of," that he was "slowly [...] 'coming alive' with the garden" (247). The first moment of that recognition comes during an extended visit at Lake Como where he spent his time walking in the hills around the lake; with that exercise he thinks: "Perhaps [...] my body is growing stronger," a fact that the narrator confirms before adding that "his soul was slowly growing stronger too" (248). The pattern so visible in Colin of physical health bringing spiritual health in its wake is repeated with the father, Mr. Craven. The next stage is his restoration to relationship with his son through his full acceptance of the meaning of his wife's life and death within the ecosystem of the garden. That acceptance comes in the form of a dream:

> He did not know when he fell asleep and when he began to dream; his dream was so real that he did not feel as if he were dreaming. He remembered afterward how intensely wide awake and alert he had thought he was. He thought that as he sat and breathed in the scent of the late roses and listened to the lapping of the water at his feet, he heard a voice calling. It was sweet and clear and happy and far away. It seemed very far, but he heard it as distinctly as if it had been at his very side.[34]

The voice is his wife's, and when he heard it in his dream, "[H]e thought he sprang to his feet not even startled. It was such a real voice and it seemed so natural that he should hear it." It is not necessary to attribute that voice as one that has transcended the grave, the voice of a spirit hovering near its beloved to draw him back to embracing life after a decade of fixating on death; the voice could more plausibly had welled up from his own mind, his returning bodily and spiritual health having cleared the paths of memory. He had shuttered the garden and made it off-limits to everyone because it was the place where his wife had died; it was also her most beloved place, which they had shared together. For him to understand the full meaning of his wife's life and death, then, he has to return to the garden at her behest to embrace their son. So in his dream, he asks the voice, "Lilias, where are you?" The reply, "[I]n the garden [...] came back like the sound from a golden flute." The "golden flute" dimly echoes Dickon's playing on a rustic pipe, reinforcing the notion of the voice calling Mr. Craven back to a community bound together by the garden and by history.

That latter point emerges through Mr. Craven's self-questioning as he travels back to Misselthwaite Manor. He wonders why driving "across the wonderfulness of the moor" gave "him a sense of homecoming which he had been sure he would never feel again—that sense of the beauty of the land and sky and purple bloom of distance and a warming heart at drawing nearer to the great old house which had held those of his blood for six hundred years?" (252). One answer to that question may be that his home has already been reconstituted. He thinks he will need to find the key to the garden, "to try to open the door" although he does not "know why" (253). As he approaches the garden, however, the door opens from the inside, and Colin dashes out, unwittingly running into him. Colin, Mary, Dickon and the others subsequently lead him into the garden, which Mr. Craven thought "would be dead," where he finds "[L]ate roses climbed and hung and clustered and the sunshine deepening the hue of the yellowing trees made one feel that one stood in an embowered temple of gold" (257). The garden, the individual bodies of the core family—Mary, Colin and Mr. Craven—the community and the continuity of history in the permanent return of the Master of Misselthwaite with his healthy and strong son with "eyes full of laughter" close the novel with an image of, to coin a new term, "magical naturalism." The natural world, cultivated and uncultivated, and the creaturely human community are bound together through the vital magic that produces ecological unity. The health of the land, the health of the body, the health of the community and the possibility of an open-ended, renewable historical future are all contained in Burnett's conception of the garden as both a real, tangible, life-enhancing place and as a metaphor for the world.

VI

The Secret Garden is the fullest realization of Burnett's interest in the interdependence of human environments, the natural world, human community and individual health, the components of the ecosystem that guarantees order and harmony among all those elements. Clorinda's efforts to rebuild the village dependent on Wildairs Hall, Emily Fox-Seton's rebuilding of the abandoned farmhouse for the Osborns on her husband's estate, and the comprehensive efforts of Bettina to rebuild the gardens, house, stables and so on of Stornham Court all point toward the concentrated core myth, which is built on the textured realities of the material world, in *The Secret Garden*. In each case Burnett exposes and celebrates aspects of human relations that, in their closeness to the animating energies of nature and to the elemental requirements of the human body in relation to others, are independent of rigid, atrophied social conventions. Even though, for example, the social conventions in *The Secret Garden* are reinstated in the end, the patriarch reunited with his son to restore order to the manor, that outcome is an effect not a cause, nor is it a goal. It is subordinated to the cross-class quality of relationships between the working class (Mrs. Sowerby, Dickon, Martha and Ben Weatherstaff) and the gentry (Mary, Colin and Mr. Craven). In those relations social conventions have meaning insofar as they sustain healthy individuals and by extension healthy community. But it seems only in the carefully circumscribed world of *The Secret Garden* can social conventions as such lose their power to distort human relations, poison human minds and weaken human bodies. In Burnett's next novel, *T. Tembarom*, she returns to the transatlantic, Anglo-American world in what she calls in Chapter XXXV of that novel "merely a study of the manner in which untrained characteristics and varied limitations of one man adjusted or failed to adjust themselves to incongruous surroundings and totally unprepared-for circumstances" (437). That mere study resulted in a more than five-hundred-page volume that on the surface reprised the little Lord Fauntleroy story with the lead character an adult. The repetition, however, is repetition with a difference.

The reviews tended to be positive although none took the book very seriously. The *New York Times* reviewer called the book "interesting, full of its hero's friendly spirit, and like all this author's books, written in an exquisitely simple, pellucid style,"[35] and the *Boston Transcript* reviewer wrote: "It is an old-fashioned tale that is sometimes romantic, sometimes realistic, sometimes plausible, sometimes incredible but always enjoyable" (cited in Thwaite, 225). The British paper, *The Saturday Review*, ended its one-paragraph notice with, "[I]ncidentally, the book provides a real insight into American life and manners."[36] There was even a rhymed review in *Life* (1883–1936), which summarizes the novel in verse and begins: "He peddled papers; next he won/ The journalistic job he sighed for./ A helpful youth and full of fun,/ He mostly earned the things he tried for."[37] Ann Thwaite writes very little about the novel, but Gretchen Holbrook Gerzina offers this observation: "Indeed, the modern reader is led, erroneously, to believe that its Dickensian characters and obvious intrigue mean a predictable ending. [Burnett] recognized the danger and thwarted all those expectations, deciding to build toward melodrama and then subvert it. It is a modern story, her first real twentieth-century one" (269).

The titular character is the Brooklyn-born only child of English parents, who died by the time he was 10. His father had come to the United States to make his fortune, and failing that, he became "a resentful, domestically tyrannical immigrant Englishman" (4). T. Tembarom, whose full legal name is Temple Temple Barholm, grows up on the street; in his early twenties he had worked his way into a newspaper job with ambitions to write the uptown society page for the Sunday edition. "He was a common young man," Burnett writes, "who was not marked by special brilliancy of intelligence, but he had a clear head and a good temper, and a queer aptitude for being able to see himself in the other man's shoes—his difficulties and his moods" (8). When the novel opens he is living in a rundown "third-rate boarding-house" (9) where he meets the daughter of an English inventor, who had come to New York to find a wealthy backer to invest in his invention. As Tembarom's father had done, he too had failed. Tembarom falls in love with the daughter. On his way home from a day of scrounging for society news, Tembarom encounters a man suffering from amnesia and obvious trauma. Tembarom brings the man to the boarding house and provides him shelter, paying with the substantial amount of money the man had pressed into his hands while still out on the streets. That is the situation when a representative from the Temple Barholm estate in Lancashire arrives to inform Tembarom that he is the only surviving heir and has inherited an estate that generates some $350,000 annually. Because Tembarom loves his life in New York, his speech bursting with the local slang that overflows with the life of the city, he is reluctant to take up his inheritance. He is obliged to do so, however, so having exchanged a pledge with Ann Hutchinson, the English inventor's daughter, and arranged for his amnesiac "friend" to accompany him, he takes on his duties as heir to the Barholm estate. Within that basic plot the melodramatic potential consists in the seclusion of the amnesiac friend and the discovery that the most direct heir to the estate may not have died in an accident as was generally believed. Might the man in seclusion be the true heir? If so, can that be proven? How can his identity be determined as long as his memory is gone? Might the young American interloper be trying to ascertain his identity while holding him against his will for fear of losing the estate? Questions such as these drive the story. When the questions are answered, the unsettling implications of the questions disappear, for it turns out that Tembarom wanted to prove the man with amnesia was in fact the true heir. Once that could be established, Tembarom would be free to return to New York. Here is how one character describes the denouement:

> It struck me as a sort of wild-goose chase [Tembarom's search for the man's identity] at first. He had only the ghost of a clue—a mere resemblance to a portrait. But he believed in it, and he had an instinct [...]. The dullest and most un-melodramatic neighborhood in England has been taking part in a melodrama—but there has been no villain in it—only a matter-of-fact young man, working out a queer thing in his own queer, matter-of-fact way. (505)

The melodrama in such a scenario is a function of the various projections of desire and anxiety by the English characters in the novel who are unable to recognize simple honesty for what it is. As the narrator says of Captain Palliser, who tries to convince Tembarom to invest in a dodgy speculation, he believed that "everyone was scheming for something" (246), so he assumes that Tembarom "must want something and it would be discreet to find out what it chanced to be" (247). That belief also seems a part of the other characters' basic orientation to Tembarom, if not always toward each other. To glance back at Burnett's formulation quoted above, Tembarom is the one with "untrained characteristics," and, in the satiric trope of the unlettered innocent exposing the corrupt delusions of a self-proclaimed sophisticated elite, he becomes the one who, without specific intent, reveals the moral worth for good or ill of the other characters.

As Little Lord Fauntleroy had done, T. Tembarom inherits a grand English estate, but unlike Fauntleroy, who will restore the moral integrity and physical vitality of the estate, Tembarom helps heal the body and mind of the English heir before surrendering the estate and returning to New York. That difference marks a change in Burnett's imaginative interests. In *The Shuttle* the idea of American enterprise, optimism and physical vitality fuses with a mythic–historical British past in a project of Anglo-Saxon restoration through an Anglo-American alliance. In *T. Tembarom* the Anglo-American alliance figured in the marriage of Tembarom and Ann Hutchinson is subordinated to the problem of imagining ordinary people carving out a meaningful life in a world where the ordinary is devalued, overlooked or simply impossible for some to understand. Burnett articulates this idea in the novel's opening chapter:

> No one has ever made a collection of statistics regarding the enormous number of perfectly sane, kind, friendly, decent creatures who form a large proportion of any mass of human beings anywhere and everywhere—people who are not vicious or cruel or depraved, not as a result of continual self-control, but simply because they do not want to be, because it is more natural and agreeable to be exactly the opposite things; people who do not tell lies because they could not do it with any pleasure, and would, on the contrary, find the exertion an annoyance and a bore; people whose manners and morals are good because their natural preference lies in that direction […]. When a combination of circumstances sufficiently dramatic brings one of them into prominence, he is either called an angel or a fool. He is neither. He is only a human being who is normal. (5–6)

In the course of the novel, Tembarom is called both an angel and a fool before he is recognized as simply a "matter-of-fact young man," a normal human being who wants happiness for himself and does not begrudge happiness to anyone else. When Lady Joan Fayre struggles to understand that Tembarom "had determined to do her—in spite of herself—a good turn," her comprehension is not up to the task. "I don't understand you," she tells Tembarom, who replies: "I know you don't. But it's only because I'm dead easy to understand. There's nothing to find out. I'm just friendly […] that's all" (385). Such an exchange is in danger of descending to the bathetic, but in contrast to those who live "like a fellow in a novel," as Tembarom puts it, and who think that in order to make "noble sacrifices" they must "walk all over a woman because they won't do anything to hurt her" (387), Tembarom's instinctual, unpremeditated friendliness highlights the most essential element missing from most of the relationships in the novel: the unequivocal acceptance, even celebration of the humanness of others. Social conventions reinforced by the tropes found in romantic novels where men end up abusing women in their efforts not to hurt them so encrust the mind that mutual human recognition, when it comes, arrives like a revelation. Consequently, when Little Ann Hutchinson and T. Tembarom marry and choose to spend their honeymoon in the small fourteenth-floor apartment above 150th Street in Harlem that, in the beginning of the novel, they had dreamed about occupying "like birds in a nest," their final exchange affirms the absolute centrality of simply being. "'You *are* there, ain't you?' said Tembarom in a half-whisper. 'Yes—I am,' murmured Little Ann" as she falls asleep with her head on his shoulder (518). The image of the pair announces at novel's close, if simply being is good, being in relation is best.[38]

Notes

1 "Little Lord Fauntleroy." *The Eclectic Magazine of Foreign Literature* (November 1886): 715.
2 "Little Lord Fauntleroy." *The Book Buyer* (December 1, 1886): 430–32.
3 "Fauntleroy." *New York Times* (October 31, 1924): 18.
4 "Mrs. Burnett, 'Fauntleroy' Author, Dies." *Chicago Daily Tribune* (October 30, 1924): 1.
5 Arthur Bartlett Maurice. "Best Sellers of Yesterday: V. Frances Hodgson Burnett's 'Little Lord Fauntleroy." *The Bookman* (September 1911): 35–45; John Nicholas Beffel. "The Fauntleroy Plague." *The Bookman* (April 1927): 133–38.

6 Alex Zwerdling. *Improvised Europeans: American Literary Expatriates and the Siege of London.* New York: Basic Books, 1998. The quotation from Yeazell comes from the back matter of Zwerdling's book.
7 William Thomas Stead. *The Americanization of the World.* London: Horace Markley, 1902, p. 2.
8 Christopher Hitchens. *Blood, Class, and Nostalgia: Anglo-American Ironies.* New York: Farrar, Straus & Giroux, 1990, p. 5.
9 The record of journalism and popular literature on the idea of an Anglo-Saxon alliance in the 1890s and through the early years of the twentieth century is extensive. To provide the flavor of how that idea was expressed in popular literature, I offer the penultimate paragraph from Louis Tracy's *The Final War: A Story of the Great Betrayal.* London: C. Arthur Pearson, 1896.

> Thus, as life becomes more complex and harder grows the struggle, there is no escape for peoples not fitted to bear its strain. The Saxon race will absorb all and embrace all, reanimating old civilizations and giving new vigour to exhausted nations. England and America—their destiny is to order and rule the world, to give it peace and freedom, to bestow upon it prosperity and happiness, to fulfil the responsibilities of an all-devouring people; wisely to discern and generously to bestow. (372)

The pernicious mixture of race pride, social Darwinism and utopian dream in that passage is characteristic of the literature.
10 Anna Wilson argues on this point that "little Lord Fauntleroy represents a boy functioning as a female substitute" as a way to external domestic authority into a masculine world by way of the rhetorical tools of sentiment (235 and 236). In her reading, Fauntleroy's feminized appearance is a foreign invasion that must be expunged by a nativist male reassertion of authority. The tension between Wilson's reading and mine is less a literary disagreement than it is a mark of the incoherence of discourse associated with the idea of an Anglo-American/Anglo-Saxon alliance. *Little Lord Fauntleroy* was the locus of a convergence of contradictory social forces in Anglo-American relations, layers of which can be uncovered by feminist, queer and social–political readings. See Anna Wilson's "The Darling of Mothers and the Abomination of a Generation," *American Literary History*, vol. 8, no. 2 (Summer 1996): 232–58.
11 For a concise discussion of the term and its significance for understanding English and American literature around the turn of the century, see Thomas Recchio's *Elizabeth Gaskell's Cranford: A Publishing History.* Farnham, Surrey: Ashgate, 2009, pp. 156–58 especially.
12 See Recchio, pp. 157–58 on the Boas studies.
13 This panic found its most extreme expression in popular apocalyptic dystopian/utopian fantasies such as Tracy's *The Final War* and Henry Standish Coverdale's *The Fall of the Great Republic* (circa 1887, General Books reprint 2009). In that latter volume the United States falls at the hands of "immigrants from the most dangerous classes of Europe," which just happen to be from Central and Eastern Europe (2).
14 Stephen Arata. *Fictions of Loss in the Victorian Fin De Siecle: Identity and Empire.* Cambridge: Cambridge UP, 1996, p. 1.
15 Anna Wilson interestingly notes that Fauntleroy's velvet suit and lace collar and cuffs have clear Wildean qualities, and she reminds us that Wilde talked with Burnett socially in Washington DC on at least one of his trips to the United States. Burnett, Ann Thwaite reports, "was delighted with him" (71).
16 See Mary Fanton Roberts's "Mrs. Burnett's Rose Garden in Kent: Evolved from a Centuries-Old Orchard" in *The Craftsman* of August 1, 1907. The article recounts Roberts's visit to Maytham Hall and is supplemented by eleven photographs, nine of them full page, of the house and gardens. Early in the article Roberts writes of the orchard that Burnett converted to a rose garden: "It is this old orchard which fell under the observant eyes of Mrs. Frances Hodgson Burnett shortly after she became the chatelaine of Maytham Hall." See Thwaite for an overview of Burnett's time there, especially pp. 178–83.

17 For a fascinating discussion of atavism and Mr. Hyde, see Arata, chapter 2, "*The sedulous ape: atavism, professionalism, and Stevenson's* Jekyll and Hyde" (33–53).
18 Sir Charles Wentworth Dilke. *Greater Britain: A Record of Travel in English-Speaking Countries during 1866 and 1867*. London: Macmillan, 1869.
19 It is interesting to note that in the supplemental volume Dilke published in 1890, he is careful to distinguish British North America from the United States, for which no chapters are dedicated. Sir Charles Wentworth Dilke. *Problems of Greater Britain*. London: Macmillan, 1890, pp. vii–viii.
20 Ralph Waldo Emerson. *Nature*. Boston: James Munroe, 1836, pp. 1, 5.
21 Thomas Carlyle. *Sartor Resartus. Carlyle's Complete Works: The Sterling Edition*. Boston: Estes and Lauriat, n.d., c. 1880, p. 54.
22 While the reviewers almost uniformly discuss transatlantic marriage as a central theme in *The Shuttle*, and while Burnett uses two such marriages in contrast as a structuring devise in the novel, transatlantic marriage serves a much broader theme engaged with questions of atavism, degeneracy, evolution and revitalization in terms of race and nation. For a comprehensive view of transatlantic marriage, see: Gail MacColl and Carol McD. Wallace. *To Marry an English Lord: Tales of Wealth and Marriage, Sex and Snobbery*. New York: Workman, 2012; Elizabeth Eliot. *The All Married Well*. London: Cassell, 1959; and Brandon, Ruth. *The Dollar Princesses: Sagas of Upward Nobility 1870–1914*. New York: Alfred A. Knopf, 1980.
23 Burnett's take on the paradox of a female patriarchy has conceptual affinities with what Rosemarie Bodenheimer would later call "the romance of the female paternalist." Bodenheimer argues that the thing that makes the story of female paternalism a romance is that it is a "fantasy of female intervention without power; it wishes for protectionist forms of class relations free from the taint of male power or social dominance" (23). Burnett is less interested in social reform as such; her focus is on English village life, and her vision is based on the Victorian fantasy of organic, medieval community.
24 Toward the end of the novel the features highlighted in the two passages just quoted are repeated in a compressed and poignant form:

> Each creature she passed was a sort of friend who seemed almost of her own blood. It had come to that. This particular existence was more satisfying to her than any other, more heart-filling and warmly complete. "Though I am only an imposter," she thought; "I was born in Fifth Avenue; yet since I have known this I shall be quite happy in no other place than an English village." (451)

25 "Sketch: Frances Hodgson Burnett." *Harper's Bazaar* (February 24, 1900): 160. Cited in Gerzina 212.
26 "Mrs. Burnett's Book is Called a Fairy Story for the Discouraged." *Chicago Daily Tribune* (November 16, 1907): 10.
27 "American Girl Abroad [...] Did a Woman Novelist Ever Invent a First-Class Villain?" *New York Times* (October 18, 1907): 19.
28 Gerzina suggests that Townsend compelled Burnett to divorce her husband by threatening "to go public with stories about their [Burnett and Townsend] relationship" (218). Gerzina goes on the explain that "Although she was careful to cover her tracks, Frances seems to have been a woman with a past, something even her descendants quietly acknowledged even though no names were attached to the accusation." The danger of Townsend's threats was that "[T]o be denounced as a married woman consorting with another man, and that man one who claimed to know something damaging about her past, would have sounded the death knell of her career" (220).
29 It is also worth noting that Burnett's last two novels are both set squarely in Britain (England and Scotland) and have only one American character who is alluded to but not a real presence in the narratives (203).
30 The critical literature on *The Secret Garden* is extensive. A review of the nearly forty critical pieces listed in the Modern Language Association International Bibliography lists work that addresses

such matters as the garden as utopia, the use of dialect, manhood, myth, metaphysics, anti-empire, sexuality and so on. My interest is on the place of *The Secret Garden* in the development of Burnett's novels written for adults. Consequently, I focus on the story as the culmination of a thematic thread that appeared as early as *A Lady of Quality* and that accumulated a deeper resonance by the time of *The Shuttle*.

31 M. H. Abrams. *Natural Supernaturalism.* New York: W.W. Norton, 1971, pp. 65 and 68.
32 See his "Preface to *Lyrical Ballads*" for a full articulation of that point.
33 William Wordsworth. "Tintern Abbey." *British Literature 1780–1830*, Anne K. Mellor and Richard E. Matlak (eds.). New York: Harcourt Brace, 1996, pp. 571–73.
34 Dreams as a mode of communication play a crucial part in the denouement of Burnett's final novel, *Robin*. A couple of distinctions are in order: first, while mind is emphasized throughout *The Secret Garden*, it is discussed in terms of keeping one's thoughts healthy, whereas in Wordsworth mind functions more unconsciously, the forms of nature shaping the mind rather than the will of the individual controlling it. Second, dreams seem to function in *The Secret Garden* the way mind does in "Tintern Abbey." In *Robin* Burnett coordinates dreams, mind and nature in ways that reconcile the tensions I am positing here between her fiction and Wordsworth's poetry (248).
35 "Fact and Fairy Tale: Mrs. Burnett's 'T. Tembarom" A Delightful Blending of Familiar Modern Conditions and Romance." *New York Times* (October 26, 1913), Book Review, p. 573.
36 "T. Tembarom." *The Saturday Review* (January 3, 1914): 22.
37 "Rhymed Reviews: 'T. Tembarom.'" *Life* (December 11, 1913): 1055.
38 A poignant marginal notation from a former pair of readers in my copy of the novel obliquely echoes that point. The notation in a rather shaky hand written in blue ink reads: "Read—Nov. 10, 1951. ANC. GOC." The sameness of the final letter in the pair of initials suggests that the notation covers two readers—a newly married couple perhaps?—having read the book together.

Chapter Five

AFTER THE GREAT WAR: EMERGING FROM THE WASTELAND IN *THE HEAD OF THE HOUSE OF COOMBE* AND *ROBIN*

I

Burnett's transatlantic novels articulate the core of her essentially optimistic vision. From Fauntleroy's rebuilding of the workmen's cottages on the Dorincourt estate to Bettina's comprehensive restoration of house, stables and gardens at Stornham Court to T. Tembarom's restoration of the physical and mental health of the rightful heir to the Temple Barholm estate in Lancashire, those novels assemble the elements of what in *The Secret Garden* is rendered as a myth of ecological wholeness, where the natural world and human community achieve elemental attunement and in the process enable the healthy renewal of the land and of the human body and mind. In that group of novels Burnett subordinates her interest in the economic, political and social mechanisms that disrupt the possibilities of such ecological wholeness, which she had explored in her industrial, political and historical novels, even as those disruptive energies still linger in the a-perceptive background through such figures as the false claimant in *Little Lord Fauntleroy*, Nigel Anstruthers in *The Shuttle* and Captain Palliser in *T. Tembarom*. Such figures in various ways both abuse nature and disrupt generative human relationships, but their power to overcome what Burnett presents as the forces of evolutionary ecological growth and health is limited. In her work from the 1890s to 1914 Burnett's optimism intensifies, her faith in the possibilities of Anglo-American life to continue to develop along the lines of a version of romantic naturalism seems unshaken. That changes with the events in Sarajevo on July 28, 1914, when Gavrilo Princip assassinated Archduke Franz Ferdinand, heir to the Austro-Hungarian crown, and his wife, the Duchess Sophie. With Britain's entry into the Great War on August 4 of that year, as has been well documented in scholarship, in the press and in popular culture, everything changed. The fabric of relationships that comprised Burnett's ecological vision was torn to shreds with the natural world becoming the backdrop to the slaughter of human bodies, the dominant image in cultural memory being of poison gas and rows of crosses in symmetrical array across fields of green. There was no place for any garden, secret or otherwise, during and in the aftermath of a war that seemed to have left the world in ruins.

As Paul Zweig observed in the opening sentence of his review of James Webb's *The Harmonious Circle*: "We have tended to view the aftermath of World War I through the dusty lens of T. S. Eliot's 'Waste Land': an exhausted civilization inhabited by people without roots or hopes."[1] The line "These fragments I have shored against my ruins"

(l. 431) captures Eliot's project in that poem, which could be characterized as piecing together religious, literary and cultural referents in an effort to fathom the depth of a lost coherence in a world drained of vital energies (particularly regenerative, sexual energies), a world whose organic and aesthetic ecosystems have become mere husks, the natural world drained of meaningful life even as literary culture has crumbled into pieces that may be retrievable but are impossible to reassemble. Meaning survives only in shards; the best that can be done is to look back to a lost past and make peace with the loss. Hence, the final words of the poem are "Shantih shantih shantih" (l. 434).

Zweig's characterization of European civilization appearing in "the aftermath of World War I" "exhausted" and without hope in Eliot's rendering applies with equal aptness to the world Burnett figures in her postwar novels, *The Head of the House of Coombe* and *Robin*. In those novels religion, literature and culture appear drained of substance; any meaning still attached to those things lingers via an association with a past that feels increasingly distant, irrelevant and powerless to provide a vision for the future. And even though the world in those novels seems drained of the same regenerative, sexual energies so painfully absent in *The Wasteland*, Burnett does not reach toward the past in an effort to make peace with irretrievable loss; she instead tests the capacity of the maternal body to regenerate actual life. In their nearly simultaneous responses to the cataclysm of the Great War, Eliot turned to high culture and Burnett to the female body, a contrast that maps precisely with the distinction, discussed in the opening of this book, that Andreas Huyssen makes between high modernist art as masculine and art that appeals to mass culture as feminine. Huyssen's argument fuses gender hierarchies onto the purist–profiteer contrast Peter D. McDonald makes, wherein the purist who is dedicated to the aesthetic demands of high art chooses the long-term validation of critical, cultural memory over the short-term enjoyment of riches garnered from wide sales to a semiliterate mass audience. With those distinctions in mind, it comes as no surprise that Burnett's postwar novels were dismissed (though not universally) as "the apotheosis of Burnettian slush" (cited in Thwaite 240) while Eliot's poem has become a cultural tour de force, whether loved or hated taken with the highest seriousness. Both writers, however, were responding to the same cultural conditions at the same historical moment, both were reeling from their knowledge of the brutalities of the war and both responded in ways both culturally conservative and artistically radical, Eliot by means of the highest of high modernist poetic technique and Burnett by means of a popular romance that could look fearlessly at the pervasive violence against women on the domestic front, the brutalities of mechanized killing on the battlefield and the persistence of the instinct for life despite the most vile of depredations on the body. Through high art Eliot chose culture; through popular art Burnett chose the spiritual life of the body.

The Wasteland was published in December of 1922, the same year as the publication of *The Head of the House of Coombe* and *Robin*. At this late stage in Burnett's career (she died in 1924), the post-Fauntleroy dismissal of her as having sacrificed her highest talents for easy popular acclaim had so set in among some critics that their reviews were, at best, lazy. They tended to offer bald summaries of plot lines followed by snide dismissals in ways that often made no sense at all. The review of *Robin* in the American magazine, *Life*, for example, opens with this: "The other day in the city of Bath, Me., our critic saw a young girl driving a taxi. You can form some idea of the consequent feminist reaction, when I tell you that he went right home and read the latest work of Frances Hodgson Burnett." The critic then offers this two-sentence summary: The novel

> is so violent about the war that almost anyone would suspect her of a job on the general staff. But the hero isn't really killed and the heroine brushes her tears aside as she works on the 'tiny garments' and the conversation is awfully aristocratic and a shocking liaison turns out to have been a secret marriage all the time.

In those sentences Burnett's engagement with the enormity of violence in the first modern, mechanized war is dismissed as pointless propaganda while her rendering of the drive of life to persist within that violence is ridiculed in a series of simple sentences joined by the word "and," suggesting through the critic's stylistic choice the association of Burnett with children's stories. When we compare the sentiments in the opening sentences, where, for 1922, the unconventional act of a woman driving a car for money is associated with Burnett and ridiculed as a consequence, with the one-paragraph review's final sentence, it is hard to know exactly what the critic objects to most: Burnett's long literary record of constructing strong, independent women characters or what was taken as her narrative conventionality, suitable for children's stories and dismissed under the modernist notion of the hopelessly smug and naïve Victorian period. "'Robin'," the reviewer observes in closing, "very well written, is no duller than usual and would have meant a lot to Queen Victoria. All wool, a yard wide and a bit thick."[2] It would be hard to find a starker critical contrast with the lean poetic assemblage of *The Waste Land*.

That contrast can be seen most forcefully in Edmund Wilson's December 1922 review of Eliot's poem in *The Dial* in a review titled "The Poetry of Drouth."[3] Wilson grounds his review on the idea that "Eliot uses the Waste Land as the concrete image of a spiritual drouth" (5), the consequences of which extend to the physical. In the first section of the poem entitled "The Burial of the Dead," the dead body planted in the garden evokes the consequences of that spiritual drouth: "Hereafter," Wilson writes, "fertility will fail; we shall see women deliberately making themselves sterile; we shall find that love has lost its life-giving power and can bring nothing but an asceticism of disgust" (7). As I will demonstrate in some detail below, spiritual emptiness and a failure of fertility through cold indifference and violence permeate the narrative in *The Head of the House of Coombe*, but in *Robin* love refuses to surrender its power to give and sustain life. In those novels, asceticism is not of disgust, it is of fashion, which in its consequences produces a moral disgust. But spiritual drought in Eliot's poem and in Burnett's novels does more than create a fissure between the spirit and the body through failed fertility; the drought permeates all of modern life. Here is Wilson on that point:

> And sometimes we feel that he [Eliot] is speaking not only for a personal distress, but for the starvation of a whole civilization—for people grinding at barren office-routine in the cells of gigantic cities, drying up their souls in eternal toil whose products never bring them profit, where their pleasures are so vulgar and so feeble that they are almost sadder than their pains. It is our whole world of strained nerves and shattered institutions, in which "some infinitely gentle, infinitely suffering thing" is somehow being done to death. (10)

Wilson suggests that what seems merely personal in Eliot's poem should be considered as representative; the dryness of soul that emanates from the poem cannot be reduced to autobiography, the personal finding in the images of the poem an "objective correlative" that makes personal emotion bred of particular experience broadly accessible. The poem, then, does not speak for the poet as an individual; it speaks to how social experience can be understood. Wilson does not read the weariness of pointless labor and "strained nerves" as symptomatic of Eliot. Wilson instead is offering a view that accounts for Eliot's understanding of how art works, be that art poetic or narrative.

Because Eliot was firmly ensconced as a personage in the world of actual literature, the critical assumption in Wilson's representative review is that the work must be read as a serious aesthetic engagement with ways to understand the particular historical and cultural moment, ways that also reveal something significant about human experience transhistorically. But because Burnett's novels had been read sometimes as literature and sometimes as popular romance (and sometimes as both), her work among critics seemed to oscillate between the literary and the popular; her place in the literary field was unstable. Ann Thwaite has posited a narrative of steady decline. She notes that *The Head of the House of Coombe* and *Robin* "had the worst press of any [novels Burnett] had written. Her day was over, her powers declining [...]. [I]f she had died at forty-five, before she had written *Little Lord Fauntleroy*, she might well have had a reputation comparable to Mrs. Gaskell's" (240). Thwaite then defends the novels on the basis of what they reveal about Burnett's own life. "From a biographical point of view," she writes, "there is much of interest," the central interest being how the neglectful mother called "Feather" in the novels "is like a caricature of all the basest characteristics [Burnett] feared, of all the tendencies in herself that frightened her, of things she herself had been accused of in the newspapers" (241). Even if those observations are true enough, might we not say of Burnett as Wilson did of Eliot that Burnett was writing not only of her personal distress; she was exploring aspects of the same historical moment, diagnosing what she perceived as the "starvation of a whole civilization" in the years before and during the Great War when "'some infinitely gentle, infinitely suffering thing' is somehow being done to death" (Wilson 10). One contemporary reviewer for the *Los Angeles Times* captured something of this fusion of the intimately personal, the historical and the transhistorical in a piece that suggests how, through the form of popular narrative, Burnett intimately explored aspects of women's experience on the home front in a time of war to powerful literary effect.

The review I am referring to is the one I quoted in the opening of the Introduction to this book. There I suggested that the reviewer's praise of the "consummate art" of *Robin* for the lovers of Romance is a way to denigrate the literary quality of the novel by faint praise. However, the details that precede that conclusion of the review belie the implication of its damning praise, for those details point to the way Burnett evokes the experience of war for women at home, whose suffering can be understood as profoundly as that of the men suffering, wounded and killed on the front. Women too experience a form of shell shock just as the men returning from the front do. Here is how the reviewer puts it:

> The war itself comes into the story only through its effects on its victims, civilian as well as the mutilated and shell-shocked soldiers thrown from its discard. But all the heart-breaking

uncertainty, the grief for those killed or maimed or missing, the horror and the cruelty of war are held within these pages, like a haunting evil spirit bringing blight to the world.[4]

Those killed include Robin's governess, who had returned to Belgium just before the opening of hostilities and was killed when her home village was razed in battle, as well as many of the young men in the social circle that surrounded Robin in her young adulthood. It is believed that Donal, the boy and man whom Robin loved and had married before he left for the front, was also killed. Thus, the reviewer notes: "Robin, the lovely inarticulate girl who in all her lonely life has known love only through Donal, was as much shell-shocked as though she had been on the field of battle" (43). Simply registering those narrative "facts" is an implicit protest against the unfairness of the reviewer who snidely remarked how Burnett "was so violent about the war that almost anyone would suspect her of a job on the general staff." Such a remark not only denigrates Burnett's novel, it mocks the real suffering of the women on the home front who lost lovers, brothers, fathers and friends; the reality of their suffering is what undergirds the force of Burnett's presentation where her art and the world it engages inter-illuminate each other.

The depth of those novels' engagement with the war makes Burnett's most recent biographer's cursory gestures toward them a bit frustrating, but in fairness Gerzina wrote a biography not a critical study. So while she observes that Burnett "pour[ed] out her feelings about the war, about the now-lost England she had known and the new Europe that must rise from its ashes" (287), that even though "*Robin* was her most modern novel [...] its real message [...] was not modernity [...] but the way the world now embraced notions of psychic phenomenon," she offers little detail to reveal how Burnett did those things. Nonetheless, Gerzina's observations are suggestive. For instance, she notes: "At a time when high modernists were tackling the war in startling new ways in works such as *The Waste Land* and *Jacob's Room*, [Burnett] turned to the occult to define the modern sensibility" (299). In that sentence, Gerzina suggests that Burnett's last two novels should not be read strictly in terms of realism and/or popular romance. Like Eliot and Woolf, she is doing something different, and while both the realism of significant visceral detail and the romance of idealization are central aspects of her final novels, those recognizable forms are framed by what I would call a mystic–ethical drive to make readers feel that hard to define energy that animates matter (what we might call spirit) and that transcends its individual manifestations, that energy, for example, that Bettina could perceive in the growth of a rose through close, still and silent observation in the garden, which is, of course, the same energy that permeates *The Secret Garden*. It is that energy that is under assault in *The Head of the House of Coombe* and in *Robin*. We can perceive the assault in the combination of neglect and subtle violence perpetrated against Robin as an infant and child, and later in a direct attempt by a man to take literal possession of her body in a context that connects his attempt at personal, domestic violence to the extreme mass violence enacted in the war. We can see it metaphorically in the physical resemblance between Robin's mother Feather and the woman Coombe had loved in his youth; that woman was abused to the point of death by her aristocratic English husband, something Coombe could neither prevent nor compel a legal prosecution to bring him to justice, the killer as it were being protected by his high social standing and his gender.

The war itself, in every aspect, is inimical to life and thus an assault on the vital energy that animates nature and the human body. Ultimately, the combination of direct assaults on Robin's body and the deaths of so many of her peers in the war produces a form of psychological passivity, akin to death, something that in the past would have been called despair, which Robin must either succumb to or resist by managing to keep alive the vital energies that link the mind and body to those forces that stir "dull roots with spring rain" (Eliot l. 4). That thing that keeps vital energies alive in defiance of the entropic forces of war and death is what Gerzina refers to above as psychic phenomenon, which is a theme that pervades much of *Robin*. We might say, then, that for Burnett, nothing, not even war, is powerful enough to destroy the forces that bind mind and body together, linking each individual to the current of energies that sustain life. A garden, she might suggest, can thrive over time on the top of a battlefield. The challenge is to keep the human connected to the garden.

II

As Paul Fussell has shown in his magisterial *The Great War and Modern Memory*, the sense of complete desolation associated with the Great War was taking shape in British culture as early as the 1870s, the decade in which Burnett began her literary career. Fussell opens his book with reference to a piece Lytton Strachey had published in the *New Statesman* on December 19, 1914, in which Strachey, according to Fussell, focused on "the tragedies of whole lives and the long fatalities of human relationships. His language was dark," Fussell continues, "He spoke of events *remorseless, terrible, gruesome*. He noted that 'the desolation is complete' and recalled a phrase from Gibbon's appropriate to the kind of irony he was contemplating: 'the abridgement of hope.' 'If there is joy […], it is joy that is long since dead; and if there are smiles, they are sardonical'" (3). After that characterization of Strachey's piece, Fussell points out there is not a single reference to the war that had already shocked British expectations and sensibilities over the previous four months. Strachey was writing instead a review of Thomas Hardy's volume of poems, *Satires of Circumstance*, where, in Fussell's words, many of the poems "emanate[d] from Hardy's personal experience as far back as 1870" (3). The trajectory of Hardy's increasing pessimism that can be tracked through novels such as *Tess of the D'Urbervilles* and *Jude the Obscure* and through his poetry well into the twentieth century can be read, then, as a counterweight to Burnett's trajectory of novels that strive to anchor meaningful human lives within an ecosystem that functions as a kind of biological music, with human bodies attuned to the rhythms of the natural world as figured in images of gardens, which creates the conditions for them to be attuned to each other in meaningful and generative relationship. Zangwill's exuberant "Tess triumphant" assessment of Clorinda in *A Lady of Quality* is a useful shorthand for the contrast of feeling for the world I have tried to articulate. In writing her postwar novels, Burnett reached back to the years before the war, recognizing, as Hardy had done, that the feelings putatively generated by the war had a longer cultural history. She announces that awareness in the opening paragraph of *The Head of the House of Coombe*.

The history of the circumstances about to be related began many years ago—or so it seems in these days. It began, at least, years before the world being rocked to and fro revealed in the pause between each of its heavings some startling suggestion of a new arrangement of its kaleidoscopic particles, and then immediately a re-arrangement, and another and another until all belief in permanency of design seemed lost, and the inhabitants of the earth waited, helplessly gazing at changing stars and colours in a degree of mental chaos. (1)

The keynote struck in that opening is of unrelenting change, a world in perpetual motion where all the elements that seemed to have constituted a coherent if not necessarily orderly world keep changing their relation to each other, the people of the society revealed in the book in a sort of suspended animation staring wide-eyed at an expanding universe (figured in the stars), their minds reflecting the "chaos" of their vision. These circumstances predate the cataclysm of world war, and they are a repetition of the sense of an unstable world articulated in Carlyle's essays of the 1830s (cited in Chapter Three) and given perhaps its most poignant expression some twenty years later in Mathew Arnold's *Stanza of the Grand Chartreuse* (1855), where the speaker of the poem laments what he sees as an inevitable inner incoherence that reflects what seems to be a directionless historical moment. Contrasting the order of monastic life based on a certainty of faith to the disorder of a putatively rational world where faith has meaning only as it reveals its irrationality, the speaker sees himself "Wandering between two worlds, one dead / The other powerless to be born" (ll. 85–86).[5] For the speaker of Arnold's poem, "all belief in the permanency of design seemed lost." What stood in for that belief in the years between Queen Victoria's death and the Great War was, among the fashionable elite (either through birth, wealth or cleverness) in the London of Burnett's novels, "a singular confidence in the importance and stability of their possessions, desires, ambitions, and forms of conviction" (1). That quotation emphasizes material things, individual emotions and belief as a matter merely of form, things that contract within the individual rather than expand out to form a society or nurture a culture. We can detect a conceptual continuity from Carlyle in the 1830s to Arnold in the 1850s to Burnett in the 1920s that is not incompatible with the view of a fragmented, incoherent world that produces within the individual little more than an anguished desire for peace, as articulated in *The Waste Land*.

Burnett gives the abstractions—"possessions, desires, ambitions, and forms of conviction"—comically painful embodiment early in the first chapter in her presentation of Amabel Darrel (later Mrs. Robert Gareth-Lawless, aka Feather), the oldest daughter of a doctor on the island of Jersey. After she meets Gareth-Lawless, "who was a beautiful and irresponsibly rather than deliberately bad young man" (3), she discusses the prospects of marrying him with her younger sister Alice. Reflecting that despite the larger number of heirs standing between Lawless and the Earl of Lawdor, after all, she says to her sister, children do die of "scarlet fever or diphtheria," Amabel suggests they pray, for had not the Vicar preached that Sunday on the text " 'Ask and ye shall receive' " (6). Alice declines but Amabel

> knelt down, clasping her slim young hands and bending her forehead upon them. In effect she implored that Divine Wisdom might guide Mr. Robert Gareth-Lawless in the much-desired

path. She also made divers promises because nothing is so easy as to promise things. She ended with a gently fervent appeal that—if her prayer were granted—something "might happen" which would result in her becoming a Countess of Lawdor. One could not put the request with greater tentative delicacy. (7)

The clash between real conviction and mere form could not be greater, Amabel's desire for a husband, her ambition for rank and the implication that to secure both would also bring abundance of possessions (not least of which being an estate) overwhelming any mask of real piety. With a light touch, akin to one displayed in Elizabeth Gaskell's Mrs. Gibson from *Wives and Daughters* (1865), Burnett's character has mastered the art of rank selfishness presenting itself as delicacy of feeling; Amabel's hollowness of character produces a self-deception that leads to deception of others (it is indeed easy to promise merchants payments for things that then are never paid for); it also enables not quite willful but nonetheless devastating acts of violence (for Amabel to become Duchess of Lawdor would require the deaths of at least seven children). Lightly as such violence is alluded to in the quoted passage, violence against children and young women develops as a motif that permeates both novels.

Amabel's first prayer was granted so to speak, and she and Gareth-Lawless were married, after which Amabel was always called Feather. Then the first disaster struck: Feather gave birth. They named the infant girl Robin, "who was," the narrator explains, "an intruder and a calamity of course. Nobody had contemplated her for a moment" (9). It is as if Feather and her husband were the typist and her "young man carbuncular" (l. 231) in *The Waste Land*. The young man, in initiating sex with the "bored and tired" (l. 236) typist, "makes a welcome of [her] indifference" (l. 242) while she, "glad it's over […] smooths her hair with automatic hand, and puts a record on the gramophone" (ll. 252–56). In both cases sex is anything but generative; it functions as a barely remembered physical expression of desire and joy, with desire reduced to base impulse and joy simply out of the question. The child is the culmination of nothing. "Nobody had contemplated her for a moment." Robin is little more than a blemish on an otherwise "pure" expression of facile social display. After learning she was pregnant, Feather "cried for a week […] [but then] she managed to forget the approaching annoyance and went to parties and danced to the last hour continuing to be a great success because her prettiness was delicious and her diaphanous mentality was no strain upon the minds of her admirers, male and female" (9). Once Robin is born, her physical reality cannot be completely ignored though Feather is ingenious in her efforts to make her invisible. When asked, for example, what she will do with the child after the birth, Feather replies: "'Do!' […] 'What is it people "do" with babies? […] I wouldn't touch her for the world. She frightens me'" (10). The "do" in inverted commas indicates how unable Feather is to imagine the child as requiring some kind of active engagement that would extend Feather out of herself. Her whole response is a stolid rejection of motherhood, the refusal of touch, and her fear suggests a denial of ordinary, organic relations where parents and children are bound in a mutuality that models a miniature community. Robin threatens Feather's absolute commitment to herself, a self she defines strictly in terms of appearance.

Feather's obsession with clothes becomes her only means of self-expression and identity. "Her passion for self-adornment expressed itself in ingenious combination and quite startling uniqueness of line," the narrator explains. Feather "created fashions" that were imitated by others in her social circle too; "she was enraptured by the fact and the entire power of such gray matter as was held by her small brain cells was concentrated upon her desire to evolve new fantasies and amazements for her world" (16–17). She cannot see much beyond her own appearance as that appearance is reflected back to her by others. "She chattered so incessantly about nothing and was such an empty-headed extravagant little fool in her insistence on clothes—clothes—clothes—as if they were the breath of life" (17). But clothes as the breath of life can do nothing in the face of death; they cannot imbue life in a body. Consequently, when Feather's husband dies suddenly, the response of her social circle is silence. The narrator's commentary is focalized through their eyes: "It seemed almost indecent for Robert Gareth-Lawless to have dragged Death nakedly into their midst—to have [...] been put in his coffin and carried down the stairs scraping the wall, and sent away in a hearse. Nobody could bear to think of it" (28). Such a refusal even to think about the physical reality of death, the scraping of the coffin on the wall providing an apt image of the putative lookers-on irritation of being confronted by such a thing, has consequences for Feather; the fact of death overwhelms her power to fascinate by dress. Her power was to produce visual fantasies to amaze her "friends," not to know them, not to connect with them, not to build a community together. "She suddenly and rather awfully realized," the narrator explains, "that she did not know a single person whom it would not be frantic to expect anything from" (41). Amazement only goes so far.

Feather's self-obsession, her inability to form meaningful relationships, provides the grounding for her daughter's vulnerability to violence, and within the logic of a literary text, it functions as a metonymy for the inability of those in Feather's fluid and amorphous social circle to form meaningful relationships as well. Through the self-obsession of individuals who tend to circulate among each other (I am avoiding the word relation), they enable violence to flourish as that violence is rendered in the child Robin's experience; they also themselves become vulnerable to violence, a violence that comes to fruition when they respond to war as simply another aesthetically pleasurable experience.

The development of neglect into a form of violence occurs soon after the death of Robin's father. He left Feather with nothing but debt, and the servants, seeing no future with the widow, simply leave. Feather is alone and experiences a sense of solitariness that is a perverse echo of her self-obsession. With no one to amaze and no resources at hand, she could not "even vaguely put to herself any question involving action, [which] would not have been within the scope of her mentality" (42). The only thing her mind drifts toward is the prospect of being saved somehow by someone. She concludes that she will entreat Lord Coombe to save her as she drifts off to a self-protective sleep, all the while giving no thought to her now fully abandoned infant locked away in an upstairs room. "And then she was disturbed——started out of the divine doze stealing upon her—by a shrill prolonged wailing shriek!" (45). Her response to her infant's cries is "not to stir from her [own] bed" but rather to hold her "pillow closer to her ears" (46); she assumes that Robin will simply cry herself back to sleep, which Robin does, but not before she experiences her abandonment as a form of physical and spiritual torment. The following paragraph is focalized through Robin, the narrator's words giving expression to what she can only feel.

> No one came. The discomfort continued—the blackness remained black. The cries became shrieks—but nothing followed; the shrieks developed into prolonged screams. No Louisa, no light, no milk. The blackness drew in closer and became a thing to be fought with wild little beating hands. Not a glimmer—not a rustle—not a sound! Then came the cries of a lost soul—alone—alone—in a black world of space in which there was not even another lost soul. And then the panic of which there have been no records and never will be, because if the panic stricken does not die in mysterious convulsions he or she grows away from the memory of a formless past—except that perhaps unexplained nightmares from which one wakens quaking, with cold sweat, may vaguely repeat the long hidden thing. (47)

The source of Robin's cries, of course, is her feeling of bodily discomfort; she is hungry, her clothes most likely soiled, as she waits for the nursery maid Louisa, who has left with the other servants, to bring light and food. (Earlier the narrator observes that "Robin knew only Louisa, warmth, food, sleep, and waking" (46).) The image of the "little beating hands" punctuating an existential panic visible to no one communicates a depth of trauma that "unexplained nightmares" in later life "may vaguely repeat." The emotional void that Robin experiences as internal violence is so powerful because it is deeper than words; the imagination quells before the prospect of nothingness, a prospect that Burnett renders through the body of the infant, whose "awful little sobs [were] shuddering through [her] tiny breast and shaking the baby body. A baby's sobs are unspeakable things—incredible things" (47). Struggling through such sobs, an "uninfantile druglike sleep came" to Robin, the denial of connection her body so craved resonating beyond infancy through her whole life. During that scene of psychic torture, which Feather could have ameliorated with a touch, "Feather's head was still burrowed under the soft protection of the pillow" (47). But in the morning, Feather decides she must do something, saying to herself: "'I suppose she would starve to death if I didn't give her some food—and then I should be blamed! People would be horrid about it'" (50). She manages to find some food for the baby, soothing her not out of care but in a further act of self-protection. It is a question of how she would appear to others.

Lord Coombe does, in fact, save her, after Feather entreats him with these words: "'I would do anything—*anyone* asked me, if they would take care of me.'" Those words, coming from a beautiful young widow bereft of resources and obtuse to the moral and physical debasement her words imply, move Lord Coombe in a strange and complex way: "[I]n the remoteness of his being, a shuddering knowledge that it was quite true that she would do anything for any man who would take care of her, produced an effect on him nothing else would have produced." The coupling of the words "shuddering" and "knowledge" suggests the possibility of Feather's potential for future debasement were a man to save her on the terms most obvious for those in Feather's social circle, and the reference to "the remoteness of his being" implies that Coombe knows the consequences of such potential, a knowledge he has found so painful that he can approach it only from a distance. The comparison that then comes to his mind captures the moral instability of his historical moment: "Also a fantastic and finely ironic vision of Joseph and Potiphar's wife rose before him and the vision of himself as Joseph irked a certain complexness of his mentality. Poignant as the thing was in its modern way, it was also faintly ridiculous" (63). Joseph, though accused of adultery by Potiphar's unnamed wife, is innocent as Coombe will be when he saves Feather without requiring anything from her; her body remains hers to dispose of as she wills. He is "irked," however, because the Joseph comparison can carry no ethical weight; Feather's situation may be "poignant" and Coombe's assistance may make their relation appear more intimate than it is, but false knowledge that Coombe is buying a concubine as it were and the truth that he is simply saving her from being victimized by others cannot be morally distinguished. Both would be judged as simply ridiculous despite the fact that "he was [...] in this particular case an entirely blameless character" (68).

While Coombe's assistance saves Feather from what she most fears, which is not to be able to live a fashionable life, and while it does enable Feather to hire a "respectable" nursery maid, it does not protect Robin from more direct forms of violence. It will take Coombe's intervention to provide such protection. The newly solvent Feather needed to find a replacement for Louisa; she "found a young person [named Andrews] who looked exactly as she should when she pushed the child's carriage before her around the square" (72). It seems appearance and the ability to keep Robin quiet and out-of-the-way were the primary qualifications for the job. Andrews was required to keep Robin in an upstairs bedroom out of sight of her mother, whose identity Robin did not know. Robin knew Feather instead as "the Lady Downstairs" (76). Robin thus begins to grow up with an ignorance worse than not knowing who her mother is; she does not know what a mother is. She admires Feather from a distance; Andrews, at Feather's behest, arranged matters so that Robin spent most of her time "quite by herself." Robin was made to understand that "'being good' could only mean being passive under neglect and calling no one's attention to the fact that she wanted anything from anybody" (73). If she in any way drew attention to herself, Andrews would put an immediate stop to the behavior.

> She once had a little black and blue mark on her arm for a week where Andrews had pinched her because she had cried loud enough to be heard. It had seemed to her that Andrews twisted and pinched the bit of flesh for five minutes without letting it go and she had held her large hand over her mouth as she did it.
>
> "Now you keep that in your mind," she said when she had finished and Robin had almost choked in her awful little struggle to keep back all sound.
>
> The one thing Andrews was surest of was that nobody would come upstairs to the Nursery to inquire the meaning of any cries which were not unearthly enough to disturb the household. So it was easy to regulate the existence of her charge in such a manner as best suited herself. (74)

As the detail in Burnett's explanation demonstrates, the regulation of Robin's existence involves nothing less than physical and verbal abuse, a double layer of violence that closes off any avenue of expression and suppresses any ordinary impulses to gratify Robin's most basic desire for the loving touch of another human being. The violence closes off all normal structures of human interaction; Robin is deprived of both the concept of love and the experience of a physical bond that could express that love, having no experience of a mother. She is raised, then, as a bundle of unstructured and not understood desires that she is taught through force to suppress. As the narrator puts the point in broad terms: "That which automatically becomes the law at the dawning of new-born consciousness remains, to its understanding, the Law of Being, the Law of the Universe" (78). For Robin, that law is repression.

When Robin was 8 years old, Andrews took her to the local garden. There she meets, unknown to Andrews, a 13-year-old boy with "wide, glowing, friendly eyes." When those eyes meet hers, she smiles as a preliminary to some childish play. The children, the narrator explains, were "drawn" to each other as the boy teaches Robin to create patterns in a leaf by using a pin. In an instant—although Robin could not conceptualize such a thing for herself—her "Law of Being" was challenged. She felt what she felt without fear and without constraint.

> She had never been happy before in the entire course of her brief existence. She had not known or expected any conditions other than those she was familiar with—the conditions of being fed and clothed, kept clean and exercised, but totally unloved and unentertained. She did not even know that this nearness to another human creature, this pleasure in the mere warm closeness of a friendly body, the exchange of companionable looks, which were like flashes of sunlight, the mutual outbreaks of child laughter and pleasure were happiness. To her, what she felt, the glow and delight of it, had no name but she wanted it to go on and on, never to be put an end to by Andrews or anyone else. (84)

This sudden experience of relation functions as an epiphany, an instant apprehension of the possibility that she was not by nature consigned to a life of isolation. Her encounter with Donal Muir (the boy's full name) on "that early summer morning in the gardens of a splendid but dingy London square" was something "as clear and simple as spring water and as warm as the sun" (90–91).[6] While for the boy "[L]ove and caresses were not an amazement [...] [but were] parts of the normal joy of life," Robin found the normality of human encounter to be an "absolute wonder" (92). As the children meet in the gardens over a two-week period, "[T]he boundaries were removed from Robin's world. She began to understand that there was another larger one containing wonderful and delightful things she had known nothing about" (97). Through that understanding Robin begins to turn her repressed desires outward, first in the form of resistance to Andrews's abuse and later as she grows in the form of looking outward into the world to find a place for herself.

Through her encounter with Donal, Robin meets his mother and thus learns what a mother is before she discovers that the Lady Downstairs is her own mother. Because of Coombe's dubious and exaggerated reputation and of the common belief that Feather was his kept woman, Donal's mother prevents her son from seeing Robin. Robin finds herself again alone but with a fuller knowledge of what being alone means for a normal human being. Her response to losing Donal is diagnosed, by the doctor called in to evaluate her increasing lethargy, as "shock" (132). That shock, as Robin learns more about the reasons for Donal's removal from London, stirs her to anger. That anger finds a stimulus for expression when Robin is brought downstairs to be displayed at one of her mother's domestic social events. There she sees Coombe and overhears the story of his being the cause of her loss of Donal. She refuses then to shake Coombe's hand when her mother orders her to do so, after which she is sent back to her upstairs room to be at the tender mercies of Andrews; Robin shouts, "Andrews will pinch me!" before she meekly follows her from the room. The guests are all struck by "the queer flame in the child's face," a flame that Coombe perceives as "that of an obstinate young martyr staring at the stake" (143). Robin knew only too well from experience what a pinch from Andrews entailed; the image of her as a 5-year-old martyr (to her mother's vanity) is very much to the point. As the narrator observes, however, despite her awareness that "she was nothing" in comparison to Andrews's violence, yet "out of the wonders she had begun to know, there had arisen in her before almost inert little being a certain stirring. For a brief period she had learned happiness and love and woe, and, this evening, inchoate rebellion against an enemy" (145). Robin rebels by crawling under the bed to avoid Andrews's attack. "She was actually unreachable, and she lay on her back kicking madly, hammering her heels against the floor and uttering piercing shrieks" as she resists by also reenacting her original bodily objection to the torment of her mother's neglect in her infancy. But now she has an emergent sense of what might be called justice: "In her overstrung little mind there ruled for this moment the feeling that if she was to be pinched, she would be pinched for a reason" (146). She is no longer a passive victim and begins to assert her own dignity. But the wounds of her earlier childhood are deep; the snatching away of Donal makes them hard to heal. In addition, Andrews succeeds in dragging her from under the bed. "Holding her between the iron knees, she put her large hand over her mouth" (148), preparing to do more than pinch her. Then, Lord Coombe intervenes.

From that moment, he decides to refocus his protection from Feather to Robin. He has Andrews removed and hires a mature, professional, compassionate nursery maid named Dowson whose "respectability [was] far superior to smartness" (167). Dowson learns from the other servants how Robin had "been taken care of by the clock and dressed like a puppet, but she's not been treated human[…]. She's lived upstairs like a little dog in its kennel" (171). The night of Robin's resistance had wrought a change in her, however. "From that hour [Robin's] softness had become a thing of the past." When Dowson then takes charge of her, she finds a "brooding, little, passionate being" (179), whom she envelops with compassion and care. The center of Robin's double trauma—emotional and physical indifference of her mother and physical abuse of her nursery maid—remains, but it is in tension with a felt possibility of happiness born of relation to another. Hence Robin's brooding and passion weigh inwardly even as they push outwardly. Coombe, it seems, wants to cultivate the latter, to connect Robin to a social world grounded on care, curiosity, openness and possibility. What motivates him more deeply, perhaps, is his knowledge of a woman's vulnerability. As he puts it to Feather when she asks him why Robin's life matters to him: "The situation interests me. Here is an extraordinary little being thrown into the world. She belongs to nobody. She will have to fight for her own hand. And she will have to *fight*, by God! With that dewy lure in her eyes and her curved pomegranate mouth! She will not know, but she will draw disaster!" (187). The already damaged Robin, without explicit protection, would be the object of male sexual aggression in what the novel shows as an increasingly predatory world. On the most basic level, Coombe is thinking about the integrity of Robin's body and the fact that in isolation she would be powerless, as she was against Andrews's pinching, to protect herself from male violence.

When Coombe hires a Belgian woman Mademoiselle Valle as governess for Robin, she seeks initial guidance from Dowson, who observes that Coombe is "the only creature [...] that remembers that child's a human being. Just him" (195). The use of the word creature in a context in which the word would generally be applied to a woman registers Coombe's sensitivity to the physical vulnerability of women in his world while also identifying him with that vulnerability. Three narrative threads intersect in the use of that single word: the history of Robin's developing awareness of herself as a physical being, the reconnection of Coombe to an ethic of bodily care from which he had been alienated because of an earlier trauma and the story of how their histories intersect to provide a vision of future possibility in the wake of war.

III

As Robin matures, she gains in beauty and indeed "draws disaster." The first indication of her potential danger comes from the unwanted attention she attracts on the street. "She was not a self-conscious creature, but the time came when she became rather disturbed by the fact that people looked at her very often, as she walked in the streets" (226). At first Robin perceives no distinction between the looks of women and men, so she thinks there must be something amiss in her dress. But the male gawkers quickly overwhelm the female looks of interest. Mademoiselle Valle was usually with her on walks, and on one occasion in quick succession two men in a cab lean out toward her, one saying something to the other just as "three young men" pause to stare at her before moving on; she is entangled among five male gazes, and her reaction to the latter three is to find them to be *"rude"* (227).

> They were carelessly joyous and not strictly well-bred youths, who were taking a holiday, and their rudeness was quite unintentional and without guile. They merely stared and obviously muttered comments to each other as they passed, each giving the hasty, unconscious touch to his young moustache, which is the automatic sign of pleasurable observation in the human male. (227)

The narrator here takes on an objective, nearly scientific diction, the young men becoming representative of "the human male," their gestures an "automatic" response. That diction conveys how ordinary the stares, muttered comments and gestures are, an ordinariness in tension with Robin's indignant reaction. "'If she had had companions of her own age, she would have known all about it long ago,' Mademoiselle [Valle] was thinking" (227). Innocent as the moment is, it suggests that Robin is more vulnerable than other girls for her lack of social connection and experience. She has trouble reading the intentions of others. As Mademoiselle Valle and she talk further about Robin's beauty,

Valle tells Robin that she "should thank Heaven for it and make the best of it without exaggerated anxiety." But as she reflects further on Robin's particular circumstances, Valle hesitates about the wisdom of the advice she just offered. Robin "was a warm, intensely loving, love compelling, tender being. Having seen much of the world, and of humanity and inhumanity, Mademoiselle Valle had had moments of being afraid for her" (228). Youthful innocence meeting youthful innocence is one thing; youthful innocence as object of mature and calculating desire reinforced by worldly experience is something else. It is when Robin becomes an object for such calculating desire that Valle's and Coombe's worst fears for her begin to be realized. As Lord Coombe puts the point: "'She is [...] as ignorant as a little sheep—and butchers are on the lookout for such as she is. They suit them even better than the little things whose tendencies are perverse from birth" (233). The man who pursues her with cool and paradoxically cold-blooded desire, the man who desires to possess the physical fullness and beauty of Robin's body because of her innocence, is more than representative of a certain kind of bad man; that man represents a peculiar type produced by nationalistic, military culture on the continent. His efforts to control Robin through confinement, which perversely echo Feather's consigning Robin to the upstairs room in her early childhood, links domestic violence to currents of violence in European history that flowed through the first half of the twentieth century.

The man in question "was an occasional visitor of [Robin's] mother's—a personable young Prussian officer of high rank and title" (236) named Count von Hillern. One critic calls the sequence of events associated with von Hillern as "yellow and theatrical"[7] while another describes the sequence as a "bizarre kidnapping and rescue [that are] out of tone with the rest of the pathetic idyl [sic] of Robin's life."[8] Such assessments ignore how central von Hillern is as a link between the domestic and historical threads of the novel; they also ignore the depth of psychological probing Burnett provides as she analyzes the intersection among patriarchy, militarism and misogyny. Consider the deft way Burnett introduces von Hillern as he is focalized through the perceptions of Fraulein Hirsch, Robin's German tutor, who, in sync with the spy fever in England at the time of the novel's events, is also part of the German espionage efforts in the years before the war.[9] "She was in England under orders," Burnett writes, "because she was unobtrusive looking enough to be a safe person to carry on the work she had been given to do" (241). Hirsch's physical appearance may have rendered her all but invisible (and by implication asexual), but her inner life is infused with the psychosexual, ideological currents of her national moment:

> She lived in small lodgings in a street off Abbey Road, and, in a drawer in her dressing table, she kept hidden a photograph of a Prussian officer with cropped blond head, and handsome prominent blue eyes, arrogantly gazing from beneath heavy lids which drooped. He was of the type the German woman, young and slim, or mature and stout, privately worships as a god whose relation to any woman can only be that of a modern Jove stooping to command service. In his teens he had become accustomed to the female eye which lifts itself adoringly or casts the furtively excited glance of admiration or appeal. It was the way of mere nature that it should be so—the wise provision of a masculine God, whose world was created for the

supply and pleasure of males, and especially males of the Prussian Army, whose fixed intention it was to dominate the world and teach it obedience. (239–40)

The dynamic between patriarchal arrogance and misogynistic submission that bubbles within the caricature of the sexually repressed and deprived older woman embracing the young, powerful male only in her fantasy life cannot be so easily dismissed as merely "yellow and theatrical"; the passage captures qualities in German military training that produced figures like von Hillern and generated the psychosexual mixture of violence and intimacy that the German social theorist Klaus Theweleit so comprehensively explores in his two-volume *Male Fantasies*, a study to put it as simply as possible, of fascist psychology with an emphasis on the male body, male bonding, and the subordination and rejection of, in addition to the desire for, women.[10] Early in Chapter 1, "Men and Women," Theweleit explains his choice to explore "the soldier male's relationship to women," wherein he draws on novels and memoirs written by former members of the *Freikorps*, German veterans of the Great War who fought against left leaning forces in Germany and Eastern Europe between 1918 and 1923.[11] Struck, in that material, by "the peculiarities of passages in which women were mentioned," Theweleit highlights the "strangely ambivalent emotions" he sees in the texts. Those emotions "vacillate," he writes, "between intense interest and cool indifference, aggressiveness and veneration, hatred, anxiety, alienation, desire," and they serve as a starting point for his larger project to understand "the matter of the 'White Terror'" (24). The passage from Burnett above suggests how such a mixture of emotions does not only circulate among men; as part of a larger cultural system, they shape the self-perception of women as well. And since that peculiar emotional concoction is a product of a particular version of patriarchy, namely fascism, resistance against such figures as von Hillern not only is a necessity for individual integrity (not to mention survival), it is emblematic of a larger international struggle for a cultural, political and national future.

The stakes are clearly high, and Burnett renders how those stakes permeate the most ordinary of experiences in the normal course of social life. Here is how Robin describes her first encounters with von Hillern, who had become a regular at her mother's social gatherings for "two or three seasons" (237). Robin is most put off by what von Hillern does with his eyes when he sees her. "I suppose they are handsome eyes," she says to Mademoiselle Hirsch. "They are blue and full—rather too full. They have a queer, swift stare—as if they plunged into other people's eyes and tried to hold them and say something secret, all in one second. You find yourself getting red and trying to look away" (236–37). In order to get at a richer understanding of Robin's words, we can draw on Theweleit's incisive reading of the conflation of "woman as love object" and "violence" that he finds in a text by Ernst Junger. Junger writes: "I plunge my gaze into the eyes of passing women, fleeting and penetrating as a pistol shot, and rejoice when they are forced to smile." Theweleit then observes of Junger's conflation of women and violence that "[A] pistol shot and a young girl's smile are brought into association, as if that were the most natural thing in the world" (38). Though more elaborated than Junger's simile of the gaze as a pistol shot, Robin's description evokes similar images: the plunging stare could be figured as a knife or a bullet, the secret bonding the aggressive gaze with the passive victim in a moment of forced, unwanted intimacy, and the blood rushing to Robin's face evoking what happens to a body wounded by a bullet.

Von Hillern's default mode of figuratively wounding (and not with the dart of love) women who fall under his gaze functions as a metaphor in the novel for Germany's orientation toward England or any other nation. In a conversation between Lord Coombe and his closest friend the Duchess of Darte, Coombe shares this observation of what they both allude to as "It" in reference to Germany under the rule of Kaiser Wilhelm:

> "Through three weeks I have been marking how It grows," he said; "a whole nation with the entire power of its commerce, its education, its science, its religion, guided towards one aim is a curious study. The very babes are born and bred and taught only that one thought may become an integral part of their being. The most innocent and blue eyed of them knows, without a shadow of a doubt, that the world has but one reason for existence—that it may be conquered and ravaged by the country that gave them birth." (207)

By the logic of that passage, von Hillern looks upon anything and anyone he sees in England as simply his by right. Women in particular exist for him only insofar as they are able to gratify his whim. The arrogance of the national and personal positions here is laughable, a quality that, in Coombe's understanding, makes the attitudes even more dangerous, for the Kaiser's "pretensions seem too grotesque to be treated seriously. And, while he should be watched as a madman is watched, he is given a lifetime to prepare for attack on a world that has ceased to believe in the sole thing which is real to himself" (208). Reasoned analysis reveals a potential so grotesque (and unreasonable) that reason cannot lead to belief. It defeats itself in the face of a parodic Nietzsche-like drive for dominance. Just as "England comfortable in stolidity" believes enough in a world civilization to blind itself to the threat to that civilization taking clear form in Germany, so Robin and her caretakers miss all the signs that would warn them of von Hillern's real intentions.

Rape is at the core of those intentions just as rape is central to the thematic concerns of *The Waste Land*. That latter point is less an esoteric critical point than it is a commonplace shared by general readers of literature today as suggested by Roz Kaveney in *The Guardian* (April 17, 2014). Of *The Waste Land* she writes:

> This is a poem full of rape—we get the story of the abused and mutilated Philomel, who became the nightingale, and the seduced, abandoned and mad Ophelia, whose 'good night, sweet ladies, good night, good night' follows on from the bickering cockneys' chatter of abortion and adultery, and the story of the typist aggressively taken by her dinner guest. (n.p.)[12]

In that catalog of rape-related items from the poem, the focus fluctuates among seduction and abandonment, mechanical sex performed with mutual indifference, adultery and abortion, and straightforward physical violence. In each case, any possibility of sex as a source of joy in the production of future life is simply unthinkable; sex is subordinated to a drive for dominance and self-aggrandizement. In *The Head of the House of Coombe*, sex as it is connected to German expansionism requires not just male dominance but the willing abasement of the woman as object of desire as that desire can be expressed only through violence. In a grotesque version of that abasement Fraulein Hirsch plays the lead role as she "crawled upon her poor, large-jointed knees to adore" von Hillern (242), who responds to her adoration with the self-gratifying indifference of cold "annoyance" (243). In their official meeting—"the sole link between them was the asking of questions and the giving of private information" (244)—Hirsch accepts the fact of von Hillern's frigidly repressed gratification as she recognizes that "[I]t was Robin he was enclosing in his network of questions" (244).

From Hirsch he learns that if Robin should choose to go to Berlin as a governess, "her mother [would] not feel any anxiety about her," nor would Lord Coombe bother to search for her, if she were in the possession of a "young man who was her lover" (246). The import of such half-true information becomes unambiguous at the end of their meeting when von Hillern reveals his intentions toward Robin and exults in the prospect of making his action representative of those of his brethren.

> "If she were missing, no particular search would be made then," he said. "She is pretty enough to suit Berlin." He seemed to think pleasantly of something as he stood still […] his eyes on the floor. When he lifted them, there was in their blue a hint of ugly exulting, though Mathilde Hirsch did not think it ugly. (246)

In those lines his intentions as a rapist rip away any veneer he has been polishing of himself as Robin's potential young lover. His task will be to subdue her, to produce in her the same abjectness, despite her youth and beauty, so evident in every gesture from the older Hirsch. And that task would simply be a part of the larger national purpose, to make all of England abject as embodied by physically inferior English men and especially by English women:

> "It will be an exciting—a colossal day when we come to London—as we shall. It will be as if an ocean had collected itself into one huge mountain of a wave and swept in and overwhelmed everything. There will be confusion then and the rushing up of untrained soldiers—and shouts—and yells—"
>
> "And Zeppelins dropping bombs," she so far forgot herself as to pant out, "and buildings crashing and pavements and people smashed! Westminster and the Palaces rocking, and fat fools running before bayonets."
>
> He interrupted her with a short laugh uglier than the gleam in his eyes. He was a trifle excited.
>
> "And all the women running about screaming and trying to hide and being pulled out. We can take any of their pretty, little, high nosed women we choose—any of them." (247)

Robin may be von Hillern's most immediate object, but she will be but the first of many to experience rape as a weapon of war. The language of sexual excitement collecting itself into an overwhelming wave conflates killing with ejaculation, the military bodies of the German soldiers with their phallic bayonets penetrating the flabby English "fat fools" masquerading as soldiers as a preliminary to debasing the "high nosed women" whose faith in the safety of their social rank would be shown to be as flimsy as their fashionable clothes. The fact that Burnett is doing more than indulging in anti-German propaganda is confirmed late in the second novel, *Robin*, when Feather is blown to pieces (only one hand adorned by a ring remains) after she and her friends rush out to observe German Zeppelins bomb London, as if the bombing were nothing more than a thrilling spectacle. That event in addition to Robin's being a specific target of von Hillern's related to the impending war are parts of Burnett's fusion of the domestic and the martial, the reality of war being accessible by attention to experiences on the home front. That fusion is also suggested by the sequence of Robin's isolation as a child being enforced by violence, a pattern that is then repeated in von Hillern's plot.

In order to isolate Robin, von Hillern's plot exploits her hunger for independence from her mother (and by extension from Lord Coombe) and her deeper, repressed hunger for intimacy with another human being. Her early encounter with Donal of which the reader is aware while von Hillern is not, creates the psychological conditions that make von Hillern's scheme plausible. Deploying two women in service to him and the German state, von Hillern arranges for Robin to interview as a governess for an only child whose circumstances on the continent parallel Robin's in England. Lured to a house by someone Hirsch has introduced to her as Lady Etynge, Robin expects to be interviewed for the job and to meet the child, Helene. As she waits to meet the mother and child (all the while unknown to her as she is being locked in a strange house), her thoughts exult in what looks to her like a prospect for a new life defined by relationship.

> What good luck and how grateful she was! The thought which passed through her mind was like a little prayer of thanks. How strange it would be to be really intimate with a girl like herself—or rather like Helene. It made her heart beat to think of it. How wonderful it would be if Helene actually loved her, and she loved Helene. Something sprang out from the depth of her being where past things were hidden. The something was a deadly little memory. Donal! Donal! It would be—if she loved Helene and Helene loved her—as new a revelation as Donal. (261)

Just as Donal had opened up the prospect of a world of human connection different from anything she had known, the thought of Helene beckons. But her memory of connection is overwhelmed by her memory of loss, a return to isolation, which was mitigated by the care of two hired women but unredeemed by any relation to anyone, male or female, near her own age with whom she could make sense of the world as something more than a mere accumulation of experiences. Her "deadly little memory" that frames her hope for a loving relationship with Helene suggests that however wonderful she imagines the potential "new […] revelation" to be, that revelation can only be glimpsed, never realized. That memory also evokes her subsequent pain, physically through the abuse of Andrews and psychologically through the loss of Donal. In that sense the new revelation could mean nothing more than renewed pain.

Helene it turns out is only a fiction, and almost immediately after Robin's thoughts are rendered in the passage above, she is locked into the house by a footman whose "unprofessional bad manners," which included subjecting her to his masculine gaze of sexual assessment, she "resented" (261). Still feeling a sense of gratitude toward the false Lady Etynge, however, Robin is fearful of doing anything that would show impatience or distrust, so she waits, and even after she learns that she is locked in, she thinks there may be "a dozen ordinary reasons" for it (266). Then she discovers that all the bell ropes used for summoning servants were out of order; with that discovery she knows that "[I]t has been done on purpose," and she struggles to reconcile her interaction with Lady Etynge with the reality of her confinement. "She saw her gentle face and almost affectionately watching eyes. She heard her voice as she spoke of Helene; she felt the light pat which was a caress." Each of those small things had fed her hopes for a loving relationship with Helene, and with Robin's understanding of their insincerity, their use for an intentional deception, she experiences the same anguished passion she had done with the disappearance of Donal. "It was the same kind of passion—the shaken and heart-riven woe of a creature who has trusted and hoped joyously and has been forever betrayed" (266). Once she understands the falsity of Lady Etynge, she recognizes that "Fraulein Hirsch had *known*!" (268). Then when the "leering footman" responds to her 30-minute beating of the door panels by telling her to "keep still" because "no one's going to bother taking any notice" (269), she acknowledges the fact that she is trapped, but she does not accept being so. "She told herself that she was strong for a girl—that she could tear with her nails, she could clench her teeth in flesh, she could shriek, she could battle like a young madwoman so that they would be forced to kill her." In an echo of her resistance to Andrews as a child, the direction of Robin's rage moves outward with those words. Her passion is not self-consuming; she imagines the physical details of fighting for her life, as a soldier does in war, the image of her sinking her teeth in flesh capturing to some degree the debasement and brutality of war. The idea of a woman fighting to the death in her resistance to rape in a time of war carries with it too a very long history,[13] which Burnett evokes as she describes Robin's "prayer": "Her hands were clenched together hard and fiercely, as she scrambled to her knees and uttered a sort of prayer—not a child's—rather the cry of a young Fury making a demand." Rather than demanding vengeance, as would be the wont of a Fury, Robin demands that she simply be acknowledged as a human being, that her experience of the physical fact of a woman's defenselessness in the face of organized male violence be accepted as real just as she, in her own consciousness and body, is real: "'Perhaps a girl is Nothing,' she cried, '—a girl locked up in a room! But, perhaps, she *is* Something—she may be *real* too!'" (278). That declaration functions as an act of defiance on two fronts: toward male oppression in whatever form it is manifest, and especially toward the irrational male prosecution of war.

Robin's defiance directed at male oppression, however, obscures what she should have understood once she discovered Lady Etynge's and Fraulein Hirsch's complicity in her confinement: for male oppression to be effective, it requires the cooperation of women. In the context of the shadow war already apparent in Britain pre-1914, those two German women are combatants, Hirsch through her coordinated activities with the military man von Hillern and Etynge through her long career as a tool of Kaiser Wilhelm. When Coombe intervenes to prevent von Hillern from carrying out his planned rape and abduction of Robin, she misconstrues his actions, thinking he was behind her kidnapping. Reluctantly she accepts his help and is reunited with Mademoiselle Valle while Coombe informs Etynge of her imminent arrest with these words: "You are not young and you are facing years of life in prison. Your head will be shaved—your hands worn and blackened and your nails broken with the picking of oakum. You will writhe in hopeless degradation until you are done for [...]. Women such as you should learn what hell on earth means. You will learn" (284). Coombe's words could be taken as little more than a standard misogynist judgment of a woman acting outside the pale of domestic life; a woman who dares to be as active in the interests of a national cause as a man, however aggressive that cause may be, deserves anything she gets. But even though Coombe offers no parallel judgment about the intentions and actions of von Hillern, he utters his judgment of Etynge in the context of a series of geopolitical discussions he had been having with the Duchess of Darte. Those discussions conflate Coombe's personal history with what he calls "the overwhelming forces of Fate" (324) that will demand that he, and every one of his time and place, commit to a life determined by the necessities of a national community over the desires of the self. Those forces of fate are manifest in the stirring precedent to war. Consequently, Coombe's words function as evidence that the battle has already been joined, that war has permeated the realities of everyday life in Britain and on the continent. For Coombe, the changes he foresees both geopolitically and domestically are fueled by the idea emerging from Germany of a society organized on a military model, war being the fuel that energizes public feeling and national action.

In the second of a series of conversations with the Duchess of Darte on "the black tragedy for which they believed the world's stage was already being set" (324), Coombe reflects on the "responsibilities" he believes will be "demanded" of those with material resources and social rank. When the Duchess asks exactly "*what* will be demanded," Coombe replies that he does not know; he does know, however, that there will be a major "readjustment" in geopolitical relations, which will extend through the social relations within England itself. "But before the readjustment," he says with a sense of foreboding, "there will be the pouring forth of blood," leaving in its wake "many a house left without its head." But that's the least of the danger. For when war comes, men "[I]n all their young virility and promise for a next generation—the strong young fathers of forever unborn millions" will simply be gone. "And it will be so not only in England, but all over a blood drenched world" (324). A country laid waste, a continent laid waste, a world laid waste through the killing of a generation of young men certainly captures the feeling of those who survived the Great War, a feeling rendered with such cultural comprehensiveness in Eliot's poem where fertility is both lamented and feared. ("April is the cruelest month" because it still stirs with life through a soft though insistent pulse that can jog the memory but not stimulate the body, "breeding / Lilacs out of the dead land" rather than a new generation of people or anything warm of blood at all.) Coombe's prewar assessment (which is, of course, Burnett's retrospective view) probes the causes behind the impending bloodshed and its concomitant erasure of fertility as not merely a cultural feeling but the result of actions and actors that can be named and resisted. Here is how Coombe puts it after one of his frequent visits to the continent:

> Above all the common sounds of daily human life one hears in that one land the rattle and clash of arms and the unending thudding tread of marching feet [...]. Two generations of men creatures bred and born and trained to live as parts of a huge death dealing machine have resulted in a monstrous construction. Each man is a part of it and each part's greatest

ambition is to respond to the shouted word of command as a mechanical puppet responds to the touch of a spring. To each unit of the millions, love of his own country means only hatred of all others and the belief that no other should be allowed existence. The sacred creed of each is that the immensity of Germany is such that there can be no room on the earth for another like itself. Blood and iron will clear the world of the inferior peoples. To the masses that is their God's will. Their God is an understudy of their Kaiser. (325)

Coombe's analysis, with its emphasis on the absolute authority of a single leader as the head of a racist, martial social order where the individual's highest goal is obedience, peels back the layers of a German fascist state; his analysis captures qualities of that state, which, from our post-World War II perspective, reveal the continuity in German culture from Kaiser Wilhelm to Adolf Hitler.

The shift in terms in the previous sentence—from state to culture—is not accidental. As Theweleit suggests in the second volume of *Male Fantasies* in the chapter called "The Mass and Its Counterparts," in the years designated above, the norms of masculine life in the German military became the norms by which culture writ large was understood. According to Theweleit, the "concept of 'culture'" served as an umbrella term that designated "the whole welter of soldierly traditions in a single word" (62).

All the army's norms and code of honor, the social conventions observed in the barracks or the casino, on maneuvers, the battlefield, in theater stalls, at commanding officers' receptions, in cafes and bordellos—all are succinctly contained in this one term, culture. The high regard in which "culture" is held in Germany springs from a veneration of male dominance and militarism. There is no contradiction at all in the fact that men who hate and prosecute free thought and activity, threatening its practitioners with exclusion from their professions (*Berufsverbot*), expulsion, or death, are able to do so in the name of the German culture they love and revere. The man of culture is defined as the man who knows the difference between first-lieutenant, major, and captain; a barbarian is a man who feels no love either for uniforms or death. And the "highest" form of cultural celebration is war. (62–63)

In the context of Theweleit's formulation, von Hillern is the man of culture, who abuses women as he oils the gears that he controls in the machinery of death, and Coombe the barbarian, indifferent to rank and solicitous of life. Burnett's critics may have seen *The Head of the House of Coombe* as a throwback to the Victorian era as suggested by the title of the review in *Outlook* called "Back to the Victorian" cited above and by Gerzina's characterization of "the postwar intelligentsia, who rejected what they saw as the wordy sentimentalism of the Victorians" (299) in Burnett's final novels, but such critical dismissals miss the clear-eyed realism with which Burnett confronted not just the prelude and impact of the Great War but the fascistic forces still at work during the time of her writing, whose damage to the world order—and obliteration of millions of lives—was not yet complete. Like her hero Coombe, Burnett was afraid, and their fear was not abstract. It was tied to the beauty, power and fragility of the human body.

That latter point emerges with some force in the fate of Coombe's youthful love and in his later anxiety about the effects of war on the body of his heir, Donal Muir. Coombe was in love with a young woman attached in some capacity to the English court. For reasons of national expedience, she was compelled to marry a man connected to the German court, an innocent enough arrangement given the historical and literal family connection between the English and German aristocracy. Coombe had been assigned as an aide to the German aristocrat, who, as he relates years later to the Duchess, was "a brute incarnate, mad with unbridled lust and drink and abnormal furies" (298). Stories of the aristocrat's brutalities toward his young wife circulated at the time, and when the Duchess asks if they were true, Coombe confirms their truth in harrowing and intimate detail: "I myself," he explains,

> by royal command, was a guest in the Schloss in the Bavarian Alps when it was known that he struck her repeatedly with a dog whip. She was going to have a child. One night I was wandering in the park in misery and I heard shrieks which sent me in mad search. I do not know what I should have done if I had succeeded, but I tried to force an entrance into the wing from which the shrieks came. I was met and stopped almost by open violence. The sounds ceased. She died a week later. But the most experienced lying could not hide some things. Even royal menials may have human blood in their veins. It was known that there were hideous marks on her little dead body. (299)

The parallels between what Coombe describes in that passage and the thwarted rape and kidnapping of Robin reinforce Burnett's critique of German militarism and misogyny as a fundamental denial of life. Although Robin was not raped, beaten and killed with her bruised body discarded, the elements were in place for a repetition of the fate of Coombe's youthful love: a German aristocrat whose very identity is tied to his capacity for violence, and especially violence against women, singles out an innocent English girl as an object for the gratification of his violent pleasure. For him the girl is merely a body, the fact of her pregnancy an affront, for the pregnancy insists that there is another, much larger significance for the girl's body. Killing her is a rejection of fertility, which, given Coombe's desire for marriage and family with the girl, is more than simple murder. The unnamed aristocrat and von Hillern venerate, as Theweleit might put it, masculine dominance and militarism. Their culture is a culture of death. And that is what frightens Coombe and the Duchess.

In a later conversation between Coombe and the Duchess, the Duchess articulates her own fear, which Coombe then amplifies and applies to himself. Speaking of the uses of nationalism to incite the population in Germany, Coombe says that the Kaiser dangles nationalism (the idea that all good things spring from Germany) "before his people to arrest the attention of the simple and honest ones as one jingles a rattle before a child. There are those among them who are not so readily attracted by terms of blood and iron." The Duchess responds with: "'But they will be called upon to shed blood and to pour forth their own [...] lads with ruddy cheeks and with white bodies to be torn to fragments.'" She ends with, "'I am afraid,'" to which Coombe responds: "'So am I.'" But, he goes on to say, fear "clears a man's mind of rubbish and nonessentials. It is because I am *afraid* that I accuse myself. And it is not for myself or you but for the whole world which before the end comes will seem to fall into fragments'" (327). For Coombe fear is tied to the simultaneous potential and frailty of the body; just as he had witnessed the violation of his beloved's body in his youth, he imagines the dismemberment of young men, English and German, with the beauty and vitality of his heir. The element of escape in Coombe's formulation, however, lies in the word "seems." His youthful loss is in reality not universal loss; it is partial, and he will not concede fully that representative bodies necessarily mean all bodies. English and German youth may "fall into fragments," but not all of them. The war is not absolute; it is a prelude to a "readjustment." As he says toward the end of the conversation: "The [human] race is an undeveloped thing. A few centuries later it will have evolved another sense. This century may see the first huge step—because the power of a cataclysm sweeps it forward" (328–29). That "other sense" is both residual and emergent, primitive and evolutionary at the same time, and its contours and complexity are suggested in the childhood connection between Robin and Donal, and its power for life and regeneration is implied in their experience in and survival of the war. *The Head of the House of Coombe*, in fact, closes with the juxtaposition of the reunion between Robin and Donal and the commencement of hostilities that became the Great War. Having met by chance at a social event organized by the Duchess of Darte, for whom Robin has been hired as a companion and secretary, Robin and Donal lose themselves in their reunion as they dance. But before the dance ends, word arrives of the assassination in Sarajevo. "In the shining ball room the music rose and fell and swelled again into ecstasy as he took her white young lightness in his arm and they swayed and darted and swooped like things of the air—while the old Duchess and Lord Coombe looked on almost unseeing and talked in murmurs of Sarajevo" (374). The final image of the book, then, emphasizes the ethereal in a style that is childlike in its directness (note the sevenfold repetition of the connective "and," for instance), the figures of Donal and Robin like "things of the air" blending with the "murmurs of Sarajevo." What emerges in the blending of the physical compulsion for relationship and the destructive powers of war becomes the burden of Burnett's final novel, *Robin*.

IV

The romance of Robin and Donal is framed in Chapter Two of *Robin* by the impact the war has on ordinary life. Here is how the chapter begins:

> If some uncomplex minded and even moderately articulate man or woman, living in some small, ordinary respectable London house and going about his or her work in the customary way, had been prompted by chance upon June 29th, 1914, to begin to keep on that date a day-by-day diary of his or her ordinary life, the effects of huge historic events, as revealed by the every-day incidents to be noted in the streets, to be heard in his neighbours' houses as well as among his fellow workers, to be read in the penny or half-penny newspapers, would have resulted—if the record had been kept faithfully and without any self-conscious sense of audience—between 1914 and 1918 in the gradual compiling of a human document of immense historical value[...]. But it must have been begun in June, 1914, and have been written with the casualness of that commonplace realism which is the most convincing realism of all. (9)

In the modesty of its claims to an unselfconscious realistic depiction of ordinary life as that life is impacted by the events of world war, Burnett articulates what amounts to an immodest ambition: to write a romance as a vehicle of a "commonplace [...] [and] convincing realism," romance providing, in that formulation, a narrative grammar that facilitates human relations. War, of course, is the antithesis of romance, which is one explanation for why in fact and fiction individual stories of romance in war time emphasize haste, the drive to bond being an act of defiance to events against which one feels helpless. *Robin*, then, "is not," as the narrator puts it,

> a "war story." It is not even a story of the War, but a relation of incidents occurring amidst and resulting from the strenuousness of a period to which "the War" was a background so colossal that it dwarfed all events, except in the minds of those for whom such events personally shook and darkened or brightened the world. (13)

The Great War in this, Burnett's last, novel may permeate every aspect of life, but it is not all of life. War may have an impact on daily life, making war a preoccupation realized most commonly as speculation and gossip,[14] but when war directly reshapes particular lives through separation, death, injury, and mental and physical trauma (and conceivably the potential for reunion and healing), the irreducibly personal nature of such events overwhelms the abstract comprehensiveness of war as a singular world historical event. The idea here is that Burnett's insistence that the meaning of war can be best felt on the pulses of individual human beings most deeply affected by it subordinates the significance of war to its effects. The narrator gives voice to that idea when observing the following about Coombe's travels in Germany just before the war.

> He had been through the monster munition works at Essen several times and he had heard technical talks of inventions, the sole reason for whose presence in the world was that they had the power to blow human beings into unrecognizable, ensanguined shreds and to tear off limbs and catapult them into the air. He had heard these powers talked of with a sense of natural pride in achievement, in fact with honest and cheerful self gratulation. (19)

Though voiced by the narrator, the passage is focalized through Coombe, and it captures the tension between war as abstraction that stimulates a weird form of "creativity" but is realized most concretely in the bloody fragments of human bodies personally known and loved by someone. The "cheerful gratulation" that Coombe hears is a form of gossip, a hyper-interested though distanced verbal play directed at a subject (as object) powerless to respond.

Given what I am presenting here as Burnett's thoughtful and complex engagement with the Great War, it comes as some surprise that *Robin* and *The Head of the House of Coombe* appear nowhere that I can find in the criticism on the Great War and literature.[15] That is the case even though Burnett's take on some of the standard tensions engaged in the criticism is ambitious and provocative. To develop that point, I focus on one representative example, Sharon Ouditt's *Fighting Forces, Writing Women: Identity and Ideology in the First World War*.[16] Ouditt's book is theoretically sophisticated and exciting. In it she explores the role of women as nurses, workers (factory and beyond), political actors (maternal pacifists against the war) and emergent new literary forms in the work of Virginia Woolf. "[T]he central chapter of [her] study," however, is called "Women at

Home: Romance or realism" (89), a title that echoes the polarities of the popular and the purist even as the argument in the chapter emphasizes the interplay between romance and realism within rather than between novels. Ouditt frames her discussion of Great War novels written by women within the context of less sustained and more diffuse forms of popular expression. "Many of the popular songs, posters, and postcards of the war," Ouditt writes, "reveal that romance was necessary as a life-enhancing counterpoint to the brutalities and degradations of war[…]. Romantic love seemed to offer both soldiers and civilians some continuity and order in their lives" (89). Implicit in Ouditt's argument is that romance was not an escape from reality; rather, it served a genuine psychological function that could be reinforced in fact, through actual relationships and marriages no matter how short-lived. Not only that, however, "the ideality of romantic love, while frequently conservative, can offer a pathway to a vision of an alternative value system preferable to that dominated by war" (90). One example of such a value system is a model of communication predicated on an "image of spiritualized maternal love" (113).

In her analysis of Rebecca West's first novel, *The Return of the Soldier* (1918), Ouditt explores West's ironic rendering of the English country house as refuge from war overseen by a glittering angel in the house. The house according to Ouditt has all the upmarket sparkle of a *Vogue* presentation house, and the angel in it, Kitty, appears as a "stiff and lifeless icon" that West describes in this way: "she looked cold as moonlight, as virginity, but precious; the falling candlelight struck her hair to bright, pure gold" (West, 56–57 cited in Ouditt 111). The irony of what amounts to a "frigid felicity" is counterpoised to the unironic presentation of the maternal woman, Margaret, who, although fitting "an alternative stereotype of femininity" to Kitty's, has undeniable "healing powers" for the wounded soldier returned to his estate. That soldier, Chris, returns from war crippled with anxiety (a form of shell shock). On one occasion he walks with Margaret, his former lover, beyond the boundaries of the estate, where they recline, Chris's head on Margaret's lap, in the woods. Observed by Jenny, the narrator and Chris's cousin, the pair seem to communicate in a way that erases any barriers of gender, experience and social convention. For Jenny the couple revealed how "the woman has gathered the soul of the man into her soul and is keeping it warm in love and peace so that his body can rest quiet for a little time. That is a great thing for a woman to do" (West 144, cited in Ouditt 113). In that moment, Ouditt argues, "Margaret represents timeless values: an abstract reality that finds articulation in concrete acts of love," in contrast to the idea presented above as the abstract idea of war realized in its unspeakable impact on individual bodies. Unlike war, which achieves a perverse unity through utter destruction, where even bodily parts cannot be differentiated, "concrete acts of love" symbolize "a land of no differentiation; a magic state like the semiotic, where substances merge and the laws of the physical universe melt into an imaginative, sensual haze" (113). A spiritualized union of imagination and sensuality experienced in bodily relations where the distinction between self and other dissipates in a speech-defying sense of wholeness is the dream vision the narrative offers in reaction to and correction of the life-denying energies of war. That sentence not only summarizes my reading of Ouditt's interpretation of West's novel, it serves as a characterization of the imaginative core of Burnett's *Robin*.

After Robin and Donal are reunited and they confess that in the intervening years they could not "stop thinking" of each other (31), and after it becomes clear that Donal must serve in the war, the narrator describes the quality of their connection through the image of their eyes:

> There has never been a limner through all the ages who has pictured—at such a moment—two pairs of eyes reaching, melting into, lost in each other in their human search for the longing soul drawing together human things. Hand and brush and colour cannot touch That which Is and Must Be—in its yearning search for the spirit which is its life on earth. Yet a boy and a girl were yearning towards it as they sat in mere mortal form on a bench in a London square. And neither of them knew more than that they wondered at and adored the beauty in each other's eyes. (31–32)

That passage captures the evolutionary energies that drive Robin's and Donal's desires as their bodily awareness of each other melts into a singular unity; the soul or spirit that impels the body to thirst for a full life in union with another functions in the novel as the primary thing war destroys. The conceptual center of the passage posits a larger soul, one might venture to say an Emersonian *Oversoul*,[17] as a life-affirming force that unifies the experience of the senses with an apprehension of a comprehensive spirit. The image that carries the burden of the passage is the interlocking gazes Robin and Donal share, gazes characterized by wonder and adoration. The image of two figures on a London bench serves as a metaphor for the general position of youth in the early stages of the Great War.

As word filters back to London with increasing frequency of the number of casualties and their relative youth, Coombe observes how young men have become hyper-aware of the fragility of their hold on life. "The young ones know" they will be the first to die in the war, Coombe asserts; therefore, "they clutch the most frantically" at life.

> That is what I am seeing in young eyes everywhere. Mere instinct makes it so—mere uncontrollable instinct which takes the form of a sort of desperateness at facing the thousand chances of death before they have lived. They don't know it isn't actual fear of bullets and shrapnel. Sometimes they're afraid it's fear and it makes them sick at themselves and determined to grin and hide it. But it isn't fear—it's furious Nature protesting. (37)

Coombe's words extend the earlier description of Robin and Donal to others; while they remain a special case (being the focus of the novel), they are also representative, their love and predicament common. That great soul "drawing together human things" becomes, again in Emersonian idiom, simply "Nature"; the apparently metaphysical is a manifestation of the irreducibly physical, the boundaries dividing human beings, nature and spirit blurring into a single life-affirming dynamic.

My reading of the sequence of passages above would seem to reinforce Gerzina's contention that the "real message" in *Robin* concerns "the way the world now embraced notions of psychic phenomenon" (299). Although Burnett does introduce a particular kind of psychic phenomenon as an aspect of Robin's and Donal's story, to limit the novel to an argument in defense of the reality of such phenomenon is reductive and begs a key question. First, as I have suggested in my allusions to Emerson above, Burnett draws on transcendental concepts firmly embedded in the Anglo-American literary tradition. Second, *Robin* is a novel, which by definition indicates that even the most straightforward gestures toward mimesis also carry metaphorical weight. Therefore, the question Gerzina's generalization begs concerns the figurative significance of the psychic in the novel. In the context of the collision of ideologies and social discourses that characterize the novel as a genre,[18] what social discourse does the language of psychic phenomenon clash with and in what thematic direction does it move? Specifically, given the novel's emphasis on how the war is part of a process of social upheaval, disorientation and ultimate change (in the most optimistic form, change means growth, the expansion of human capacity for sympathy and solidarity), what role does the discourse of psychic phenomenon play in the *longue duree* required for such change? If resistance to the values of war is part of that role, what social realities does war symbolically evoke in the novel? If the Great War assists "Nature" in giving "a new impulse to the race," if "[M]en and women are being dragged out of their self-absorbed corners and stirred up and shaken" (35) as the novel through Coombe suggests, we need to think about the war and the social placement of men and women that preceded the war as a function of the old impulse. In my reading, Burnett's novel identifies that old impulse with the idea of the patriarchy she has been resisting from her earliest novels: an asymmetrical social order organized by male violence and sustained by a language that masks and naturalizes that violence.

The first stage of the disruption of the social order in the novel is its depiction of the well-documented historical phenomenon of women taking on male roles and responsibilities during the first mass mechanized world war.

> Women were doing astonishing work and revealing astonishing power and determination. The sexes mingled with a businesslike informality unknown in times of peace. Lovely girls went in and out of their homes, and from one quarter of London to another without question. They walked with a brisk step and wore the steady expression of creatures with work in view. (44)

Note how that brief passage registers women's power and determination as something revealed, not discovered or learned under stress. Women working are people working, the sexes sharing the domestic business in support of the war while the view of women in public being little more than objects of sexual interest for men is suspended if not definitively superseded. Even the conventions of wartime romance are changed. When Donal and Robin meet for the second time after their reunion at the house party, Donal asks: "'Ought I to ask you to come and meet me—as if you were a little housemaid meeting her life-guardsman?'" Robin replies: "'Yes, you ought' […] [but] [t]here are no little housemaids and life-guardsmen now. It seems as if there were only—people'" (45). Robin's erasure of the most ordinary markers of social placement in the name of the equality of all human beings is an extension of what the narrator defines as her full, unalloyed "pure acceptance" of Donal as he is; their attunement with each other functions as a metaphor for a larger attunement in social relations, distinctions of class, culture, wealth, sect and so on being absolutely subordinated to something more than mere survival.

The novel extends the metaphor of attunement. "The whole world seemed a great musical instrument, overstrung and giving out previously unknown harmonies and inharmonies. Amid the thunders of great clashing discords the individual note continued its vibrations" (46). In the grammar of those lines the inharmonies are associated with "great clashing discords" (i.e., the masses on the battlefield) while the harmonies evoke "the individual note" (the simultaneously common and peculiar relations between individuals). The implication is that the threat of war to any particular life is a threat to life itself. "'It is as if a gigantic wall were piling itself up between us and Life,'" Donal says to Robin. He then "gently put out his own hand and took in it the slim gloved one and looked down on it, as if it were something quite apart, and wonderful—rather as if hands were rare and he had not often seen one before" (47). Donal's response to the war, then, is not to project hatred toward the Germans or revel in jingoistic rhetoric about the superiority of the British. He turns to the facts of the living body as in and of itself extraordinary; he desires to be on the side of life, which he sees as possible only if he can imagine life apart from all social determinations, especially the social determinations of language. Consequently, when he tells Robin that he wants her to himself, he qualifies his words by saying that what he means "is a little different" than what his words seem to denote. He explains further: "'I want [...] our being together in this way—our understanding and talking—to be something that belongs to *us* and no one else[...]. Nobody else *could* understand it. Perhaps we don't ourselves—quite!'" (49). Donal is groping for a new language, words whose meanings are not already predetermined by social usage. "I can't bear the thought of other people spoiling the beauty of it [their being together] by talking it over" (49). In his struggle to use a symbolic medium (i.e., language) to take on meaning outside the symbolic order (patriarchy), Donal rejects Robin's effort to understand what he means. When she asks whether what he is talking about is "like a secret," he says "No"; it is, rather, "a sort of sacred, heavenly unbelievable thing we own together" (49). "Sort of sacred," "unbelievable," "thing," do not point to any precise object; the language is vague, teasingly suggestive. Consequently, they did not "express [...] in any common mental form the fact that they were 'in love' with each other." They merely were borne on the "swelling waves" of the tide of life, "as though they were leaves" (50). The image of the swelling waves projects Robin's soon to be realized pregnancy; her maternal body, in the narrative logic of the novel, becomes an expression of her and Donal's and their generation's defiance of the logic of war.

Beginning with the material disruptions of war, Burnett deepens her effort to shape a vision of human relationship independent from the social conventions that have served to define the range of possibilities in advance. One of the most challenging aspects of that effort is to imagine a pregnancy outside of conventional ways of thinking about it, be the pregnancy a fulfillment of social expectations or a violation of them. On its deepest level, Burnett is working within what Julia Kristeva has defined as the semiotic, which is a "mode of signification other to the Symbolic Order" (Ouditt 132). Rendered through gesture, nonverbal sound, metaphor and art, the semiotic is a mode of resistance to patriarchy that opens a way to begin to imagine alternative forms of social relations emergent from experience.[19] With war as the ultimate expression of and, paradoxically, challenge to the inherent violence of patriarchy, Burnett writes her Great War novels in an effort to give shape to a semiotic resistance to patriarchal violence in its most extreme form, and she found her richest vein of semiotic energies in a form of psychic phenomenon.

V

Burnett's interest in psychic phenomenon, or what was called during her lifetime "New Thought," became most evident to her readers with the publication of her story, *The Dawn of a To-morrow* (1906). Writing for the *New York Times* under the pseudonym "Pendennis," the reviewer entitled his interview with Burnett on that story, "Mrs. Frances Hodgson Burnett Finds a New Field for Her Pen."[20] But in the course of the interview, the definition of that new field never emerges. Asked whether the story is theosophy, Burnett replies: "Why give it a name." Asked then whether "it is Christian Science [she] wish[ed] to point out," Burnett says "[I]f I were a Christian Scientist that might be, but I am not" (3). What she does acknowledge, however, is that her subject matter unsettled her. Pendennis put the point this way: "[W]hen 'The Dawn of a To-morrow' first quivered into manuscript form, like Mrs. Shelley's 'Frankenstein,' it overwhelmed her intellectual discretion and compelled her to seek the advice of a literary physician" (i.e., her editor at Scribner's). Pendennis then quotes that editor, paraphrasing, one can only assume, what Burnett told him the editor advised.

> You have come across one of your big subjects, Mrs. Burnett; by no means neglect its bringing up. It is a story that will be far-reaching in its ethical effect. Nurture it carefully, but let it have its own way. (3)

At the end of the interview, Burnett acknowledges that she followed her editor's advice. "It would be quite impossible to make it clear to a promiscuous public just how obstinately the story worked its way out, entirely away from the intentions with which I sat down to write it" (3). The key terms in the above exchanges—theosophy, Christian Science and ethics—and the fact that Burnett felt some lack of control over her material—suggest the emergence in Burnett's art of spiritual concerns for which she was struggling to find, if not exactly a language, an appropriate literary orientation.[21]

Gretchen Holbrook Gerzina, in her discussion of *The Dawn of a To-morrow*, offers a starting point for thinking about the nature of Burnett's engagement with the "new thought":

> New Thought was a spiritual movement that was gaining in popularity in America at that time [c. 1906], even though it had its roots in the mid-nineteenth century with thinkers such as Emanuel Swedenborg, Ralph Waldo Emerson, and the magnificently named Phineas Pankhurst Quimby. Henry James's brother, the Harvard professor William James, was also associated with New Thought, which had certain affinities with Christian Science. Its basis was in the link between spiritualism and the physical world, the power of belief and the power of the human mind. Both were metaphysical in nature […]. [Burnett's] fictionalized formulation of her 'new thought' planted the seed that would influence her writing for years. (241)

While one can quibble over the association of Swedenborg with the mid-nineteenth century (he published his most influential work, *Heaven and Hell*, in 1758), the idea that there are deep intellectual antecedents to the conceptual river associated with New Thought, of which theosophy and Christian Science are merely tributaries, opens the probability that Burnett's engagement with the intersection between "spiritualism and the physical world" is as much a literary as it is a biographical phenomenon. In other words, New Thought may have spoken to a deep personal need in Burnett, but it also provided a wide field for her to structure in literary form ideas and configurations of human relationship that break out of conventional modes of thought and story. We might say that for Burnett New Thought functioned as a generative grammar that could help her art project possible futures at a time when the world seemed to be heading toward a form of suicide in the realities of the war that would break out fewer than ten years after the writing of *The Dawn of a To-morrow*. Though this point may be obvious, the story hinges on the fact that the central figure in that story, a famous, wildly successful man of business, is saved from his well-thought-through plan to commit suicide by his happenstance engagement with a group of struggling, impoverished others, who, despite their limiting circumstances, live their lives with an open hopefulness for the potential of the future. In other words, their basic spiritual orientation, even in the face of death, is to embrace life. Their faith, insofar as it can be defined, has nothing to do with dogma and everything to do with the acknowledgment of the primacy of the reality of every individual, who, by definition as a human being, is embedded in the natural world. When, for example, the suicidal protagonist Antony Dart is asked what he was looking for, he responds: "'Failing brain—failing life—despair—death!'" To that his interlocutor Miss Montaubyn replies: "'None of 'em's comin'—if yer don't call 'em. Stand still an' listen for the other. It's the other that's *true.*'" The other, in the logic of that reply, can only be life, a point reinforced by the narrator's comment, focalized through Dart's point of view, that "[S]he [Miss Montaubyn] was without doubt amazing. She chirped like a bird singing on a bough, rejoicing in token of the shining of the sun" (120). She may respond to Dart in words, but rather than words he hears bird song and sees the brightness of the shining sun; his senses respond to the sound of her voice more than to the sense of her words.

The new literary orientation that one might claim in the partial reading of *The Dawn of a To-morrow* above, wherein Burnett seems to be reaching for ways to make language signify something beyond itself or, as Kristeva might have it, prior to itself, by way of the New Thought may seem fresh in the context of the overt thematics of Burnett's work before 1906, but it may not be so singular when placed in the context of Burnett's literary ancestors, particularly at the time of the publication of *Robin*, the maligned Victorians and among some of Burnett's more prominent contemporaries, Henry James by way of his brother William, Arthur Conan Doyle and the poet William Butler Yeats, to name just four. The terms New Thought, the occult, spiritualism, metaphysics, theosophy and so on designate a huge range of belief, phenomenon, thought and practice about which there is a long history. Particularly in the years between 1850 and 1914, as Janet Oppenheim has thoroughly documented, spiritualism as a practice and psychical research as an area of inquiry that focused the methods of science on the study of psychic phenomenon experienced a sustained surge of interest.[22] With a focus specifically on mesmerism, Alison Winter characterizes that surge of interest as follows:

Over the past fifteen years historians have developed the makings of a dramatically new account of how people in the past understood mental powers. Far from exhibiting the stifling conformity long associated with the period, Victorian England is now recognized as having been populated by phrenologists, plebian spiritualists, mediums, and psychic researchers. They lived in a broth more exotic than the so-called Monster Soup of the Thames: a potent concoction of magnetic fluids, vital powers, and swarming spirits. So did many of their more familiar physiologists, physicians, social scientists, and writers: Thomas Carlyle looked around him to find friends "sleeping magnetic sleep," George Eliot shaved her head for a phrenological reading, Herbert Spencer wrote articles for a mesmeric journal, Michael Faraday built an apparatus for experiments in table turning, and spiritualism inspired the famous logician Augustus De Morgan to question the nature of scientific proof.[23]

Although that passage implies a tension between psychic phenomenon and science in De Morgan's skepticism about scientific proof when that proof is placed against such phenomenon, it captures in the range of its examples and through its gastric metaphors of broth and soup a more productive interrelationship between science and the occult in the period that spanned Burnett's career, an interrelationship that was explored in novels ranging from Charlotte Bronte's *Jane Eyre* (1848) to Thomas Hardy's *Tess of the D'Urbervilles* (1891), as demonstrated by Anna Neil in *Primitive Minds*.[24]

As we saw in Burnett's representation of Lord Mount Dunstan in *The Shuttle*, Burnett evoked two contradictory energies in her description of the nature of his character. On the one hand, he is represented as the First Man, a primeval figure whose humanness is elemental in that it precedes a fully developed social order to define it in advance. But his attraction to Bettina Vanderpoel associates him with the evolutionary process Burnett connects to Bettina's family history. Thus, the atavistic First Man is also the evolutionary man still to come; in both conceptions Mount Dunstan represents qualities that are independent of the social order while being at the same time necessary to sustain the health of the social order. In *Primitive Minds*, Anna Neil conjures a similar tension between atavism and evolution in her exploration of novelistic engagements with the intersection between the occult, what she broadly defines as "spiritual experience," and evolution, an intersection that places the a-temporal states of a range of spiritual experiences in productive tension with the temporality of evolutionary process. Neil dissents from the idea that the definitive narrative model for the spiritual in the Victorian novel has its origins in John Bunyan's *The Pilgrim's Progress* (1678), which presents a narrative of linear spiritual progress for the development of the protagonist Christian. Rather, Neil argues, "there are numerous Victorian literary accounts of spiritual experience that suggest not species progress but rather the evisceration of the very entities—self, other, space, and time—around which our perception of reality is organized and whose existence is evidence of the complex achievements of consciousness" (7). The "evisceration" of "self, other, space, and time" may glance back toward a primeval timelessness, but as an achievement of consciousness such an evisceration also gestures toward the visionary. With the annihilation of the boundaries between self and other along with the constraints of space and time, such spiritual experiences fall squarely within the realm of the semiotic, a sphere where a sense of wholeness depends on the difference from any preexistent social order. The spiritual and semiotic serve as utopian spaces where the world can be made new.

Neil focuses on a specific category of spiritual experience, what she calls "dreamy disturbances of consciousness" (8), which she shows are part of both "evolutionary-materialist and spiritual explanations for the human mind and its relationship to the world it mediates." Dream states, she suggests, suspend "the brain's higher conscious activity" and are, as a result, associated with a "rudimentary stage of mental development." A form of atavism, the "marvelous events associated with dreamy mental states [point] to the nervous pathologies of lower nervous arrangements, but they also [reveal] latent mental powers as forgotten elements of the physical history of the species" (9). There is an odd oscillation between the idea of development (e.g., "latent mental powers" that can be brought out into the open for development) and retrieval ("forgotten elements [...] of the species") that parallels Burnett's deployment of the atavistic in her novels. Burnett, however, does not conceive of dream states in the way that Neil explains them. For example, in her discussion of "Rapture and Realism in *Jane Eyre*," Neil argues that "much of the spiritual work [in the novel] occurs in a dream or in a dreamlike state, suggesting that, despite Jane's developing capacity for self-control, the mind's path to God involves those regions of mental experience that remain ungoverned by the faculties of will and judgment" (47). Dream states in that formulation remain separate from cognition; they are independent of individual volition and function via a form of receptive passivity. Dream states in *Robin*, however, do not necessarily function as a form of suspension or transcendence of consciousness; rather they form a space where consciousness can function more fully and freely, where the affordances of the mind can intersect with the possibilities embodied in the myriad forms of the natural world in a way where dream and intellect, body and mind, consciousness and nature function as a continuous whole. What *Robin* adds to Burnett's various renderings of how atavistic elements function as residual fuel for future transformations of the human body and mind, as they evolve toward a fuller realization of human potentialities, is the intentional, active and cognitive cooperation of individuals in that evolutionary process. The romance of Robin and Donal serves as an evolutionary metaphor in defiance of the regressive violence of the Great War. Central to that metaphor is Robin's maternal body, which becomes the point of intersection of vital energies focused on that body as the locus of meaning while the war, though unheard, still rages.

VI

Robin's maternal body is representative of the significance placed on how that body must be enabled to fulfill its function despite social rules and other forms of artificial constraint. In the context of war, women as bearers of life serve as both a metaphoric rejection of war even as they quite literally make a future possible. In a conversation between the Duchess of Darte and Lady Lothwell, the significance of the proliferation of love children (also called in the conversation "illegal" babies) is suggested to be as a result of transpersonal forces in reaction to war. "There ought to be a sort of moratorium in the matter of social laws," the Duchess states. "The old rules don't hold. We are facing new conditions. This is a thing for women to take in hand, practically, as they are taking in hand other work" (90). Out of context, the Duchess's words could be drawn on to support the notion that women must give birth in order to produce more soldiers to defend the nation (and the empire); maternity is just another form of work, just the same as any other work related to the necessities of war. At such times, the Duchess goes on to say, "[T]here is only time to heal wounds and quiet maddening pain and save life" (90). Therefore, the bearing of children, legal or illegal,

> involves issues the women who can think must hold in their minds and treat judicially. One cannot moralise and be shocked before an advancing tidal wave. It has always been part of the unreason and frenzy of times of war. When Death is near, Life fights hard for itself. It does not care who or what it strikes. (91)

Though somewhat out of sequence, the logic of the Duchess's words is that in wartime social rules must be suspended; instinct can be trusted to guide a life-affirming response to the realities of war. As a consequence, those with social power should not use that power to condemn women who ignore social norms; nor should those women judge themselves. Life makes demands prior to social decorum. As is the case with war, life "does not care who it strikes," or when.

The general discussion between the Duchess and Lady Lothwell provides the discursive context for Robin's and Donal's stolen and solitary meetings in a nearby wood during the time between their reunion and his being shipped off to France. In that time, life, of course, had struck her, and with his departure and the prospect of his being killed in battle, as almost all the young men from the house party had been, life is struck by war; Robin separates her pregnancy from the "tidal wave" of life; the stirring life within her becomes something for which she must struggle. After she learned of his departure, she went to her room and "fell down on the floor and sat there," drawing a comparison between her current loss and their initial separation when she was a child: "Long ago his mother had taken him away from her. Now the War had taken him. The spectre stood straight in the path before her" (96). In that series of simple sentences, the hyper-socially conscious motives behind Donal's mother's actions are equated with the violence of war as both constitute the "spectre" (of death, of all forces social and martial opposed to the freedom and fullness of life) that Robin must confront or succumb to. Her mind then oscillates between what she is compelled to read about the atrocities of war and the time she and Donal had spent in the wood, a time that plays in her mind like a dream.

Just before the start of the war, the Duchess of Darte had hired Robin to be her companion and personal secretary. One of her duties once the war started was to read the daily newspaper accounts of battles, casualties and the like, but during her off days, she and Donal would meet in "the deep wood" where they "walked [...] night after night when the stillness was like heaven itself" and where it felt to them both as if "there was no longer war in the world." The sexual element in their meetings is rendered in the sensitivity they each show to the literal rhythms of each other's heartbeats: "'Do you hear my heart,'" Donal asks Robin, to which she replies: "'I feel it'" (87–88). Sound is rendered as feeling; the dream of their time in the wood is anchored by their acute attunement with each other's bodies. After Donal leaves for the front and Robin must read account after account of battlefield horrors, their mutual bodily awareness constitutes her most powerful (counter)-memory:

> As there came surging in day by day bitter and cruel waves of war news—stories of slaughter by land and sea, of massacre in simple places, of savagery wrought on wounded men and prisoners in a hydrophobia of hate let loose, it was ill lying awake in the dark remembering loved beings surrounded by the worst of all the world has ever known. Robin was afraid to look at the newspapers which her very duties themselves obliged her to familiarize herself with, and she could not close her ears. With battleship raids on harmless coast towns, planned merely to the end of the wanton killing of such unconsidered trifles of humanity as little children and women and men at their every-day work, the circle of horror seemed to draw itself in closely. (100–101)

The descriptions of war are generalized of necessity since they are not the product of first-hand observation, unlike these lines from Wilfred Owen's "Dulce et Decorum Est": "If you could hear, at every jolt, the blood / Come gurgling from the froth-corrupted lungs, / Obscene as cancer, bitter as the cud / Of vile, incurable sores on innocent tongues" (ll. 20–24). Nonetheless, the rabid image of the "hydrophobia of hate" and the manner in which the passage is focalized from the point of view of the German aggressors (e.g., "unconsidered trifles of humanity") combine to present an equally jarring sense of horror, Owen's lines through the specificity of the suffering of the body and Burnett's paragraph through the deft rendering of the scope of the killing and the quality of mind that would revel in it.

Reminded each day of the endless and comprehensive killing, Robin's mind reaches for the comfort of her memory of her dream with Donal in the wood. But she doubts the reality of that memory ("Had there been a dream" (101), she wonders) until she recalls his words: "'Can you hear my heart beat?'" Then the feel of that experience suffuses her body: "It had been a rapture to lay her cheek and ear against his breast and listen[...]. They had been so still [...] for pure joy in their close, close nearness." That physical memory, however, is overwhelmed by her imaginative projection of what his body may now be experiencing in the war. She wonders where Donal might be among the "millions of men marching [and] [...] thinking of nothing but killing." She knows that since he is among such men, and that "[I]f he were a brave soldier" then he too "must only think of killing and not be afraid because at any moment he might be killed too." Her body responds to that thought as she "clutched her knees and shuddered, feeling her forehead grow damp." Then she imagines "Donal killing a man—perhaps a boy like himself—a boy who might have a dream of his own! How would his blue eyes look while he was killing a man?" (102). Petrified as those thoughts make her, there is more fearlessness and honesty than self-pity in Robin's imaginings; her bodily connection to Donal connects her thinking to his capacity to exert the force of his body onto another even as she registers his vulnerability to be the victim of that other, his physical double. In a sense her mind fills in the personal detail that the newspaper accounts absorb in the mass. Then her thoughts circle back to the dream: "'Do you hear my heart beat? There is no time—no time!' these two things had been the beginning, the middle and the end" (104). Those lines contain two contradictory qualities: as the beginning, middle and end, the shared heartbeats have no chance to be sustained for "there is no time"; in contrast, "there is no time" can also suggest timelessness, a sense of the eternal, figured in the shared heartbeat that is sustained through the maternal body, in generation after generation. The heartbeat Donal and Robin shared in the wood is echoed by the heartbeat of their child, whom we do not see until the novel's end.

The wood, which had seemed like a fairy wood to the young lovers, is called Mersham Wood where an old woman, Mrs. Bennett, serves as caretaker. Drawn by her heartbeat-inflected memory of the safety, lushness and solitude of the wood, Robin returns to visit the old woman, "whose three grandsons had been killed within a few days of each other." Their deaths coupled with Robin's daily anxiety about the fate of Donal change the face of the wood from a refuge to a wasteland. For Robin, "There was no fairy wood any longer, there were only bare branched trees standing, holding out naked arms to the greyness of the world" (108). But at that point Mrs. Bennett's grief is greater than hers, her loss real in its finality, death having had the last word. For Robin the wood may come to life, may come to itself again. When she returns to the Duchess's house after the visit, however, the news she most feared arrives: "A shell had fallen somewhere and when it had burst Donal was 'blown to atoms'" (115). With that news her inner world reflects the emptiness she had already been confronted with in the outer world, and when she again seeks refuge in the wood, hoping against hope that there will be some echo of her dream, she hears and feels nothing, not even the life that is beginning to stir in her womb. No words can bring her comfort, and she can shape no words of her own. Her expressiveness is limited to "her sobbing," and this, the narrator explains, is what "her sobbing said": "'All the world is covered with dead—beautiful boys! [...] All alone and dead—dead!'" (169). The worst of that thought for Robin lies not in the fact of death alone, but in her knowledge that in being "blown to atoms," Donal leaves nothing. There had been and were yet to be many "strange and cruel tragedies" for England in the war, but Robin's pain over Donal's death and the fate of his body was a domestic tragedy "near enough to seem even worse—if worse could be" (182). As Coombe says to a Vicar later in the narrative: "In this—holocaust—she [Robin] needs protection," to which the Vicar replies: "It is a holocaust" (200). The holocaust reference encompasses the battlefields on the continent and the death-in-life of grief in England. As one of the reviewers of the novel noted, Robin is herself "shell-shocked." Indifferent to her own health, unresponsive to the fact of her pregnancy, her physical vitality simply drains away. There is not even a "Murmur of maternal lamentation" (*The Waste Land*, l. 368); Robin's inner world shrinks as she waits for her body to runs its course to silence, unable, even, to pray for peace.

Robin waits as one walking in her sleep. She eats and speaks very little as she loses weight and goes about her work in a mechanical fashion, like Eliot's typist but without the sex. In their search for the trick that would, as one doctor puts it, create conditions where "she would wake up" (222), Coombe sends Robin to an isolated, "small ruin" called Darreuch Castle in Scotland to be cared for by her old nurse, Dowie, who would shield her from hearing about the war so that she could, Coombe and the Duchess hope, begin to turn away from her grief and attend to the prospect of her impending motherhood. After some weeks there, however, "she had not 'wakened up,'" as Dowie put it, which shook Dowie's belief "that it would be only 'Nature' that she should" wake up, responding to the insistence of the life stirring within her. But Robin had "the look of a young thing who had done with Nature—and between whom and Nature the link had been broken" (223). As her weakness increases, Robin asks that she lie by the open window of her bedroom where she can look "[A]t the end of the heather" on the moor because she feels "as if something is there" (225). That something, it turns out, is the thing that reconnects her to nature: it is the warm, living body of Donal who comes to her that night in her dream. Her dream is the inverse of her real experience with Donal in Mersham Wood, which she remembers as a dream: in that case reality became a dream; in the second her dream is her reality. The hidden and vibrant, occult energy, which fuels the green growth over former battlefields, links the spirit and the body in doing the work of nature, connecting bodies in a generative dance that will not be stopped by the violence of war. Infused with that energy, Robin's body and mind heal rapidly as night after night she and Donal commune through the mysterious, psychic power that the novel suggests not only emanates from nature but ties nature to the human body and mind.

The link between the occult and nature is made explicit on the morning after Robin lay at the open window. That morning, the narrator notes, "came the 'waking up for which Dowie had so long waited and prayed. But not as Dowie had expected it or in the way she had thought 'Nature'" (226). Dowie had thought nature could work only one way, through the body alone. For Robin, nature compels through her body in synchronization with her spirit, the blurring of dream and the real being a metaphoric rendering of that blurring. When Robin informs Dowie that in the night, "Donal came," Dowie asks: "In a dream?" "I don't think it was a dream," says Robin. "It wasn't like one. I think he was here." Robin then recounts stories she has heard whispered to the Duchess of how, "[S]ince the War there have been so many stories about things like that." Dowie then observes that "[P]erhaps they are true" before she asks Robin whether she "could eat a new-laid egg and a shred of toast" (229). The fusion of her "real" spiritual experience with her bodily need for food, which precede her assertion that "I will [...] I *will*" to Dowie's question, connects her spirit, her body and her will in a unified embrace of life, which is figured in the way in which "the faint colour on her cheeks deepened and spread like a rosy dawn." That infusion of life into Robin's nearly emaciated body Dowie finds both exhilarating and "alarming." For Robin, however, her coming alive is the result of intimate, human relations that have meaning in how those relations are part of a larger web of connections that constitute a nation. "Donal was not dead," she tells Dowie, "He was not an angel. He was Donal" (229). Those facts anchor and renew her intimacy with him. Then Donal extends that relation to their child and to the nation. "He told me things about England—needing new souls and new strong bodies—," Robin explains, before affirming that Donal had come back for them "*both*" (230). Dowie remains hesitant in her response to Robin, not knowing how much to believe as real or whether she should pretend belief for the sake of Robin's physical health.

> Dowie bustled about with inward trembling. Whatever strange thing had happened it had awakened the stunned instinct in the girl—perhaps some change had begun to take place and she *would* eat the bit of food. The test would be the egg and the crisp toast—the real test. (230)

The test of the occult energies animating life is in the real: spirit has meaning insofar as it is tied to the body, which itself, then, is part of a web of relations. That web of relations is not only suggested by Donal's words about England, it is rendered in the novel through the representative positions of those around Robin, who share in her hopes and support her healing: science and the professions in the figure of Dr. Benton who is charged with her care in Scotland, the labor sustaining domestic life in the figure of Dowie and the traditional social order in the figure of Lord Coombe.

When Dowie explains to Dr. Benton that Robin believes Donal had actually come to see her in her dream, the doctor is gravely concerned, for, he explains: "One can't say what it [Robin's belief in seeing Donal] may lead to." His obvious concern for her mental health is offset when Dowie describes Robin's renewed interest in care of her own body in the form of food and exercise. "I was afraid of—what you're afraid of, sir," Dowie says to Benton; rather than mental imbalance and excess excitement, Robin spoke "in her natural voice," and she seemed above all else to Dowie simply "*happy*." "That's what she looked and what she was," Dowie concludes. After Benton's "longer than usual" examination of Robin, during which he did not, as he had promised Dowie, ask about her "dream" (234), "he drove down the moor thinking of curious things" (235) that were increasingly becoming a part of his experience as one who had served in the war and as one who has been charged with the care of military and domestic casualties.

> The agonized tensions of war, he told himself, seemed to be developing new phases—mental, nervous, psychic, as well as physiological. What unreality—or previously unknown reality—were they founded upon? It was curious how much one had begun to hear of telepathy and visions. He himself had been among the many who had discussed the psychopathic condition of Lady Maureen Darcy, whose black melancholia had been dispersed like a cloud [...]. He also was a war tortured man mentally and the torments he must conceal beneath a steady professional calm had loosened old shackles. (235)

The terms associated with mind in that passage, "mental" and "psychic," are balanced by terms that link to the body, "nervous" and "physiological," in order to suggest how comprehensive the disruptions in ordinary human functioning are, which Benton had begun to observe. His initial response to see those disruptions as a mark of "unreality" turns almost immediately into the notion of "previously unknown reality," opening a path of thought from the occult and paranormal as strange and unreal to things natural, "new phases" of evolutionary development. Belief in that possibility is anchored on practical results. "'Good God! If there is help of any sort for such horrors of despair let them take it where they can find it,' he found himself saying aloud to the emptiness of the stretches of heath and bracken" (235). Given his own struggles with despair, he too has begun to "take it where he can find it" in his observation of the impact of expanded mental/spiritual experience on the health of the body. As he asks himself later in the novel: "How closely involved physiology and psychology were after all! Which was which? Where did one end and the other begin? Where was the line drawn? Was there a line at all?" As he observes Robin's returning health and considers the fact that it was based on the "curative agency that she believed that her husband, who had been blown to atoms on the battle field—held her in her arms[...]. And there you were—thrown upon occultism" (263).

The progression of mind evident in Benton's reflections above is given more homely and direct expression in the narrative's representation of Dowie's "wholly untranscendental mind," which having been "long trained by patent facts and duties" found "any suggestion of the occult [to be] vaguely ominous."

> She had spent her early years among people who regarded such things with terror. In the stories of her youth those who saw visions usually died or met with calamity. That their visions were, as a rule, gruesome and included pale and ghastly faces and voices hollow with portent was now a supporting recollection. (236)

In Dowie's youth the occult was associated with death, connected with satanic threatening and ghostly terrors. Robin's occult experience in contrast brings signs of life; it turns her mind back to the earth, to the requirements of her body through the presence of another human being, whom she loves. As she contrasts her youthful fear of the occult with her present observations of Robin, Dowie hears her "undoubting voice" declare: "'He was not dead. He was not an angel. He was Donal.'" Those three declarative sentences, in addition to the fact that "she had stood the test—that real test of earthly egg and buttered toast" (236), fold the occult in her mind into the elements that constitute nature. When Robin's baby comes, Dowie thinks, she would "forget less natural things," those things being the residue of her prior fears of the occult rather than Robin's occult encounter with the life she so deeply desires and requires. For Robin's experience of the occult is her relationship with Donal.

Lord Coombe's engagement with the occult is more indirect and complex. He had given up his London house for the purpose of nursing the wounded and shell-shocked soldiers newly returned from the front. Because he "had seen what was left of strong men brought back from the Front, men who could scarcely longer be counted as really living human beings"; and because "he had talked to men on leave who had a hideous hardness in their haggard eyes and who did not know that they gnawed at their lips sometimes as they told the things they had seen" (251–52), Coombe ached to understand the meaning of such living death and self-devouring life. He would walk into churches, becoming "only part of some surging misery." He also "heard weird stories again and again of occult happenings." His skeptical turn of mind turned not to the easy solution to understanding the current misery of the world by believing nothing and covering himself in despair. Rather, "[H]e was one of those who have advanced through experience to the point where entire disbelief in anything is not easy." From first hearing stories of occult events, he turned to research, reading the best books he could find on what was later called "psychical research."

> He was amazed to discover that for many years profoundly scientific men had been seriously investigating and experimenting with mysteries unexplainable by the accepted laws of material science. They had discussed, argued and written grave books upon them. They had been doing all this before any society of psychical research had founded itself and the

intention of new logic was to be scientific rather than psychological. They had written books, scattered through the years, on mesmerism, hypnosis, abnormal mental conditions, the powers of suggestion, even unexplored dimensions and in modern days psychotherapeutics. (252–53)

That rather daunting list of occult subject matter can be read as apt verification of Alison Winter's occult "Monster Soup of the Thames" metaphor for the extent of interest and activity related to psychic activity in the Victorian and Edwardian periods. To mix metaphors, the occult was in the air of Coombe's times, and he somewhat belatedly breathed it in, careful to sift out the good from the bad. "The cheap, modern popular form [of the occult] is often fantastic and crude," he comments, "but there remains the fact that it all contains truths not to be explained by the rules we have always been familiar with" (253). Prepared by his reading and thinking about what he has seen of the effects of war on the body and mind and the dearth of readily explicable explanations for the amelioration of those effects, Coombe keeps his mind open and is thus prepared, when Dowie writes to him, to credit Robin's experience as real. After reading Dowie's letter, Coombe "thought it out":

> If it had not been for the tea and egg and buttered toast she would have been sure the poor child was mad [...]. An egg and a slice of buttered toast guarantee even spiritual things. Why not? We are material creatures who have only material sight and touch and taste to employ as arguments. I suppose that is why tables are tipped and banjos fly about for beginners. It's because we cannot see things, and what we cannot see—Oh! Fools that we are! The child said he was not an angel—he was himself. Why not? Where did he come from? Personally, I believe that he *came*. (255)

With those words, Coombe adds his endorsement to the novel's search for an articulate and paradoxically nonverbal space to communicate something that is both fully human and freed from the constraints of encrusted conventionality of belief and thought. And that is despite the fact that on the surface, Coombe is throughout the novel the last vestige of Victorian patriarchy in his defense of the English state through his diplomatic work, in his effort to ensure that the "house of Coombe" will have an heir and in his overtly protective role of the women in the novel, first Feather and then Robin.

All those things upon which he centered his life become subordinate to what turns out to be the emergence of instincts aligned with changes he feels happening in the world, but for which he has no proof. "We are living in a changing world," he says to the Duchess, "and new things are happening" (259), and one of those new things is happening within himself for, as he puts it, the "emotional upheaval of the times has broken down all my artificialities," which is to say, his hyper-adherence to social form. The metaphor he chooses to amplify his point has to do with the breaking of conventions: "Shrines are being torn down and blown to pieces all over the world," he explains. "And I long for a simple shrine to cleanse my soul before" (260). The "simple shrine" he has chosen, of course, is Robin, so when she requests that he come to see her in Scotland, he readily agrees because, the narrator explains: "The thing which had always touched him most in her was her simple obedience to the laws about her. Curiously it had never seemed insipid—only a sort of lovely desire to be in harmony with all near her—things and people alike" (266). The vagueness of the use of the word "laws" and its linkage to "harmony" in that sentence convey an idea akin to the laws of music, being attuned to the non-semantic sounds and natural energies (human and nonhuman) in one's environment. With that in mind, Coombe's "centuries old instinct that a House of Coombe must continue to exist" (268) begins to slacken as he realizes that in the face of the Great War in order "to rebuild, to reinspire [sic] with life, to heal unearthly gaping wounds of mind and soul" (269) attunement to the expanding laws of nature is the first requirement.[25] For the remainder of the novel, he focuses his thinking on Robin as a shrine to such attunement, she, who had "passed to places where vision revealed things as they were created by that First Intention"—before convention, before patriarchy, before war.

That turn in Coombe's thinking marks a transition in the emphasis in the novel from a benign traditionalism that served as a counterweight to the irresponsible selfishness embodied in Robin's mother to an implicit utopian future that cannot be fully imagined but only gestured toward in the qualities associated with Robin and Donal, who, while clearly not fully representative, open doors through which the outlines of that future can be dimly discerned. The novel offers three perspectives that ground responses to the war: one is to aestheticize it, another is to hold on to traditional values and the other is utopian, an effort to embrace life as fully as possible and to give one's self to its future development based on an expanded definition of human possibility. While Coombe moves from the traditional to the utopian in his thinking, Feather embraces the aesthetic possibilities of the war and remains in opposition to her daughter's role in a possible utopian future. Burnett captures the perverseness of the aesthetic response, as suggested earlier, in the way in which Feather's "slice of a house" in Mayfair becomes a social center that "within the memory of man" had never before "been so brilliant" (288). As Feather tells Coombe: "I consider that my best War Work is giving as many dinner parties as possible, and paying as little attention to food restrictions as I can manage by using my wits" (289). Feather then avers later that "I *like* the war" (295), which for her and her circle has become a superior form of entertainment. To aestheticize the war is to embrace the war and then to become a product of the war as a dead body, which in Feather's case, as we know, was in the form of a hand, a ring and a fragment of purple scarf. In contrast to her embrace of death is Robin's maternity with its symbolic resonance of human relation and generation with an orientation toward the future. It is Robin's experience of the expanded possibilities for the maintenance, expressiveness and connectedness of life through her meetings with Donal in her dreams that carries the symbolic burden of the novel in the end. For Donal had not been killed; he had been badly wounded and was taken prisoner. During his captivity he shared confinement with an American, who had joined the fight by enlisting in Canada, before the United States had officially entered the war. That American, who was versed in "New Thought" (340), taught Donal "how to concentrate on dreaming," and by that means to find his way "near" Robin. Within the logic of Burnett's novel, Donal's effort is the next stage in a literary history of "mystic" romantic relations that connect lovers at great distances at the most critical moment in their lives. The most obvious example is Jane Eyre's hearing Rochester's voice calling out to her as she struggles with St. John Rivers's insistence that she share his life as a missionary in India. In despair, Rochester cried out to Jane, and in her need she heard him, the particulars in the event becoming clear in retrospect. In *Robin* Donal learns to coordinate his will with the mystical energies that are manifest and can be transmitted through dreamlike states, and in so doing he shows the possibilities of the human capacity to fuse cognition and the spirit in the service of life.

Donal tells his tale at the end of the novel, and Robin confirms his experience. Their mystical connection is made real in the body of their child, who comes into the world in defiance of the war, Robin's maternity functioning as an act of heroism against the logic of war. When the novel closes, the war is still going strong; the Americans have not yet committed to enter it. Given that Burnett wrote the novel after the war, her choosing to end with the war still in progress suggests that she did not see the Great War as the one to end all wars. As her insight into German militarism under Kaiser Wilhelm showed, and as that militarism had extended expression beyond the war in the activity of the Freikorps as Theweleit so comprehensively has shown, and as the rise of Hitler and the Third Reich so horrifically confirmed, the tensions between organized patriarchal violence and the imperative for the development of life through an evolutionary maternity could not be so easily resolved, not even in a work of utopian-inspired fiction. The closing paragraph of the novel presents an embryonic image as it describes Donal's reunion with Robin and his first encounter with their child: "And they were in his arm—the soft warm things—and he sat down upon the lowest step and held them—rocking—and trembling still more—but with the gates of peace open and earth and war shut out" (343). Note how there is no exchange of words. The novel's final sentence is dominated by touch, movement, connection, those elements associated with the preverbal wholeness of the semiotic out of which a social future other than the dominant patriarchal order can take shape. (See tailpiece for an illustration of Robin and her child.) One way to read the trajectory of Burnett's novels as a whole is as a series of variations on the possibilities of women—Joan Lowrie, Rachel Ffrench, Octavia Basset, Bertha Amory, Clorinda Wildairs, Emily Fox-Seton/Walderhurst, Bettina Vanderpoel and Robin Lawless/Muir—shaping a life for themselves that is neither dependent on the power of men nor subject to the pernicious ideology of an inherently unequal complementarity. Her work can be read as a celebration of the full humanness of women and, at times, men.

Notes

1 Paul Zweig. "Cosmic Freedom" a review of James Webb's *The Harmonious Circle: The Lives and Works of G. I. Gurdjieff, P. D. Ouspensky, and Their Followers. New York Times* (March 30, 1980), "Book Review," p. 3.
2 S. H. "The Latest Books: The Ladies Pageant." *Life* (September 14, 1922): 22.
3 Edmund Jr. Wilson. "The Poetry of Drouth." *The Dial* (December 1922): 4–10.
4 Thomas F. Ford and C. Lillian. "A Chronicle of Young Love." *Los Angeles Times* ("The Literary Page) (August 20, 1922): 36 and 43.
5 Arnold Matthew. "Stanzas from the Grand Chartreuse." *New Poems by Matthew Arnold*. London: Macmillan, 1867, pp. 208–19.
6 In these novels the garden, rather than being the center of community as in *The Secret Garden* or the literal manifestation of social renewal as in *The Shuttle*, is surrounded by the city, a pocket of natural growth struggling to maintain itself against the depredations of urban sprawl and, as the novel progresses, bombardment from the skies.

7 "The Book Table: Back to the Victorian." *Outlook* (March 21, 1922): 350.
8 Fanny Butcher. "Tabloid Review." *Chicago Daily Tribune* (February 5, 1922): G14.
9 For a summative view of the role of German spies in English fiction and the uneven, and at times comic, British government response to German spies real and imagined, see David French's "Spy Fever in Britain, 1900–1915." *The Historical Journal*, vol. 21, no. 2 (June 1978): 355-70.
10 Klaus Theweleit. *Male Fantasies*, vol. 1 and vol. 2. Translated by Stephen Conway (in collaboration with Erica Carter and Chris Turner). Minneapolis: U of Minnesota P, 1987 and 1989.
11 For a brief history of the *Freikorps* see Barbara Ehrenreich's "Foreword" to Volume I of *Male Fantasies*, especially ix–x.
12 https://www.theguardian.com/commentisfree/belief/2014/apr/17/ts-eliot-waste-land-radical-text-wounded-culture Accessed June 19, 2019.
13 Consider as just one example the ubiquity of artistic images based on the story of the rape of the Sabine women in classical Rome, wherein the term rape extends to both abduction and sexual violence. See Jacques-Louis David's 1799 painting and Giambologna's sixteenth-century sculpture, "Abduction of a Sabine Woman" to get a sense of the dense aesthetic history of rape and abduction of women as weapons of war.
14 Burnett captures how war becomes the occasion for gossip *par excellence* as follows: "People were talking—talking—talking. Ordinary people, common people, all kinds of classes. The majority of them did not know what they were talking about; most of them talked either uneducated, frightened or blustering nonsense, but everybody talked more or less" (15).
15 On women, the Great War, and literary and social history see, for instance: Margaret Randolf Higonnet, et al. *Behind the Lines: Gender and the Two World Wars* (Yale UP, 1987); Rosa Maria Bracco. *Merchants of Hope: British Middlebrow Writers and the First World War 1919–1939* (Berg, 1993); Sharon Ouditt. *Fighting Forces, Writing Women*. (Routledge, 1994); Dorothy Goldman. *Women Writers and the Great War* (Twayne, 1995); Sharon Ouditt. *Women Writers of the First World War* (Routledge, 2000); Angela K. Smith. *The Second Battlefield: Women, Modernism and the First World War* (Manchester UP, 2000) and Ed. *Women's Writing of the First World War: An Anthology* (Manchester UP, 2000); and Susan R. Grayzel. *Women and the First World War* (Pearson, 2002). What is noteworthy about Burnett in relation to that list is that not only does she not appear in the literary, cultural and historical studies of the period, her Great War novels are not listed in Ouditt's annotated bibliography nor is any material drawn from those novels included in Smith's anthology. Even in the study on middlebrow writers, which would be the most conventional of classifications in the critical history of Burnett as popular novelist, Burnett's Great War novels are ignored. Perhaps those omissions reflect the fact that the heyday of Great War fiction occurred in the latter part of the 1920s. Burnett may have been writing at a time when the psychic wounds from the war in England were still too fresh.
16 Sharon Ouditt. *Fighting Forces, Writing Women: Identity and Ideology in the First World War*. London: Routledge, 1994.
17 In his essay on the oversoul, Emerson offers this definition: "Within man is the soul of the whole; the wise silence, the universal beauty, to which every part and particle is equally related; the eternal ONE." If that soul emerges, it cannot be distinguished; they exist in a singular unity. Within man is the eternal ONE. *Essays First Series*. "The Oversoul." *American Transcendentalism Web*: http.www.vcu.edu/engweb/transcendentalism/authors/emerson/essays/oversoul.html.
18 See M. M. Bakhtin. *The Dialogic Imagination: Four Essays*, especially "Discourse in the Novel." Austin: U of Texas P, 1992.
19 According to Kristeva, however, there is no purely semiotic mode of expression even as there is no absolutely symbolic patriarchal totality. Individuals—men and women—are interpolated by the symbolic order even as their presymbolic biological drive toward bodily integrity and uncompromised, nonhierarchical relation permeates their being: "Because the subject [i.e. the individual human being] is always *both* semiotic *and* symbolic," Kristeva writes, "no signifying system [e.g. the novel] he [she] produces can be either 'exclusively' semiotic or 'exclusively'

symbolic, and is instead marked by an indebtedness to both" (Kristeva 24). Burnett's occult turn can be read as an effort to get beyond the symbolic.

20 Pendennis. "Mrs. Frances Hodgson Burnett Finds a New Field for Her Pen." *New York Times* (May 20, 1906): SM 3.

21 Burnett's emergent occult literary engagement found expression in scenes in earlier novels, such as Walderhurst's calling Emily back from death after she gave birth to the first of their children and Mount Dunstan's hearing Bettina's prayers in his illness, calling him back to life. Among her children's stories is the weird *In a Closed Room* (1904), where a dead child leads another to the other world, leaving a second set of parents in grief; and in 1917 she published *The White People*, a novella about a young girl with the visual power to see the physical forms of the dead, who linger near their loved ones after death. In those latter two tales, one can see Burnett's personal anguish over the death of her son Lionel at 16, but in her full-length novels for a literary readership, Burnett's commitments are more literary than they are personal (though they certainly are that as well).

22 Janet Oppenheim. *The Other World: Spiritualism and Psychical Research in England, 1850—1914*. Cambridge: Cambridge UP, 1985.

23 Alison Winter. *Mesmerized: Powers of Mind in Victorian Britain*. Chicago: U of Chicago P, 1998, pp. 9–10.

24 Anna Neill. *Primitive Minds: Evolution and Spiritual Experience in the Victorian Novel*. Columbus: Ohio State UP, 2013.

25 Imagining a "new planet" that will emerge after the war, Coombe concludes that "[O]n the new planet one ceases to feel the vital importance of 'houses'" (288). That sentiment marks a moment when the utopian future the novel implies diminishes the traditional values that had carried the burden of Coombe's common sense through the majority of the narrative.

She held her baby in her arms, and to Donal her cheeks and lips and eyes were as he had first seen them in the Garden.

The tailpiece is from the serial publication of The Head of the House of Coombe in The Pall Mall Magazine February 1922. The illustrator is Fred C. Yohn.

BIBLIOGRAPHY

Abrams, M. H. *Natural Supernaturalism*. New York: W.W. Norton, 1971.
"American Girl Abroad … Did a Woman Novelist Ever Invent a First-Class Villain?" *New York Times* (October 18, 1907): 19.
Anesko, Michael. *"Friction with the Market": Henry James and the Profession of Authorship*. New York: Oxford UP, 1986.
Arata, Stephen. *Fictions of Loss in the Victorian Fin De Siecle: Identity and Empire*. Cambridge: Cambridge UP, 1996.
Armstrong, Nancy. *Desire and Domestic Fiction*. New York: Oxford UP, 1990.
"A Speech by Mrs. Burnett." *New York Times* (August 16, 1896): 23.
"A Tale of Queen Anne's Reign." *New York Times* (March 8, 1896): 31.
Bakhtin, M. M. "Discourse in the Novel." In *The Dialogic Imagination: Four Essays*. Edited by Michael Holquist. Austin: U of Texas P, 1992, pp. 259–422.
Beard, R. O. "A Certain Dangerous Tendency in Novels." *Dial*, vol. II, no. 30 (October 1882): 110–12.
Beffel, John Nicholas. "The Fauntleroy Plague." *Bookman*, vol. 65, no. 2 (April 1927): 133–37.
Belloc, Marie A. "Mrs. Hodgson Burnett: A Famous Authoress at Home." *Idler*, vol. 9, no. 5 (June 1896): 644–48.
Bending, Lucy. "From Stunted Child to 'New Woman': The Significance of Physical Growth in Late Nineteenth-Century Medicine and Fiction." *Yearbook of English Studies*, vol. 32 (January 1, 2002): 205–16.
Bixler, Phyllis. *Frances Hodgson Burnett*. Twayne's English Authors Series. Boston: Twayne, 1984.
Black, Clementina. "The Novels of Frances Hodgson Burnett." *Time*, vol. 12, no. 1 (January 1885): 72–85.
Blair, Sara. *Henry James and the Writing of Race and Nation*. Cambridge: Cambridge UP, 1996.
Bodenheimer, Rosemarie. *The Politics of Story in Victorian Social Fiction*. Ithaca: Cornell UP, 1988.
"Books of the Week." "Mrs. Burnett's New Novel." *Chicago Daily Tribune* (December 9, 1899): 10.
Bourdieu, Pierre. *The Field of Cultural Production*. New York: Columbia UP, 1993.
Boyle, Thomas. *Black Swine in the Sewers of Hampstead: Beneath the Surface of Victorian Sensationalism*. New York: Viking, 1989.
Bracco, Rosa Maria. *Merchants of Hope: British Middlebrow Writers and the First World War, 1919–1939*. Oxford: Berg, 1993.
Braddon, Mary Elizabeth. *Lady Audley's Secret*. New York: Oxford World Classics, 2012.
Brandon, Ruth. *The Dollar Princesses: Sagas of Upward Nobility 1870–1914*. New York: Alfred A. Knopf, 1980.
Browning, Robert. *The Ring and the Book*. London: Penguin Books, 1989.
Burlingame, Edward L. "Art. VI.—New American Novels." *North American Review*, vol. 125, no. 258 (September–October 1877): 309–21.
Burnett, Frances Hodgson. *In the Closed Room*. New York: Grosset & Dunlap, 1904.
———. *In Connection with the De Willoughby Claim*. New York: Charles Scribner's Sons, 1899.
———. *The Dawn of a To-morrow*. New York: Charles Scribner's Sons, 1906.
———. *A Fair Barbarian*. Boston: James R. Osgood, 1882.
———. *Haworth's*. New York: Charles Scribner's Sons, 1879.

———. *The Head of the House of Coombe*. New York: Frederick A. Stokes, 1922.
———. *His Grace of Osmonde*. New York: Charles Scribner's Sons, 1897.
———. *A Lady of Quality*. New York: Charles Scribner's Sons, 1896.
———. *Little Lord Fauntleroy*. New York: Charles Scribner's Sons, 1886.
———. *A Little Princess*. New York: Charles Scribner's Sons, 1905.
———. *Louisiana*. New York: Charles Scribner's Sons, 1880.
———. *The Making of a Marchioness*. New York: Frederick A. Stokes, 1901.
———. *The Methods of Lady Walderhurst*. New York: Frederick A. Stokes, 1901.
———. *The One I Knew Best of All*. London: Frederick Warne, 1893.
———. *Robin*. New York: Frederick A. Stokes, 1922.
———. *The Secret Garden*. Norton Annotated Edition. Edited by Greatchen Holbrook Gerzina. New York: W.W. Norton, 2007.
———. *The Shuttle*. New York: Frederick A. Stokes, 1907.
———. *Surly Tim and Other Stories*. New York: Scribner, Armstrong, 1877.
———. *T. Tembarom*. New York: The Century, 1913.
———. *That Lass O'Lowries*. New York: Charles Scribner's Sons, 1877.
———. *Through One Administration*. New York: Charles Scribner's Sons, 1883.
———. *The White People*. New York: Harper, 1917.
———. *A Woman's Will or Miss Defarge*. London: Frederick Warne, 1887.
Butcher, Fanny. "Tabloid Review." *Chicago Daily Tribune* (February 5, 1922): G 14–15.
Carlyle, Thomas. "Characteristics." In *The Emergence of Victorian Consciousness: The Spirit of the Age*. Edited by George Levine. New York: Free Press, 1967: 39–68.
———. *Sartor Resartus. Carlyle's Complete Works: The Sterling Edition*. Boston: Estes and Lauriat, n.d., c. 1880.
Carpenter, Angelica Shirley. *In the Garden: Essays in Honor of Frances Hodgson Burnett*. Lanham, MD: Scarecrow Press, 2006.
Casey, Ellen Miller. "'Our Transatlantic Cousins': The Battle over American Analytic Novels in the *Athenaeum*." *Studies in American Fiction*, vol. 21, no. 2 (Autumn 1993): 237–46.
Cazamian, Louis. *The Social Novel in England 1830–1850 Dickens Disraeli Mrs Gaskell Kingsley*. London: Routledge & Kegan Paul, 1973.
Clark, Suzanne. *Sentimental Modernism: Women Writers and the Revolution of the Word*. Bloomington: Indiana UP, 1991.
Collins, Wilkie. *The Moonstone*. London: Penguin Books, 1998.
———. *The Woman in White*. London: Penguin Books, 2003.
"Copyright—Dramatization of Novel—Injunction." *Albany Law Journal: A Weekly Record of the Law and Lawyers*, vol. 38, no. 13 (September 29, 1888): 256–58.
"Correspondence. Mrs. Burnett and the Century." *The Literary World* (March 6, 1886): 82.
Coverdale, Henry Standish. *The Fall of the Great Republic*. Boston: Roberts, 1885.
Crosby, Christina. *The Ends of History: Victorians and "the Woman Question."* New York: Routledge, 1991.
"Current Fiction." *Literary World*, vol. 12, no. 9 (April 23, 1881): 146.
"Current Fiction." *The Literary World; a Monthly Review of Current Literature* (1870–1904), vol. 11, no. 10 (May 8, 1880): 153.
Cvetkovich, Ann. *Mixed Feelings Feminism, Mass Culture, and Victorian Sensationalism*. New Brunswick: Rutgers UP, 1992.
Daly, Nicholas. *Modernism, Romance and the Fin De Siecle: Popular Fiction and British Culture, 1880–1914*. Cambridge: Cambridge UP, 1999.
Dames, Nicholas. *Amnesiac Selves: Nostalgia, Forgetting, and British Fiction, 1810–1870*. New York: Oxford UP, 2001.
Dickens, Charles. *Bleak House*. London: Penguin Classics, 1996.
Dilke, Sir Charles Wentworth. *Greater Britain: A Record of Travel in English-Speaking Countries during 1866 and 1867*. London: Macmillan, 1869.

———. *Problems of Greater Britain*. London: Macmillan, 1890.
Easley, Alexis. *Literary Celebrity, Gender, and Victorian Authorship, 1850–1914*. Newark: U of Delaware P, 2011.
Edel, Leon. *Henry James: A Life*. New York: Harper & Row, 1985.
Eggleston, Edward. "Some Recent Works of Fiction." *The North American Review*, vol. 129, no. 276 (November 1879): 510–17.
Eichelberger, Clayton L. (ed.). *A Guide to Critical Reviews of United States Fiction, 1870–1910*, vols. I and II. Metuchen, NJ: Scarecrow Press, 1971.
Eliot, Elizabeth. *They All Married Well*. London: Cassell, 1959.
Eliot, T. S. *The Waste Land* in *The Complete Poems and Plays 1909–1950*. New York: Harcourt, Brace & World, 1971.
Elliott, Emory (ed.). *Columbia History of the American Novel*. New York: Columbia UP, 1991.
Emerson, Ralph Waldo. *Nature*. Boston: James Munroe, 1836.
———. "The Oversoul." *Essays First Series*. American Transcendentalism Web: http:/www.vcu.edu/engweb/transcendentalism/authors/emerson/essays/oversoul.html. Accessed July 2, 2019.
"Fact and Fairy Tale: Mrs. Burnett's 'T. Tembarom" A Delightful Blending of Familiar Modern Conditions and Romance." *New York Times* (October 26, 1913): BR 573.
"Fauntleroy." *New York Times* (October 31, 1924): 18.
Felski, Rita. *The Gender of Modernity*. Cambridge, MA: Harvard UP, 1995.
"Fiction." *The Academy* (December 14, 1901): 592.
Fleishman, Avrom. *The English Historical Novel: Walter Scott to Virginia Woolf*. Baltimore: Johns Hopkins Press, 1971.
Ford, Thomas F. and Lillian C. "A Chronicle of Young Love." *Los Angeles Times* ("The Literary Page") (August 20, 1922): 36 and 43.
French, David. "Spy Fever in Britain, 1900–1915." *The Historical Journal*, vol. 21, no. 2 (June 1978): 355–70.
Fussell, Paul. *The Great War and Modern Memory*. New York: Oxford UP, 1975.
Gabin, Jane S. *American Women in Gilded Age London: Expatriates Rediscovered*. Gainesville: UP of Florida, 2006.
Gallagher, Catherine. *The Industrial Reformation of English Fiction 1832–1867*. Chicago: U of Chicago P, 1985.
Gaskell, Elizabeth. *Cranford*. New York: Oxford World Classics, 2011.
———. *Mary Barton*. A Norton Critical Edition. Edited by Thomas Recchio. New York: W.W. Norton, 2008.
———. *North and South*. A Norton Critical Edition. Edited by Alan Shelston. New York: W.W. Norton, 2005.
———. *Wives and Daughters*. London: Penguin Books, 1995.
Gerzina, Gretchen Holbrook. *Frances Hodgson Burnett: The Unexpected Life of the Author of* The Secret Garden. New Brunswick: Rutgers UP, 2004.
Gilder Collection, New York Public Library.
Gilder, Jeanette L. "'A Lady of Quality' by Frances Hodgson Burnett." *Chicago Daily Tribune* (March 1, 1896): 40.
Gissing, George. *The Odd Women*. London: Penguin Classics, 1994.
Goldman, Dorothy with Jane Gledhill and Judith Hattaway. *Women Writers of the Great War*. New York: Twayne, 1995.
Grand, Sarah. *The Beth Book*. Fairford: Echo Library, 2009.
Grayzel, Susan R. *Women and the First World War*. New York: Longman (Pearson), 2002.
Guy, Josephine M. *The Victorian Social Problem Novel*. London: Macmillan, 1996.
Hammond, Mary. *Reading, Publishing and the Formation of Literary Taste in England, 1880–1914*. Aldershot: Ashgate, 2006.
Harkins, E. F. *Famous Authors (Women)*. Boston: L. C. Page, 1901.

Hawthorne, Julian. "Trips to Bookland: Frances Hodgson Burnett Creates a New Type in Fiction—and of a Woman, at That." *Los Angeles Times* (March 16, 1902).

Hay, John. *New York Daily Tribune* (December 25, 1881): 8.

Herrick, Mrs. S. Bledsoe. "Frances Hodgson Burnett." *The Southern Review*, vol. 25, no. 49 (January 1879): 87–117.

Heywood, Christopher. "Frances Hodgson Burnett's *The Secret Garden*: A Possible Source for T.S. Eliot's 'Rose Garden.'" *The Yearbook of English Studies*, vol. 7 (January 1, 1977): 166–71.

Higonnet, Margaret Randolph et al. *Behind the Lines: Gender and the Two World Wars*. New Haven: Yale UP, 1987.

Hipsky, Martin. *Modernism and the Women's Popular Romance in Britain, 1885–1925*. Athens: Ohio UP, 2011.

Hitchens, Christopher. *Blood, Class, and Nostalgia: Anglo-American Ironies*. New York: Farrar, Straus & Giroux, 1990.

Hughes, Winifred. *The Maniac in the Cellar: Sensation Novels of the 1860s*. Princeton: Princeton UP, 1980.

Huyssen, Andreas. *After the Great Divide: Modernism, Mass Culture, Postmodernism*. Bloomington: Indiana UP, 1986.

James, Henry. *The Portrait of a Lady*. Boston: Houghton Mifflin, 1963.

John, Arthur. *The Best Years of the Century: Richard Watson Gilder, Scribner's Monthly, and Scribner's Magazine, 1870–1909*. Urbana: U of Illinois P, 1981.

Keating, Peter. *The Haunted Study: A Social History of the English Novel 1875–1914*. London: Fontana Press, 1991.

Kestnor, Joseph. *Protest & Reform: The British Social Narrative by Women, 1827–1867*. London: Methuen, 1985.

Knezevic Borislave. "An Ethnography of the Provincial: The Social Geography of Gentility in Elizabeth Gaskell's Cranford." *Victorian Studies*, vol. 41 (Spring 1998): 405–26.

Kristeva, Julia. *Revolution in Poetic Language*. New York: Columbia UP, 1984.

Levine, George (ed.). *The Emergence of Victorian Consciousness: The Spirit of the Age*. New York: Free Press, 1967.

"Literary Gossip." *The Art Interchange: A Household Journal*, vol. 10, no. 6 (March 15, 1883): 67.

"Little Lord Fauntleroy." *The Eclectic Magazine of Foreign Literature* (November 1886): 715.

"Little Lord Fauntleroy." *The Book Buyer* (December 1, 1886): 430–32.

Lucas, John. *The Literature of Change: Studies in the Nineteenth-Century Provincial Novel*. Sussex: Harvester Press, 1980.

MacColl, Gail and Carol McD. Wallace. *To Marry an English Lord: Tales of Wealth and Marriage, Sex and Snobbery*. New York: Workman, 2012.

McAleer, Joseph. *Popular Reading and Publishing in Britain 1914–1950*. Oxford: Clarendon Press, 1992.

McDonald, Peter D. *British Literary Culture and Publishing Practice 1880–1914*. Cambridge: Cambridge UP, 1997.

Maher, Susan Naramore. "A Bridging of Two Cultures: Frances Hodgson Burnett and the Wild West." *Old West—New West, Centennial Essays*. Edited by Barbara Howard Meldrum. Moscow, Idaho: U of Idaho P, 1993.

Maurice, Arthur Bartlett. "Best Sellers of Yesterday: V. Frances Hodgson Burnett's 'Little Lord Fauntleroy." *The Bookman* (September 1911): 35--45

Michie, Helena. *The Flesh Made Word: Female Figures and Women's Bodies*. New York: Oxford UP, 1987.

Moers, Ellen. *Literary Women*. New York: Knopf Doubleday, 1976.

Molson, Francis. "Frances Hodgson Burnett (1848–1924)." *American Literary Realism, 1870–1910*, vol. 8 (1975): 35–41.

Moore, R. Laurence. *In Search of White Crows: Spiritualism, Parapsychology, and American Culture*. New York: Oxford UP, 1977.

Moore, Rayburn S. *The Correspondence of Henry James and the House of Macmillan 1977–1914*. Baton Rouge: Louisiana State UP, 1993.

Morse, James H. "The Native Element in American Fiction." *Century Illustrated Magazine*, vol. XXVI, no. 3 (1883): 62–75.
"Mrs. Burnett, 'Fauntleroy' Author, Dies." *Chicago Daily Tribune* (October 30, 1924): 1.
"Mrs. Burnett's Book is Called a Fairy Story for the Discouraged." *Chicago Daily Tribune* (November 16, 1907): 10.
"Mrs. Burnett's New Story." *New York Times* (March 1, 1902): BR 2.
Neill, Anna. *Primitive Minds: Evolution and Spiritual Experience in the Victorian Novel*. Columbus: Ohio State UP, 2013.
"New Books: A Little Fiction." *The Interior* (April 9, 1896): 473.
Nietzsche, Friedrich. "Prologue." *Thus Spoke Zarathustra*. Translated by Thomas Common. New York: Modern Library, 1917.
Noonan, Mark J. "Modern Instances: Vanishing Women Writers and the Rise of Realism in the *Century Illustrated Magazine*." *American Literary Realism*, vol. 42, no. 3 (Spring 2010): 192–212.
———. *Reading the* Century Illustrated Monthly Magazine: *American Literature and Culture, 1870–1893*. Kent, Ohio: Kent State UP, 2010.
Nord, Deborah Epstein. *Walking the Victorian Streets: Women, Representation, and the City*. Ithaca: Cornell UP, 1995.
Nordeau, Max. *Degeneration*. London: William Heinemann, 1895.
"Novels." *The Saturday Review* (January 25, 1902): 115.
"Novels of the Week." *The Athenaeum* (May 12, 1883): 600–601.
Oppenheim, Janet. *The Other World: Spiritualism and Psychical Research in England, 1850–1914*. Cambridge: Cambridge UP, 1985.
Ouditt, Sharon. *Fighting Forces, Writing Women: Identity and Ideology in the First World War*. London: Routledge, 1994.
———. *Women Writers of the First World War*. London: Routledge, 2000.
"Our New York Letter." *The Literary World: A Monthly Review of Current Literature* (January 23, 1886): 28.
Overton, Grant M. *The Women Who Make Our Novels*. New York: Moffat, Yard, 1918.
Owen, Alex. *The Darkened Room: Women, Power and Spiritualism in Late Victorian England*. London: Virago Press, 1989.
Phillips, Jerry. "The Mem Sahib, the Worthy, the Rajah, and His Minions: Some Reflections on the Class Politics of *The Secret Garden*." *The Lion and the Unicorn*, vol. 17, no. 2 (December 1993): 168–94.
Preston, George. "His Grace of Osmonde." *The Bookman* (December 1897); 355–56.
———. "Mrs. Burnett's New Book." *The Bookman* (April 1896): 156–57.
Quinn, Arthur Hobson. *American Fiction: An Historical and Critical Survey*. New York: D. Appleton-Century, 1936.
Radford, Andrew. *Victorian Sensation Fiction: A Reader's Guide to Essential Criticism*. Basingstoke: Palgrave/Macmillan, 2009.
Rance, Nicholas. *Wilkie Collins and Other Sensation Novelists*. Rutherford, NJ: Fairleigh Dickinson UP, 1991.
Recchio, Thomas. "'Charming and Sane': School Editions of *Cranford* in America, 1905–1914." *Victorian Studies*, vol. 45, no. 4 (Summer 2003): 597–623.
———. "Elizabeth Gaskell as 'A Dramatic Common': Stanley Houghton's Appropriation of *Mary Barton* in *Hindle Wakes*." *The Gaskell Journal*, vol. 26 (2012): 88–102.
———. *Elizabeth Gaskell's* Cranford: *A Publishing History*. Farnham, Surrey: Ashgate, 2009.
"Recent Literature." *Atlantic Monthly*, vol. 40 (November 1877): 626–36.
"Recent Literature." *The Manhattan* (1883–1884), vol. 2, no. 1, 7 (1883): 88.
"Recent Novels." *The Nation* (October 23, 1879): 277–79.
"Recent Novels." *The Nation* (June 28, 1883): 552–54.
"Reviews": "Fauntleroy in Later Life." *The Chap Book* (February 1, 1898): 251.
"Rhymed Reviews: 'T. Tembarom.'" *Life* (December 11, 1913): 1055.

Richardson, Angelique. *Love and Eugenics in the Late Nineteenth Century: Rational Reproduction & the New Woman*. Oxford: Oxford UP, 2003.
Ripley, William. *The Races of Europe*. New York: D. Appleton, 1899.
Roberts, Mary Fanton. "Mrs. Burnett's Rose Garden in Kent: Evolved from a Centuries-Old Orchard." *The Craftsman* 12.5 (August 1, 1907): 537–55.
Runciman, James. "King Plagiarism and His Court." *Fortnightly Review* (March 1890): 421–39.
Schmidt, Barbara Quinn. "Introduction, *The Cornhill Magazine*: Celebrating Success." *Victorian Periodicals Review*, Special Issue, *The Cornhill Magazine* (Fall 1999): 202–8.
S. H. "The Latest Books: The Ladies Pageant." *Life* (September 14, 1922): 22.
Showalter, Elaine. *A Literature of Their Own: British Women Novelists from Bronte to Lessing*. Princeton: Princeton UP, 1977.
Shumaker, Jeanette Roberts. "A Secret Garden of Repressed Desires: Frances Hodgson Burnett's *That Lass O'Lowries. Dickens Studies Annual: Essays on Victorian Fiction*," vol. 32 (2002): 363–78.
"Sketch: Frances Hodgson Burnett." *Harper's Bazaar* (February 24, 1900): 160.
Smith, Angela K. *The Second Battlefield: Women, Modernism and the First World War*. Manchester: Manchester UP, 2000.
———. *Women's Writing of the First World War*. Manchester: Manchester UP, 2000.
Smith, Herbert F. *The Popular American Novel 1865–1920*. Boston: Twayne, 1980.
Spofford, Ainsworth R. "Directions and Volume of Our Literary Activities." *Forum* (January 1894): 598–604.
Stead, W. T. *The Americanization of the World*. New York: Horace Markley, 1901 and 1902.
Stegner, Wallace (ed.). *The American Novel from James Fenimore Cooper to William Faulkner.* New York: Basic Books, 1965.
Stoddard, R. H. "Frances Hodgson Burnett." *The Critic*, vol. 1, no. 25 (December 17, 1881): 345–47.
"Talk About New Books." *The Catholic World* (May 1896): 63–64.
Tennyson, Alfred. *In Memoriam*. A Norton Critical Edition. Edited by Erik Grey. New York: W.W. Norton, 2003.
"That Lass O'Lowries." *Southern Review*, vol. 24, no. 48 (October 1878): 491–96.
The Academy Fiction Supplement (December 11, 1897): 122–23.
"The Book Table: Back to the Victorian." *Outlook* (March 21, 1922): 350.
"The Modern School of Fiction." *Chicago Daily Tribune* (October 29, 1882): 4.
"The New Publications." "Strong Work in Mrs. Burnett's Latest Novel." *The Hartford Courant* (December 16, 1899): 17.
Theweleit, Klaus. *Male Fantasies Volume 1: Women Floods Bodies History*. Minneapolis: U of Minnesota P, 1987.
———. *Male Fantasies Volume 2: Male Bodies: Psychoanalyzing the White Terror*. Minneapolis: U of Minnesota P, 1989.
"Through One Administration." Saturday Review of Politics, Literature, Science and Art, vol. 55, no. 1444 (1883): 837–38.
Thwaite, Ann. *Waiting for the Party: The Life of Frances Hodgson Burnett, Author of* The Secret Garden *and* A Little Princess. Boston: David R. Godine, 1991.
Tilley, Arthur. "The New School of Fiction." *The National Review*, vol. 1, no. 2 (April 1883): 257–68.
Tillotson, Kathleen. *Novels of the Eighteen-Forties*. Oxford: Oxford UP, 1956.
Tracy, Louis. *The Final War*. London: C. Arthur Pearson, 1896.
Tromp, Marlene, Pamela K. Gilbert, and Aeron Haynie (eds.). *Beyond Sensation: Mary Elizabeth Braddon in Context*. Albany: State University of New York Press, 2000.
Trotter, David. "Modernism and Empire: reading *The Waste Land*." *The Critical Quarterly*, vol. 28 (1986): 143–52.
———. *The English Novel in History 1895–1920*. London: Routledge, 1993.
"T. Tembarom." *The Saturday Review* (January 3, 1914): 22.
Vedder, Henry C. *American Writers of To-day*. New York: Silver, Burdett, 1895.

Waller, Philip. *Writers, Readers, & Reputations: Literary Life in Britain 1870–1918* Oxford: Oxford UP, 2006.
"Western Town has Literary Censors." *New York Times* (July 6, 1902): 9.
Williams, Raymond. *Culture & Society, 1780–1950*. New York: Harper & Row, 1958.
Wilson, Anna. "Little Lord Fauntleroy: The Darling of Mothers and the Abomination of a Generation." *American Literary History*, vol. 8, no. 2 (Summer 1996): 232–58.
Wilson, Edmund, Jr. "The Poetry of Drouth." *The Dial* (December 1922): 611–16.
Winter, Alison. *Mesmerism: Powers of Mind in Victorian Britain*. Chicago: U of Chicago P, 1998.
Wordsworth, William. "Tintern Abbey." *British Literature 1780–1830*. Edited by Anne K. Mellor and Richard E. Matlak. New York: Harcourt Brace, 1996, pp. 571–73.
Zangwill, Israel. "Without Prejudice." *The Pall Mall Magazine*, vol. 9, no. 37 (May 1896): 153–56.
Zlotnick, Susan. *Women, Writing, and the Industrial Revolution*. Baltimore: Johns Hopkins UP, 1998.
Zweig, Paul. "Cosmic Freedom." *New York Times Book Review* (March 30, 1980): 3.
Zwerdling, Alex. *Improvised Europeans: American Literary Expatriates and the Siege of London*. New York: Basic Books, 1998.

INDEX

Abrams, M. H. 161
Academy 125
The Academy Fiction Supplement 111
accent 49–50
acculturation 35
Adam Bede 3, 17
Adams, Henry 60
adult novels 8–10
Alcott, Louisa May 135
Alien Nation: Nineteenth-Century Gothic Fictions and English Nationality 126
allegorical frame 19, 45, 61, 101–2, 104, 110, 131
The American 1, 56–57
American fiction 8, 10, 58
American literary culture 19
American literary magazines 24
American literary publishing 24–25
American literature 8, 24, 51, 168
American regional fiction 18–19
amorality 74–75
Anesko, Michael 59
Anglicization 138–39
Anglo-American alliance 157–58, 166–67
Anglo-American character 45
Anglo-American future 48
Anglo-American literary field 2, 24–25, 49
Anglo-American literary tradition 198
Anglo-American literature 24–25
Anglo-American modernism 137
Anglo-American rivalry 48
Anglo-American tradition 24
Anglo-American unity 48, 159
Anglo-American world 66, 165
Anglo-American/Anglo-Saxon unity 147
Anglo-Saxon alliance 168
Arata, Stephen 140, 144
Arnold, Mathew 177
The Art Interchange 55
The Athenaeum 83
Atlantic 23, 51
The Atlantic Monthly 3, 11, 24, 57

Austen, Jane 3
The Awakening of Women; or, Women's Part in Evolution 93, 142

Bakhtin, Mikhail 100
Ballou's Magazine 23
Beard, R. O. 79
Beffel, John 136–37
Belloc, Marie A. 93–96
The Beth Book 112–13
Birch, Reginald 136
Bixler, Phylis 9
Black, Clementina 49–50, 54
Blake, William 111–12
Bleak House 110
Boas, Franz 139
Boccaccio, Giovanni 93
Bodenheimer, Rosemarie 169
The Bookman 96, 111, 136
Boston Transcript 165
Bourdieu, Pierre 2
Braddon, Mary Elizabeth 3, 121
Britain literary field 24
British industrial fiction 10
British literary modernism 7
Bronte, Charlotte 3, 17, 23, 202
Bronte, Emily 23, 103
Browning, Robert 110
Bunyan, John 73, 202
Burlingame, Edward 56–57
Burnett, Frances Hodgson 1, 7, 25
  adult novels 9
  body for 87
  Century "friends," 85–86
  childhood 23–24
  children's literature 7–8
  cultural visibility 8
  discovery of sensual beauty of man's
  explicit ideas about gender 98
  feminist stance 11
  girl's composure depiction 13
  ideals 95–96

Burnett, Frances Hodgson (*cont.*)
  interest in psychic phenomenon 200
  and James 4–7
  literary career 1–2
  patterns 10–11
  publication and critical history 8–9
  romanticism 11
  sense of Anglo-American alliance 158
  on writing for children 93
Burnett, Lionel 4
Burnett, Swan 159
Burnett, Vivian 136

Carlyle, Thomas 121–22, 150–51, 161
The Catholic World 96
The Century Magazine 19, 35, 55, 57–58, 121
Changes in Bodily Form of Descendants of Immigrants 139
The Chap Book 112
character types 36
Chicago Daily Tribune 3, 97, 117, 136, 158
A Child's History of England 89
Chopin, Kate 93
Christianity 32–33
chronology 18
Clark, Suzanne 8
Clay, Bertha M. 3
Collins, Wilkie 10, 110, 121
Columbia History of the American Novel 8
Conrad, Joseph 2
consummate art 12
convention 35
  of marriage 79–80
conventional gender constructions 34–35
Corelli, Marie 7, 17
The Cornhill Magazine 121
Cranford 10, 19, 45, 53
Critic 11
The Critic 54
Crosby, Christina 99
cross-class romance 27–28
cross-class sexual relations 31
Culture and Society 1780-1950 35–36

Daly, Nicholas 8
The Dawn of a To-morrow 10, 20, 200–201
Decameron 93
Degeneration 133, 140
degeneration theory 140–43, 150
The Dial 79, 173–74
dialect speech, verbal texture of 27

Dickens, Charles 3, 23–24, 26, 49, 89, 110
Dictionary of Races of People 139
Dilke, Sir Charles Wentworth 146–47, 169
domestic fiction 10
domestic realism 18, 20
Doyle, Arthur Conan 20, 201
dramatic intensity 12
dramatic scenes 36
dreams 170, 203

The Eclectic Magazine of Foreign Literature 135
Edel, Leon 59
Editha's Burglar 93, 97
Eliot, George 1, 3, 17, 24–25, 50, 55, 83, 99, 172–76, 202
Eliot, T. S. 10, 17, 20
Ellis, Havelock 20
The Emergence of Victorian Consciousness 122
Emerson, Ralph Waldo 24, 147, 213
The English Novel in History 1895-1920 8
Esmeralda 4, 86
Evans, Augusta May 3
evolution/evolutionary 148, 150
Examiner 53
The Examiner 54

A Fair Barbarian 8, 10, 18, 45–47, 49, 53, 89, 135
fallen woman 27–28, 37
Felski, Rita 7, 17, 51
female patriarchy 169
feminine 103
feminine sentimentality 14
feminist allegory 19
'feminized' popular literature 7
Fighting Forces, Writing Women: Identity and Ideology in the First World War 195–96
film adaptations 8
The Final War: A Story of the Great Betrayal 168
Fleishman, Avrom 99
Frances Hodgson Burnett: The Unexpected Life of the Author of The Secret Garden 8
Friction with the Market 59
Fussell, Paul 176

Gaskell, Elizabeth 3, 9–10, 18–19, 23–27, 35–39, 41–43, 45, 47–49, 51, 53, 83, 89, 93, 97, 121, 178
gender 30
gender ideology 16
gender markers 114

INDEX 227

gender roles 34
generic variety 18
German militarism 186, 193, 212
Germany 81–82, 139, 147, 155, 186–87, 191–93, 195
Gerzina, Gretchen Holbrook 4, 7–8, 26–27, 45, 79, 84, 86, 88, 98–99, 117, 159, 165, 169, 175–76, 192, 197–98, 200
Gilder, Helena 87
Gilder, Jeanette L. 97
Gilder, Richard Watson 19, 36, 83–85, 121, 159
 and Burnett 87
Gillette, William 86
Gissing, George 123
God 110
 and force 150–51
Godey's Lady's Book 23
Grand, Sarah 112–13
Great War 10, 20, 25, 172, 174, 176, 186, 192, 194, 196, 198, 211–13
The Great War and Modern Memory 176
The Guardian 187

Hammond, Mary 7–8
Hardy, Thomas 93, 95, 176
The Harmonious Circle 171
Harper's 23–24
Harper's Bazaar 158–59
Harper's Monthly 24
The Hartford Courant 117
The Haunted Study: A Social History of the English Novel 1875-1914 8
Haworth's 1, 10, 18, 26, 36, 38–43, 45, 51, 53, 82, 84, 89, 135
Hawthorne, Julian 15–16, 121–22
Hay, John 59
The Head of the House of Coombe 10, 20, 172–77, 179–81, 183–85, 187–95, 197–98, 206, 208–11, 214
Helen Fleetwood 26
heroines 14–17, 99
Herrick, S. Bledsoe 12
high modernism 25
Hipsky, Martin 2, 7, 9, 24–25
His Grace of Osmonde 10, 19, 67, 70–74, 76, 106–16, 118, 132–33, 140, 142
historical fiction 10, 18
historical novels 19
Hitchens, Christopher 138
Holland, Josiah 24
Household Words 89

Howells, William Dean 10, 57–58
Hughes, Thomas 24
Hughes, Winifred 126
human body 18, 94, 110–12, 140, 159, 164–65, 171, 176, 192, 195, 203, 207
humor 153
Huyssen, Andreas 4, 172
hyperbolic humor 6

The Idler 93
The Impressions of Theophrastus Such 1
Improvised Europeans: American Literary Expatriates and the Siege of London 8, 137
In a Closed Room 20, 214
In Connection with the De Willoughby Claim 10, 19, 88, 116, 121, 159–60
In Memoriam 107
incongruity 29
industrial novels 18, 26, 36, 42
 narrative elements 27
The Interior 95
irrational reproduction 20

Jacob's Room 175
James, Henry 1–2, 4, 10, 19, 55–59, 83, 94, 201
 and Burnett 4–7
 Guy Domville
James, William 20, 201
Jane Eyre 3, 17
John, Arthur 24
Jude the Obscure 93, 95, 97–98, 176

Kaveney, Roz 187
Keating, Peter 8
Kingsley, Charles 24
Knezevic, Borislave 45
Kristeva, Julia 199, 213–14

A Lady of Quality 8, 10–11, 14–16, 19, 90, 93–100, 110–12, 114–15, 130–33, 135, 140, 142, 170, 176
language 99
Levine, George 122
Libbey, Laura Jean 3
Life 172
The Life of Frances Hodgson Burnett author of The Secret Garden and A Little Princess 8
literary authority 24
literary modernism 7, 51
literary practice 36
literary workforce 25

The Literary World 49, 84–85
Little Lord Fauntleroy 1, 3, 7–11, 15, 61, 89,
    91, 93–95, 97, 112, 134–41, 165–68,
    171, 174
Little Lord Fauntleroy (films) 8
Little Lord Fauntleroy (television production) 8
A Little Princess 1, 7, 21
A Little Princess (films) 8
A Little Princess (television production) 8
Longfellow, Henry Wadsworth 24
Los Angeles Times 1, 3, 15, 121, 174
Louisiana 10, 19, 53–55, 84, 89–90,
    116–17, 121–22
Lowrie, Joan 50

Macmillan's Magazine 57
magic 161–62
magical naturalism 164
The Making of a Marchioness 10–11, 19, 121–22,
    125, 134
male dominance 17
Male Fantasies 186, 192
Manchester Guardian 25–26, 36
The Maniac in the Cellar 126
Mary Barton 18, 23, 25–29, 31–32,
    34–37
masculine 103, 111
masculine vigor 12
Maurice, Arthur 136
McAleer, Joseph 8
McDonald, Peter D. 2, 8, 172
McTeague 93
melodrama 3, 59, 83, 125–26, 129,
    136, 165–66
melodramatic writer 3
Meredith, George 2
The Methods of Lady Walderhurst 10–11,
    15–16, 19, 93, 121–32, 134,
    140, 212
Michie, Helena 17–18
middle-class feminine ideal 35
middle-class model of womanhood 35
mid-Victorian realistic mode 11
Mitford, Mary Russell 10
A Modern Instance 57
modernist romance 18
modernist romance mode 11
modernity 37
Moers, Ellen 7
Molson, Francis J. 8, 11
moral judgment 39
Morel, Benedict-Augustin 140

Morris, William 24
Morse, James Herbert 49, 55

narrative closure 35
narrative elements 19, 26–28, 36, 43
narrative vocabulary 27
The Nation 82–83
The National Review 57
Neil, Anna 202–3
new fiction 10
new heroine 27
"new woman" novel 14
New York Daily Tribune 59
New York Times 97, 99, 122, 125–26, 136, 159,
    165, 200
Nietzsche 94
Nietzschean 97–98
Nietzsche-like individualism 14, 97, 116
Noonan, Mark J. 34–35
Nordau, Max 133, 140
Norris, Frank 93
North American Review 1, 3, 56
North and South 18, 36, 40
nostalgia 151–52

occult 207–10, 214
The Odd Women 123
Of Queens' Gardens 16
The One I Knew the Best of All 13
The Ordeal of Richard Feverel 2
Ouditt, Sharon 195–96
Our Village 10
Outlook 192
Owen, Wilfred 205

Pall Mall Gazette 4
Pall Mall Magazine 14
patriarchal system 101
patriarchy 110, 156
physical force 12–13, 94, 110, 132, 142
physical realities of female body 17
physical strength 15–16, 18, 32, 101–2, 104,
    111, 113, 118, 131
The Pilgrim's Progress 73, 202
plot elements 36
political novel 19
popular culture, as feminine 4
popular fiction 17
popular modernism 17
popular romance 51, 172, 174–75
popular sublime 51
The Portrait of a Lady 51

The Portrait of a Lady 19, 57, 60
post-World War I English society 20
The Prelude 161
Preston, George 96, 111
Primitive Minds 202
profiteers 2, 55, 57, 88
purists 2, 55, 57, 88, 172, 196

Quinn, Arthur Hobson 83

race 142–43
race panic 140
The Races of Europe 139
Radcliff, Ann 3
Radford, Andrew 126–27
rape 187, 213
rational reproduction 19–20
Reade, Charles 89, 97
realism 83, 111, 175
reconciliation fantasy 138
The Return of the Soldier 196
Rich, Adrienne 17–18
Richardson, Angelique 19, 106, 142
The Ring and the Book 110
Ripley, William 139
Roberts, Mary Fanton 168
Robin 1, 3, 9–10, 20, 161, 170–76, 178–90, 193–99, 201, 203–12
romance 2, 9, 42–43, 167
rural American story 19
Ruskin, John 16, 24
Ruth 37, 53

Sara Crewe 93, 97
Sara Crewe (television production) 8
Sartor Resartus 150
Satires of Circumstance 176
Saturday Review 55
The Saturday Review 165
Schayer, Julia 86
Schmitt, Canon 126
Scott, Sir Walter 23
Scribner's Magazine 19, 23–24, 51, 83–84
Scribner's Monthly 36
The Secret Garden 1, 7–9, 21, 51, 70, 116, 136, 159–62, 164–65, 169–71, 175
The Secret Garden (films) 8
The Secret Garden (television productions) 8
semiotic mode 196, 199–200, 202, 212–14
sensation novels 20, 90, 121, 125–26, 133–34, 149
serious lady novelist 3

sex 187–88
sexual distinctions of biological bodies 28
Showalter, Elaine 7
Shumaker, Jeanette 34–35
The Shuttle 8, 10, 20, 61, 132, 135, 137, 139, 141–43, 145–47, 149, 151, 153, 155, 157–61, 163, 165–67, 169–71, 202, 212
Smith, Reginald John 121
social and verbal textures 36
social conventions of gender and woman's bodily composure, tensions between 30
social novels 19, 36
social realism 19
social reform 36
social-sensation novels 20
Southern Review 1, 3, 12
Southworth, E. D. E. N. 3
spiritualism 11, 96, 102, 104, 140, 163, 172–73, 180, 200–203, 207–8, 210, 214
Spofford, Ainsworth R. 50
St. Nicholas 89
Stanzas from the Grand Chartreuse 177
Stead, William 138–39
Stillman, William James 24
Stoddard, Richard Henry 54–55, 136
Stokes, F. A. 121
Stone, Elizabeth 26
Strachey, Lytton 176
Surly Tim and Other Stories 84
Swinburne, Algernon Charles 24
Swiney, Frances 142–43

T. Tembarom 10, 20, 135, 137, 139, 141, 143, 145, 147, 149, 151, 153, 155, 157, 159, 161, 163, 165–67, 169–71
Tess of the D'Urbervilles 176
Thackeray, William Makepeace 23
That Lass O'Lowries 1, 3, 8, 10–12, 14–15, 18, 21, 25–26, 28–29, 31, 35–37, 39–40, 51, 56, 83–84, 89–90, 97, 118
Theweleit, Klaus 186, 192, 212
Thomas, Katherine 159
Through One Administration 10, 19, 51, 54–55, 57–58, 60, 63, 66, 73, 76, 79, 82–86, 88–90, 93, 116–17, 135, 140
Thus Spoke Zarathustra 94
Thwaite, Ann 3–6, 8–9, 11–12, 25–26, 36–37, 54, 60, 84, 87–88, 93, 117, 165, 168, 174
Tilley, Arthur 57–58
Time 49
Times Literary Supplement 9

Tonna, Charlotte Elizabeth 26
Townsend, Stephen 159
Tracy, Louis 168
traditional mistrust 48
traditional village fiction 10
The Tragic Muse 59
transatlantic literary field 50
transatlantic marriage 169
transatlantic novels 10, 18, 20
transcendence 7
Trollope, Anthony 17
Trotter, David 8
Twayne's English Authors Series 9

Übermensch 94, 98
unsentimental romance 125
upper class 30–31, 37

Victorian consciousness 122, 134
Victorian domestic fiction 17
Victorian domestic realism 18
Victorian domestic realistic novels 18
Victorian female characterization 16
Victorian novels 9, 25, 90, 202, 214
Victorian realism 9–11, 17–18, 23–24, 51, 57, 97
Victorian romance mode 11
Victorian sensation 149
Victorian society 35
Victorian works 17
Villette 17
virility and femininity 15

Waller, Philip 8
The Waste Land 10, 20, 172–73, 175, 177–78, 187
Webb, James 171
West, Rebecca 196
The White People 10, 20, 214
Whittier, John Greenleaf 24
Wilde, Oscar 133, 140
William Langshawe, the Cotton Lord 26
Williams, C. D. 121
Williams, Raymond 35–36
Wilson, Anna 140, 168
Wilson, Edmund 173–74
Winter, Alison 201–2, 210
Wives and Daughters 178
The Woman in White 110
woman's character, integrity of 75–76
woman's defiance to convention 15
A Woman's Will or Miss Defarge 10
women romance writers 9
Wordsworth, William 16, 161–62
working class 25–26, 28, 30–31, 35, 37
Writers, Readers, & Reputations: Literary Life in Britain 1870–1918 8
Wuthering Heights 103

Yeats, William Butler 201
Yeazell, Ruth Bernard 137

Zangwill, Israel 14–16, 19, 94, 97–98, 102, 110, 116, 131, 176
Zweig, Paul 171–72
Zwerdling, Alex 8, 48, 137–38, 141

www.ingramcontent.com/pod-product-compliance
Lightning Source LLC
Chambersburg PA
CBHW021825300426
44114CB00009BA/329